This unusually accessible account of recent Anglo-American philosophy focuses on how that philosophy has challenged deeply held notions of subjectivity, mind, and language. Where some have concluded that this challenge must inevitably lead to antirealism and relativism, Frank Farrell argues that the rejection of certain metaphysical notions leads to a more acute sense of realism, or as he puts it to the "recovery of the world."

The book is designed on a broad canvas in which recent arguments are placed in a historical context (in particular they are related to medieval philosophy and German idealism). The author then explores such topics as mental content, moral realism, realism and antirealism, and the character of subjectivity. Much of the book is devoted to an investigation of Donald Davidson's philosophy, and there is also a sustained critique of the position of Richard Rorty. A final chapter defends the realist position against objections from postmodern thought.

As a rigorous and historically sensitive account of recent philosophy, this book should enjoy a wide readership among philosophers of many different persuasions, literary theorists, and social scientists who have been influenced by postmodern thought.

SUBJECTIVITY, REALISM, AND
POSTMODERNISM – THE RECOVERY
OF THE WORLD

SUBJECTIVITY, REALISM, AND POSTMODERNISM – THE RECOVERY OF THE WORLD

FRANK B. FARRELL

State University of New York at Purchase

 CAMBRIDGE
UNIVERSITY PRESS

Published by the Press Syndicate of the University of Cambridge
The Pitt Building, Trumpington Street, Cambridge CB2 IRP
40 West 20th Street, New York, NY 10011-4211, USA
10 Stamford Road, Oakleigh, Melbourne 3166, Australia

© Cambridge University Press 1996

First published 1994
First paperback edition 1996

Printed in the United States of America

Library of Congress Cataloging-in-Publication Data is available.

A catalog record for this book is available from the British Library.

ISBN 0-521-44416-0 hardback
ISBN 0-521-56832-3 paperback

To KAZUMA,
whom I can never thank properly
for his great generosity and his
companionship over many years

and to my parents,
G. FRANK FARRELL and AGNES COONEY FARRELL

Contents

Acknowledgments

I began this project in 1987 when I was granted a semester's leave as part of a program of awards for junior faculty development established by President Sheldon Grebstein of the State University of New York at Purchase. I finished it during a sabbatical leave granted to me by the college in 1991–2. I am grateful to the college administration for unqualified support during the time I have spent there. My habits of doing philosophy still owe very much to several of my graduate school professors, and I would like to express my gratitude to Ruth Marcus, Scott Soames, Jonathan Lear, Karsten Harries, and Harry Frankfurt. I remain thankful also for the support I received for dissertation writing from the Mrs. Giles Whiting Foundation. I have been fortunate to benefit from many discussions of Hegel with my colleague Ken Dove. Those at Cambridge University Press have been extremely helpful and I am indebted to Terence Moore, to Louise Calabro Gruendel, to Cynthia Insolio Benn, and to two anonymous readers of an earlier version of the book whose evaluations proved very useful.

Introduction

My initial motivation for beginning this project was a belief that Richard Rorty, in his various writings, has given an unreliable account of recent philosophy. He gets certain figures wrong, Davidson in particular, but more important is that he is wrong about the positions we are led to as a result of that work. There have been a number of important recent challenges to our philosophical understanding of mind, subjectivity, and language. (In considering these challenges I shall speak of a "disenchantment of subjectivity.") Rorty is sensitive to those developments, but he believes they lead to a picture of free-flowing cultural conversations for which there is no constraint that the world itself provides on what "getting matters right" will be. I think, in contrast, that they lead to more realist accounts and to what we might call the recovery of the world. There are two senses, as I shall tell the story, in which we may speak about that recovery. The alienated self of modernity is assured that its concepts are at home in the world as it is, and the world itself recovers from a process of thinning out and contraction that it suffered in relation to the powers of the modern subject.

Besides having the plan of giving a counternarrative to Rorty's, I also thought it would be worthwhile, especially as we approach the century's end (a point however arbitrary), to try to give a summing up of what I take to be the "state of the argument" in several important areas of philosophy. There has been much interesting work over the last couple of decades, but it is often difficult to comprehend the place of that work in a wider philosophical setting. Yet if it is important, one ought to be able to show why it is so to those not already committed to the particular research program in which the argument occurs. So I thought it would be beneficial to look at the field more broadly than is usual, and to show where I think a number of the important debates have ended up, while introducing arguments of my own on the various issues.

A third motivation was that I am uncomfortable with certain artificial barriers in philosophy: between studying the history of philosophy and engaging in the practice of it, and between studying the typical work done at English and American graduate institutions and studying work more likely to be done in Germany or in France. It seems that it ought to be possible to develop a style that moves without too much strain among the different ways of doing philosophy, and that remains clear and accurate in the process. Most of the book will be a study of recent Anglo-American philosophy, in the areas of philosophy of mind, philosophy of language, metaphysics, and ethics. Yet I shall set the stage for that treatment in a perhaps unexpected manner, by beginning with a chapter on medieval philosophy and on Hegel, and I shall examine what I take to be the inertia of "religious" patterns of thought that developed in late medieval and early modern philosophy. And I shall end with a chapter that considers a number of thinkers often called postmodern.

I think that much of the recent work in philosophy will be of interest to those in related disciplines, especially as many in literature and political science and anthropology are now engaging in theoretical discussions about subjectivity, meaning, and rationality. I have tried to present the arguments clearly, and in a manner more accessible than is the case with typical journal articles. Yet much of what follows is difficult. One just cannot present certain philosophical arguments accurately without presenting their difficulty, and omitting the more demanding arguments would give a truncated picture of the state of the discussion. (I am not suggesting that philosophy is more difficult than these other disciplines, but merely that it has, as they do, its own sort of difficulty.)

1

"Theological" Subjectivity and the Hegelian Response

Disenchantment of the World and of Subjectivity

Those who examine conceptions of thinking in modern philosophy often trace the models they investigate back to Descartes. But there is an earlier history to those conceptions and we need to look at medieval philosophy if we wish to understand it. The metaphysicians of that period were interested in what God's thinking and willing could be like, and there were religious pressures toward intensifying the innerness of the self, since God's presence was somehow more immediate in that interior space, and since confession and other practices gave it a depth needing exploration. I believe there are models of subjectivity, and of the mind's relations to the world, that were shaped by those theological and religious considerations; that were present in a more secular form in modern philosophy; that still shape certain contemporary positions; and that are now being widely challenged.

I recognize that establishing that claim properly would require a lengthy study of causal influence, and I am not prepared to do that here, if anywhere, because my purpose is to give an account of philosophical work over the last few decades. But I have found it helpful, in looking for patterns in the recent work, to make note of analogies between medieval conceptions and various notions in contemporary thought having to do with the mind, subjectivity, and realism. (We can specify, for example, a certain "theological" notion of subjectivity that has application well beyond theology.) I want to give just a very brief survey of some of the conceptions that I have found helpful, so that I shall be free to make reference to them in the chapters to follow. Even without the sort of scholarly investigation that a different book might undertake, the reference to religious and theological pictures will provide, I think, an interesting narrative frame, and a spur to look for patterns that other accounts of the material I am treating are likely to miss. (Most of what I say about the arguments of recent philosophy stands independently of that narrative.)

One theme I shall be referring to is that of a disenchantment of subjectivity. That notion is meant to recall Weber's theme of the disenchantment of the world. (My emphasis in using that term is more on the world's or subjectivity's loss of its "enchanted" status than on the disillusionment experienced by the modern self.) We can follow a process by which nature, once ensouled and the abode of deities, becomes, for modern thinkers, a neutral material for instrumental action, with nature's meaning and value determined by values we impose. Ancient philosophers began a disenchantment of nature, in saying that natural processes, rather than personal gods, would account for the phenomena of nature. But while losing its gods, nature retained for many thinkers several features of the divine. It was the deepest ground of rightness and necessity, and the rational order of things showed its "divine" character in being eternal.

The full process of dedivinizing that natural world was aided when it could be seen in relation to a subject that was itself divine. Suppose that the Aristotelian god, the fullest actualization of the highest activity in nature, comes to be seen instead as a consciously willing subject creating the world from a point beyond it. Then everything in the world can be an object of the divine intellect and will. In order that God's power would be absolute, nature had to lose its necessity and eternity, its determining power as a region where entities had, on their own, their substantial natures and their proper values. These traits would have to be thought of as really "in" the divine thinking and not as independent sources of determinacy. In the late medieval period this process was exaggerated. A world where things have their proper natures and proper modes of actualization seems to place undesirable limits on God, while a fully nominalist world of individuals will allow the determining power to reside in an unencumbered act of divine willing. (One medieval philosopher, Nicholas of Autrecourt, favored an atomist account, not for scientific reasons, but because it was the sort of neutral universe that offered the widest play to God's freedom.)

In the modern period the finite human thinker takes over some of God's functions as subject. The qualities that things once were taken to have on their own migrate across the subject/object divide and are seen to be determinations imposed by the self (secondary qualities, substance, causality, value, and the like). The world becomes ever more neutral and insubstantial as the environment in which human willing makes itself real. Heidegger argues that the contemporary world has even lost its status as objective, and is now no more than an inventory of things ready for calculation and arrangement.[1] It seems that we have repeated the cycle of medieval philosophy, only with ourselves in the place of God. And we have ended, as they did, with a nominalism that makes the

---

[1] That is his general theme in "The Question Concerning Technology," in Martin Heidegger, *The Question Concerning Technology and Other Essays* (New York: Harper & Row, 1977), pp. 3–35.

world the sort of "thinned out" region that puts the least constraint on our willing and ordering.

A condition of this disenchantment of the world, and of the evacuation of various qualities from it, was that subjectivity itself remain in an important sense absolute, since it is relative to the power of the subject that the world loses its intrinsic substance and value. The human subject is the origin of unity, determinacy, necessity, rules of ordering, and values. Its absolute status is shown in the difference (noted by Hegel) between ancient and modern skepticism.[2] Whereas the ancient skeptic recommended withholding judgment about any proposition, his modern counterpart is skeptical about the world in a way that he is not skeptical about the contents of inner life. Things in the world may be worthy of doubt in every respect, but at least my ideas give themselves to me as what they really are, and while natural entities can no longer have natures, the inner objects do have natures, in that it is clear to the thinker what to count as the same idea reappearing. There may be no necessary connections in things, but if I observe my ideas I can see that some are necessarily related to others. Or necessity will be thought to reside in one's language, in the connections it supports by its conventions; then that necessity is projected onto the things and relations of the world. We still find in subjectivity the necessity, the intrinsic natures, the autonomy, the constructive power, the role as an always present conserver of determinacy, that earlier we had located in God. (Recall how, still earlier, some of those features had remained in nature, even after its partial disenchantment. Here too, in the modern self, there is a partial disenchantment, a secularization, of divine subjectivity, one that still leaves many of its divine features intact.)

We can, in this context, now conceive of a further process: a complete disenchantment of subjectivity that will match the complete disenchantment of nature that has already occurred. This would mean reaching a stage resembling late medieval nominalism, only now in relation to the mental and semantic items of the subjective realm instead of in relation to the natural world. These items will then lose their intrinsic natures and will not, in themselves, determine what will count as a reappearance of the same thought or as an expression of the same meaning. The mental and semantic realms will be "nominalist": a collection of individual items or tokens that do not intrinsically classify themselves, and do not intrinsically represent one thing rather than another. What they are will depend on what an interpreter can take them to be, through considering their causal relations to surrounding environments. No amount of inspection of any such item will determine what another item in the

---

[2] See Michael N. Foster, *Hegel and Skepticism* (Cambridge, Mass.: Harvard University Press, 1989), pp. 9–35.

future will have to be in order to be a repeating of an utterance or of an earlier act of referring. The subject can no longer have a theological power to confer meaning on its utterances and to project determinacy on what is real; there will no longer be the same motivation to find onto-logical determinacy, necessity, and value as really "in" subjectivity rather than in the world.

By the "disenchantment of subjectivity" I shall mean the removal from our conceptions of thinking and experiencing of the residual in-fluence of theological and religious models. One claim I find interesting and shall investigate is whether that double disenchantment, both of the world and of subjectivity, will lead to indeterminacy and relativism, as many postmodern thinkers believe, or will lead instead to more realist conceptions of a "thicker" world, since the world became "thinned out" earlier only in relation to a divinized subject.

The Subject as External and Arbitrary Determiner

The act of creation and the Incarnation are, insofar as the character of the world is concerned, arbitrary and external. The medieval wish to guarantee God's free willing power at all costs meant that God could intervene in the world at any time and that his willing must be unfath-omable. Earlier there was the Greek sense of things as showing them-selves and as having a natural accessibility to the inquiring mind. But with the Judeo-Christian God as a personalized source of the deter-minacy of things, one must rely on a freely willing thinker who may will to reveal matters or to keep their status hidden. Ockham gives as one of the reasons for his anti-Aristotelianism the desire not to constrain God's freedom in creating; if there were essential forms either prior to creation or in members of a species, then God would be constrained by such forms in creating further members of a species.[3] So the world has its intelligibility and determinacy from a source with absolute arbitrary power, a source that must remain to us deeply inscrutable and un-motivated by the character of what is determined. Morality indeed has its only foundation in God's arbitrary willing; acts in themselves do not have properties that make them inherently moral or immoral. (One may, of course, emphasize God's rationality and his willingness to keep the natural and moral orders stable.)

---

[3] "An individual of any species can be created afresh, however much other previously created or produced individuals of the same species persist. But creation is absolutely from nothing, so that nothing essential or intrinsic to the thing precedes it in real being. Therefore, no non-varied thing pre-existing in any individual belongs to the essence of this freshly created individual, since if anything essential to this thing preceded it, then it would not be created." Ockham, *Commentary on the Sentences*, Book One, Distinction Two, Question 4, in *Philosophy in the Middle Ages*, Arthur Hyman and James Walsh, eds. (Indianapolis: Hackett, 1973), p. 663.

It then becomes useful to ask whether the voluntaristic arbitrariness of the medieval God repeats itself in the activity of the modern subject. There are, again, ways of trying to limit that arbitrariness. One may see the subject (like Leibniz's God) as constrained by a certain rational necessity. The transcendental deduction in Kant, for example, attempts to show that there are necessary categorial structures that will be imposed by any thinker who experiences an objective world through the forms of space and time; and there will be a similar necessary structure imposed by rationality upon our acts of moral choice. But the progress of modern philosophy follows to some degree that of its medieval counterpart, which in its later stages emphasized that the determining power of God might be external, arbitrary, and variable. The Kantian model raises the issue of whether alternative conceptual schemes might be used in ordering the sensory information, and later philosophers would pick up on that possible variability. Moral value, in a similar manner, will arise from the imposition of a moral scheme upon the world and there will be a variety of such schemes that might be imposed. As with God's Incarnation or his bestowal of grace, there will be no moral character of the world that demands the application of one scheme rather than another. In Nietzsche, we have a structure that is in one respect like that of the late medievals. He sees the world as offering a minimum possible constraint on the self's capacity freely to create conceptions of the world that enhance its power. (I am not here endorsing Heidegger's picture of Nietzsche as a metaphysician of the will.)

God's creating is inscrutable for the later medievals because the world that appears by no means expresses fully the infinite character of his willing.[4] That willing has a depth that exceeds whatever we might learn about it through the appearances it produces. Now the modern subject also takes on a certain unplumbable depth (though certainly not for Nietzsche, who strongly rejects the notion of a hidden willing behind the scenes). Its willing produces various appearances in the world, but those appearances are consistent with quite different acts of intending, meaning, and willing, and we might never comprehend just what another subject is really referring to, or really means, or is really thinking. For all we know, it will be said, others might inhabit different worlds that they have constructed through their schemes, even though we are able to interpret their behavior well enough to get along with them efficiently. As with the medieval God, there is an excess of determining power beyond what appears. We cannot know whether someone is truly doing

[4] There is an excellent discussion of this issue in Hans Blumenberg, *The Legitimacy of the Modern Age*, Robert Wallace, trans. (Cambridge, Mass.: MIT Press, 1983), pp. 549–96. I have been influenced by Blumenberg's work throughout the present chapter. He gives a compelling account of the theological absolutism of the late medieval period and of the early modern responses to it on pp. 125–226.

addition, since his behavior is consistent with his willing different mathematical functions, and we cannot know, through watching some-one apply an expression, whether he projects that expression to future cases in the way that we do, or in a manner that would strike us as bizarre.[5] Which scheme is he really applying? He must come across as an arbitrary and hidden determining power whose effects in the world fall so short of that arbitrary power that I might never know what he is taking the world to be. And subjectivity and personal identity will themselves have an absolute character, even if all the observations available are insufficient to determine where one consciousness, or one person, leaves off and another begins.

Taking a nominalist stance toward the subjective realm will be an important step in undermining any role for an arbitrary subjective determiner, one that would impose its structures and schemes from without, in perhaps unfathomable ways, upon the world it experiences. If mental and semantic items have no intrinsic character on their own, independently of their links to the world and to interpreters, then the way is open to claiming that there is no fundamentally hidden depth to subjectivity, and that the relations between the world and what believers are believing, and between believers and what others interpret those beliefs to be, must be far more internal than has usually been assumed. The determinacy-conferring power of subjectivity, rather than being a hidden source behind the scenes like the voluntarist God, will exhaust itself in the sort of behavior it could display to an interpreter. We shall also be readier to see the world itself as guiding and constraining our accounts of it, in such a manner that the notion of a scheme imposed by thought or language upon a largely indeterminate world will become very much less appealing. And consciousness may lose its absolute character, as determining its own identity from within.

Aquinas and the Self-relating God

The Aristotelian divine activity, as the highest actualization of the best activity, governs by the desire for further actualization that it inspires in entities that are less developed; it is a perfect thinking about thinking. The Christian God, on the other hand, is characterized by freedom of the will, by the initiation of action, and by love and care for each creature individually. The God who knows what each creature does, even a sparrow falling from the sky, cannot, it seems, have the self-

---

[5] I shall be examining Wittgenstein on rule following in Chapter 2. For a discussion of the issues concerning the projectibility of a predicate to new cases in what we take to be a bizarre manner, see Nelson Goodman, *Fact, Fiction, and Forecast*, 3rd ed. (Indianapolis: Bobbs-Merrill, 1973), pp. 72–81.

containment that Aristotelian perfection requires. For God to know what a creature does is for him to be moved as a knower from potency to act by something external to that knowing, so that he must earlier have been less than fully actualized and so less than fully perfect.

Aquinas's solution is to see God's relating to what is other, to creatures, as actually a species of self-relation. The essence of each creature is God's own essence in one of the infinite number of possible ways in which it could be participated in by creatures whose act of being is limited. God, says Aquinas, "knows all things by knowing his own essence," and "sees everything in one, namely, in himself alone."[6] "The essence of God contains what is of value in other things, and much more besides, and so God can know things other than himself with proper knowledge. The proper nature of each consists in this, that in some degree it participates in the divine perfection."[7] So God in knowing creatures is actually knowing his own essence, his own ideas, and is not being brought from potency to act by an external other. Even his willing to create other entities might be taken as a willing of his own essence. (Some medieval philosophers, in order to place no limit on God, saw his creation not as done for the sake of man, but as an act of self-love.)

Whatever may be the philosophical merits of that solution, it sets in play a conception that will haunt the history of the modern subject: a picture of what an unconditioned autonomy must be like, and a model for the kind of self-relating-in-relating-to-otherness that might occur when we know. (Perhaps that picture is much more vivid in German philosophy than elsewhere.) It is not just that the thinker or willer wants a certain independence from the world. The goal is rather to be fully engaged in the world (like the Christian God) in such a way that the relation to what is other turns out to be a self-relating. One recognizes in what is other one's own working, one's own determining, the principles of one's own inner life at work.

We shall get a number of versions of that conception of autonomy: Kantian, Hegelian, existentialist, and others. The common theme is that one's knowing is ultimately a self-knowing; one's freedom lies in a willing that is an unconditioned self-willing. More than this, the medieval God presents a picture of a taking of otherness into the structure of one's own self-relating while letting the other remain *other*. Creatures do not become part of God even while his knowing of them is a knowing of himself. If one loses the delicate balance of Aquinas's structure, then pantheism is a threat, and if one loses the delicate balance of various secular versions of that structure of subjectivity, then there will seem to

[6] Thomas Aquinas, I *Summa Contra Gentes*, 58, in *St. Thomas Aquinas: Philosophical Texts*, Thomas Gilby, trans. (London: Oxford University Press, 1951), p. 100, and *Summa Theologica*, 1a. xiv. 7, ibid., p. 101.
[7] Aquinas, *Summa Theologica*, 1a. xiv. 6, ibid., p. 105.

be a swallowing up of the world into the activity of thinkers. One begins by saying that in encountering the world we are really encountering our own cultural structures and determinations projected out before us. And soon the world is too insubstantial to have any character of its own and becomes an inert material for our theological determining, as pansubjectivism rather than pantheism becomes the danger. (The subject with that power may be, for certain thinkers, Language or discursive practices rather than the human self.)

That "divine" self-relational structure may have the tendency to re-order a field of objects into a starkly oppositional pattern. Determinacy-conferring power flows to one point in the field, and the contours of a pluralist universe may be flattened out into a realm of items defined just by their opposition to that point. We can see that outcome in Kantian ethics. There is the moment of the self-willing rational will, imposing its rational structures on action, and then all other considerations relevant to agency, in being opposed to that self-relational willing, count as "merely" inclinations. Whatever cannot be made rational in that way, and determined by that sort of willing, counts as an expression of force. The thick ethical universe of the ancient world is flattened into one whose character can be determined from out of that divinized structure.

The Consolidation of a Free-standing Interior

John McDowell has recently challenged the notion of mind as an auton-omous inner space.[8] He traces that notion to what he sees as the Cartesian desire to mark off a certain mental realm for scientific study, as a realm of physical bodies in motion had been similarly marked off for the physical sciences.[9] That desire leads to the conception of an inner space the character of whose objects is transparently available for introspection, with the further condition that such introspection could present the objects in just the same way no matter how things were varied in the world around. But we need to go back well before Descartes to understand the factors behind the consolidation of the mental as a self-standing inner space. There was, for example, the Stoic notion of inner concepts that have their own reality independently of how matters stand in the world, and Augustine's work displays the neo-Platonic notion of the purification of the soul from the body and Christianity's taking over of the idea of knowledge through divine illumination. It is typical of Augustine's thought that he assigns to things in the world a reduced causal role in our experiencing of their features. He accepts the

---

[8] McDowell, "Singular Thought and the Extent of Inner Space," in *Subject, Thought, and Context*, Philip Pettit and John McDowell, eds. (Oxford: Clarendon Press, 1986), pp. 137–68.
[9] Ibid., pp. 152–5.

neo-Platonc picture which holds that the higher order of thinking cannot be passive in relation to the lower order of the physical. Happenings in the body are the occasion of an active self-affecting on the part of the mind, as it causes sensory images in itself by its way of actively attending to disturbances in the body. He holds that we can easily become lost in the world because our self-loving becomes mixed with the love of things, and he asks us to withdraw to a purer self-knowing in which there is no such undesirable admixture.[10]

So the mind is active and self-affecting and its self-presence is more original than, and not dependent upon, its knowing of the world; in knowing other things it is always self-relating. Now if one is familiar with recent claims about the externalism of mental content, then one shall at least wish to ask (even if one finds those claims unacceptable) what gives Augustine the assurance that a mind so withdrawn from the world, supposedly into its own self-presence, can have any content at all. McDowell will make the claim (we shall see it later) that a mind so cut off goes "dark."[11] But it is clear that Augustine will not worry about that outcome, for the mind is lit up within by a divine illumination. The propositions that I know I know through the illumining power of the divine ideas, so that I can arrive at certainty and universality and an understanding of eternal truths, such as those of mathematics, even though the world around me could not support knowledge of that kind. "But when we have to do with things which we behold with the mind, that is, with the intelligence and with reason, we speak of things we look upon directly in the inner light of truth which illumines the inner man and is inwardly enjoyed."[12]

Subjectivity can then be thought of as possessing an awareness of content independently of how things happen in the world, and as secure in a rich self-presence, because of its relation, implicit or explicit, to a divine reality. Aristotle, in contrast, thought of the mind as actualizing itself in raising to explicit universality the intelligible forms of things.[13] Aquinas tried to reconfirm that Aristotelian linkage, but late medieval nominalism moved rather in a different direction. I have mentioned Ockham's claim that only a universe of individuals without natures or essences allows God full freedom in creating. Each created individual is unique, with even its individual idea coming into existence at the moment

[10] Some of Augustine's views of the mind as active and self-relating can be seen in his *On the Trinity*, ch. 8–9, selections in *Philosophy in the Middle Ages*, Hyman and Walsh, eds., pp. 70–1.

[11] McDowell, "Singular Thought and the Extent of Inner Space," p. 158.

[12] Augustine, "The Teacher," in *Philosophy in the Middle Ages*, Hyman and Walsh, eds., p. 32.

[13] For a very helpful treatment of Aristotle on knowing, see Jonathan Lear, *Aristotle: The Desire To Understand* (Cambridge: Cambridge University Press, 1988). pp. 116–51, 293–309.

of creation, so that God, unlike the Platonic demiurge, is not constrained by any essential forms in creating. Now that sort of universe will not be one in which Aristotle's account of knowing could be correct. For Aristotle, the mind in knowing shares the intelligible form of the thing known; there is a built-in sameness that holds together the act of knowing and what is known. But Ockham will allow no such built-in identity in his universe; the concept and the thing are two items that have no intrinsic relation, and the former has to do with our mental acts or habits, and not with the Aristotelian form abstracted from things. So the moment of self-relating seems to come apart from the moment of relating to otherness. Instead of mind as actualizing the universal aspect in things, there are two regions of items whose relationship may end up being a puzzle.

If the act of experiencing and the thing experienced are distinct items in a nominalistic universe, then it ought to be the case that one could always be present without the other. God, bound only by the law of noncontradiction, could easily produce the perception of whiteness without any whiteness being present. (Ockham granted that possibility, given the absoluteness of God's freedom, but it did not raise serious skeptical problems for him. He was confident about our knowledge of individual existents in the world.) Now such a conception might be thought both to favor and not to favor the Augustinian autonomy of mind. On the one hand, mental items or acts will have no intrinsic connection with things. But on the other hand, the privilege and autonomy given to the mind's self-relating activity appears to be in jeopardy. For my act of perceiving or believing will be distinct from my reflection on that very act. If these are individual acts, one of which could appear without the other, then my reflective awareness that I perceive or believe could occur, perhaps through God's intervention, even without my perceiving or believing actually occurring. So I would be in no better position concerning internal activities or objects than concerning objects external to the mind.

It is instructive to see just that issue arising for the late medievals, in a letter from Nicholas of Autrecourt to Bernard of Arezzo.[14] Nicholas is offering a skeptical challenge to some of Bernard's claims about our knowledge of things. But what is more interesting is that for polemical reasons he pushes to extremely skeptical conclusions certain premises accepted by Bernard, especially the premise that intuitive cognition does not necessarily require the existing thing. "But what is even harder to uphold, you must say that you are not certain of your own actions – e.g. that you are seeing, or hearing – indeed you must say that you are not

[14] Nicholas of Autrecourt, "First Letter to Bernard," in *Medieval Philosophy*, Herman Shapiro, ed. (New York: Modern Library, 1964), pp. 510–16.

sure that anything is perceived by you, or has been perceived by you."[15] Autrecourt also says that "it follows that if you were asked whether or not you believed some articles of the Faith, you would have to say, 'I do not know,' because, according to your position, you could not be certain of your own act of believing."[16] Indeed, says Nicholas, Bernard could not be certain that any cognitions or propositions existed at all.

Though one of the most skeptical thinkers of the later medieval period, Autrecourt seems to resist those conclusions and to accept the empiricist position that we have certainty about the reports of our senses and about our own inner acts: "And so, in order to avoid such absurdities, I maintained in my disposition at the Sorbonne that I am evidently certain of the objects of the five senses, and of my own acts."[17] Why did he not extend his skepticism to the self-relating interior life of the mind? Perhaps at least part of the answer (I am following Hans Blumenberg here) lies in the desire of the medievals not to make God responsible for sin or error. Instead of accepting the Gnostic claim that world was made by an inferior god different from the God of salvation, Augustine accounts for evil by taking human free will to be responsible. A similar outcome will then be suggested to later thinkers for the problem of error. If my mind, in its most immediate operation of registering sensations and inner happenings, could be making mistakes, then God must have made the knowing instrument badly. But if, on the other hand, error enters only when our judging faculty has gone into operation, then the error is our own responsibility, for in judgment our free will is active.[18] It is in Descartes that we see this solution being adopted as he enters the space constituted by late medieval thought and shows the consolidation of an interior realm that can resist skeptical doubt, if one uses one's free will properly.

The Aristotelian account of knowing does not fit so neatly into this project of saving God's goodness by attributing error to man, because it does not have the proper room for our active willing. A consequence of the project is that we shall not be in error when we are at our most passive, before the activity of judging has come into play. So we can have certainty in the passive registering of sensations; the very proper question (raised but dismissed by Autrecourt) of whether we should be just as skeptical about our seeing of inner objects will become a live issue in twentieth-century philosophy. But we can see in the late medieval

---

[15] Ibid., pp. 513–14.
[16] Ibid., p. 514.
[17] Ibid., p. 516.
[18] Blumenberg is again helpful. "Thus the deception can only be indirect, as the production of a perception, since the responsibility for the error then remains with man in his, so to speak 'overshooting' in the act of judgment. Thus the Augustinian model of theodicy, assigning to man the responsibility for the evil in the world, is held to here also." Blumenberg, *Legitimacy of the Modern Age*, p. 194.

developments, and then in the early modern response to them, the gradual development of the sort of interior space with which modern philosophy is familiar. (By limiting the world to individuals, Ockham had not only supported his empiricism but had also understood the relation between conceptual and real as a relation between the interior realm and the exterior one, rather than as a metaphysical relation present in reality itself.)

In the fourteenth-century thinker Gregory of Rimini we see coming together the strands of a conception of mind that has much in common with the Cartesian one. Gregory combines Ockham's empiricism with an Augustinian view of an inner realm some of whose ideas are innate. He says that the image or species is the immediate object of perception rather than the thing itself, and also allows for immediate awareness of mental states. In Gordon Leff's words, he "makes the intelligible a self-contained realm, owing no dependence to external reality."[19]

God's-eye View and a "Human" Realism

Blumenberg says that the late medieval emphasis on God's absolute power and freedom did not lead to despair but rather paved the way for modern science. Once we recognize that we cannot hope to understand what the world is like in itself (for that would mean understanding God's willing), one response might be what Blumenberg calls self-assertion.[20] In that world without Aristotelian natures, we shall try to make the movements of bodies predictable insofar as they affect our desires and our projects. We shall assert our power to bring matters under control, to define things not by what they are like for God or in themselves but by our own procedures for producing their occurrence reliably. So the modern conception of an object as what can be reliably, repeatably constructed or produced by the communal subject of science takes shape and develops. Such an objective world, many will grant, is not the world as seen from God's viewpoint, or noumenally. But that conception is what we need to assert ourselves as able to manage our surroundings from our human point of view.

Hegel saw as one of the chief claims of his system that it could overcome that unbridgeable gap between finite and infinite, and human and divine, by showing how finite human thinking, properly understood, transformed itself into the infinite, circular activity of self-relating thought. It is not that we become gods, and the distinction between finite and infinite remains, but as in Aristotle, the thinking we are able to

[19] Gordon Leff, *Gregory of Rimini* (Manchester: Manchester University Press, 1961), pp. 50–1. I have used Leff's account in portraying Rimini's position. See Leff, pp. 29–74.
[20] Blumenberg, *Legitimacy of the Modern Age*, pp. 125–226.

engage in, though intermittently, is not a second-best kind but is properly "divine." A similar theme occurs, in a very different account, with Davidson. We know the world roughly as it is, and while others may be smarter or have more true beliefs, our thinking is accompanied by an Aristotelian confidence that the kind of thinking we do is fit to grasp the determinations of things as they are. Even an omniscient god, interpreting us, would have to conclude that our conceptual scheme is not different in kind from his or her own.[21] Putnam, in contrast, offers us an internal realism that involves relativity to our scheme and that is opposed to a God's-eye realism.

I think there may be a residue of the religious picture in positions that emphasize their "realism with a human face." On the one hand, much is made by such positions of a contrast between their accounts and accounts supposedly committed to a omnipotent seeing of which only God is capable. And that contrast suggests why *our* knowing must be characterized as a pragmatic or instrumentalist self-assertion rather than as a grasping of things as they are. It is also the case that the medievals said, against certain Aristotelians who claimed that God's self-sufficiency would not let him know particulars, that God had to know the world and its creatures because he had made them. The *demiurgic* role of the modern subject gives it cause to make the same claim: that it must know what it has made, with the suggested addition that it does not know that in which its making has failed to play a part. But if we reject the notion of a voluntarist origin of determinacy, one that could vary unpredictably such that only God could know what is really the case, and if we reject the theological picture of the self as constructing its objects, then we need to ask what role can be played, if any, by the sort of oppositions that we employ in talking about a merely human realism. (I am not claiming that no legitimate role can be played by those oppositions, but I shall consider the way they can be used to support a picture of a thinned-out world upon which we impose our constructions.)

Human labor takes on a new significance in a world made radically indeterminate by the thought of theological absolutism. Hegel says that the Catholic worships Christ in an external thing, the host, while Luther recognizes the principle of interiority: Christ is received only on condition of our internal act of faith in him, our taking him to be present, which itself is due to God's grace.[22] The Catholic believes that the actions of priests, taken by themselves, will bring about certain sacra-

---

[21] Donald Davidson, "A Coherence Theory of Truth and Knowledge," in *Truth and Interpretation*, Ernest Lepore, ed. (Oxford: Blackwell, 1986), p. 317.

[22] Hegel, *The Philosophy of History*, in *The Philosophy of Hegel*, Carl J. Friedrich, ed. (New York: Modern Library, 1953), p. 106. The selections from the Introduction are translated by Carl Friedrich from the text of Georg Lasson (2nd ed.). The second part consists of selections translated by Paul Friedrich, and revised by Carl Friedrich, and are based on the translation of Sibree from the German of Karl Hegel.

mental effects, while the Lutheran demands an immediate relation to Christ in spirit.[23] The Romanic peoples, who remained Catholic, leave their spiritual life "over there," in an alien form, in the Church, and "since that which they have to do is not self-originated and self-prescribed, not their very own, they attend to it in a superficial way."[24] The Frenchman, in attending Mass, "reiterates words without much attention, while yet the necessary is being done," while the German Protestant requires inwardness.[25] The Catholic is even willing to have grace gained for him by the good works of others, through the Church's granting of indulgences.

The self in Protestant thought combines a passivity in relation to God's enabling grace with an emphasis on one's active making of the world through one's work, in accord with one's calling. In much of modern philosophy, we see the claim that anything objective must be constituted and secured as such by subjective activity. Political institutions, for example, are legitimate when we can take them to be so as autonomous rational citizens. Some recent debates about meaning and mental content may be seen to repeat, much transformed, the pattern of the Hegelian comparison of Lutheran and Catholic. Does the content of my beliefs or the meaning of my expressions depend just on the meaning I can take them to have? The greater a role I grant to the world and to the abilities of others in determining what I mean, the more I may seem to be in the position of Hegel's Frenchman, for whom "the necessary is being done" in some way external to him, or in the position of Hegel's Catholic when, in the manner of accepting indulgences, I accept my words to mean more than my own activities and abilities can make them mean.

The Aristotelian picture adopted by many medievals (it was rather a neo-Platonized Aristotle) not only allowed that things had their proper forms, independently of what we took them to have, but also that divine activity worked through proper channels, that is, through the lower spheres. The Church could imitate that structure through supposing that divine grace arrived through the channels of the priestly hierarchy. But for the Protestant, God's intervention is more immediate and interior. One possible outcome is that the world itself becomes a desacramentalized realm that has to have its meaning and value and objectivity established through our labor. One appealing idea, then, is to suppose that the real is what can be secured and ordered through our mental work, through the way that subjectivity "mixes its labor" with the world.

Our conception of our relationship with God may have an additional philosophical influence. The virtuous life for Aristotle is one that re-

[23] Ibid., pp. 107–8.
[24] Ibid., p. 126.
[25] Ibid., p. 126.

quires good practices of self-formation when one is young. The Christian, on the other hand, believes that God's grace can intervene in the world at any time and turn even the worst sort of person into a saint. So there is a sense that what I really am, the self as it is in relation to God, is not to be identified with a particular situation, character, habits, and training. I might be temporarily identified with a particular set of those, but the possibility of a very new self emerging through grace gives me a more abstract sense of what I really am. My immediate relation to God and my distance from a particular situatedness may also fortify my position as a demiurge securing the objective status of the world from outside it. With that position, I shall be much less disturbed than is the late-medieval Aristotelian by scientific studies that challenge my place at the center of the natural universe.[26] The self as demiurgic subject has a stance outside the world, instead of a localized position within it, and therefore is capable of a certain kind of reflection on his society from a point external to it.

There are other connections that might be drawn between religious and theological notions and our thought about subjectivity. But even this very brief survey will suggest certain issues for us to focus upon: the problem of the linkage of a free-standing mental space to the world; the emptiness and loss of content when that space is no longer secured by a relation to the divine; the thinning out of the world in relation to the power of subjectivity; the difficulties that arise from the notion of an external and arbitrary determiner; the problematic structure of an autonomous self-relating that can include a relation to, without swallowing up, what is other to it; the issue of how we might overcome the implicit comparison of our sort of knowing with a standard set by God's; the problem of the antirealism implicit in the emphasis on work and on our securing of objectivity by what we take matters to be. We shall see how Hegel attempted to solve some of these problems; then we shall look in detail at recent philosophy.

Subjectivity and the World in Hegel

There arose, even within the theological idiom, suggestions for solving the difficulties that the late medieval picture had raised. We might reduce the metaphysical insecurity of the medieval account, both Bruno and Spinoza suggest, by eliminating God as a transcendent will who might vary his determining power arbitrarily. Suppose there is instead an *immanent* God identified with the logico-metaphysical order that

---

[26] See Hans Blumenberg, *The Genesis of the Copernican World*, R. Wallace, trans. (Cambridge, Mass.: MIT Press, 1987), pp. 200–8.

makes things what they are. Then the role assigned to the divine activity will not be one that makes the world's own ontological stability any less. That is the strategy of Spinoza, while in Bruno the answer is to see the world as the self-exhaustion of God.[27] Suppose that God in creating expressed his power fully in an infinity of worlds spaced out over the universe. Then there is no leftover power still waiting to be expressed, and there is no place for the intervention of an arbitrary divine will into nature or into history. (Bruno accepted what turned out for him to be the painful consequences of the Christology that resulted from that claim.)

Hegel is, I think, the most interesting modern figure who rethinks the structure of subjectivity and its relation to the world, so that the problems caused by an alienated and demiurgic subject will not be a matter for concern. A recovery of the world is necessary in two senses, I have said, if we want to challenge the configuration set in place by the medieval and modern picture of subjectivity. The thinker must recover the world and be at home again among things as they are, and the world itself must recover at least a fair share of its metaphysical status, after having been thinned out by the migration of its features to the subject. Let us see how Hegel attempts to bring about that double recovery.

We need to look first at the issue of in just what sense he is an idealist. He holds that thought is the ground of the determinacy of the real, not just of the world as it is experienced by us, but of anything at all that is determinate. Thought, says Hegel, "is the constitutive substance of external things" (*EL* §24Z).[28] A claim such as that appears to make a strong commitment to idealism, until we note that Hegel uses 'thought' in an unusually broad fashion. The logical structure of thought seems to be present, on his account, wherever there is any kind of self-unifying or self-determining going on. So when the strong realist claims that reality articulates itself into units and sorts, even apart from how humans think, it seems that Hegel would see such a realist as granting the presence of

---

[27] I am again following Hans Blumenberg on this point. He has a chapter on Bruno entitled "The Nolan: The World as God's Self-exhaustion," in *Legitimacy of the Modern Age*, pp. 549–96.

[28] The longer version of Hegel's argument is *The Science of Logic*, A. V. Miller, trans. (Atlantic Highlands, N.J.: Humanities Press, 1990; from the Allen and Unwin edition of 1969). An abbreviated version is in the first part of Hegel's *Encyclopedia of the Philosophical Sciences*. That part, often called the *Encyclopedia Logic*, is published separately as *Hegel's Logic*, William Wallace, trans. (Oxford: Clarendon Press, 1975). I shall make citations to those sources in the text itself, using the following abbreviations. The *Science of Logic* will be abbreviated as *SL* and I shall use the page numbers of the English text. The *Encyclopedia Logic* will be abbreviated *EL* and I shall use the standard *paragraph* numberings in my references. This version of the *Encyclopedia Logic* contains the *Zusätze* or additional notes compiled by Leopold von Henning from lecture notes of Hegel and his students. When a citation is from these I shall use Z following the paragraph number: for example, §206Z.

thought in the world, in the very way in which things are determinate. Hegel, in fact, says that all philosophers are idealists ("Every philosophy is essentially an idealism or at least has idealism for its principle" *SL* 154–5), and some commentators, given the way Hegel defines his idealism, call him among the most realist of philosophers.[29] He does not make reality dependent on *thinkers*, as Berkeley does. The structure and activity of thought can be present before there are rational beings thinking, though in a manner that can be seen by the philosopher as a not fully developed form of the self-determining activity that is more explicitly present when we think.

Consider the perfectly natural way in which we speak of biological entities as actively maintaining themselves against other entities and against their environment. The living thing maintains itself as the same while going through changes that are determined from within, in accord with its own nature, instead of externally, as when I divide up a piece of land into quantitatively determined units, or add to or subtract from a heap of sand. But for Hegel that activity of self-maintenance through distinguishing itself from what is other, so that change comes about through internal development instead of through external determination, embodies a pattern we will find fully developed in thinking, when we examine the structure of self-relating-in-relating-to-otherness that characterizes thought. So logical notions can be seen as "immanent" in living things:

Since the Notion is immanent in it, the purposiveness of the living being is to be grasped as inner; the Notion is in it as determinate Notion, distinct from its externality, and in its distinguishing, pervading the externality and remaining identical with itself. (*SL* 766)

Hegel takes the self-mediating, self-differentiating activity in *biological* entities to exemplify the sort of logical relations that occur in syllogisms. To get going at all on this analogy, Hegel must make a great deal out of the "mediating" function of the middle term in the syllogism. Just as the middle term links universal and particular terms in the well-formed relations of certain syllogisms, so a biological entity is a self-unifying whole that joins in a successful "mediation" a universal character and particular differences or determinations. Because living things embody, so he believes, those patterns of logical activity, Hegel feels free to say that they are "thoughts" or "syllogisms." (". . . a living being is a syllogism" *EL* §217). It is not that thinkers must think of them or that the patterns of thought are projected upon them. If living things were not actively *self*-articulating, if they were only articulated by thinkers,

---

[29] "And if terms are used in their usual senses, it must be said that Hegel's System is 'realist'." Alexandre Kojève, *Introduction to the Reading of Hegel*, James Nichols, trans. (New York Basic Books, 1969), p. 150.

then they could not embody those thought-patterns, so that Hegel's form
of idealism seems to require a commitment that is not only more common
to the realist, but that renders antirealist and projectivist accounts unacceptable. On the other hand, it is important to the character of Hegel's
argument that we do not arrive at this logical category by describing
living things empirically and by then seeing analogies with patterns of
thought. If the logic is to be successful, then the *idea* of life must be
generated as a logical notion solely by the internal relations that develop
among the various notions themselves, by an internal momentum within
the logical realm, as we consider ways in which reality can be understood
as determinate. (See *SL* 762.) But we are not thereby engaging in a *merely*
categorial analysis; the kind of determinacy that the category of 'life' gets
through its logical relations will capture the sort of determinacy had by
real living things, so that our description of them in terms of thought-
structures will be an adequate one. (I shall be saying more about Hegel's
defense of that claim.)

There is a certain Aristotelian move in Hegel's conception of how
mind is related to the rest of reality. A common picture in modern
philosophy is that the mind is a realm of particulars situated in one place
and the rest of the world a realm of particulars situated across from it,
and the problem is to show why the former should be taken as giving us
any information about the latter. But that, believes Hegel, is the kind of
crude picture one gets when the categories one is working with are inadequate. Far better is the Aristotelian account that understands thinking
as a fuller actualizing of that which in things gives them unity and
determinacy, as the raising of that which makes something what it is to
fully explicit universality. But even in Aristotle, the understanding of that
relation has not developed to its proper completeness; the Aristotelian
notion of *form* does not fully capture the structure of free subjectivity that
only the modern Christian world, so Hegel believes, can make explicit.
So when he wants to follow the Aristotelian move that takes thinking to
be the actualizing of the thought-character of things, that is, of their
unity and universality and determinacy, he must look in the world for a
more complex structure than that of Aristotelian form. He must find
there in less fully actualized fashion the mediating structure of self-
relating-in-relating-to-otherness, or the "negative unity" with self, that
keeps repeating itself in his philosophy and that is the structure of
subjectivity and of thought as "spiritual."

Hegel is often seen as making outlandish metaphysical claims. He is
said, for example, to hold that everything real expresses the thinking of a
single supersubjective entity, one that generates versions of itself in the
world, thus accounting for nature and for history. But while his theological images will mislead, Hegel does not take thinking to be a constructing of objects. That model, based on the medieval God's relation as

creator to the world, is rejected by him in favor of the more Aristotelian account, one that holds thinking to be the *telos* of a process of development ("it is the *result* which appears as absolute ground" *SL* 72). There is no need to assume some creative or constructive activity that lays out the structure beforehand; that is precisely one of the accounts of determinacy he rejects. We can be misled in the way we take Hegel to be an idealist because as medieval/modern thinkers, we expect satisfying accounts to be in terms of *origins* (a divine act of creation that makes the universe what it is; the Cartesian pure origin or starting point for thinking; the original state of nature in Locke and Hobbes; the quality of the act of intending in Kantian ethics). So we think that his idealism must involve the activity of thinking as the causal origin of whatever determinacy we find. But Hegel's Aristotelianism is expressed in his holding that we understand the determinacy, sameness, and objectivity in things by understanding any activity of self-articulation in terms of the *most developed* form of it, that is, in terms of the structure of thought.

Hegel wants to redescribe generally accepted beliefs in his logical vocabulary, I think, rather than to put forward strange metaphysical claims. We do not need to see him, for example, as making the dialectic of thought the driving force behind history. His claim is instead that something's determinacy is defined in terms of what it is when it is fully developed, as I know what it is to be an apple by knowing what a fully actualized version of an apple is supposed to be. In a similar way, he believes, political institutions, if they actualize fully their rational potential, will come to embody a particular logical structure. But some apples fail to develop, and political institutions may fail to develop as well.

It is true, on the other hand, that Hegel's idealism is in many respects controversial. Even if his interest is in redescription rather than in metaphysical grandiosity, still the fundamental claim of his logic, and the basis for his redescriptions, is that every form of determinacy, in nature or culture or elsewhere, expresses an undeveloped or partly developed form of the logical structure that is proper to thinking or subjectivity:

The negative of the negative is, as *something*, only the beginning of the subject [Subjekt] – being-within-self, only as yet quite indeterminate. It determines itself further on, first, as a being-for-self and so on, until in the Notion it first attains the concrete intensity of the subject. At the base of all these determinations lies the negative unity with itself. (*SL* 115)

what seems to occur outside it, to be an activity directed against it, is its own doing, its own activity, and substance shows that it is in reality subject.[30]

Hegel does not (as the caricature goes) try to deduce all empirical facts from his logic, but he does grant a crucial role in his account to a

---

[30] Hegel, *The Phenomenology of Mind*, J. B. Baillie, trans. (New York: Harper, 1967), p. 97.

priori reflection. This issue is a subtle one. He believes that we can investigate the conditions of the determinacy of objects in a way that is not, in the end, empirically constrained. It is not that we can start from a realm of pure thought and can then deduce, autonomously from that realm, the logical categories outright. The philosopher begins instead in a world where such categories have already worked themselves out in discourse about nature and psychology, in our cultural and political life as well, and in earlier philosophy. She will then take the various ways we have come to talk about the world, and she will make explicit the patterns of logical development that relate these ways of talking one to another. (It should be clear that Hegel is not giving us a *formal* logic; he is rather relating different conceptions of what reality is like and he claims that there are internal relations among them, since some express in a more explicit way relations at work in, but hidden by, the earlier ones.) But there is a further and important demand. The philosopher must be able to relate those logical patterns so that they form themselves into a self-contained development within the logical sphere itself, a development that no longer depends on how or when logical categories arose in history, or on patterns that might occur in nature or in psychology:

For the reality which the Notion gives itself must not be received by it as something external but must, in accordance with the requirement of the science, be derived from the Notion itself. (*SL* 587)

The logical categories must become determinate not through the way they are anchored in the natural or historical worlds, but through their internal relations in an autonomous unfolding. Not only are the determinations internal to the logical sphere, but the standard for arranging them in an order is one that the order is able to put forward for itself. Only when that criterion is met will Hegel feel that his account is satisfactory. Yet it seems that making the logic of subjectivity autonomous guarantees that its application to the world must forever be in jeopardy.

Beyond Kantianism and Empiricism

Robert Pippin argues that Hegelian philosophers have not generally seen the degree to which Hegel continues Kant's program of transcendental investigation.[31] Kant had challenged the dogmatic metaphysicians by demanding that any conception of the world take into account the role of our *taking* the world to be such. Experience can be unified, says Kant, because in every experience of objects there is an apperceptive taking of ourselves to be so experiencing the world. The necessary conditions for

---

[31] See Robert Pippin, *Hegel's Idealism* (Cambridge: Cambridge University Press, 1989), pp. 16–41.

that apperceptive taking of the world to be objective will be conditions for any experience at all, so certain rules for determining objects will be present whenever we experience. Hegel, says Pippin, believed himself to be continuing Kant's work, even if he was dissatisfied with the limitation of Kant's findings to the world as it appeared, and with Kant's manner of deriving the categories. He thought of his self-determining logic of categories as playing the role of the transcendental unity of apperception in Kant.[32] But many Hegelian scholars today, says Pippin, treat Hegel as having fallen back into the dogmatic metaphysics it was Kant's entire purpose to overturn.

Now it is true that it is wrong to portray Hegel in the fashion Pippin opposes. He is not trying to describe the world, and to assign metaphysical categories to it on the basis of that description. The relation between thought and the world will not be shown through a *discovery* of what the world is like, but through an examination of the different ways we can *take* the world to be determinate, and through locating certain *internal* relations among them. Yet one may leave Pippin's overall reading wondering just why Hegel thinks that he has overcome the alienation between the categories of thought and the world as it is. By the time we finish the *Logic*, we are supposed to be convinced that the categories we have uncovered in our investigation are not imposed on the world but are an exhibiting of its own ontological character. While we have not gone about our business by comparing our categories to how things stand in the world, we have discovered an internal momentum among the various ways of understanding the determinacy of reality. Those ways of understanding present themselves as having various inadequacies, and we are led along by that natural momentum until we arrive at the Hegelian conception of the thought/world relationship. That final understanding shows that our fundamental concepts must capture the world as it is, and even more, must be an explicit actualizing of "logical" patterns that are in some sense present in things and institutions themselves, making them determinate.

the Notion is to be regarded . . . not as the subjective understanding, but as the Notion in its own absolute character which constitutes a stage of nature as well as of Spirit. (*SL* 586)

If, however, an existence contains the Notion not merely as an abstract in-itself, but as an explicit, self-determined totality, as instinct, life, ideation, etc., then in its own strength it overcomes the limitation and attains a being beyond it. The plant transcends the limitation of being a seed, similarly, of being blossom, fruit, leaf. . . . (*SL* 135)

The mechanical and chemical object . . . do not, according to their various natures, have their Notion existent in them *in its own free form.* . . . (*SL* 756–7)

<hr>

[32] Ibid., pp. 175–88.

Now the Notion, in Hegel's terminology, is the self-determining system of categories that he uncovers in his logical investigations. So the preceding passages can only mean that those logical relations, even if we define them and justify them in an a priori investigation of ways of taking the world to be determinate, are not just features of how we look at the world, but are in some sense present in a more primitive form in the very ways in which things articulate and exhibit themselves as having a determinate character.

Hegel believes he can give a comprehensive account of our metaphysical conceptions. The significantly different ways in which things can be self-articulating, can be determinate, can have conditions of sameness and difference, will be included in a progressive ordering. That ordering will be able to describe all these ways of being determinate as partial and less developed forms of the patterns of relationships, properly comprehended, that characterize his own conception of reality. His account will have included its possible opponents as employing notions of determinacy that, once their implicit structures are teased out of them, transform themselves into Hegel's account. The measure of his success, the sign that his progression is complete, is that the accounts can be reconstructed as part of an autonomous logical progression governed only by the demand to make explicit what is implicit in, or taken for granted by, earlier accounts. Even the position of the Kantian objector will supposedly have been included and surpassed. Instead of being a still viable position from which we can confront Hegel after he has finished, it will have been shown to transform itself into Hegel's own position, as soon as we demand that it display the logical structure that is, in the way it presents itself, implicitly present.

(The idea is that a metaphysical account can turn into a different one, not through being opposed from without, but through our pressing it to take to their logical outcome its own internal principles. That may seem an odd strategy to the Anglo-American philosopher, but let me give an example that is in some respects analogous. Davidson starts with Quine's principle of the inscrutability of reference, then says that some read Quine as using that principle to argue for ontological relativity. But if we push through to its logical outcome that notion of the inscrutability of reference, then there is no place from which we can support a claim that there are different reference schemes at work. So the relativist position turns itself into a more realist one when we put pressure on it and demand that it display its consequences explicitly. I shall look at this case further in my chapter on Davidson.)

Hegel's project is then more sophisticated than that of the empiricist, who wants to start from a position that is immediately self-certifying. Critics of empiricism will be quick to claim that much has been taken for granted in the background in order to make that "immediate" experience possible. It is "mediated" (Hegel's term) by that conceptual background, and it can be a determinate experience only when we consider the network of oppositions that is helping to constitute it. Hegel, in contrast, understands and makes explicit those hidden patterns of mediation and opposition, the structures that are taken for granted in various accounts of reality and of thought's relation to it. (That is the plan.) As each account puts itself forward, it turns out that there is another and richer account that puts the first in its place by making its character explicit, or that brings out a logical movement that was operative at the earlier categorial level but hidden, and that could not be explained with the logical resources of that level.

But by the time we reach the end of the logical progression, there will be no more mediating/opposing positions that remain external, so as to undermine the claim of a position to be self-legitimating. That ending account, Hegel's own, will have made the entire structure of mediation and opposition internal to itself; the very moves that would define Hegel's position by finding a stance external to it, one from which it could be given a determinate status, have supposedly been included *within* his complex conception. His conception cannot, then, be given its determinacy through an opposition to something *else*. It is made determinate through its own internal oppositions and mediations and is thus, in a genuine sense, self-determining. (That is, at least, the extremely ambitious goal.) There can be no higher grasp of reality such that Hegel's categories can come off as giving just a very limited and distorted purchase on the world. The measure again is that our categories have circled around on themselves in a now complete, autonomous movement.

So while Pippin is right to stress the Kantian sort of logical deduction in Hegel, he does not seem to grant that such a Kantian investigation leads, in Hegel, to a picture that is as Aristotelian as it is Kantian. Thus Hegel commends the "ancient metaphysics" for holding

that thinking (and its determinations) is not anything alien to the object, but rather its essential nature, so that things and the thinking of them ... are explicitly in full agreement, thinking in its immanent determinations and the true nature of things forming one and the same content. (*SL* 45)

Thoughts, according to Kant, although universal and necessary categories, are only our thoughts – separated by an impassable gulf from the thing, as it exists apart from our knowledge. But the true objectivity of thinking means that the thoughts, far from being merely ours, must at the same time be the real essence of things, and of whatever is an object to us. (*EL* §41Z)

As we go along in the Logic, other conceptions of the determinacy of what is real display themselves as suggesting, in more primitive and one-sided versions, the final Hegelian conception of a well-mediated self-relating-in-relating-to-otherness. Atomist accounts, for example, will have a one-sided emphasis on the self-relational aspect, the moment of self-identity, but then the relation to otherness comes off as empty and illusory, as with Leibniz's monads:

The diversity is only ideal and inner and in it the monad remains related only to itself; the alterations develop within the monad and are not relations of it to others. (*SL* 162)

Or (a different kind of one-sidedness) causal explanations emphasize the relation to something other, namely, to the effect that is produced by the cause. But in relating to the effect as its other, the cause is expressing itself as a cause, and is relating to that which allows it to be actual as a cause in the first place, so that there is implicitly here a relation of the cause with itself, and thus a self-relating that has not been adequately expressed. (See *EL* §153–4.) And so on until we arrive at Hegel's own conception, in which the entire structure of self-relating-in-relating-to-otherness is expressed in a perfectly explicit display, one that no longer has any impulse toward a more adequate expression. (In becoming *other* than itself, thought is unfolding its *own* character.) Some may find the use of that sort of vocabulary, and of that sort of argument, very unappealing, and perhaps not even comprehensible. But it may be unfair of me to separate out those analyses from the context in which Hegel has set them.

The finally adequate account may remind the reader in some respects of Aquinas's conception of God, as I described it earlier in the chapter. (This is not a surprise, in that both thinkers are Aristotelian.) The activity of thought remains autonomously self-relating in any relating to otherness. The conditions for categorial adequacy are set by itself, not empirically, so that in being sensitive to the ontological character of things, the thinker is relating to features that express his own character as a thinker. God's thought for the medievals involved a thinking of ideas that were his own essence, so that every thought of a creature was really a self-relating, God's thinking of himself; but also the metaphysical forms making things what they are were an embodiment, in a finite way, of those divine ideas. In Hegel's not quite fully secularized version of that structure, there is no longer a *transcendent* God. But thought relates to itself in relating to things because it relates to an embodiment of the very structure that it exhibits to itself internally. We can see the theological analogy in Hegel's claim that "God is, therefore, *for* himself in so far as he himself is that which is *for him*" (*SL* 159). That, in fact, is just the structure that Hegel takes thinking itself to have. The Hegelian category of the idea is explicitly that logical structure in which it is expressed that the categories at work are both subjective and objective, so that any relationship of logical or conceptual categories to what is objective must ultimately be thought's self-relating. We also have the Aristotelian result that our thinking, while its categories have the autonomy just described, does not occur in a separable autonomous space; it actualizes itself in bringing to explicitness and fully articulated development the categorial features of reality.

Let us express matters one more way. One difficulty for a philosophical account of reality is that it seems to lie open to a worrisome objection: that it may not match up with how things really are because it may always be contrasted with a God's-eye view of matters. Without the theological overtones, the claim is just that we cannot be sure that very substantial increases in our various intellectual abilities would not make available to us a fundamentally different account of what reality is like. Hegel's response to this claim (as we might put it too simply) is to display the God's-eye viewpoint, the divine contemplation of things as they are, as appearing within his system as its culmination, so that the contrast can no longer be made with an unincluded "divine" way of seeing. By what criterion can we be sure that we have arrived at such a position? The criterion will emerge through an unfolding of what previous accounts of God's thinking have presented. Our thinking must take on the qualities of autonomy, self-sufficiency, self-relating-in-relating-to-otherness, absolute self-grounding, and so forth, that the tradition has marked out for God's thinking. And that is just what Hegel believes has occurred in his systematic account. (Hegel overcomes many aspects of the theological and demiurgic model of subjectivity, but the self-relational activity of thought retains important features of the divine.)

Hegel will show us, as it were, the construction of the God's-eye view itself. The Kantian God who knows the noumenal world must be able to say *something* about it, minimally that it *is*. But Hegel can then supposedly show that implicit in an acceptance of that minimal category is already the set of oppositions and relations that will be effective in the culminating position of the logic. So the "divine" activity of thinking and determining unfolds in an immanent development. There is no space left for the external and arbitrary determiner that theological voluntarism made us worry about, and not any space left for the modern subject to take up such a stance from which it could project the world's determinacy upon it.

So we have seen roughly the form of Hegel's claim that self-relating selves are, in being such, fully in touch with things as they are. We do not assure the application of our categories through generating a constructed world that stands over against the world as it really is, nor do we contract the world on the basis of the evidentiary requirements of our sensory faculties. We are sure of being at home in a world that has, on its own, a rich determinacy. It is worth asking where the weaknesses in the program are mostly likely to be found. What will strike the reader first is that his argument places enormous pressure on his redescriptions. He must redescribe the various sorts of determinacy things may have in terms of the logical categories that he will later find to characterize the self-determining logic of thought. He has no hope, without doing that, of showing that the logical categories that emerge when we think are an exhibiting, in a more fully explicit form, of that which makes things themselves determinate. But the redescriptions are into such an exotic and highly abstract vocabulary that it will be very hard to convince us that they are not forced on the material by the needs of the Hegelian argument. Someone who approaches the project with a considerable degree of skepticism will be very unlikely to agree that Hegel is just making explicit what was implicit in earlier accounts.

And suppose I agree that every general form of determinacy appealed to in human accounts so far can be redescribed in the Hegelian manner and placed in his progression. Still that may indicate a limit in the way the human mind or our conceptual scheme works and not some deeper feature of reality itself. Perhaps I can recognize only those ways of being determinate that fit a logic programmed into our brains, and perhaps, additionally, we are good at making up narratives that hold the parts together in a rational sequence. So if there were other ways of understanding determinacy, including some that truly explain how things are, I just could not recognize them as candidates, but given ways of the sort I can recognize, I shall be able to tell a story in the Hegelian fashion. In addition, Hegel's analysis of our ways of talking about the world seems too much linked to the concepts available in the textbooks of his time, and in the history of philosophy up to the time of his writing. But the natural sciences, and the philosophy of science accompanying them, have changed significantly, and there have been developments in logic itself.

But I am not looking here to do that sort of evaluation of Hegel's claims. I do not think the project works, but working through Hegel's writings may spur us to be aware of, and also to offer resistance to, patterns of thought that modern philosophy would have us take for granted. (It is perhaps an irony that while such awareness and resistance might have caused earlier analytic philosophers to give up many of their projects, more recent philosophy in England and America has in some respects already worked through, on its own, "Hegelian" criticisms of that earlier work.)

Transition to Contemporary Philosophy

Hegel believes that the conceptions we find in empiricist and Kantian philosophies, and in their many variants, are not rigorously enough examined. One tries to break off some moment from the larger structure of self-relating-in-relating-to-otherness, and to grant it a determinate status independently of the mediations and oppositions of that structure.

One may hope to find, for example, experiences of immediate confrontation with the world that make certain base-level sentences true, or one may suppose that linguistic schemes can be made determinate on their own and can then project a determinate order on a more nebulous realm encountered in experience. Hegelian habits of mind, if not always his specific arguments, would make us far more skeptical about how these moments of confrontation or these linguistic schemes will themselves, cut off in that way, be determinate.

The Hegelian strategy for showing what reality is like, and how our thinking is at home in it, will then not appeal to theories of reference, of epistemic anchorage, of construction by a scheme. It will not seek to have the "fit" between the two sides secured either through having points where experience flows against the mind, or through having our categories impose their structure on a recalcitrant world. Hegel will instead try to examine, more reflectively and rigorously, what our general metaphysical and epistemological conceptions themselves are like, and how there is something primitive and "unthought" in them, even when we try to accept them on their own terms. Somehow a reflective inquiry that looks at internal relations among our conceptions will be able, just on the basis of those internal connections, to guarantee the correspondence of our categories to what is real, because the whole question of such a correspondence can no longer be a worry. (I shall be interested in a different sort of argument, offered recently by Donald Davidson, that likewise tries to secure that correspondence without depending on a comparison of thought and the world.)

The picture of an alienated and demiurgic subject reflecting on its own inner space may appear to be more advanced, and more persuasive, than what we are given with naive realist accounts. But that picture can remain attractive (the Hegelian suggests) only if it avoids having to account for itself, only if it fails to reflect carefully on the conditions for such a subject's having thoughts in the first place. As we press our inquiry more deeply, we end up not with that sort of alienation of thought but with a more sophisticated realism, and with the assurance that in making manifest the relations among our most basic logical/ metaphysical categories, we are making manifest the large features of the world. Just that claim is made by Davidson,[33] who will be one of the contemporary thinkers I find as continuing some of the Hegelian themes, if from a very different background and with arguments of a very different nature. Hegel attacks the Kantian philosophy for holding "that we place our thoughts as a medium between ourselves and objects, and that this medium instead of connecting us with the objects rather cuts us

[33] Donald Davidson, *Inquiries into Truth and Interpretation* (Oxford: Clarendon Press, 1984), p. 199.

off from them" (*SL* 36), while Davidson will say that "language is not a screen or filter through which our knowledge must pass."[34]

Hegel holds that neither the idealist nor the realist is correct:

> It is just as one-sided to represent analysis as though there were nothing in the subject matter that was not *imported* into it, as it is one-sided to suppose that the resulting determinations are merely *extracted* from it. The former view, as everyone knows, is enunciated by subjective idealism, which takes the activity of cognition in analysis to be merely a one-sided *positing*, beyond which the thing-in-itself remains concealed; the other view belongs to so-called realism which comprehends the subjective Notion as an empty identity that *receives* the thought determinations into itself *from outside*. (*SL* 788)

I do not want to overplay that comparison with Davidson, for the differences go deep as well. Hegel would find it unsatisfying, for one thing, that Davidson and others focus on causal relations between mental states and the world in order to show that their relationship is an internal one. Understanding the mind–world relation causally is still an undeveloped form of thinking for Hegel, one more primitive than the Aristotelian account of the actualizing, in a free and explicit form, of the thought-character of entities. But I believe that if we move to a somewhat higher level of resolution, we can see very real parallels between the anti-Kantian and antiempiricist moves in Hegel and quite a number of moves in recent philosophy, moves that ultimately support more realist conceptions. For the recent thinkers are often arguing against linguistic versions, put forward earlier in the century, of the Kantian and empiricist pictures that Hegel opposed. And what will interest me, in Davidson for one thinker, is the attempt to secure the adequacy of our concepts not through any empiricist anchorage in the world, but through rethinking the conditions for the realm of thought having the determinacy it does in the first place. We do not look for some kind of evidentiary linkage to the world. Rather we consider various conceptions of how thought is related to reality and try to show that these conceptions collapse when we press them to account for what they take for granted. Someone who proposes that our thoughts might be the same no matter how the world itself varied has not asked in a sufficiently radical way how those thoughts come to be the thoughts they are.

We saw earlier one of the problematic issues that medieval thinkers had left to their modern counterparts. They constituted an energy field one point of which had such an unlimited power against all other points that it was bound to suck into itself all activity of determination, and to leave the rest of the field thoroughly evacuated of power, meaning, and value. The modern subject's power, if not unlimited in that way, has at least a similar status. Hegel's solution is a clever one in that he accepts

---

[34] Ibid., p. xviii.

the modern turn to subjectivity and then proceeds to remake our conception of subjectivity so that its structures and patterns can count as already at work in the self-articulating of things. Then the determinative power can again be nicely distributed across the field, and there will not be the emptying-out rush to the single point of determination. If we cannot accept his solution, we shall need a different one for the redistribution problem, a different way of checking the inertial patterns of the medieval-modern energy field. We need to see whether a full disenchantment of subjectivity, and a consequent rethinking of the involvement of subjectivity in the world, will allow us to find ourselves in a world whose order and value we contribute to but do not constitute.

Ultimately Hegel wants to defend the claim that mind can grasp the world as it is. But he goes about his task, it seems, by releasing radical forces of instability, negation, and relativism into his system. All anchorage points and starting points and external stances that one might think necessary as an origin of determinacy are undermined in the movement of his logic. Yet he tries to show that it is these very negative forces that finally make possible the confidence of the mind in its grasp of things as they are. By using a strategy that is in some ways analogous (perhaps I am stretching here), Davidson establishes a conservative and even realist position, though he may be unwilling to describe it in those terms. He does not try to establish a stable point that can withstand the arguments by Quine and others for indeterminacy, but rather pushes even more radically the Quinean claims, through showing that relativists (like the skeptics in Hegel) have not been radical enough. (I am going to be developing that thought in Chapter 3.)

I have picked out these themes of subjectivity, mind, and realism, because I am now going to turn to a discussion of them in recent analytic philosophy, in thinkers such as Davidson, Putnam, McGinn, Wiggins, Rorty, McDowell, and many others. If Hegel's project had been successful, then we would have solved the problem of the recovery of the world, in the two senses that I have specified. Now we shall see if we can find, by other means and other arguments, positions that satisfy some of the hopes that Hegel had for showing how self-relating selves are at home in a world that retains, against the sort of pressures common in modern philosophy, its thick ontological and ethical character.

2

The Disenchantment of Mind

Externalism about Mental Content

Certain pictures of the mind's interiority, and of what God's thinking and willing must be like, helped to shape modern conceptions of the mental, and in so doing raised difficulties for situating mind in the causal order. The challenging of such religious and theological models I have called the disenchantment of subjectivity. The project of disenchantment is ubiquitous today but is carried out differently in different traditions. One may try to reduce the psychological to a level of description more firmly grounded in the scientist's understanding of nature; or one may talk of subjectivity as a construction out of the public practice of language. Perhaps an appeal to computers will seem the best way to go in explaining what it is to have a mind; perhaps the analogy will be instead to the construction of a self in literary texts or through relations a psychoanalyst might uncover. However the projects may go, the point is to challenge the autonomous, alienated, original, and demiurgic power of subjectivity. Often it seems that we are left with very little that could count as genuinely subjective; that outcome may suggest there are aspects of the topic we have not properly treated. Let us see how some of the relevant arguments go; my focus here will be on recent work in the Anglo-American tradition, though I think the results are of interest to those whose work lies elsewhere.

Medieval and modern thinkers gradually made more plausible, though they did not originate all aspects of, a picture of the mind such that worldly objects and mental contents could vary independently. My perceptions and beliefs might change radically without the world changing at all, or the world might be made to vary radically and things could seem to me, from the inside, just the same. It is not just the worries about skepticism that are a problem here; there is also the issue of whether the mind could be as alienated as that from the rest of the universe.

One way of asking if that account is correct is to investigate just what it is that makes the content of our mental states determinate. A feature of the mind is that at least many of its states are *about* something external to them. Our beliefs take the world to be a certain way, our intentions aim at making it be a certain way, and so on through other states of that sort. These are, in the philosophical idiom, *intentional* states, and we need to ask how it is that they have the particular content they have. Suppose it is the case that how matters stand in the world is an essential factor in the fixing of that content. In other words, suppose that the proper description of how I am *taking* the world to be depends on what is there to be thus taken. Then our mental life will fit into the world in a way that it could not do so on the Cartesian picture.

But that strategy will have no chance of being successful unless certain features of the modern conception can be challenged. For it seems that mental states are determined as what they are from within, and that we do not need to take the world itself into consideration in asking what someone is taking that world to be like. Such a response, call it an *internalist* one regarding mental content, may base itself on any of several accounts of how it is that content is fixed. Perhaps whatever vehicles in the mind carry intentional content do so intrinsically; they are not like written characters or spoken sounds that might carry, depending on who is using them, quite different meanings. Or perhaps it is the case that while the shapes or sequences of the inner representational medium do not have their content intrinsically, still there are mental acts of meaning-bestowal that fix what they mean in a finally determinate way. Or perhaps there is a privileged reader of those shapes, either the believer himself or a divine being who illumines the interior realm and sees into its depths.

There has been much work in recent philosophy that aims at defeating such internalist accounts. It is natural, in the first place, to do here what scientists do, and that is to isolate causal factors by conducting experiments that keep some factors fixed while letting others vary. These will be thought experiments, given the nature of our subject matter. One imagines a situation in which such a controlled variation has taken place and then tests one's intuitions about how to describe that situation and others that resemble it. There are some who have little patience for such a way of doing things, and it is true that it is easy to parody some of the less skillful or more bizarre examples. But well done they are a proper part of doing philosophy.

It is clear how one might attack the internalist. The latter must say that if you fix someone's internal happenings from the skin inward, as it were, insofar as these can be described independently of the world or of other believers, then you have fixed as well the content of his intentional states. So a thought experiment will try to keep internal happenings fixed, while varying some other factor, such as causal connections to things in the world. If the person's beliefs or intentions change as a result of that variation, then the external factor must play a role in determining the content of psychological states.

That is just the sort of experiment proposed by Hilary Putnam; it is among the best-known in recent philosophy.[1] I may imagine that there is someone just like me, molecule for molecule, on a planet that is just like the earth, except for one fact. On that planet, Twin Earth, water has a different chemical composition, XYZ instead of H_2O. Let us suppose further that I and my twin, living in 1750, know nothing about that hidden chemical structure. We may ask then whether we have the same thoughts and beliefs, and whether we mean the same thing by 'water' (for he speaks Twin English). Putnam believes our answer should be negative. The actual chemical composition of what I am talking about helps to define what I mean, and that fact in turn helps to define the beliefs and thoughts I express. So I and my twin have different beliefs, at least in the case of beliefs about the waterlike substance that each of us is confronting. Yet the experiment was set up to make us the same in our physical states, in our qualitative feels, in our discriminatory abilities, and in our dispositions to produce motions. (Since our physical states contain molecules of water, my twin and I must have some physical differences, but they should not be relevant to the determination of content.) So it must be the world that is making the difference in what mental states we have ended up having.

Putnam seems to suggest the conclusion that our psychological states could not determine what we mean and refer to since the psychological states have remained the same while meaning and reference have varied.[2] But he has shown rather that the psychological states have varied as the world did, so we cannot draw a conclusion based on a supposed failure in their covariance.[3] What the argument shows, if it works, is that facts internal to me fix neither meaning nor psychological states. That conclusion expresses a position regarding mental content that we shall call an *externalist* one.

Putnam's example concerns a natural kind, but the form of the argument is thought by many to allow a more general conclusion. Even a superintelligent observer, it will be said, if she had access to all the inner goings-on of a person, would be unable identify his beliefs and intentions. That would be like having access to spoken utterances or to written characters without seeing how the one producing them is speaking a particular language, and is engaged with a particular environment. The inner patterns of the mind are not intrinsically meaningful. They become meaningful only when light from the world, as it were, shines across them, when we see how they are triggered in regular ways by regular features of the world.

---

[1] One version of the experiment is in Hilary Putnam, *Reason, Truth, and History* (Cambridge: Cambridge University Press, 1981), pp. 22–5.

[2] Ibid., p. 23.

[3] On this issue, see Tyler Burge, "Other Bodies," in *Thought and Object*, Andrew Woodfield, ed. (Oxford: Clarendon Press, 1982), pp. 100–3.

A related argument holds that meaning, belief, and intention are public in nature. Meaning and belief, as Quine and Davidson argue, must be displayable to an interpreter, at least in principle. For it is in situations of the public availability of evidence that our psychological and semantic vocabularies have their place, and gain whatever legitimacy they can possess. And the interpreter, in assigning psychological states to a speaker and meaning to his utterances, will have some leeway in making holistic adjustments for the evidence. So there cannot be internal states that carry their content intrinsically; indeed the basis of the interpreter's assignment will be an assessment of how utterances and behavior make sense relative to the causal environment.[4] (I shall say more about that argument in the next chapter, on Davidson.)

Externalism will not likely be true for the case of pains, but our topic here is those mental states that have *aboutness*, an other-directed content. Regarding some inner states we may expect there to be considerably more controversy. We readily accept the world to be articulated into natural kinds in ways that our present understanding may not capture, so that our vocabulary reaches out towards being fixed by what other investigators, perhaps in the future, will discover. But then there is the content that is more proper to the mind's interiority, namely, how the world *seems* to us when we perceive it. My beliefs about titanium or ospreys may depend on discriminations that I am unable to make, but it appears that how the world seems to me is a function of my actual causal powers to make discriminations. So it will be argued that it is less likely the case that the world itself must figure in the determination of that sort of content.

We might ask, then, whether a reference to something external to the mind is implicit in the fixing of the character of our perceptual states.[5] This topic connects with earlier and difficult issues in the philosophy of mind, and it challenges the often limited powers of our imaginations to think of what might be the case in contrary-to-fact situations. So my consideration of the topic will be brief. Could the sensation that is now in me an appearing of something as green have been the appearing of something as red? Suppose that I woke up after a minor accident to the head and my perception had changed so that (formerly) red things appeared to me green and vice versa. At first, I would likely take the conservative route and say that what it is for something to *appear* green remains the same but that I am consistently misperceiving colors. But I

[4] The Davidsonian account of interpretation can be found in two of his essays, "Radical Interpretation" and "Belief and the Basis of Meaning." Both are reprinted in his *Inquiries into Truth and Interpretation* (Oxford: Clarendon Press, 1984) (henceforth: *Inquiries*).
[5] I recommend the discussion of this topic in Colin McGinn, *Mental Content* (Oxford: Blackwell, 1989), pp. 60–94.

might well come to feel, as I adapted over time, that since my apparatus still works well at making the color discriminations that need to be made, I should stop thinking of the apparatus as guilty of consistent misperception. I should say instead that what it is for something to appear green has changed.

I might begin to look on the vocabulary of my "qualitative feels" as to an important degree nonnatural, and think it no odder that appearing green now has a different "feel" to it than that the language I speak may come over time to change the meaning of some of its utterances, so that certain sounds now carry a different semantic content. The inertia of wanting to continue my agreements with others and to count the world itself as relatively stable may also work in favor of that conclusion. So the way the world appears to *other* color discriminators, and their habits of engaging in color discourse as well, would be (externalist) factors in the identification of just what sensory states I am having. The claim will be made that even my most thorough awareness of the feel of my internal states, and of my dispositions to produce utterances and other behavior, would be insufficient to fix how the world *seems* to me. (Unlike with the case of natural kinds, so long as I cannot discriminate between different ways in which the world seems, then there is no difference; the world is not such, in the case of sensory content, as to fix kinds in a way that transcends my own abilities to discriminate. But it may happen, on the present suggestion, that *what* perceptual content gets mapped onto the space articulated by my discriminatory abilities may depend on how others experience, and on how they speak about it as well.)

Now some will believe it just an unacceptable outcome that I might be wrong not only about how the world is, but also about how it seems. In the case above, I might wake up in a daze sometime and forget whether the sensation I am having is an appearance of something as red or is an appearance of something as green. Is that a real possibility or is there something odd about thinking of matters in that fashion? And the preceding example does not show that all internal states have remained the same, while content changed, since my dispositions to behave and to appreciate colored objects may change along with the character of the sensations. (That is a significant contrast with Putnam's Twin Earth case; perhaps we could make further adjustments to remove that complicating factor.) But I shall leave this particular topic. I do not have the confidence in my intuitions here that some others have, though I do think we shall be able to push the externalist position rather far into our account of how the world seems to one perceptually. One's externalism will be stronger or weaker depending on how extensively across the field of mental phenomena one supposes Putnam's results to apply, and sensory content will be an important area of controversy.

There is a difficulty generally for someone who wants to base a theory of content on regularities in the causal triggerings of internal states.[6] We make perceptual *mistakes* very often. A stick may lead me to take the world as containing a snake, and there will likely be cases where a perceptual belief will be triggered a majority of the time by objects that will make us count that belief to be in error. But it is unclear on just what basis we can suppose that there are indeed errors in such cases. An externalist, causal account of content should, it would seem, define a belief's content on the basis of what actually triggers it, so that the very process of defining content seems to guarantee that whatever triggers the belief must be counted as *properly* triggering it. Thus the concept I express through uttering 'snake' will have the disjunctive content 'is a snake or is a snakelike stick.' Then when I take the stick as falling under that concept I am correct.

But that cannot be right. The content of my belief states fits into the larger picture of what I am aiming at in being engaged with the world. The strict causal theory of content makes me too passive; it does not acknowledge that my *taking* of the world to be such-and-such is some-thing that I do, relative to my interests. So our account of content needs to become teleological as well as causal, not in any extravagant sense but in the sense familiar to the biologist. Certain internal mechanisms of an organism may have the evolutionary advantage of making it sensitive to features of the environment that affect its success in living and reproduc-ing. But those mechanisms may not be fine-tuned enough to distinguish between the environmental features associated with that evolutionary advantage and other features that are very similar. So the organism can make "errors." Once we have an entity advanced enough to count as having internal states with genuine semantic *content*, then causation plus teleology will give us an account of that content that still favors the externalist, and that shows how very substantial error is possible.[7]

Attempts at a Retreat Inward

Now one frequent response of analytic philosophers to these externalist pressures is to make a tactical retreat inward and to try to find new boundaries for the mind whereby its contents will be unaffected by the external features. The idea is that a theory of the mind will be done, insofar as content is concerned, in two distinct stages. First we shall account for what is genuinely inner about the mind by letting no external content-determining factor play a role in what we articulate the mind's

[6] For a discussion of this topic of error and causal theories, see Jerry A. Fodor, *Psycho-semantics* (Cambridge, Mass.: MIT Press, 1988), pp. 97–127. I cannot recommend his solution.

[7] For a biological account of content see Ruth Millikan, *Language, Thought, and Other Biological Categories* (Cambridge, Mass.: MIT Press, 1984).

contentful states to be. Here we shall uncover "narrow" or pure intentional states that are what they are apart from how matters stand in the world. Then in a second step we shall bring in those connections to a particular world that, when added to the narrow intentional states, produce full-blooded beliefs and intentions, of the sort that Putnam is worried about in his Twin Earth experiment.

I want to look at this strategy for just a bit, for it is notable that philosophers should find it important to discover such a purer content that is genuinely inner to the mind. The motivation may in some cases be the desire to construct a science of the mental (I shall be examining this issue), but I wonder if there is as well a residual effect of the religious notion of an interiority visible to God, of the Protestant notion of individual responsibility for the contents of consciousness, and of the demiurgic picture that we know what we have made. Our autonomy and self-knowledge as individuals seem at risk under the externalist account. Even if many of my beliefs are false, still it seems that the fact that they mean what they do is, if anything is, an individualist undertaking of mine.

So let us consider the strategy of pulling the defensive perimeter inward, and of establishing precisely what the individual contributes to the content of his intentional states. At first glance this strategy seems promising. Suppose we have Oscar and his twin on Twin Earth. There is something different about what the two believe (that was Putnam's point), but there is also something that is the same in their psychological states. If you transported Oscar to Twin Earth he would behave in just the way that Twin Oscar does there and vice versa. And the strategy of a certain kind of retreat from the world has more general support. It is true that we can make our descriptions identity-dependent in that the content will depend on what is out there causing the description. But we can also make our descriptions identity-independent by taking content to remain the same even as it comes to be about situations that are different.[8] Thus I may use 'the man who won the New York lottery yesterday' as a way of picking out a particular individual in order to say about him that he is short and fat. But I may also use that phrase in a way that is detached from the picking out of any particular individual but that applies to *whoever* it is that falls under the description, so that the phrase might have the same semantic content even as it is used to pick out different individuals in different possible worlds.

So the idea would be this. We might talk of *modes of presentation* of the world that are not linked to particular referents in the world and that are definable just on the basis of the discriminatory abilities and causal

---

[8] I am depending here on distinctions made by Simon Blackburn, *Spreading the Word* (New York: Oxford University Press, 1984), pp. 302–40.

powers internal to the individual. Sameness and difference of (narrow) mental content would be based just on these modes of presentation. So we can ignore the kind of worries that Putnam introduces. There will be two kinds of beliefs, then, based on different principles of individuation, of counting beliefs as the same and as different. Narrow beliefs are what are the same in Oscar and Twin Oscar and wide beliefs are what are different. The former can help specify an autonomous mental realm where content is what it is without reference to anything external.[9]

But has that strategic retreat inward been successful? Note how very much we take for granted in deciding what the same narrow belief will be in Oscar and in his twin. We ignore the molecular structure of water and of XYZ and focus instead on their shared belief in a waterlike substance that satisfies thirst, that is good for cleaning, that provides coolness in summer when it is present in amounts large enough for swimming. But just how were we able to assign that very rich semantic content to their mental states? Only by assuming their residence in worlds with very much in common, worlds that could be used as the taken-for-granted background that had to be present for interpretation to go on. We did not turn inward away from the world; we just ignored some distinctions in the world to which the two knowers had no access. Perhaps we turned inward enough to make sameness of psychological state depend on the actual discriminatory abilities of Oscar and his twin. But then the overall assignment still depended on letting the world cast its shadow across those internal states, to make them able to bear content at all.

Suppose instead that we wanted to make the retreat to the interior a more honest one so as to arrive at a genuine mental autonomy, in order to know precisely how much of the content of an individual's states is due to what is going on in him and not to the world. Then we could not yet take for granted anything about the worlds in which Oscar's mental functioning might be meaningful. We would have to worry about the possibility that a range of Twin Oscars might inhabit quite different worlds from that of earth and still function appropriately in them. Then the narrow content we ascribe to Oscar would have to abstract not only from the differences between water and the watery substance on Twin Earth, but also from a wide range of other differences as well. (This point is a difficult one to make, so let me do more to set up the claim.)

It may have seemed from what we said earlier that once we bring considerations of teleology into the picture, then it will be clear just what narrow content is to be assigned to a believer. For the inner discriminations and dispositions will be appropriate for the satisfying of a very particular set of interests. But that answer may be insufficient here. Let

[9] For a discussion of narrow and wide content, see Burge, "Other Bodies," pp. 107–16.

me refer to an example put forward by Colin McGinn, though I shall be using it for a different purpose. (Again I ask the reader to be patient with these thought experiments. They do have a point, and they raise issues that can be raised in no other way that I know of.) McGinn asks us to consider the frog's mechanism for perceiving bugs darting across the visual field and for using its tongue to capture the bugs.[10] An accurate account of what the frog is about when carrying out its functions properly must take that mechanism as a bug-catching mechanism; that is what the mechanism has been designed through its evolution to do. Now imagine placing that frog from birth in an environment where certain dark spots are flashed across a large screen that is one wall of its world. The frog snaps its tongue at the spots just as it is programmed by evolution to do, though these, unfortunately for it, are not bugs. Yet the spots are not only the typical cause of the frog's perceptions and tongue movements; they are the only cause, since the frog is never allowed to see bugs. So it seems that a causal theorist about perceptual content ought to say that the frog is correctly perceiving the world as containing such dark spots, rather than systematically misrepresenting the world as containing bugs. But that seems an odd conclusion, since a million years of evolution went into designing the mechanism as a bug-perceiving mechanism; that is what it does when it is thriving as what it is. So McGinn concludes that the straightforward causal theory must be wrong.

We have earlier taken just such a teleological turn in response to the simpler account of the causal theorist. Often we must give a story of causal genesis of internal states that goes well beyond the immediate environment of the representer, and that may include the causing of internal states in other perceivers now absent (as, for example, earlier members of the species). But now let us ask whether we might see an alternative teleology that would make the frog's behavior appropriate in its new environment. The facts about evolution ought not, on their own, to persuade us. For biological organisms can find new uses for mechanisms that revolution has designed for other purposes, and if such uses prove appropriate in new natural or cultural environments, we shall likely see them as functioning successfully by the new standard rather than badly by the old. So imagine that the dark spots moving across the screen register the elevated presence of a dangerous substance in the air of the new environment, one that could kill the frog. (This is the way the designers have set things up.) When it strikes at one of the spots with its tongue, it causes another substance to be released that counteracts the dangerous one.

At first, we might say that the frog is simply being fooled into aiding

---

[10] McGinn, *Mental Content*, pp. 78–80.

itself. But suppose large colonies develop over many generations in this environment. They never see bugs in the air and are provided their food in an alternate manner. Wouldn't we eventually see a new teleology in the activity of the frog? It would no longer be misperceiving the world as containing bugs; the very same perceptual mechanism would now be a registering of spots that warn it of a dangerous substance in the atmosphere. (I recognize that the example is strained but it is, of course, difficult to think of alternate teleologies that would affect just one small aspect of an organism's life.)

The issue then is whether the same internal happenings and dispositions to produce motions might count as carrying out rather different teleologies, in different circumstances or in different worlds. If so, then our assignment of narrow beliefs, as defined above, would have to be neutral regarding the effects of those different teleologies on the determination of content. For the assignment of narrow content is not yet supposed to be taking an engagement with a particular world into consideration. Instead of just withdrawing to a semantics that included most of what we know about water but was neutral regarding the distinctions in molecular structure between water and XYZ, we would have to come up with a far more abstract description of content, one that was consistent with all the successful assignments of content to all the Twin Oscars in all their different worlds. And it should be clear what the danger is: A level of abstraction will soon be reached that means there is nothing left that could genuinely be called a psychological state. We would end up not with narrow beliefs but with vague abstract structures whose content might be filled in rather differently in various environments.

Perhaps we should not be so ready to draw that conclusion. It is easy to think of a certain sequence of characters as meaning one thing in English and another in another language, and we have been supposing that the representational medium of the mind has a similar kind of plasticity. But suppose we keep increasing the length of the sequences to include, say, all of Shakespeare or a standard encyclopedia. The more complex we make the interconnections among the characters in the sequences, the harder it becomes to believe that someone could take those sequences to belong to a language different from English that is talking about a very different kind of world. The parallel will be that the more intricately connected are the internal happenings and states and dispositions that are relevant to an individual's mental states, the harder it is to believe that the individual could, while possessing such internal features, be functioning well in worlds very different from the present one. (The follower of Derrida will note how that comparison emphasizes what Derrida calls the "written" character of mental activity.)

Here is one way of thinking about this issue. (It is suggested by Daniel

Dennett.[11]) Let us see what remains constant, as the individual's "organismic" contribution to the content of belief, as we allow the natural and social words to vary as radically as we wish. We pluck someone from his natural and social environments and present him to a super-intelligent interpreter. That interpreter, we may imagine, is also a super-powerful demiurge, and can create radically different possible worlds as situations in which to test the believer plucked from his home environment. The interpreter is not allowed any knowledge of that home environment, but is allowed to examine the individual's responses to any possible world in which he is placed, and thus his current total dispositional state. (Again there may be readers hostile even to thinking about this sort of thought experiment. But how else are we to specify just what supposedly comes from the individual himself and what from the world in the determination of mental content, once we have rejected the notion of a mysterious meaning-conferring activity that comes from within? We have to show by argument what goes wrong, and why it does so, when we try to purify a genuinely inner realm that is what it is apart from its connections to the particular world in which the owner of that inner realm is positioned. We should not simply move on to antiinteriority positions because of their popularity. We have to ask if after we give up the notion that mental states have their content intrinsically, there will remain a basis, in the very complexity of the internal states and their connections to bodily motions, for a unique assignment of content.)

The interpreter's strategy, says Dennett (I have been modifying his experiment), would be to try to guess what would be the optimum environment for the believer being examined.[12] The situation will be like coming upon a machine that is no longer in its environment, and trying to guess what it is by testing it in a variety of environments and seeing what it is good for. The interpreter will not be looking for the best possible world for the subject, but rather for the world for which his discriminatory abilities seem best fitted. We thus have a Davidsonian situation of radical interpretation, only with much greater freedom.[13] Dennett's interpreter here will be able not only to adjust belief, meaning, and desire relative to one another, but also to vary the natural and social environments (so as to get at what mental content is independently of those environments).

Now here I am at something of a loss, since I think such a thought experiment is the proper way of isolating precisely what we should count as genuinely "inner" to the individual, yet I also think it moves us to a level where our intuitions are not likely to be much good. Who has any

---

[11] Dennett, "Beyond Belief," in *Thought and Object*, Andrew Woodfield, ed., pp. 36–48.
[12] Ibid., pp. 41–2.
[13] See Davidson, *Inquiries*, pp. 125–40. I shall be considering Davidson's work in the following chapter.

sense at all what superintelligent interpreters might be able to assign as suitable possible worlds to someone whose internal states, and whose dispositions to produce movements, are functioning in just the way that mine are? Who can even begin to tell just how much those interpreters will be constrained in making such assignments? For they might take motions that seem inappropriate for a particular natural environment and count them as expressions of social rituals in just such a world. There are not obvious limits on the kinds of compensations one could make, when interpreting another in this thought experiment, in order to count a mind as fitting an environment. I do not take our difficulty here to mean that the thought experiment is a foolish one. Perhaps beings with a higher intelligence and much more powerful imaginations than ours would be able to draw plausible conclusions from the situation described. The experiment does the right job of trying to isolate out just what all the inner goings on in the individual contribute to fixing the content of his psychological states. But it also presents to us a situation for which our own intuitions will take us only a very short way down the path to a solution.

If we are looking for a two-stage psychology, as above, and the first stage requires a retreat to the genuinely inner, then the considerations now in place do not show us how to get that first stage done. They show us that we should not expect it to be something that we can make very good sense of doing at all. Either we end up with extremely abstract content descriptions that fail to count as intentional states at all, so that there is nothing left that can properly be called mental; or we appeal to a distinction that depends on a thought experiment that we cannot even begin to think about with any precision. I think our conclusion ought to be that it is not of much use, and should no longer be of much interest, to look for some genuinely autonomous region of mind where the individual determines the content of his mental states, however narrowly conceived. The self as having intentionality is essentially " in the world," as the Heideggerian would want to put it. If we try to think of the self as on its own and worldless, we end up with no subjectivity whatever, but with an isolated engine producing shapes and sequences that can have no meaning at all.

This is not to say that the distinction between narrow content and wide content is never useful. Sometimes our interest in assigning beliefs is in making the other's behavior predictable, and then we are interested in his own discriminations and causal powers, so that Putnam's distinction between what Oscar believes and what Twin Oscar believes will be unimportant. At other times we are more interested in beliefs as carrying a content that can be communicated among believers with different sorts of information. Then we may focus on connecting the belief to worldly features of which the believer may be partly ignorant. But it is important to see that when we make that distinction between narrow and wide content, we are not isolating an autonomous sphere in which the individual from within determines the contents of his mind. We are just distinguishing between two ways in which the world comes into play in our assignment of content.

I have been considering externalist claims about the role of the world in determining intentional content. There is another externalist argument having to do with whether the linguistic practices of *others* play a role in fixing the semantic content of an individual's beliefs. (We may contrast socialist and individualist positions on the matter of content.) This argument has its own importance but I am postponing the issue to the following chapter. There I shall be considering Davidson's general account of meaning and language, and as his position is a central one in that debate about content and is linked with much of the rest of his philosophy, it will be more appropriate to treat the issue in the course of a larger treatment of his work.

Interiority and Following a Rule

There is a different argument against the notion of individual autonomy regarding meaning and belief. It is an argument different versions of which can be found, I think, in Wittgenstein and Derrida, though I shall be considering work by the former, and shall save my comments on the latter until the final chapter. The general argument claims that essential to that which makes any semantic content determinate is an insertion in a chain of possible repetition. A meaningful utterance is determined to have the meaning it has only if it is determined what counts as a saying of the *same* thing on another occasion. But nothing about the original saying can fix in advance just what can serve as a repeating of it, as a going on in the same way. And the chain of repeatings may include not only the utterer's future sayings but also those of other speakers whose practices of saying and interpreting will help fix what was originally said, by contributing to the determination of what counts as a repetition. Making content determinate involves a reference to an elsewhere whose character cannot be controlled in advance. So the "divine" act of meaning-bestowal by a subject becomes instead an activity dispersed along a chain that one can never take to have ended. Once we accept that utterances do not get their meaning by expressing an ideal semantic content or through being a product of a privileged activity of mind, then identity and sameness for mental or semantic items must depend on what practices come to count as such.

Wittgenstein asks what gives determinacy to a semantic rule that is supposed to govern future uses of an expression.[14] I learn how to use an expression by encountering a limited number of applications of it to the world, but those limited applications allow of different possible ways of extending usage to absent and to future cases. We might think of an image of a railroad track that diverges at some point in the distance, and then ask what will count as a continuing of the same route and what as a change to a different one. Even in the case of arithmetic, says Wittgenstein, a limited number of applications, during a process of learning, cannot fix how future cases of the chain of applications must go in order to be a doing of the same thing. No matter how many cases we consider in advance, there will be a multitude of mathematical functions that agree in their assignments of values for the cases so far considered, but that diverge regarding cases not yet encountered. How can there be a fact of the matter as to which function we are computing when our only experience is with those encountered cases?

An appealing response is to say that the problem described holds for the outside observer, who has available to her only the limited number of applications that I have made in following the rule. But I know what I shall do in the future; I know how I am interpreting the rule that I have inferred from the practice around me. Perhaps I did not learn the rule properly, but I know what I am *taking* the rule to be as I follow it. I can display it in my mind and know automatically how to go about governing my practice on the basis of what is thus displayed, and I might attach a handy recipe to the rule's representation, so that there is a step-by-step procedure for making correct applications. Or I might visualize what I shall do in various circumstances.

But I have not thereby made the semantics of the rule finally determinate, even to myself. Neither the display of the rule nor the attached recipe nor the representation of future applications will be enough to fix future use. For the displays and recipes and representations themselves need to be interpreted; they are not self-interpreting. There is no mean-

---

[14] Wittgenstein has remarks relevant to the issue of rule-following throughout *Philosophical Investigations* and *The Blue and Brown Books*. See especially the *Investigations* (Oxford: Basil Blackwell, 1953), sec. 147–242. There has been a great deal of recent discussion of the topic. Here are just a few of the important treatments: Saul Kripke, *Wittgenstein: On Rules and Private Language* (Cambridge, Mass.: Harvard University Press, 1982); Colin McGinn, *Wittgenstein on Meaning* (Oxford: Basil Blackwell, 1984); Crispin Wright, *Wittgenstein on the Foundations of Mathematics* (London: Duckworth, 1980); David Pears, *The False Prison*, Vol. II (Oxford: Clarendon Press, 1988), pp. 423–501; G. P. Baker and P. M. S. Hacker, *Scepticism, Rules, and Language* (Oxford: Blackwell, 1984); S. H. Holtzman and C. M. Leich, eds., *Wittgenstein: To Follow a Rule* (London: Routledge and Kegan Paul, 1981); Simon Blackburn, *Spreading the Word* (New York: Oxford University Press, 1984), pp. 69–109. I have found Kripke's discussion especially useful in thinking about the present section. But I am not in agreement with his account of the relationship between repeatability and actual community practice.

ing-conferring power in the mind that can give a determinate meaning to any of the representations we might bring forward. If I define addition in terms of a counting procedure, my representation of the counting procedure will be consistent with different ways of going on to do the same thing in unencountered cases. Even for the future cases that I do now picture to myself, there will remain the question of what it takes to make a certain behavior in the future count as a doing of the *same* thing as what I now picture. Just what ultimately is supposed to be grounding those judgments of sameness? If I try to define what I take my subjective states to be in terms of *more* subjective states that I present to myself, I shall still leave matters indeterminate. Everything depends on making determinate our application of the vocabulary of sameness and difference to semantic sequences, and no amount of building up representations in the mind, or of producing public representations, will make that determination a final one.

The Wittgensteinian pushes an opponent into the position either of accepting the given account of rule-following, and of granting the indeterminacy Wittgenstein has proposed, or of appealing to an utterly mysterious way by means of which one might confer a determinate meaning on one's intentional states. (Some believe that we understand subjectivity so poorly even today that we should not rule out the possibility of a meaning-conferring activity that must appear as mysterious to our very limited minds, but that could be readily understood by much more intelligent beings.)

Now the result of Wittgenstein's rule-following considerations is unthreatening, because it undermines a picture of semantic determinacy that was not at all needed. The mistake was to suppose that what makes our practices work is that we are governed by inner representations of the rule, such that it is a sameness of internal entities that guides our common practice, and makes us all go on in the same way to new cases, so that semantic indeterminacy at *that* level would be a serious problem. What makes rule-following successful, says Wittgenstein, resides at the noncognitive level, in the habits and biological propensities that make us count the same things as the same, and so make us go on in the same way when a limited number of applications have been presented. My taking of a rule to mean something is part of my active engagement in practice, and is not something definable as an adding of new items to the set of internal representations. But then it appears that we do after all determine internally what rule we are following, and that is by the causal powers of the machinery that is operating in us to fix what we shall take to be the same. That answer will not do. For any machine can make mistakes, and we need to distinguish between the machine's running properly and its being in error. One cannot appeal then to the causal powers of the machine itself as a criterion for making that distinction. (Nor can one, on the communal level, let the causal powers of cultural practices be an ultimate criterion of rightness.)

I shall not take a final position on the rule-following argument because I am not sure what final position to take. I do find persuasive the claim that mental and semantic items do not have an intrinsic content that can be determined by some interior activity, and the claim that repeatability, if not actual repetition, is a necessary condition for content and cannot be fixed in advance by the features of earlier utterances or of earlier mental states. If we return to the metaphor of an engagement with a set of railroad tracks that diverges somewhere in the distance, then it seems correct that a multiplication of mental or semantic items cannot fix the character of that engagement, in such a way as to determine, on their own, what it is to follow the tracks along the same route. On the other hand, I do not believe that from this conclusion it follows that the individual's own understanding of what he means and believes is bypassed in the determination of semantic content. What we must grant, rather, is that to the extent that what we take ourselves to be saying fixes what we are indeed saying, that very activity of taking ourselves to mean something will itself be determined as what it is under the same Wittgensteinian conditions of repeatability. I shall argue in the next section, indeed, that Wittgenstein's argument is consistent with the claim that we can be confident that it is addition that we are doing when we put numbers together in the familiar manner.

On the other hand, I am unsure of what is finally the best account of why addition seems to us, when compared with other mathematical functions that diverge from it only with very big numbers that humans have not yet put together, the "natural" way of going on, so that we are not surprised when we all, upon finally coming to these numbers, go on in just the same way. It is hard to avoid the strong intuition that something about reality itself makes that way of determining sameness more natural, so that an interpreter will interpret us on that basis, even if there is no determinacy-conferring move that we can make that fixes that particular function as the one we are computing. The idea would be that sameness in these cases is not simply a creature of our biological propensities for counting as the same, but has at least some basis in the actual world in which we are engaged or in mathematical reality. Then that contribution by the world could help fix what it is to go on to do the same thing, and what an omniscient interpreter would interpret us as doing, even if the individual's production of tokens or sequences could not by itself do so. But I do not know how to make that argument and shall leave the issue there.

There is a related argument that is raised (by Dennett, for one) concerning the problem of the *homunculus*. The interior states of a believer or perceiver are not self-interpreting, so they need to be read. We explain our seeing of the world by proposing an internal seeing that requires a "little man" in there to read the images. Or we explain the ability of our subjective states to confer meaning upon the world by supposing that the subjective states themselves have their meaning conferred upon them by a further little man inside. There is an answer to the homunculus problem in cognitive science, and it trades on the nature of writing a program for a computer.[15] We consider a task at a high level of description where the principal steps in the task, supposedly going on in the machine, must be performed by very intelligent homunculi. But we continue to break each subtask down further into tasks that can be performed by very many homunculi who are considerably less intelligent than the first ones. Eventually the analysis of the task reaches a level where it is being performed by many thousands of quite stupid homunculi whose tasks are on the order of "if positive current comes in both wires, then send out positive current, otherwise send out negative current." But at this level all the stupid homunculi can be replaced by physical mechanisms. So the operations become, as we might put it, self-reading.

But of course they are self-reading only as the computer's strings of output are being interpreted in relation to the world or to some practice. We solved the problem of an internal seeing not by locating a mysterious subjective intervention, but by seeing even reflective activity, our seeing and reading of the interior representations, as itself no more than the further production of strings of shapes that can affect what happens with other strings of shapes. The reflective move, on this model, does not uncover a special power that gives subjective states their content. It just adds items and operations that must themselves be interpreted on the basis of their linkage to the world and to other items and operations. (It is said that in Alan Turing's code-breaking operations during the second world war, he first needed many human readers who would read and interpret machine output before giving further instructions to the machine. Gradually more and more of those activities of reading and interpreting were incorporated into the machines' own functioning.)

Let us note a similarity between Wittgenstein on rule-following and the cognitive science handling of the homunculus problem. Both reject a theological solution, one that accounts for determinacy by appealing to a meaning-conferring power whose own determinacy we must take for granted. Such a power will no longer be outside the network of signs, interpretation, practices, and world, will not be "outside the game," as the Derrideans put it, but will be immanent in, and dispersed across, that network. The homunculus was absorbed into the operations of

---

[15] This point is made nicely by Dennett in *Brainstorms* (Montgomery, Vt.: Bradford Books, 1978), pp. 122–5.

syntactic shapes upon one another; Turing's machine readers were absorbed into the machines' own functioning; the modern subject's productive activity from without is absorbed into the sort of network of signs it was supposed to be determining. (It is important that the reflective, self-relating, self-knowing subject does not disappear in that absorption. I spend a later chapter showing that an acceptance of certain attacks on interiority does not license positions that take subjectivity to be easily dismissed, through considering it a product of language or culture or of mechanical operations.)

That result is consistent with the process that I called the disenchantment of subjectivity. That process leads to a nominalist mental universe of individual items that do not have anything like natures or essences to give them a determinate identity apart from a practice of counting as the same. I should perhaps grant that there are large debates about just what conclusions we are supposed to draw from Wittgenstein's rule-following arguments, or from Saul Kripke's revival of them in recent years. There are questions, for example, of the degree to which, and of the manner in which, community practice is essential to one's utterances or thoughts being able to mean anything at all. My own reading emphasizes the notion of *repeatability*, of the deferral of semantic determinacy along a chain of utterances. That condition will be present even in the case of a Robinson Crusoe who has been isolated from others since birth and who has learned to speak or to write on his own. This reading, I have suggested, brings Wittgenstein in some respects close to Derrida, though certainly not in others. Some who have been influenced by Derrida, perhaps in ways that Derrida himself would disavow, suppose that challenges to metaphysically deeper notions of subjectivity, interiority, and autonomy will leave us generally with skeptical, antirealist, and irrationalist positions. It will be one of the themes of this book, pursued in subsequent chapters, that such is not the case.

Externalism, Science, and Self-knowledge

Some believe these externalist findings regarding mental content, if they are accepted, threaten important features of our understanding of the mind. Let me consider three of these features: the possibility of constructing a science of the mind, the status of the believer's self-knowledge, and the notion that externalism about content makes the subject too passive in setting the conditions of his engagement with the world.

Jerry Fodor's motivation for securing a region of narrow content is, as he says, to guarantee the possibility of a science of psychology. Scientific laws must articulate a subject matter into kinds on the basis of the causal powers of the objects that are studied. Causal powers themselves will be based on local physical structure. So no factor is relevant to the classifying of psychological kinds unless it is capable of having an effect on the local physical structure of the entity whose psychology is being examined.[16] But in the Twin Earth cases, it appears, there is, mysteriously, an action at a distance. The character of a substance in the world is supposed to be a factor in determining the psychological kinds present in the believer, even when that character has no causal effect on the believer's physical structure. We know this is so because if we remove Oscar from earth to Twin Earth, we change his psychological states even as he remains the same, molecule for molecule. So then we need, supposes Fodor, a notion of narrow content that can be scientifically hygienic, without any appeal to classifications that do not supervene on local causal powers.

But I do not see that Fodor's worry need trouble us, and we do not have to come up with strange molecular configurations to make the point. Consider again Oscar and his twin as they learn to play tennis and follow religiously the instructions of their professionals. Each hears his teacher say "it is very important to learn a drop shot," so each develops an intention that he expresses by saying "I intend to learn a drop shot." All each knows about the shot is that his teacher has mentioned it and that a tennis player will do well to learn it. Again make them molecule for molecule the same, but on Twin Earth, the word 'drop shot' developed as the name of what on earth we have learned to call a 'lob.' Thus English and Twin English are slightly different but due to their ignorance Oscar and Twin Oscar can remain the same in spite of that public difference. So the physical states of the two can be made, for the thought experiment, just the same, and it is true that if one were transported to the place of the other, he would produce just the same behavior. Yet the causal powers of their psychological states cannot quite be counted as the same. For the intention of one will make him learn a very different tennis shot from what the intention of the other, realized in just the same physical configuration, will soon make him learn.

The result seems to be exactly the circumstance that Fodor has found worrisome. Causal powers do not supervene on local physical structure. But of course there is no mysterious action at a distance in the case of the tennis players. For even if physical structure is just the same in the two at the moment, the difference in their environment is going, in the future, to impinge on that physical structure so that different physical operations will result from their respective intentions (different arm movements as well as different internal states as the two learn more about drop shots). The point is that two psychological states may be realized in the same physical states in the present, and yet the continua-

---

[16] Fodor's argument here is from *Psychosemantics*, pp. 33–44.

tion of those psychological states as the same into the future may involve a realization then in *different* physical states, in a way that would make us say that the two psychological states should be counted as of different kinds. As each of the two tennis players comes to understand the content of his own intention more fully (an intention whose content is at first parasitic on the knowledge of others), he comes to have different internal physical states from those of the other. And that future difference is enough to make the psychological states different, since it is their continuing as the same that gives them their identity, not a snapshot of their present (and inadequate) physical instantiation. So causal powers remain local; the future difference in local causation rather than some mysterious action at a distance comes into play in determining whether contents are the same or are different.

In Putnam's case, the difference between water and XYZ-water will eventually be recognized through advances in science. So the two substances would produce different psychological states in Oscar and Twin Oscar if they lived long enough to come to understand the chemical differences. Many beliefs have a built-in teleology; we leave a blank, as it were, to be filled in later, when our information is better. A superintelligent interpreter, taking that teleology into consideration, will have good reasons for assigning different states to Oscar and to Twin Oscar, even before the time when their internal states concerned with the watery substance, or the internal states of much later members of their two communities, have begun to diverge physically and causally. There is nothing at all mysterious here, no violation of the rule that useful kinds will supervene on local powers, on the discriminatory abilities of which individuals are capable. It is just that sometimes an interpreter who knows more than the believer may take into consideration, in a decision as to whether contents are the same, future states that will count as a continuing of the present states at issue, and the external causes that will affect what those future states turn out to be.

I think our conclusion ought to be that too much has been made of Putnam's thought experiment as a threat to psychology. It may seem odd that the articulation of psychological states may sometimes be future oriented, toward what those states will be as filled in by later information. But that is the nature of intention and belief and human subjectivity in the first place, and a theory that cannot make sense of that is not a theory of human psychology.

Externalism also seems to many to threaten our self-knowledge. There must be something, it will be felt, to our sense that first-person authority and self-knowledge are features of our subjectivity. The idea of objects in a self-standing interior realm has seemed a good way to show how such authority is possible. Let us come at that issue in the following way. There are two intuitions that seem to put contrary pressures on the identification of beliefs and meanings. One intuition, the externalist one, emphasizes the pressure coming from the world, while the other intuition emphasizes a pressure from the opposite direction. Surely (one will say) my beliefs have the content I take them to have because whatever language they are expressed in, whether a mentalist one or my idiolect of a public language, the sequences of that language will mean only what I take them to mean. How could I misuse words that are from the start my own, and that get their life from the way that I use them? We have, then, three levels: the world, my intentional states that take the world to be a certain way, and my understanding of the content of those intentional states. One of our intuitions tries to underwrite a certain attachment between levels 1 and 2. If there remains a discrepancy to be explained, one will let a gap open between levels 2 and 3; our beliefs succeed in being about the world, but we may not know just what beliefs they are. The other intuition, very common in the modern period, is to secure an attachment between levels 2 and 3, and to let any needed gap open between levels 1 and 2. We know what we mean and believe, but perhaps our beliefs succeed very poorly at being about the world.

But let us make use of some of our earlier results about how the assignment of intentional content will go. Suppose that we pursue the disenchantment of subjectivity only halfway in our analysis of the mind. Then we let the world's influence on mental content get in as far as helping to determine what we mean and what we believe. But we shall suppose that further in, what we take ourselves to mean and to believe has its own determinate character, independently of the connection to the world. Then the factors that make determinate my taking of myself to mean something are external to the factors that determine what I mean, and the two aspects might vary independently. But then I have no right to have confidence in my knowledge about what I mean and believe.

I can regain that confidence, oddly enough, if I let the disenchantment proceed in a more thorough fashion. Then even what I take myself to mean has no determinate character on its own, except through its links to a mind-transcendent world. The world's role in determining content goes *all the way in* to our very activity of self-knowing, to what we have marked out as the level 3 of our analysis. But now the same world-involving factors used in fixing what I mean will be used as well in fixing what I *think* I mean. The three levels that we described will have their determinate character only in the context of conditions of interpretation that bring about a rough matching of all three.[17]

---

[17] I am following Davidson's suggestion here, but I want to postpone consideration of his positions until the following chapter, which will treat only his work. See his Presidential Address to the American Philosophical Association, "Knowing One's Own Mind," in *Proceedings and Addresses of the American Philosophical Association*, 60, no. 3 (1987): 441–58.

Consider in this regard, as Davidson does, the Twin Earth case mentioned earlier. It may seem that neither Oscar nor Twin Oscar understands what he believes. Oscar has a belief about H_2O-water rather than about XYZ-water, but, as it appears, he does not understand himself to have such a belief, since he knows nothing about the molecular structure of what is before him. One factor that makes his belief what it is is unavailable. But now suppose that Oscar were to state explicitly what he means in the form of something like a Davidsonian theory of meaning. (I shall be describing what such a theory will be in the following chapter.) He therefore says, " 'Water,' as I use it, refers to water." If we have been persuaded by Putnam, then we hold that Oscar's term 'water,' as it appears in his beliefs, is about H_2O-water. But then we should use that interpretation all the way in, applying it even to his own statements about what he means, to his own self-understanding, and thus to the statements in which he expresses what he takes to be the semantic content of his utterances. H_2O-water is what is there in the world; H_2O-water is what Oscar's beliefs are about, and H_2O-water is what he *thinks* his beliefs are about.[18] No gap has to open either between levels 1 and 2 or between levels 2 and 3.

The same will apply, of course, for Twin Oscar. When he forms the utterance " 'Water' as I use it refers to water," an interpreter will consider the XYZ in the environment as helping to determine the meaning both of the word used and the word mentioned, so that Twin Oscar has a correct belief about what he means. Oscar's correctness here does not derive from his observations of his own behavior, or from a special ability to read off the value of internal entities, but rather from the conditions on assigning content to his statements about what he means. And when I say that the rule I am intending to follow is the one for *addition*, then whatever comes into play (as the chain of rule-following instances builds up) to specify my practice as one of doing addition will also come into play in specifying the meaning of 'addition,' as I use it, so that I am correct in saying that it is addition that I am doing. The Wittgensteinian argument does not show that I might generally be mistaken in identifying the rule-following practices in which I am engaged.

Yet we should acknowledge how weak is the sort of first-person authority about meaning that has here been defended. Knowing the content of one's beliefs ought to entail a richer body of knowledge than is reflected in the ability to produce bare claims about what one means or is referring to. Many of my beliefs contain blanks, we have said, to be filled in as I come to have a better understanding of just what it is to have such beliefs. And there is the issue as well of the pressure of what other speakers know and mean on what beliefs I shall be taken as

[18] Ibid., p. 451.

holding and expressing. Suppose I say that a particular piece of music is a sonata, but I have some misconceptions about what a sonata is. I might be interpreted as holding the same belief that others more knowledgeable would express by claiming that something is a sonata, or I might be interpreted as having a belief determined by the meaning that I (mistakenly) apply to the term. As I shall be treating the topic of the social pressures that fix semantic content in the next chapter, I shall postpone as well a discussion of the relations between that topic and the self-knowledge of the believer. But it should be clear already that the more we allow a social fixing of intentional content, the more severe the difficulties will be for the individual's knowledge about what he means and believes.

It may appear that in externalist atempts to shore up the authority of the knower we are just displacing, rather than removing, a certain lack of knowledge. The worry at first was that our beliefs were out of touch with the world that surrounded us. Then in externalist fashion we made beliefs generally about, and generally appropriate to, the world, but in a way that seemed to make it questionable whether we know what the words mean that express our beliefs; our beliefs might be mostly true but we might not properly know which beliefs they are. So then we make our claims about what we *mean* by our words generally true by letting world-guidedness go all the way in to our innermost subjectivity. But now it appears that while we know that our claims about what we mean and believe are generally true, we do not know which propositions those true claims are expressing. For we cannot tell the difference between expressing the true proposition " 'Water' refers to water" on earth and expressing the true proposition " 'Water' refers to water" on Twin Earth, and these are different propositions. But I do not see why a reasonable hope for self-knowledge should include the hope that my knowledge of what I mean and believe will be so comprehensive, so as to entail being able to tell the difference between the proposition I am expressing and the proposition I would be expressing in a different world. I know what I mean here: that 'water' refers to water.

Now I have spent time on that somewhat technical issue of our self-knowledge regarding what we mean and believe because it is important how self-knowledge was, in that account, secured: through global constraints on interpreting claims I make about what I mean, and not through any ability I have to survey inner objects. Such inner entities give us a dangerously inaccurate picture of what goes on when we know what we mean and believe. Suppose that Oscar and Twin Oscar had to know what they meant by examining, or by having inward access to, objects in an inner space.[19] But on Putnam's story they are the same,

---

[19] I am following here an argument by Davidson, "Knowing One's Own Mind," pp. 455–6.

molecule for molecule, from the skin inward. Objects that are genuinely inner and accessible as such ought to be, when that condition of Putnam is granted, the same from one thinker to the other. But the two are thinking different thoughts. Therefore they must not know what they are thinking; they do not have access to the external factor that, in addition to the inner objects they are surveying, makes their thoughts the thoughts they are.

But let us suppose, as above, that the fixing of content is world guided all the way in. Then the external conditions that make subjective states different will also make one's knowledge of one's subjective states different, without there being any surveyable internal object that changes in correspondence with those differences, and without the differences in one's knowledge of one's subjective states being caused by acquaintance with any inner object that has changed. So it cannot be by scanning such inner entities that I know what I believe and mean. But that turns out to be a good result that gives me more rather than less confidence in my capacity for self-knowledge.

Being a subject is something *active*. I have a perspective on the world because I set myself in relation to what is within it. I can be engaged with the world as one having intentional states because I at least implicitly take myself to be engaged with the world in a certain manner. The externalist picture of intentional states, it will be objected, makes them too passive; content happens to them from without. Now I think that objection is valid for the two-stage account of intentional content we rejected earlier, but it will not be a general objection to exernalist positions. Let us consider how one's being intentionally related to the world may turn out, on some conceptions, to be something that befalls one instead of something in which one is actively involved.

One may be tempted to suppose that subjectivity is a just a region of objects that happen to be inner instead of outer, and that it is our job to specify the inner objects in an adequate fashion. The search for genuinely inner objects, invulnerable to the Twin Earth considerations, may then appear as a way of saving the region of subjectivity. But it can only appear so if we accept a crude "objective" picture of what subjectivity is like, that is, if we think of the problem as one of relating one region of objects to another such region that is differently situated. But in seeing matters that way we are not making subjectivity *subjective* enough, and we are failing to see how it is the taking of a stance toward something that is other.[20]

Now the two-stage account of intentional content, we saw, tries to locate just such a region of genuinely inner objects and then to construct

---

[20] McDowell discusses this issue in "Singular Thought and the Extent of Inner Space," in *Subject, Thought, and Context*, Philip Pettit and John McDowell, eds. (Oxford: Clarendon Press, 1986). He there attacks the more objective conception of subjectivity.

from that beginning an account of what it is to have an intentional stance toward the world. But that project attempts to make subjectivity a composite of two features in neither of which there is anything like subjectivity.[21] First there is supposed to be narrow content. There are reasons, we have seen, for concluding that no subjectivity is left when we complete that inward turn; there is no taking of anything to be anything, no self-relating that has any content to it, just an empty and abstract processing of shapes. Then there is the work of the interpreter who, on the basis of the narow content and considering how things are in the world, assigns broader content that places the subject in relation to the world. But here too there is no genuine subjectivity. The connection to the world is done from the outside, while the narrow content is supposed to capture what things are like from the inside. (It fails to do that, we saw.) But there is no room for the subject's activity of setting itself in relation to the world, of taking itself to be so related. The relation to the world is something that simply happens to it, without affecting how things are going on inside, or that an interpreter brings about even as the inner mind is oblivious to the outcome.

The claim, of course, is that the whole picture has subjectivity in it, even if neither of the two steps has anything we could recognize as such. But then we would have to explain how subjectivity can suddenly appear in the second step, when what is added is precisely what has nothing of subjectivity in it, in that it concerns that to which the subject does not have access, that upon which the subject cannot have a perspective, since its internal self-relating supposedly (for the project under consideration) involves no intrinsic connection to the world but breaks off as an autonomous moment. The self does not seem to be relating itself to the world. It is like a computer whose output is meaningless to it but is being read by those outside it.

If you try to take the self-relating moment as autonomous, you end with a dark interior where nothing means anything, where we are not setting ourselves in relation to things in any way at all. If you then try to take the relation to the world as an independent moment that can be added on later, as an interpreter arrives on the scene, you end up with no genuine relation to the world. The self is not differentiating itself from and relating itself to any other, and without that active involvement in the self's directedness toward the world, no connection is accomplished. But that outcome does not have to follow from the adoption of an externalist position regarding mental content. Recall how in our discus-

---

[21] Again, it is helpful to look at McDowell, "Singular Thought and the Extent of Inner Space," pp. 58–61. My presentation in the next few paragraphs was considerably shaped by his arguments in that essay.

sion of self-knowledge we said that the role of the external world in fixing content should be allowed to go all the way in, to the more self-reflective activity by which we took ourselves to mean and believe some things rather than others. We can treat the subject as actively setting itself in relation to the world, and as actively setting the conditions of its engagement with the world, provided we hold as well that even that activity, if it is to be meaningful at all, must be taken as already implicated in the world-involving relations that make it possible for there to be any mental content at all. Instead of a two-step process in which there is an autonomous self-relating and then a secondary relation to the world, there is what we might call (in Hegelian fashion) a structure of self-relating-in-relating-to-the-world that comes all at once and that the externalist has no trouble endorsing. Subjectivity must collapse as an autonomous objective region, for unless it is already thought of as a standing of the self toward a particular world, there is no semantic content at all, only meaningless noise.

So we should not be concerned about what seems to be a passive structure of content-fixation in Putnam's Twin Earth example. My dependence on the world and on other speakers does not happen unbidden to a purer subjectivity. The reason that I can be taken by Putnam to be speaking about water rather than about XYZ-water is that at least implicit in my epistemic engagement with the world is a teleology that I myself breathe into my activities. I take myself to be aiming toward understanding better what I understand, toward doing better what I do, and that projection toward doing better is part of my speaking and intending. The world and others come into play in ways that make my own saying more extensive and powerful. It can be about things that I do not yet fully understand. So my dependence is part of how I am actively engaged with the world I reach out for, rather than an external happening to a passive subjectivity that has been constituted from within. When I say that an ancient thinker was talking about *our* natural kind gold, it is not that I imperialistically descend on a passive text and make it mean what I want it to mean. Rather I try to understand the sort of engagement with the world that the speaker took himself to be sharing as he spoke.

This debate opens out onto the very large issue of how much of what was important to the modern notion of the subject can be retained after subjectivity is disenchanted. That notion was of a self that was active, free, self-determining, and self-knowing, and that set the conceptual conditions to which reality had to live up. I want to devote a chapter to the question of how much of that picture can be preserved, and I shall do so later. But first I shall consider some aspects of the general project of trying to find a place for mind in the causal order described by the scientist.

Mind and the Causal Order

Philosophers have long asked how we might fit the study of mind into the picture sketched by the natural sciences. One solution might be to take the true statements of psychology and to reduce them to (that is, show them to be logically equivalent to) statements about the kinds and events studied by physics. That option seemed a good way to go for a time in twentieth-century philosophy, but there are few around now who endorse it. Even if all there is in the universe is physical stuff in various arrangements, still the kinds of patterns that we are interested in, as we use the psychological vocabulary, seem no longer to appear as significant patterns when we try to describe the world in the vocabulary of physics. What you and I have in common, in believing that Borneo is a nice place to visit, is some set of relationships with other beliefs and desires and with dispositions to behavior, and almost surely not the way the physical stuff in our brains is arranged, even if that stuff must be arranged in some way in each of us if we are to count as having the belief.

A different answer is suggested by work in formal logic and in formal semantics, and by recent developments in the field of artificial intelligence.[22] One tries to take the logical and semantic relations among sentences in an argument and to capture them in a system whose items and operations are defined syntactically, that is, in terms of their formal shapes. Without knowing what the sequences of shapes mean, you can tell how you're allowed to construct and transform them just by looking at the formal shapes and at a set of rules defined in terms of them (as if it were a chess game). If you follow these formal rules correctly, then you can arrange the strings into a series that mirrors the truth-preserving transformations of logical inference.

Suppose we really can capture the correct moves of logical inference by means of moves defined just on the basis of the formal properties of strings, on the basis of their shape or form rather than of their meaning. Then, so it seems, we have a way to give engineering reality to rational thought. We shall design a machine in which the items of the formal system can be represented, and such that the mechanical working of the machine, its operating in accord with the laws of the stuff it is made of, automatically produces operations that follow the rules of the formal system. That machine, of course, will be a computer, and the idea is that

[22] A nice introduction to this topic is provided by John Haugeland, *Artificial Intelligence* (Cambridge, Mass.: MIT Press, 1989). See also Haugeland (ed.), *Mind Design* (Cambridge, Mass.: MIT Press, 1981); Daniel Dennett, *Brainstorms* (Cambridge, Mass.: MIT Press, 1978); Jerry A. Fodor, *The Language of Thought* (New York: Thomas Y. Crowell, 1975); and Fodor, *Psychosemantics* (Cambridge, Mass.: MIT Press, 1987). A useful anthology is Margaret Boden (ed.), *The Philosophy of Artificial Intelligence* (Oxford: Oxford University Press, 1990).

the mind when it thinks is rather like such a machine. The brain is a physical engine so designed that there are sequences of physical shapes and events within it that mirror and express the logical operations of meaningful thought. The causal sequences that are due to the physical properties of the stuff the brain is made of instantiate the operations of a formally defined system, and that in turn captures the way that sentences are related to one another in patterns of inference.

The point will sometimes be put as follows. It does not really matter what material a brain is made of, so long as its mechanical operations are instantiating the operations of a "program" of rules, and such that the rules are defined in terms of how sequences of shapes get related. So mental activity is more like the running of software that can be run on quite different machines. But now we have a way of defining a psychological state such as a belief. It is an internal state defined at the level of software operations rather than the operations of physical stuff, and it is fixed as the state it is by its causal relations to other internal states and to input and output. But that way of picking out what psychological states are, it will be claimed, seems to match pretty well with how we ordinarily understand them. My belief that Borneo is a nice place to visit has whatever reality it does through its causal powers to make me adopt other beliefs and intentions on the basis of input, and to dispose me to behave in certain ways when my deliberations take it into account. We have, then, it seems, a way of showing how mind has a causal place in the natural universe, and we can understand as well why we should not expect the statements of psychology to be reduced to statements of physics. (Explaining the physics of a particular computer would not tell us much about that which makes its logical program what it is).

Those who dismiss from the start the claim that computers might tell us something about mental phenomena are narrow-minded, but it takes only a moderate degree of skepticism to worry that philosophers are too enamored with newly available models for what mind might be like. I think there are, indeed, many cases in which analogies with work in formal semantics are too seductive. Jerry Fodor, for example, has claimed that a very high percentage of our conceptual repertoire must be innate, but his argument for this claim rests on limiting the ways that new vocabulary can be formed from old to certain basic operations of predicate logic.[23] He neglects, to take just one example, how our metaphorical abilities allow us to build new concepts on the scaffolding of concepts that are more concrete.

I want to examine here the reasons we have for being skeptical that we

---

[23] That, at least, was the conclusion Fodor vigorously supported in *The Language of Thought.* I am not sure he would still support it to the same degree.

can explain mental phenomena through producing accounts of the sort just described. (They are called *functionalist* accounts.) Philosophers of the past often denied that physical machines could be the locus of mental life. The argument was that physical stuff just could not be the sort of thing that could generate the operations of a rational mind, so that another sort of stuff had to be posited. But the conceptions I shall be considering here favor a different sort of nonreducibility. They allow that there is only one kind of substance, physical substance, and that it produces various complex configurations of itself. Some of these conceptions may even allow that we can helpfully think of the human brain as running a program, as the functionalist suggests. But they go on to claim that neither a physicalist nor a functionalist account can explain what a psychological vocabulary explains. What is emergent when we come to mental phenomena is not a new kind of metaphysical stuff but patterns, vocabularies, and forms of explanation. The artificial intelligence account cannot explain what beliefs and intentions are because it cannot capture certain aspects of what it is to have a mind.

I want to investigate these arguments, but first let me mention an issue that I shall not be examining. One's skepticism about the computer model may be due to a belief about the limits of the kinds of programs by which computers operate today. In the future, it will be said, there will be programs based not only on massive parallel processing and neural networks, but also on kinds of patterns that at the moment we can hardly imagine. Only then will the operations of machines begin to mirror the kinds of operations by which human intelligence works; only then will artificial intelligence become of assistance in our understanding of psychology. The kind of claim I want to look at expresses a deeper skepticism about whether any computer model at all can *explain* what it is to have beliefs and intentions.

A common theme in those expressing this deeper skepticism is that there is something *normative* about attributing mental states to an individual.[24] One crosses over the threshold into properly having beliefs only if one's beliefs are connected in rational patterns of inference with other beliefs, and are connected to intentions and to actions through a process of rational planning. If there is not at least a modest level of rationality, then it does not make sense to suppose that it is, finally, *beliefs* that we are encountering. The attribution of beliefs works by taking a particular entity to be at least roughly approximating the operations of an ideal rational agent. As evolution comes to produce entities that are sensitive to good reasons for acting, a new kind of explanation becomes possible

---

[24] The most prominent essays framing this discussion are by Davidson. See his "Mental Events," "The Material Mind," and "Psychology as Philosophy," all reprinted in his *Essays on Actions and Events* (Oxford: Clarendon Press, 1980).

and necessary, one not reducible to descriptions of how things regularly happen.

The cognitive scientist hopes to capture the kinds of relations that make our ordinary psychological descriptions successful; she proposes to do this by coming up with a high-level program or flowchart of logical operations that supposedly shows what is going on when deliberation occurs. That program might then have quite different lower-level instantiations in individuals who are acting upon the same beliefs and intentions. But why should we suppose there will be even that higher-level sameness in a flowchart of mental operations? Perhaps once you move below the level of our everyday psychological discourse, there will be no way of picking up, by means of such a flowchart, just what individuals have in common when they have the same belief or the same intention. The functionalist level of description can then deal only with particular engineering realizations of the mental activities, and not with that which makes those activities what they are. But then we are asking the wrong question, at the wrong level, when we try to move from the belief-intention-desire sort of discourse to a discourse about flowchart operations in a particular individual.

We may insist that there is the matter of what counts as an explanation, and of what must remain in play if an explanation is to be successful. The functionalist level of explanation cannot supersede the everyday psychological one because the latter must remain in consideration if we are to know what to look for when we try to do the functionalist flowchart. Even if human thought does not approximate all that well the operations of an ideal rational deliberator, still it is only by being situated in the space carved out by the normative model of rationality that explanations in terms of beliefs and desires can be satisfying as explanations. If you wrench them free of it and focus on the causal regularities within some mechanical system that is instantiating to a rough approximation the normative model, then you will lose hold of that which made the explanations into genuine explanations, that which gave them their point. In attributing beliefs and desires to someone, we are trying to make sense of him as one acting with at least a moderate degree of rationality and purpose; we are trying to see him as one acting from reasons. It may still be the case that we ascribe mental states to him in order to make his behavior more predictable, and there may be genuine causal explanations that operate at the level of intentional description (that is, the level at which we describe beliefs, desires, intentions, and other object-directed mental states). But no description of causal regularities in a system nonintentionally described can replace the intentional vocabulary.

Consider how different this case is from what happens in the sciences when our accounts push for a deeper level of causal phenomena to explain the patterns we are investigating. When I go to the deeper causal level in trying to understand natural kinds, I can exchange my ordinary-knowledge taxonomy for one with greater accuracy. Something may have looked like gold to me but once I understand atomic structure I can classify it more accurately as not an instance of gold. I may have thought that two animals belonged in the same biological group but an examination of the genetic codes of their proteins may convince me they do not. The new taxonomies supersede the earlier ones. But it is not at all clear that we could pick up a more accurate taxonomy for psychological states by looking to a deeper causal level of explanation. Such a deeper level we might call a *subpersonal* or *subintentional* one since it is trying to explain matters beneath the level at which they are seen as aspects of the intentional life of persons. I might discover, through investigating the subintentional level, interesting facts about how certain physical entities solve the "programming" problems of engaging in the operations of thought. But it is very unlikely that with the lower-level account I would discover an articulation scheme that was self-sufficient at that level and that allowed me to correct our ordinary-knowledge taxonomy for mental states.

The problem is that it is not clear that the taxonomies relevant to and necessary for our explanations will be at all discernible when we look for causal regularities below the level of the belief-desire explanations that characterize our attribution of intentional life to persons. Intentional explanation presupposes a certain pattern of inferential relationships. Suppose a brainwashing specialist thoroughly conditions Jack so that when he has the belief that he is at the South Pole he is to take his shirt off. That connection of the belief to the action is a direct causal one that short-circuits Jack's normal process of inference. (Jack is not made, for example, to believe that the South Pole is extremely warm.) Then Jack is hypnotized and the belief is induced in him that he is at the South Pole; he begins to shiver but then he also removes his shirt. It will be true that Jack's belief that he was at the South Pole caused him to remove his shirt, but it will also be true that we do not have, in this instance, a satisfactory explanation at the intentional level of explanation. Something crucial is missing that would render the behavior intelligible by presenting Jack as approximating a model of rational decision making. On the other hand, one who gives a functionalist description of the causation of behavior cannot see anything missing; a certain internal state has played a certain causal role. There is nothing at that level of description to distinguish between the sort of (short-circuited) causation just described and the sort that the belief-desire-intention account of the mind tries to uncover. But then we cannot go from the intentional to the subintentional level of description and still pick out that which makes the intentional explanation what it is, that which determines when satisfying explanatory linkages have been made, that which separates it out from other kinds of explanation. Unlike the case of the biochemical account of reproduction, it remains here the higher-level taxonomy that is really doing the *work*, that cannot be superseded because there is nothing at the lower level to replace its articulations, no autonomous way of dividing things up that will explain why the significant patterns that appear at the intentional level of description do so appear.

Consider an analogy. We might imagine a large carpet being described in detail by someone who can look at all the knots and their colors. But suppose he is lacking the sort of pattern-recognizing sensibility that would allow him to pick out the larger figures that are represented in the carpet. Someone with that sort of sensibility, on the other hand, could show how arrangements of thousands of individual knots are producing the figures. You could not give up the higher level of resolution, the pattern-recognizing perspective, and still have any idea what one was supposed to be looking for in describing the knots. And if there is a mistake or distortion in the pattern of the knots, it will be only from the higher level of description that it can be recognized. Psychological explanation, it will be claimed, is also of that kind. Without the connection to the normative model, we lose the background against which the patterns relevant to our account become available, and on the basis of which we know what to look for when we try to specify what "program" the brain is running, as we attempt to decipher the owner's behavior.

It is not, then, that there are two vocabularies that need to be linked together in a single objective picture of reality. To give an intentional description of another is simply to be engaged in a very different sort of practice from what we do when we try to make the course of physical events more predictable. We are interested not just in what tends to happen, but also in how a kind of human activity understands itself as aiming for a certain ideal, as directed toward fitting, and being measured against, patterns that the present running of our own mental apparatus, and even the present working of our communal institutions, may not yet articulate all that well. As we come to have a better understanding of what are good reasons for belief and action, there may be gradual changes as well in our intentional explanations of others. Perhaps some behavior that once seemed caused by intentional processes in a person will be seen instead as having a nonintentional causal explanation (as we come to understand better various defects in the brain, for example); that change will be a highly significant one. But there will be nothing comparable at the functionalist level of description, since there will be no space for bringing in any consideration of how an appeal to a rational pattern of inferences, better understood, can so significantly affect the basis of our explanations in that manner.

It is a mistake, then, to think that for an understanding of our psychological vocabulary we might substitute a description of the transitions that happen to occur among inner states, whether physically or functionally described. We can see what is deeply wrong with that substitution when we note that such a physicalist or functionalist description of inner states has to work at the subintentional level; those states cannot yet be thought of as having any content determined by their aboutness, by their relations to the world. But we assign mental states to others only by supposing that certain relations obtain among those states on the basis of their content. The connections of beliefs to other beliefs and to desires and actions presumes that an interpreter can relate those states on the basis of a conception of good reasons for belief or good reasons for action. But those epistemic relations demand that we already see the states as having semantic content, as being about the world in a certain way. Otherwise the relationships are mysterious.

The functionalist seems to misunderstand the character of subjectivity.[25] While it is a phenomenon that emerges through the operations of the physical universe, and while we do not understand it at all well, still we can say, minimally, that a subject *takes* the world to be a certain way. That intentional directedness toward the world is not something that can be added on after we have given a causal account of internal states nonintentionally described. (We made that point earlier in the chapter, in a different context.) A certain global structure must emerge that includes the self's attitude of taking the world to have a certain character (and so includes relations among contentful states that are determined as such by what the world is like), and that includes as well a cultural space in which interpreters are making sense of one another as at least roughly approximating an ideal of rationality. Only with that global structure will the right sort of patterns begin to emerge that are the basis of our practice of ascribing beliefs and intentions. When we abstract from the world, and thus from content, and when we abstract from that space of interpretation, we lose hold of the conditions for the visibility of the patterns that we were after in giving psychological explanations in the first place. And with that abstraction we cannot even begin to make sense of the taxonomy of internal states that we would need to explain behavior.

One mistake here, McDowell believes, is to assume that all our accounts must fit into a single objective picture of the world, so that in making sense of inner life, we suppose the goal is to locate a region of

[25] My views here are close to those of John McDowell. That is no accident, as I have been much influenced by his essays over the years. See especially, on this topic, his "Functionalism and Anomalous Monism," in *Actions and Events*, Ernest LePore and Brian McLaughlin, eds. (Oxford: Basil Blackwell, 1985). See also the essays by McLaughlin, Jaegwon Kim, Alexander Rosenberg, and Mark Johnston in that volume.

internal *objects* whose relations and operations can fit into our general objective picture and can at the same time account for subjectivity and its achievements.[26] But we have thereby lost that which makes innerness and subjectivity what they are. We have failed to recognize that our understanding of ourselves and of one another as subjects is sui generis, even if subjectivity is itself generated by the interactions of physical stuff, the only kind there is. And that relationship between subjectivity and intentionality is such that we cannot give a proper account of beliefs and intentions if we are looking just for causal connections among internal entities. (I shall say more about that relationship in Chapter 7.)

A somewhat different kind of argument goes as follows. To assign intentional states is to interpret someone, but interpretation has certain degrees of freedom. The interests of the interpreter come into play in picking out the relevant psychological patterns of the other, and the interpreter in her psychological assignment to the other will be making a holistic adjustment in response to the evidence. The interpretive situation will help to define just what level of determinacy is appropriate here, and how rough the conditions can be for counting believers as having the same beliefs or intentions. How can a subintentional description acknowledge that role of interpretation and its freedoms? It may seem that these conditions of interpretation make it the case that the working of the intentionalist vocabulary is too much unlike the working of functionalist/causal explanations, so that the latter can never be expected to capture what is essential to the former. Yet it is possible, for all that this particular argument gives us, that once an interpreter does make an interpretation, then there will be, relative to that interpretation, a determinate way of seeing how the causal operations of the brain and its programs are realizing the mental states that the interpretation picks out. On the other hand, that response would itself acknowledge the point about the nonreducibility of the intentional. For the articulation into kinds would still require the work of an interpreter, and the interpreter's stance would remain thoroughly intentionalist.

Studying the Mind

We have looked at a range of arguments for nonreducibility, and I think that taken together they make a persuasive case. We should not expect a subintentional level of explanation to supersede the intentional one. It is not just that the belief/desire vocabulary will remain necessary to everyday communication; we shall not be able to find a grounding in another level of description for the articulations that make the intentional level what it is. But much depends on what we are now ready to say.

[26] McDowell, "Functionalism and Anomalous Monism," pp. 395–7.

Some believe the arguments make the case that we should no longer even think of doing a science of psychology; whatever it is we learn will not be relevant to our understanding of the mental. I think these conclusions are wrong, but we have to be careful how we specify the way that they are.

Let us begin with Davidson's discussion of what he calls the "anomalism" of the mental.[27] All mental events are physical events as well, according to the account that he endorses. When I make a decision to act, then what I describe as that mental event can also be described, in principle, as a physical event that will perhaps be very complex. As a physical event, it is determined by strict physical laws. Since moving toward the level of physicalist description is the only way to arrive at such strict causal laws, and since there are no "bridge laws" transforming statements about mental life into the statements of physics, then there is no hope that we are going to have laws in psychology, even if the events psychology describes are, under other descriptions, following strict causal laws. Even if an individual mental event will also be a physical event that is covered by the laws of physics, the kinds of generalizations the psychologist is interested in (what is the same when two believers have the same belief or intention, for example) will look for patterns and groupings that do not appear as such when we describe the world as following physical laws.

What are the consequences for psychology if Davidson is right? Whatever subpersonal causal regularities there are in a believer will not translate into causal laws that operate over events intentionally described. But should the psychologist worry that she is thereby driven out of business? The mental is anomalous for Davidson only in the sense that the generalizations and regularities that the psychologist studies will not have the strict legal status of the causal laws of physics. But why should falling short of that status be a problem? The way is still open to discovering very interesting truths that generally hold, and that make us understand better the nature of our intentional activities. We shall be disappointed only if we thought that we could bring all our useful explanations into a single systematic account of the world.

Some may wish to go further than Davidson and say that it will only be as a physical event that my deciding to do something will count as having genuine causal power. Then there is not, speaking strictly, mental causation. The mental is far more anomalous than has so far been suggested, for there will be no causal patterns and regularities that link mental events together as mental events, that group them on the basis of their descriptions as mental. But we are under no compulsion to

---

[27] Again, one should see the discussions in his "Mental Events" and "The Material Mind."

adopt the conception of causality that allows its application only to cases analogous to those of physics. My beliefs and intentions, *described that way*, have genuine causal power to produce changes in the world. They could not do so, it is true, if they did not have a physical instantiation. But that metaphysical dependence is compatible with its being true that causal claims in an intentionalist vocabulary have their own autonomy, one based on taxonomies that work at that level of description but that do not mirror the taxonomies of physics. Indeed, that is how our commonsense psychology works in making others comprehensible. We at least implicitly know causal generalizations that we use every day in determining that when someone has certain beliefs and desires, he will tend to act in predictable ways. These generalizations will have exceptions, and it is true that if you remain at the intentional level, you will not always be able to account for these exceptions by making your theses more refined. (The physicist, in contrast, does expect to handle such exceptions.) But that does not take away from the fact that the intentional level is an epistemically autonomous one that picks out its own causal truths, and that the psychologist can rightly hope to uncover them.

There remains the question of how useful neuroanatomical or functionalist descriptions can be to a science of the mind. We have already seen arguments to the effect that a description of subpersonal causal processes cannot supersede intentionalist discourse. But that nonreducibility of the mental is compatible with quite different positions concerning the usefulness of investigations at the subpersonal level. McDowell, for example, says the following.

Perhaps I should note that these remarks are critical of functionalism as a theory of propositional attitudes; they do not tell against functionalism as a framework for theory about how sub-personal states and events operate in the control of behavior, although they do raise a question about what (if anything) that sort of theory has to do with the mind.[28]

Now I am unsure how strongly McDowell would have us interpret the last claim in that statement. But there may be some who take him to be saying that we cannot learn anything about human believers *as believers* if we turn to the subpersonal level of investigation. Yet it seems that there is a great deal to learn about ourselves as having an intentional life, if we come to understand the engineering architecture in us for forming and representing our beliefs and for carrying out our deliberations. We can learn about biases built into that architecture that make some beliefs easier to form than others, or that make some beliefs more likely to lead to action. We can perhaps learn what kind of training is most likely to

---

[28] McDowell, "Functionalism and Anomalous Monism," p. 397.

produce, in a being with this sort of engineering, a system of beliefs that is sensitive to good reasons for believing. We might come to learn more about how information is organized in us, about how localizable the representation of beliefs is in the brain, about how much of our belief-forming system is "hard-wired" in early on and how much remains plastic. All of these things would tell us about how the mental life of human beings works, so that we shall find it surprising if such investigations have nothing to do with the mind.

Now it is not clear just how skeptical the follower of Davidson will be concerning the value, for understanding the mind, of studying neuroanatomy or artificial intelligence. But I do not see that any of the arguments of this chapter should discourage us regarding the worth of such investigations. We can look forward to learning over the next several decades how the human brain is designed to carry out some of the activities of mind. It is true that we shall be looking at one engineering instantiation of mental activity, so that the descent to the level of the biology of the brain will be unable to tell us what will be common among different minds that employ different engineering solutions for the tasks of thought. Still we are sure to learn much about what minds are like from studying the only advanced form of them around.

What of the case of artificial intelligence? Here the investigation is of a different sort. Instead of limiting ourselves to the way that evolution on this planet designed a brain, we shall try to learn something about mental activity by testing engineering solutions unlike those in the human brain, and by noting what kinds of designs seem to work well or badly for various mental tasks. The investigator here is betting that there can be interesting discoveries at this middle level between neurobiology and the intentionalist articulation of mental states. It might be the case that we just do not know enough now about how minds operate to look for such novel solutions. We shall get a much greater return from concentrating on the way the human brain functions, because it is the only example we have of something that can actually do the things we are investigating. But even in that case it appears certain there will be worthwhile collaborations between the biologists and those in artificial intelligence. Computer models can be used to see if engineering structures scientists think they are discovering in the human brain might actually do what the human brain does, and computer engineers may try to produce a design much more like that of the brain in order to handle tasks of daunting complexity.

The worker in artificial intelligence thinks that when we abstract from the "hardware" details of various sorts of brains or machines that might be taken to be engaging in intelligent activity, we shall discover interesting patterns that can be expressed as "software," as programs of formal rules for manipulating logical sequences. Here again we just do not know whether the articulation of such a middle level between ordinary psychology and the biology of the brain will be possible, or, if possible, a useful investment. Perhaps there is just not enough in common between the possible sorts of engineering solutions for us to hope that there can be interesting similarities at the level of such a program. Perhaps once you go below the level of our everyday articulation of mental states there is no further level of sameness that you arrive at among the various kinds of intelligent entities, and you have to go straight down to the level of biology. Or perhaps the logical processing of strings of syntactically defined shapes is itself a very poor model for capturing what mental functioning is like, so that even if there is that middle level between biology and everyday intentional talk, it will not be on the basis of computer programs that we come to understand it. It may be the case that some occurrent deliberative processes match up rather well with what might be seen as the running of a program by the brain, while other psychological explanations concern global patterns in behavior and do not match up with a particular set of internal happenings. We don't know how to answer those questions at the moment, but we do not have good reasons at this stage for a philosophical skepticism about the value, for the philosophy of mind, either of neurobiological research or of research in artificial intelligence. Even if the arguments in this section are correct, Fodor will not have been shown to be wrong in supposing that there are some internal states whose causal relations mirror the inferential relations picked out by belief/desire psychology.[29] But he will not thereby be reducing the intentional account to the subintentional, and he will not be able to pick out the states he is after unless he already takes for granted the intentionalist level of description, and the global structure of intentionality that makes it possible.

Less ambitious projects than that sort of reduction might seek to bring mind into the causal order of the universe. One might describe a series of steps by which, starting from simple physical entities, more and more sophisticated entities could evolve such that it will become true of some of them that they have intentional states and (eventually) a full-fledged subjectivity. It will be important that at each significant step there is no magic, no sleight of hand, no miraculous appearance of unexplained abilities. What would have to be added to a computer, it might be asked, to make it count as having beliefs or as being self-conscious? Just what thresholds would an entity have to pass over to count as having an intentional life, or a perspective on the world? I give at least a brief attention to such questions in Chapter 7. There I consider further aspects of the project of the disenchantment of subjectivity, and more general issues about the nature of what it is to be a subject.

[29] See, for example, Fodor's account in *Psychosemantics*, pp. 135–54.

It is indicative of the character of a philosophical period where it thinks its explanations may stop. And a principal model for locating such a stopping point is provided by the medieval period. A type of explanation that might threaten to lead to a regress leads instead to a reflexive, autonomous activity that can perform *upon itself* the operations to be explained. That activity is, of course, divine. The chain of events each being explained by an event outside it leads ultimately to a self-causing, a self-willing, a self-unifying, to something that can confer a status and determinacy upon itself. In the modern period that stopping point will be the human subject. (Perhaps thinkers would have had less confidence in letting explanations come to rest there if there were not already the theological model for it.) Its mental activity can confer meaning and determinacy upon itself through the very nature of its performance. Whereas shapes in the world have to be ordered and interpreted, mental activity is somehow self-ascribing, self-interpreting, self-reading. Our explanations can rest there, in a way they could not with an account of what there is in the world.

The move beyond the modern is the refusal to accept that there can be such an activity, and the demand that we explain how the mental realm itself comes to have the semantic character it has. We can still assign an important role to our self-understanding and self-ascribing, to what we take ourselves to be doing, but at the same time we recognize that these reflective acts are what can be determined as such by an interpreter who is considering a believer as in relation to a particular worldly environment. (It was just that point, the reader may recall, that allowed both Oscar and Twin Oscar to be correct in understanding what they mean and believe.)

What is no longer allowed is the entry from without, the godlike intervention into the system of semantic or mental tokens that is able to give them a fixed determinacy precisely because its own cannot be in question, because it can give itself its own content immediately. The refusal to leave any room for that sort of intervention holds together movements that may, in tone and style, be rather different. On the one hand, there is the project of naturalizing subjectivity. Once our mental activities cannot stand outside the world determining it but must be aspects of the world itself, then we have to rethink our notion of what it is for mental states or utterances to embody an ideal content. The mental acts by which such an embodiment would be effected, instead of appearing from another realm with special powers, fill up the given realm with more of the same. So you cannot expect to put your finger on any number of them and, by so doing, to specify an ideal content that determines all future cases of correct application. A finite sequence of items resident in the physical universe is not the sort of thing that can settle that in a final way.

On the other hand, in a different tradition, one finds talk about the death of the subject, as thinkers try to show the historical contingency of selves. But here too the point is that there is no place for a subjective activity that could, from a stance outside that world of cultural artifacts, confer on them a determinate meaning. Such an activity is always already caught up within the set of items it is supposed to be determining. It is as much constructed as constructing, as much written as writing. And here as in the American project of naturalization, one attempt to assimilate that outcome is to hope that mental life can be seen as a set of formal syntactic patterns that get their content from their causal ties to different sorts of objects – thus, structuralism on the one hand and artificial intelligence on the other. The differences between these traditions should not obscure their deep agreement. In both as well the self no longer has the principal divine attribute of being self-unifying, of determining its own unity from within. Our self-synthesizing, to the extent that we can indeed bring about our own unity as selves, occurs within that universe, and can effect no purer sort of unity than that universe allows.

The search for a pure interiority is, we have seen, a hopeless one. We shall not learn what it is to have a belief or an intention by describing the internal goings-on of a physical or a program-running machine. To have intentional content at all is already to be involved in a triangular situation that includes the world, the believer, and potential repeaters and interpreters of that content. One philosopher who has contributed much to our understanding of that triangle is Donald Davidson, and I turn now to a discussion of his work.

3

Davidson and the Disenchantment of Language

The Davidsonian Project

Typical patterns of thought in modern philosophy's investigations of the mind may repeat themselves in studies of language and of its relations to the world. So a disenchantment of subjectivity will do well to extend itself to work shaped by the so-called linguistic turn of twentieth-century philosophy. What we might call the disenchantment of language, the stalwart refusal to let it take on the metaphysical depth already forfeited by the Cartesian mind, is defended most vigorously in the work of Donald Davidson. That work has achieved a perhaps surprising reputation, given its density, with those in the fields of criticism and anthropology. One reason for this popularity is that Davidson has been put forward by Richard Rorty, himself widely read outside of philosophy, as the philosopher who has overcome the obsessions, in metaphysics and epistemology, that have been plaguing the discipline for centuries. In Rorty's telling, and in other books as well, Davidson appears as one who shows us how to do philosophy in a postmodern and postphilosophical age. He challenges radically a variety of semantic notions as well as the inertial influence of empiricist thought, and he may therefore seem to be supporting claims in literary criticism about the death of the subject and about meaning as indeterminate. It will be part of my argument in this chapter and the next that his conclusions fit that scheme rather poorly.

A good place to begin, in making sense of Davidson's work, is to imagine we have found an instrument from an alien civilization. It is a thermometer whose temperature lines remain visible but whose numbers have been erased, we may suppose, through constant use. If we try to calibrate the instrument so as to assign temperature numbers properly, we shall establish the identity of a given registration by seeing what temperature is its typical cause. Now humans have more sophisticated mental and cultural mechanisms for registering features of their surroundings. An alien scientist might watch us move successfully and subtly through our environment and might then classify us as belief formers who are generally good at registering truths. Imagine, then, that such an alien scientist is investigating an instrument or capacity for a particular human's registering of the world, either his verbal utterances or, should the alien have some kind of access to them, the patterns of his mental activity. How will he calibrate the instrument to determine what the various states or sounds are representing? As before, the most obvious response is that he will watch the subject operating in his natural setting, and will establish the identity of a semantic item or mental state by noting its typical cause in the environment.

To describe that strategy is to understate severely the difficulty of the task. Unlike the thermometer, the human has states and utterances that can stand for absent objects and highly abstract ideas, and there is enormous complexity in the relations of our mental states one to another. But if the alien does not begin by making the speaker a generally successful register of truths about the environment, then no assignment at all of meanings and beliefs will be forthcoming. It would be odd, in the case of the thermometer, to calibrate the markings so that the registration of temperature is usually wrong. If it is too badly off, then we should not count the mechanism in the first place as one that registers temperature. Similarly, a successful human in his environment will not properly count as registering mostly falsehoods. Either we calibrate him to be a generally successful former of true beliefs, or we should not suppose that it is belief formation that is indeed going on.[1]

That simple case presents the core of Davidson's account of belief and meaning. But the account is itself difficult because philosophers and linguists have placed obstacles in the way of our responding to the picture's natural appeal. We may imagine some immediate and typical objections to what it suggests. The utterances have a particular meaning intrinsically or by their relation to certain mental states; it may be improper, then, to let the world play, concerning their identification, the role that the Davidsonian account assigns to it. (One might want to make an analogous point about the thermometer. Some civilization produced it for that purpose, and intended the lines to indicate particular readings. So there is a correct answer as to how it is to be read, even if the interpreter has to pursue a next best strategy and see what temperature in the world is causing a particular registration.) Or someone may hold that the same linguistic behavior may express quite different conceptual schemes, and that since the interpreter does not know which scheme is being applied, she cannot know what the speaker is truly saying. Another objection will be that the utterances must be interpreted, and beliefs assigned, on the basis of conventions shared with others who are speakers of the same natural language. Perhaps the individual speaker here is misapplying his words, through misunder-

---

[1] "Once we agree to the general method of interpretation I have sketched, it becomes impossible to hold correctly that anyone could be mostly wrong about how things are." Donald Davidson, "A Coherence Theory of Truth and Knowledge," in *Truth and Interpretation: Perspectives on the Philosophy of Donald Davidson*, Ernest Lepore, ed. (Oxford: Blackwell, 1986), p. 317.

standing what they mean in his language, and the alien interpreter, in trying to match utterances to features of the environment, may again be missing badly what he means.

Note a similarity in these objections. In each case there is a semantic or mental "reification," something taken as fixed in its identity prior to, and as a check upon, the process of interpreting. One outcome of accepting these reifications, and of basing one's interpretation upon them, is that the believer or utterer may turn out to be badly alienated from how things really are. The more that is semantically fixed, the less room there is to calibrate the speaker as registering truths. And the interpreter might make excellent sense of the other's behavior, and yet miss badly in assigning the meaning of his words and in interpreting the content of his beliefs.

Davidson wants to put us as speakers and believers more confidently at home in the world and more dependably in touch with each other. (I am not suggesting that he is guided by that desire rather than persuaded by where his arguments are taking him.) He will thus attack the semantic and mental reifications we have just been describing. His attack will be, indeed, a radical one on a full range of such reifications. I think we can summarize his project as aiming to give us all of the following: truth without meanings; successful language–world connections without reference; a world of individuals without individuation by ontological schemes; communication without conventions; interpretation without shared languages; cultural differences without conceptual frameworks; sensory evidence without a "given" empirical content; beliefs and intentions without a realm of subjectivity; and epistemic success without the usual epistemic intermediaries.[2] All of those features he would do without, that is, the second member of each pairing, stand in the way of our adopting the strategy that our alien interpreter adopted earlier, and that Davidson himself wants to encourage.

Semantics without Meanings

One aspect of the disenchantment of language will be that linguistic and semantic phenomena will forfeit their metaphysical depth. Let us see how this occurs. Davidson will, first of all, give us truth without meanings.[3] One may suppose that a world of ideal entities such as senses

---

[2] A book-length treatment of Davidson by Bjorn Ramberg emphasizes his attacks on semantic reifications, especially on the notion of language itself. See Ramberg, *Donald Davidson's Philosophy of Language* (Oxford: Blackwell, 1989).

[3] Davidson has defended his account of meaning in several essays over the years. See, for example, "Truth and Meaning," "Semantics for Natural Languages," "In Defence of Convention T," and "Radical Interpretation," all in Davidson, *Inquiries into Truth and Interpretation* (Oxford: Clarendon Press, 1984).

and propositions stands as the mediating realm allowing one language to be translated into another. But Davidson (following Quine) says that ideal entities such as those can play no useful role in making our translations successful. The interpreter does not consult a field of language-neutral semantic entities so as to find statements in the two languages that express the same meaning. She looks at how the sentences of the other language are used, and on that basis connects them directly to sentences of her own.

We can best capture the notion of meaning if we see the interpreter not as compiling a manual for translation, but as using her sentences to give truth conditions of sentences of the other language, as the Davidsonian form for a theory of meaning instructs us to do. Much of the discussion of the form such a theory will take is quite technical, and requires at least some background in the semantics of formal languages. And while this project is central to Davidson's own program, and the topic of many commentaries on his work, I believe that his technical suggestions about the shape of a theory of meaning will not be what is most lasting in his philosophical output. Some of Davidson's recent work suggests, in addition, that he is no longer committed to certain earlier claims about what a semantic theory will be like. So let me give just a brief account of the overall shape of his proposal.

Consider an interpreter trying to make sense of another speaker, and imagine a situation where the former has no prior knowledge, linguistic or otherwise, of the latter. The interpreter will take as basic the speaker's assent to and dissent from statements, as well as the conditions, understood in the interpreter's own language, that typically produce such responses. She then constructs an empirical theory linking statements in the speaker's language with sentences in her own. That theory will enable her to make predictions about future patterns of assent to and dissent from statements on the part of the speaker, and she can adapt the theory depending on how well or how badly the predictions turn out. (The empirical force of the theory lies in the claim that the language the theory has specified is actually the language of the group or of the individual in question.[4]) The testable claims of the theory will be such statements as " 'Le Canada est plus grand que la France' is true in A's language if and only if Canada is larger than France," which give the truth conditions of sentences but do not talk about their meaning.

Davidson thinks that notion of what it is to give truth conditions for the sentences of a language is powerful enough to capture what we aim for in investigating meaning. It has the advantage of needing no appeal to semantic entities that are metaphysically controversial, and all it needs to get going is the notion of speakers taking utterances to be true

[4] See *Inquiries*, p. 73.

or false, and of their indicating so by recognizable behavior. The theory's semantics is *extensional* (another way of saying that it does not appeal to further semantic entities) and one cannot rely, consequently, on a notion of sameness of meaning in linking up sentences. (That notion is supposed to be an artifact of the theory's adequate completion.) The theory cannot then, starting out, be sensitive to differences of meaning, but only to differences of truth value. So it will not be able to distinguish, if the claims are seen in an isolated manner, between the predictive success of one of those "if and only if" statements (see above) whose right-hand side truly captures the meaning of the mentioned statement on the left-hand side, and another such statement that is true but seems not to capture meaning at all (such as the true statement "'Snow is white' is true in English if and only if grass is green"). But a full theory must recognize the interlocking of any single sentence of a language with many others with which it has relations of entailment, and these others will be similarly related to further sentences as the theory progresses. Once a theory has accounted for the intermeshing of a very wide range of speaker statements, believes Davidson, then the pressure of the whole will make its theorems come very close to giving us the meaning of sentences, even though no semantic notions such as meaning or sense have been used in constructing the theory.[5]

Davidson wants to circumvent the claim that an interpreter's translation might account perfectly well for a speaker's linguistic behavior, and yet be fundamentally wrong in failing to capture what the speaker really meant. If the meaning of a sentence is no more than an artifact of a theory compiled in the Davidsonian manner, then that bothersome claim can be dismissed with an easy conscience; semantic distinctions must in principle be distinguishable by an interpreter. There will not be any deeper facts about the meaning of utterances to which the semantic theory, thus constructed, will not have been faithful. Note that the elimination of the semantic reifications intended to constrain interpretation in advance does not make it the case that "anything goes" for the interpreter. Meaning rather becomes public and knowable, and amenable to investigation by science. That is a typical outcome of the Davidsonian strategy, and I have looked at his notion of a semantic theory in order to see how he brings it about.

I am optimistic about the prospects for a semantic theory that, as in the case of Davidson's, does not grant metaphysical depth to a notion of meaning. But I am less optimistic about the prospects for a theory of the specific sort that Davidson proposes. He believes that we can capture the structure of a natural language, at least in regard to its important semantic features, by systematically representing its sentences with the

[5] Ibid., pp. 73–4.

resources of a simple logical language: the first-order predicate calculus. I think this is far too logicist a picture of how natural languages hang together semantically. I have argued elsewhere, against Davidson, that metaphorical sentences, to take just one example, have a role that cannot be shunted off to the investigation of pragmatics.[6] I believe as well that a semantic theory of the Davidsonian kind, because of its focus on the logical structures of the predicate calculus, will not be able to capture the looser sort of semantic stability that characterizes much of a natural language. Perhaps there are flexible and holistic ways of relating concepts that can be picked out by highly developed pattern recognizers, but not by highly developed analyzers of the logical structure of sentences. But I shall not, or at least not here, be defending these claims. I shall just register my intuition that successful theories of meaning, whatever shape they end up taking, will not follow very closely the details of the Davidsonian model.

Reality without Reference

Theories of reference have to do with how linguistic entities hook up to the world, and these have also been popular in recent semantics. But Davidson attacks the notion of reference as that notion has typically been understood by philosophers.[7] As with the case of meaning, he is not resisting a claim that we may use the notion of reference after we have constructed a semantic theory. He is opposed rather to someone who wants to make use of reference much earlier in the game, as part of a "building-block" account of how meaning arises. Such an account, in very simple form, would be that there are basic expressions in the language that are linked, one by one, to particular items in the world. This hookup gives to those expressions a determinate semantic content, and then the meaning of other expressions can be built up from the base that we have established in that fashion.

As before with meaning, Davidson says that we cannot find any use for such a notion of reference. The speaker's behavior against which we have to test our semantic theories is assent to and dissent from statements or sentences.[8] While there is behavior that we can interpret as a speaker's attitudes toward sentences, there is no comparable behavior that specifies the reference of his terms. And all the evidence made available about those sentential attitudes will be insufficient to fix uniquely the word-to-world linkages. (There are technical arguments to

---

[6] See my essay "Metaphor and Davidsonian Theories of Meaning," *Canadian Journal of Philosophy* 17 (1987): 625–42.

[7] Here I am summarizing the argument of Davidson's essay "Reality without Reference," in *Inquiries*, pp. 215–26.

[8] Ibid., pp. 221–2.

show that there could be systematic shifts in word-to-thing hookup without affecting the overall evidence from the speaker's behavior. I shall not go into those arguments here.) We are left, as a result, with two choices. Either there is a determinate relationship of reference, but it is a metaphysically deep and even magical relation, and its preference over other candidates has no basis in the evidence. Or reference has no theoretical value in semantics, at least as an input to and constraint upon a theory of meaning.

Davidson chooses the latter route. His claim is that reference becomes useful intratheoretically: "I suggest that words, meanings of words, reference, and satisfaction are posits we need to implement a theory of truth. They serve this purpose without needing independent confirmation or empirical basis."[9] One of our tasks in constructing a theory is to account for entailment relationships and for the ability to build new sentences out of limited resources. So we break sentences into smaller units and count some of the smaller units as referential; then we use the subsentential structure to capture relationships of entailment and are able to say when we finish that " 'rabbit' refers to rabbits." But we have not thereby specified some anchorage point between an individual word and some worldly entity.[10] We have produced another sentence that our theory makes true, but we cannot conclude that the expressions in that sentence have hooked themselves to the world in a way that transcends what our intratheoretic work allows us to say.

Now that move of making reference internal to the theory's working, and the statement elsewhere by Davidson that beliefs can only be tested against other beliefs and not against the world, may entice some readers to suppose that we find here substantial support for strong claims of an antirealist sort. Those claims, put most radically, would suggest that "there is nothing outside the text." But we should be clear that Davidson's attack on reference is hardly congenial to that outcome. It remains true that a condition for the assignment of semantic content to utterances is that they are seen as directed toward a world that, from a point independent of them, is regulating their formation and can serve as a measure of their success.

It is important, I believe, that we not press a certain reading upon Davidson's work. That reading might be developed as follows. We have just seen that the articulation of sentences into smaller units taken to be referential is a "posit" of theory. Now it seems as well that it will be by means of the intratheoretic apparatus that we determine ontology: "The theory gives up reference, then, as the cost of going empirical. It can't, however, be said to have given up ontology. For the theory relates each

---

[9] Ibid., p. 222.   [10] Ibid., pp. 222–3.

singular term to some object or other, and it tells what entities satisfy each predicate."[11] Our decisions about what to count as referential expressions affect the set of items to which we are metaphysically committed, so what individuals there are in the world seems also a posit. But that outcome may appear to upset the fine balance that Davidson has been attempting to maintain against pressures that would make his position either more realist or more antirealist than he wishes it to be. He wants to restore the role of a solid independent world that manifests its character in our thinking. ("We can accept objective truth conditions as the key to meaning, a realist view of truth, and we can insist that knowledge is of an objective world independent of our thought or language."[12]) Yet at the same time he refuses to accept a "radically non-epistemic" realism, such that our understanding of the world might very badly miss how it is arranged.[13]

But now it may seem that his making of subsentential structure a posit of theory will tip the scales toward the antirealist position. Concerning ontology, Davidson says that "nothing, however, no *thing*, makes sentences and theories true. It is just that "experience takes a certain course."[14] That our skin is warmed makes the statement 'Our skin is warmed' true. The world's causal power, it seems, goes toward making sentences true, and only derivatively, as we do our intratheoretic work to get the sentence level right, toward specifying what individuals we are counting as real. And he says as well that "different theories of truth may assign different truth conditions to the same sentence ... while the theories are (nearly enough) in agreement on the roles of sentences in the language."[15] One might want to put together these various sayings of Davidson and to make from them a picture that is pragmatic, holist, and instrumentalist. Then the metaphysical distinctions and articulations we take to be significant, and see reflected in our languages, will be "merely" intratheoretic. They will be useful distinctions to make if we want to represent languages so as to account for the inferential structures that hold systems of beliefs together. Sentences are tested as a whole in terms of their usefulness in making our behavior and our predictions successful. But they should not be taken as mirroring, in their structure and their parts, real features of the world.

Davidson, on this reading, will count as having made the linguistic turn, in one of its forms, and also as having made what we might call the hermeneutic transformation of that turn. The world becomes something

---

[11] Ibid., p. 223.
[12] Davidson, "A Coherence Theory of Truth and Knowledge," p. 307.
[13] Ibid., p. 309.
[14] Davidson, *Inquiries*, p. 194.
[15] Ibid., p. 225.

of a substratum upon which linguistic distinctions are projected, but those linguistic distinctions are themselves only what can be determined as such for an interpreter. So the world's metaphysical character is a reflection of logical structure, and specifically of the structure of a language as it is available to an interpreter constructing a theory for that language.

Now it is important for my narrative that we reject that reading of Davidson. It misses from the start the situation of mutual determining that he has been careful to describe. The world must already be there, with its own well-developed contours, as a condition for counting speech as meaningful, as more than a stream of noise. Even an assignment of interests to a speaker, in order to get hold of the basis of his intentional life, will be plausible only if we assign him the interests that someone would have in that particular world, given its prominent shapes and boundaries that we can use in making sense of his discriminations. We err if we think we can divide up the contributions of world, language, and interpreter, so as to specify what the contribution of one of those sources would be, in independence of the others. A correct account of what the world is like whose articulations our language is capturing depends on what worldly contours that very language makes prominent; a correct account of what that language is like already takes for granted a well-articulated world as what is casting its shadow upon the language to make it meaningful.

Davidson rejects the realist picture of a determinate world of facts to which language can hook up causally and by so doing can get its own determinations. He accepts the various underdeterminations of belief by the world, and of interpretation by linguistic behavior. It is to some degree up to us which of the world's contours we make most important in our individuating and sorting, and it is to some degree up to an interpreter which ways of individuating and sorting she finds in a language. But on the other hand, Davidson also rejects pictures that would hold the mirroring relationship to go in the opposite direction, through some activity of projection or construction by language that is thereby reading its own articulations into the world. Davidson insists that in our practices of speaking and interpreting, the general articulations of our language are being sensitive at least roughly to the ways the world articulates itself. Metaphysics is not a child of our ways of speaking and Davidson is not a creature of the linguistic turn, at least as I am treating that turn, even if for him the right way to do metaphysics is to see what we come up with when we produce a truth theory for a language. He does not make metaphysical distinctions mirror linguistic ones, as a shadow cast by them upon a much less determinate screen. He gives us reasons instead to suppose that our language must largely be getting the metaphysical features of the world right, and it may be that the world is such as to force a further metaphysical sophistication upon a system of language that is accommodating itself to it.

We should not, then, go the route of Rorty and hold that Davidson has given up the very notion of a mirroring of the world by language, so that getting subsentential structure right is a merely intratheoretic affair. Even if we cannot arrive at that subsentential structure through a building-block approach that starts from causal ties to a fully determinate world, still the process of arriving at it is part of our holistic adjustment to worldly pressure, part of what it is to capture how matters really stand. Even if we test a truth theory for a language by considering the speaker's behavior with and attitudes toward *sentences*, still there are not two separable components here: a measuring of sentences against the world and a merely internal and instrumentalist determining of subsentential structure. It is important to Davidson's position (if I have him right) that in arriving at that subsentential structure, we are in a very general way mirroring, in our linguistic articulations, the metaphysically relevant contours of the world. To discover that getting the logical structure of a language right requires a commitment to individuals or events or times is to discover something about the world itself; it is not just to find our way about within the confines of our language. What appears in the overall character of our linguistic system and of our system of beliefs is, at least very roughly, the self-display of the world.

Neither the speaker nor the interpreter has to, or can, reach out and specify one hookup of words to the world rather than another; nor must a language determine its ontology simply from resources internal to itself. Just by using language, we all count as talking about roughly the same world of things, a world that has from the start, before all the detailed specifying we undertake, impressed itself on any language to make it meaningful. We never achieve a point from which we could project determinacy upon a worldly screen that must be, to us, indeterminate. For the very linguistic activity that would supposedly be doing the projecting will itself be indeterminate, unless there is over against it, from the beginning, a world much richer in its articulations than the projectivist picture can allow.

Ontological Relativity?

Davidson's account of interpretation gives us little support for relativism, I have been arguing, but shows how the beliefs of very different believers are about, and are guided by, the same world. But there are other considerations suggesting that claims about what is really there must end up being relative. I want to look at this issue with some care, extending the discussion of the previous section, because many believe that attacks such as Davidson's on traditional semantic notions are bound to lead to positions that support indeterminacy, antirealism, and relativism. It is important that Davidson does not go in that direction.

One way of discussing this issue is to begin with a position suggested by Carnap: that there is no world of articulated individuals, except relative to a linguistic scheme chosen by the speaker. One is ontologically committed to a certain kind of entities just by choosing a grammar that allows the formation of statements referring to them. So the world does not on its own have the sort of determinacy that would allow us to answer absolutely the question of what is really there. Ontology is relative.[16] Quine wants to do with Carnap's linguistic schemes, we might say, what Carnap attempted to do with the world itself.[17] Carnap has taken for granted, in questioning the world's determinacy, the determinacy of the linguistic schemes to which ontology is supposed to be relative. (In holding subjectivity to be determinate while saying that the world cannot be, Carnap is a "modern" thinker.) But assume we agree, says Quine, that there is no fact of the matter about what is really there, independently of the speaker's choice of a scheme. Then it is not at all clear why we should suppose that there is a fact of the matter about just what ontological scheme is really there to be applied by a speaker to the world, independently of an interpretation of the speaker's language. For words or mental tokens no more than things are self-identifying; they do not have their determinacy intrinsically, but are just utterances or marks connected to other utterances and marks and more generally to the speaker's behavior. (Again this is a move in what I called the disenchantment of subjectivity.) So now it seems the determination of ontology takes place neither on the first level (the world itself), nor on the second (the speaker's language and its ontological scheme), but on a third level (the interpreter's interpretation of the speaker's language).

That reading of Quine, perhaps not what Quine himself intended, exhibits a familiar pattern. The disenchantment of subjectivity may go only part way, as we said in Chapter 2. Then the move that makes the speaker's utterances and beliefs lose their natures is not at the same time a move back to the world, but is rather toward another layer of subjective determination. In this case the interpreter can play the demiurgic role of fixing the character of the world, by fixing the semantic character of what the speaker is saying. But (again there is something

---

[16] See Carnap's essay "Empiricism, Semantics, and Ontology." It can be found in, among other places, *Contemporary Philosophical Logic*, Irving Copi and James Gould, eds. (New York: St. Martin's Press, 1978), pp. 149–65.

[17] See Willard V. O. Quine, "Ontological Relativity," in *Ontological Relativity and Other Essays* (New York: Columbia University Press, 1969), pp. 26–68. Also see an excellent discussion of Quine's criticism of Carnap in George Romanos, *Quine and Analytic Philosophy* (Cambridge, Mass.: MIT Press, 1983), pp. 41–76.

of the religious model here) the interpreter's activity of determining appears to be determinate in a way that the rest of the system is not. It seems that we have moved, in the picture being attributed perhaps falsely to Quine, ever farther from the Davidsonian picture captured in the temperature-registering analogy, since ontology has become doubly relative, to linguistic scheme and to the interpretation of that scheme by another. Then it will be in no clear sense that I can count myself and others as able to register truths about the world and its features. The appeal of the Davidsonian project is that its success will make me as a believer at home in a solid world, one whose own character can be taken as causing my beliefs about what it is like. But now that solidity seems in danger of melting away.

It is precisely in placing that new reification at the interpreter's level, believes Davidson, that a mistake has been made.[18] Some will suppose that the interpreter (from above, as it were) can make the speaker's reference scheme determinate, at least relative to that interpretation. But if reference is truly inscrutable, it is inscrutable all the way up, and the interpreter cannot, any more than the speaker, attach the speaker's words to objects in the world, *even relative to her interpretation of them.*[19] What she can do, and all she needs to do, is to link the speaker's words with her own referential expressions.

But now it becomes more difficult to say where relativity has insinuated itself into our account. A relativist position requires that there be enough determinate stability, whether semantic or metaphysical, to support the claim that we are dealing with distinct and competing truths, so that truth value must consequently be relativized. But one does not have in the case under discussion the resources for establishing that needed determinacy, in regard to claims about reference. Within our own language, first of all, says Davidson, we cannot fix reference sufficiently to show that it is relative. If the reference of the terms of our language is what we are looking to determine, then it will hardly do us any good to *add* more of our language to the ongoing discussion. What we thereby add will be just as much up in the air concerning its anchorages to particular items in the world. So we do not have the machinery to grasp the two word-to-world linkages that supposedly encourage our belief in the relativity of reference. We shall do no better, Davidson believes, if we relativize reference to an interpreter's language or to any metalanguage at all. Reference, we said, is inscrutable all the way up, so there will be no stopping point at which reference has been

---

[18] The argument that I am analyzing here comes from Davidson, "The Inscrutability of Reference," in Davidson, *Inquiries*, pp. 227–41.

[19] Ibid., pp. 232–5. On pp. 234–5 he says: "But at no point has anyone been able uniquely to specify the objects of which a predicate is true, no matter how arbitrarily or relatively."

made determinate, even relative to a language taken for granted by an interpreter's practice. The fixing of reference will be endlessly delayed as each level, inadequate on its own to fix reference, seems to demand an activity by the level above it.[20]

Instead of specifying determinate anchorages to the world, our discussions of reference fix how to interpret one language by means of another. It looks from reading Quine that inscrutability must engender a relativist account. For reference to be inscrutable means that we cannot determine the referential scheme of another's language, and so we must make that determination relative to our own language as we use it. But to take inscrutability seriously is to see that there is not enough referential determinacy anywhere in the system so that we could see interpreters as employing fixed schemes that determined, even relatively, which particular word-to-object linkage should be assigned to a speaker's expression. The whole notion of a determinate reference scheme begins to collapse, and with it the notion of a relativity that requires, for us to make sense of it, an appeal to such a scheme.

That notion of referential inscrutability will evidently come into play when we ask what there is in the world. One argument for ontological relativity goes as follows. The world itself does not fix its units and sorts; what is there in the world is what a speaker or believer can *take* to be there, given the structure of his language. (That is Carnap's claim.) A further step is then taken after we accept Quinean indeterminacy. What a believer or speaker takes there to be is determined only relative to what an interpreter can take the character of that speaker's engagement with the world to be. So the world seems ever thinner on its own and ontology is doubly relative. But Davidson says that "ontological relativity does not follow, since it suggests that, when enough decisions, arbitrary or otherwise, have been made, unique reference is possible, contrary to our argument for the inscrutability of reference."[21] This claim is an important one in Davidson's overall program. As I have presented that program (in my terms, not his), Davidson wants to show how a full disenchantment of subjectivity, a radical attack on semantic and mental reifications, will bring about not greater relativity but greater realism, through the confidence that we are all talking about the same world and about roughly the same things within it, and that we know its features roughly as they are. (There are some accounts of realism, it is true, for which Davidson's position would fail to qualify as a realist one.)

As before, his move is to show that inscrutability is actually a weapon against relativity. Suppose we get rid of the reification of determinate reference schemes, and see the interpreter as just trying to link up the speaker's utterances with her own and with the world as she speaks of it. Without the constraint of those determinate schemes on interpretation, there will be no fact of the matter about what *objects* are being linked up to by the other's language, even relative to an interpretation; the interpreter cannot reach out and specify some such hookup. To get the other's ontology right is just to show how his language can be interpreted in our own. But now consider that the various languages, of speaker and interpreter and at whatever level, are themselves interpreted through being taken as directed toward roughly the *same* world of entities, as the world's own articulations cast their shadow on the different strings of language, and so make them capable of having semantic content, and incapable of being committed to radically different ontologies.

Perhaps I am going beyond what the Davidsonian texts strictly warrant, but I think this analysis is very much in the spirit of his philosophy. What he opposes (I am going to use my own terminology here) is a way of understanding the disenchantment of subjectivity that sees it as increasing the relativism and the thinning out of the world that the modern turn to subjectivity encouraged. That modern turn, at least in some of its forms, supported the view of a largely undifferentiated world that is given its lines when a subjective framework is imposed upon it. But now there is a further turn, as subjectivity will be disenchanted relative to the interpreter or to cultural practices, in the way that the world was earlier disenchanted relative to the subject. A believer's mental and semantic items will themselves form, then, a relatively undifferentiated realm that has determinacy only insofar as the interpreter constructs a framework and imposes it. That is a conception, I have said, that Davidson rejects. He holds that we cannot make sense of that process of constructing and imposing ontological frameworks, *either* at the level of the speaking subject *or* at the level of an interpreter of a speaker. The picture that attempts to give an account of that process assumes that once we are willing to go relativist, there is no problem with the notion of setting a *fixed* background or framework of ontological commitments, one that can be used in producing a determinate assignment of meaning to someone's utterances, or in giving an account of what there is in the world. But if the thesis of inscrutability is correct, then you will not arrive at such fixed ontological frameworks by the strategy of going one level up, from the world to the speaker and then to an interpreter of that speaker and then to an interpreter of the interpreter and so on. You can't get there from here, we might say; there are no such frameworks to be found.

But that is hardly a bad outcome. For the conception we have thus seen to fail would strongly encourage an intensification of the tendencies of the structure of modern philosophy: toward a thinning out of the world and toward relativism. But its failure opens the way for a different sort of account of what objects a speaker should be understood as talking about. Instead of ascending levels in search of a framework, we return to the world and recognize how it must have already been taken into consideration in the securing of content for any utterances, of speaker or interpreter or whomever.

Yet we should be clear about just what conclusions we are entitled to draw regarding ontological relativity. Davidson's argument is effective against those who would advance toward a defense of such relativity by way of a certain route: an account that requires that one fix, even relatively, the referential linkage of words to the world. Reference is, for Davidson, no more than an artifact of work that is intratheoretic and intralinguistic, as we try to match the articulations of the other's language with those of our own. But even in work of that sort, will not a space open up for a considerable degree of ontological relativity?

Consider the following reading of Quine's argument. He is not supposing that two interpreters can reach out and specify, for an object language, distinct schemes of referential hookup, through being able to fix one of them rather than the other as what is in play during a translation. Let him grant that reference is the theoretical artifact that Davidson says it is. Still we may imagine an interpreter who has to interpret Quine himself. She must make sense of his distinctions among rabbits, rabbit time-slices, undetached rabbit parts, and an unindividuated rabbity mass; and also of the avowal that it is the first sort of individuation that captures what we do in English. But given the complex way in which the entire apparatus of individuation works together in English, and also in Quine's own prose, it may well be that the interpreter in question and another speaker of her language will find distinct but equally satisfying ways of making all the intricate linkages between Quine's language and their own. They are both sensitive to his distinctions, but the holism of interpretation allows them to link those metaphysical distinctions differently to his actual utterances (because of compensating changes elsewhere in the translations), as those utterances get translated into their language. So they differ in just what ontological commitments they take him to be making when he avows that it is indeed rabbits that we refer to in English. Note that at no point in this argument have we appealed to any privileged ability to reach out and fix the lines of reference to the world. We have appealed only to the intralinguistic work itself.

Or perhaps two Davidsonians, while parsing the logical structure of a speaker's sentences in order to arrive at a truth theory for his language, may differ in the range of things they take the language to be committed to, because the logical representations they choose employ quantification over somewhat different sorts of entities. (Should we handle tenses by taking utterances as expressing an ontological commitment to temporal points?) Here again we do not need to make referential linkages to the world determinate in order to raise the issue of ontological relativity. (It is true that Davidson says he is "almost exclusively concerned," in making the particular argument he presents, with cases where "total ontology is assumed to be fixed."[22])

Davidson is interested in issues that arise as we adopt a certain standpoint. The question of what there is in the world, it was claimed by Carnap and others, has transformed itself into the question of what a speaker takes there to be in the world, through her choice of a scheme. And that question has supposedly transformed itself into the question of what an interpreter can take a speaker to be taking there to be in the world. Davidson has argued against a kind of relativity that might appear to open up when we consider the interpreter's work, and its underdetermination by the speaker's behavior. But we might note (this is not news to Davidson) that certain issues about ontological relativity emerge even when we are considering an earlier sort of underdetermination, that of belief by evidence when all involved have agreed that they are speaking the same language. It seems at least plausible that great technological changes, as with cloning, memory implants, and the like, might make it unclear in certain cases whether we are dealing with one person continuing as the same or with two persons (as with Quine's rabbit case). Perhaps the world is such that all the evidence it supplies is insufficient to make one of those claims true and the other false; it is to some degree up to us, and perhaps our practices will be loose enough to allow speakers to get away with both claims in many contexts, unless there are pressing legal or moral reasons for legislating one or the other. Or perhaps it is even the case that the exact boundary we draw between what is real and what is a theoretical construct is, while mostly shaped by how matters stand in the world, also influenced by the overall character of our system of beliefs. So again there will be at least some space for a modest relativity in our ontological commitments, and that space will open up even if we as speakers are speaking within our own home language, and have not yet raised the issue about what an interpreter can take us to be saying. Or we may imagine that we have arrived at the best account of what the world is like (however 'best' is determined). It may still be to some degree up to us how we should give a logical representation of those given beliefs, so that there is no precise fact of the matter as to what we are taking ourselves to be ontologically committed to, in having those true beliefs.

Davidson, I granted, is not unaware of these possibilities. His way of handling at least some of the issues associated with them shows how

---

[22] Ibid., p. 228.

central to his overall picture is his attack on semantic reifications. One of those reifications is language itself. "Our mistake was to suppose that there is a unique language to which a given utterance belongs. But we can without paradox take that utterance to belong to one or another language, provided we make allowance for a shift in other parts of our total theory of a person."[23] The physical utterance produced by a speaker does not of itself belong to a unique language. The interpreter's overall account assigns a language to the speaker, on the basis of his behavior, but there is no fact of the utterance's belonging to a language that, in advance, constrains how the interpreter must interpret the utterance. Indeed, two interpreters may take a speaker's utterances to be utterances in different languages without either being wrong in doing so, provided that the speaker's behavior is well explained:

So it seems to me that a natural way to explain the sometimes needed explicit relativization is a familiar one: we take the speaker to be speaking one language or another. If we take his word 'rabbit' to refer to rabbits, we take him to be speaking one language. If we take his word 'rabbit' to refer to things that are ϕ of rabbits, we take him to be speaking another language. If we decide to change the reference scheme, we decide that he is speaking a different language.[24]

Have we thereby taken care of the problem of ontological relativity that was raised by the Quinean thought experiment? Davidson seems to believe we have because, as he says, all theories of truth are relativized to a language.[25] It is always the case, independently of questions about schemes, that an utterance will get the value true or false only when it is specified as an utterance in one language or another. Its truth is then relative to which language it belongs to, but that is an everyday sort of relativity that no philosopher will find difficult to accept. The controversial relativism that initially threatened has collapsed back into an ordinary and nonthreatening sort. We do not arrive at a point where the ontological claims at issue here are inconsistent in a way that requires us to relativize truth. Instead of saying that the truth of a speaker's ontological commitment is relative to the scheme applied by the interpreter, we say that the question of truth does not even enter until we have specified the language to which the speaker's utterance belongs. And once we have specified that, then a nonrelativized truth value can be readily assigned and no mention needs to be made of different schemes. The truth value that might be assigned to the utterance if it belonged to a different language is immaterial.

But that is hardly a satisfactory manner of insulating the two claims from their apparent competition. There is a clear sense in which Davidson is correct that a statement's truth conditions depend on the language to which we take the statement as belonging. The utterance 'The bonnet is

---

[23] Ibid., pp. 239–40.　　[24] Ibid., p. 239.　　[25] Ibid., p. 239.

damaged' may have truth conditions referring to an automobile part when it is a statement of British English but not when it is a statement that an American would employ. But there is a great deal of strain in trying to assimilate Quine-like claims about ontological relativity to cases of that sort. In the case of 'bonnet,' to understand how the statements may belong to different languages is to understand straight off that the claims made by two speakers will not be competing ones. But consider then Quine's proposal, as it is now read by the Davidsonian. An interpreter may take speaker S to be speaking language L and thus to be claiming that there are rabbits, or he may take S to be speaking language L* and thus to be claiming that there are time-slices of rabbit. But the different individuative schemes expressed in commitments to rabbits or their time-slices remain in contention even if I take them to be expressed in different languages. Davidson's strategy is to multiply languages so as to prevent apparently competing claims from actually entering into competition. But that strategy does not seem to eliminate the problem that we presently face, nor to acknowledge that which makes it the problem that it is. It is not clear just what has been purchased if we get rid of the notion of relativity to a background scheme but replace it with the idea that a single individual on an occasion may be taken to be speaking different languages, with different ontological commitments, so that the relativity is now to which language the interpreter takes him to be speaking.

We should be aware how the Davidsonian strategy I have been discussing fits into his overall program. His point is that interpretation is holistic. The interpreter is simultaneously assigning desires and beliefs to a speaker and meaning to his utterances, and that will require deciding that they are utterances of one language rather than of a possible rival.[26] When there are differences to be accounted for by an interpreter, he may accommodate them by locating the difference in any of those features. (A simple case: Speakers who produce different utterances in a situation may have different beliefs or may have the same belief but be speaking different languages.) If we value highly an outcome that does not make ontology relative, then we locate the difference elsewhere, perhaps by supposing it to be a linguistic one. Only if we are committed to reifications such as reference schemes, Davidson will say, shall we be constrained to suppose that there are fixed and different reference schemes that make ontology relative. If we allot differences in another fashion, then we can restore the Davidsonian picture that sees us as generally successful in our registering of nonrelative truths about the world as it is.

---

[26] See Davidson's account of interpretation in his "Radical Interpretation" and "Belief and the Basis of Meaning," both in *Inquiries*.

Davidson himself seems to value very highly having different speakers count as talking about the same world of entities, and as having very roughly the same beliefs about what it is like. He assigns very little value, in contrast, to holding language or meaning the same among various speakers. His argument seems to be that being able to count others as registering truths about the same world we inhabit is the precondition for all interpretation to succeed. That is not optional, whereas interpretation could succeed even if we ended up having to assign an idiolect to each speaker, and even an idiolect for each occasion. In supporting what I have called his disenchantment of language, he wants to rid us of the notion that there are semantic natures that constrain in advance how we must use 'same' (same meaning, same referent, same language, same belief). If there are no such natures, then Davidson will feel free to apply the vocabulary of sameness and difference in the manner that best explains the other's utterances and behavior, and that best suits his own metaphysical and epistemic preferences.

His answer when ontological relativity threatens, we said, is to parse the bothersome differences as semantic ones. "Two interpreters, as unlike in culture, language and point of view as you please, can disagree over whether an utterance is true, but only if they differ on how things are in the world they share, or what the sentence means."[27] And perhaps a similar case can be made by Davidson even for the situation where I am interpreting my own language. I might generate competing logical representations of my utterances that take those utterances to embody somewhat different ontological commitments. Davidson can reply here that there is nothing odd in supposing that I might take myself to be speaking different languages; there is no fact of the matter as to the language I am speaking.

But it is difficult to suppose that if we have already found Quine's discussion of individuation to be of metaphysical interest, we shall find Davidson's solution to have satisfied that interest. If we did suppose that, then Davidson would be closer to Carnap's linguisic turn than I think he would find comfortable. Instead of the speaker's choice of a linguistic scheme, as in Carnap, there will be the interpreter's choice as to which language, with its individuative scheme, one should take the speaker as employing. But I do not think that given Davidson's own account, metaphysical issues will disappear through being counted as linguistic ones. He holds that the articulations that emerge in our language are not merely intratheoretic matters to be measured by their instrumental value; they are exhibiting real features of the world. So it says something about the world itself, and about the degree to which

[27] Davidson, "A Coherence Theory of Truth and Knowledge," p. 309.

we should count it as self-articulating and self-determining, that it can display its character in such different schemes of individuation, as embodied in different languages. We lose what is of metaphysical interest here if we let the matter be treated simply as one of choice of language, as if we were back again with the picture of a language projecting its articulations on a worldly substrate.

Now perhaps Davidson does not at all suppose that his account would reduce the interest of such metaphysical issues. Perhaps his quarry has all along been a quite specific one: the claim that ontological claims are true only relative to the background scheme of the interpreter. He has handled the relativity elsewhere, by claiming that truth is relative to the language one's utterances belong to, and that different interpreters may take one to be speaking different languages. He can count the world's underdetermination of our ontological commitments as a species of its general underdetermination of what words we ought to employ in talking about it. But then our decisions about how to speak bring with them important commitments regarding how we are taking the world to be; we are not dealing with "merely" linguistic differences as in the case of the Frenchman and the Englishman choosing different sounds to pick out the same object. My lesson then, on that reading, is not one for Davidson himself but for those who may exaggerate the outcomes, and the philosophical significance, of Davidson's attack on the notion of ontological relativity.

I believe that the difficulties posed by whatever ontological relativity we have to admit into philosophical accounts are hardly severe. Davidson himself points out that claims about differences among speakers are well supported only against a background of wide agreement. And that was the result of my explication of Davidson's argument against the notion of fixed ontological frameworks. Davidson is right that an ontological scheme cannot be a mysterious entity such that no matter how well even the most advanced interpreter accounted for all the other's behavior, she might not grasp that the other is living in a fundamentally different world, and is referring to a fundamentally different set of entities from the ones that she accepts. I do not see any argument that would make us accept ontological schemes that were reified in that fashion. The only defense we have seen of the notion of ontological differences of the sort in question makes them appear against a background of agreement, and makes them nonmysterious phenomena that are in principle available to an interpreter. (That "in principle" does carry some weight. I see no reason why it would be impossible for speakers much more advanced than ourselves to use forms of individuation and classification that our brain machinery simply isn't competent to achieve, or to recognize in others who achieved it.) Two speakers who differ in their individuative schemes will agree enough to be able to discuss those differences, if they are intelligent enough, with each able to understand the motivation of the other in making different boundaries significant.

Because the relation between language and the world is built into the very account that makes a language have semantic value, it will be the case that "when we study what our language – any language – requires in the way of overall ontology, we are not just making a tour of our own picture of things; what we take there to be is pretty much what there is."[28] The lesson of Davidson is that we can show that many features do not have the metaphysical depth that many full-blooded realists will want to grant to them, without our moving to the opposing stance of holding that the world's articulations are projected out of a constructive or demiurgic subjectivity. That is an important result and it is the picture that I develop in Chapter 5 and Chapter 6. He also denies "the possibility of discovering that others have radically different intellectual equipment."[29] It is true perhaps that the notion of simply incommensurable schemes does not make much sense if we accept Davidson's general picture. But I am wary of claims that at least seem to limit in advance how much different from humans other beings might be through having a vastly superior intelligence. Perhaps their way of doing things would be incomprehensible to us, not because it is incommensurable (they can understand us quite well as we can understand the chimp's sign-language), but because it is too advanced for our brains. Why should we suppose that Davidsonian arguments have eliminated that possibility?

While I have been focusing on the assignment of meaning to utterances, Davidson's disenchantment of subjectivity applies to the full range of mental states. He holds that these can be determinate only in the context of an overall theory that holistically assigns beliefs, intentions, meanings, and desires to the speaker.[30] One is assigned the whole system simultaneously, as it were, so that the mental features cannot serve as the basis for, and as a prior constraint upon, the construction of a semantic theory. That is a further kind of reification, then, that falls victim to the Davidsonian machinery. He does not deny that there are such things as intentions and beliefs; he remains a realist about the mental realm. The issue is rather about the point at which such mental states come to have the status they do for theory. Davidson does not see how that status could be such as to grant them sufficient determinacy, prior to theory, that fixing them could serve as a first step that would support a later semantic assignment. Again we see what I have taken to

[28] Davidson, *Inquiries*, p. xix.
[29] Ibid., p. xviii.
[30] See the essay "Belief and the Basis of Meaning," in *Inquiries*, pp. 141–54.

be the Davidsonian move of denying a certain metaphysical depth to various phenomena while holding that our accounts of them express a sensitivity to real features that regulate our conceptions of them. Here it is mental states that do not have the sort of metaphysical depth that will generate a unique correct account, and that fixes from the start what articulations our final theory must arrive at. There is, instead, some "give" in the holistic assignment of meaning, belief, language, desire, and intention. But what our theories then exhibit are real features of the mind and of practice, not instrumentally useful projections.

Against the Very Idea of a Language

Davidson, I said, tries to accommodate certain differences by counting them as linguistic ones. He can do this more readily if he takes the notion of a shared language to be itself an unneeded reification. Let me examine this feature of his work; I shall start by returning to the temperature-registering analogy that was mentioned earlier on. If we found a thermometer whose markings had no numerical values, we would define those markings so as to make the thermometer's recording of temperature at least roughly accurate, to the extent that we could do so. But now consider a different case, in which I have come across thermometers packed together in a box. Most still have the temperature numbers marked, but a few, while otherwise identical, have numbers that were blurred in manufacturing and can no longer be read. One of these few, it turns out, is way off in the way it records temperature, when compared with the others. I might decide to interpret its markings as an "idiolect" whose calibrations are different from those of the other thermometers, and might then try to assign numbers so as to make it as accurate as possible. Or I might decide, since it is a member of a batch and has the same brand name and number as the others (let us suppose), that making its conventions of recording temperature the same as the other thermometers is more important than making it accurate. I shall then be much more willing to say that its readings are highly inaccurate, and that there is a systematic defect in its temperature-registering capacity.

Now much the same choice may occur when interpreting another speaker. Sameness of brand name or batch would be sameness of linguistic community. Suppose someone says, "the carburetor in my Toyota is broken," yet it turns out that the description he associates with the term 'carburetor' contains serious inaccuracies, so that many of his beliefs about carburetors turn out to be false, if we take carburetors to be indeed what his beliefs are about. Should we then assign an idiosyncratic meaning to that expression as he uses it, in order to make more of his beliefs true? A common answer will be that he belongs to our "brand,"

and that the expression as he uses it means what it means in our language. But Davidson would generally prefer to ascribe a higher percentage of true beliefs to a speaker, even if that means accommodating differences by assigning to each his own idiolect, and even his own idiolect on an occasion. For him, we are here at the hardiest reification that can separate believers from the world around them.

The notion of a common brand, to continue the above analogy, is for Davidson one more example of the kind of thinking shown in Frege's work on senses. We try to explain linguistic behavior by appealing to some higher-level semantic natures supposedly instantiated in its patterns. In the present case a single shared language is assumed to have an ideal nature that is embodied in the linguistic activity of individual speakers, and that constrains how we may properly interpret what the speakers are saying and believing. But we have no more use for that reification, believes Davidson, than for senses or conceptual schemes. What we have actually is a more nominalist semantic universe with individual utterances that are produced and interpreted on individual occasions, without the constraint of higher-level brands to which they supposedly belong. (We shall, it is true, expect the semantic theories we need to construct for individuals of the same community to be roughly similar.) Semantically, we are in a Hobbesian state of nature without conventions, and individuals must use their overall intelligence to make sense of those they confront. If that is the case, then Davidson will have a much stronger argument for using an assignment of linguistic difference to allow for a greater ascription of true beliefs.

Davidson attacks the notion of language as "an inert (though necessarily distorting) medium independent of the human agencies that employ it."[31] If we consider language as a reification in a sense such as that, there is little reason to resist what Davidson is here recommending. But his attack on language is more radical than that quotation would suggest. He begins by asking what role conventions play in making language what it is.[32] Davidson argues that while there are clearly conventional elements in our actual linguistic practice (using the sounds we do to mean what we mean, for example), convention plays no essential role in language as an instrument of communication: "Convention does not help explain what is basic to linguistic communication, though it may describe a usual, though contingent, feature."[33]

Perhaps we can try to imagine a case in which there is communication by means of language but in which no linguistic conventions are at work. Consider a universe of two highly intelligent people who are able to

---

[31] Davidson, *Inquiries*, p. 185.
[32] See his "Communication and Convention," in *Inquiries*, pp. 265–80.
[33] Ibid., p. 280.

interpret each other but each of whom never speaks the other's language. They communicate successfully but there are no shared conventions as to how to relate meanings or intentions to the sounds or shapes being produced. We may suppose that each, in interpreting the other, forms a theory about the other's usage. Perhaps, then, the shared convention will not link meaning and the sequences actually used by the two, but rather meaning and the sequences that are common to A's speaking and to B's theory of A's speaking (and vice versa). But conventions are supposed to have some stability over time, so we may revise the experiment in the following manner. A and B are superintelligent beings who like to play with languages, for their mutual amusement. On each occasion they meet, each invents a new language to use in speaking with the other, and their intelligences are sophisticated enough, and their knowledge of each other's habits acute enough, that they can, after a time, interpret successfully, even with all the changes implied. Perhaps their circumstances are such that each has a very good idea in advance of what the other will be trying to communicate, and can use that knowledge as an aid in deciphering the other's newly created language. B's language of the moment, and A's interpretive theory of it during the time of their speaking, will not be in common long enough to count as genuine conventions governing their communication. So one could have linguistic communication without convention, in circumstances rather different from our own.

That is Davidson's conclusion and I think it is correct, but we should see that the thought experiment has little to do with actual languages as we use them. Davidson's thought, however, pushes in the direction of finding that our actual linguistic usage, much more than philosophers have generally believed, is like the austere case just described. As actual speakers we are close to the position of those speakers who have to construct new semantic theories on different occasions, as different speakers present their utterances to us in changing contexts. I think there is something right about this move in Davidson, since very often we interpret others correctly when they are misusing language, and since the linguistic knowledge that we bring into play when interpreting does shade off into our general understanding of the world. But he seriously underestimates the degree to which meaning is not only social (that it is so is central to his account, since meaning must be public and available to interpretation), but also shared.

Davidson asks what conditions something would have to meet to qualify as a language in our usual sense of the term.[34] A language would have to assign literal meanings to strings of sounds or shapes. Literal

---

[34] I am considering here the argument in Davidson, "A Nice Derangement of Epitaphs," in *Truth and Interpretation*, Ernest LePore, ed., pp. 443–6.

meaning, in such an assignment, would have to have three properties. It will be systematic, in that the meaning of much longer strings will depend on how they are constructed out of shorter ones; it will be shared, so that communication is possible between two speakers; and it will governed by learned conventions that are known in advance of any actual situation of interpreting.[35] Davidson then looks at our practices of communicating, in order to discover whether there is anything that meets all three criteria, and that can count then as the literal meaning upon which speakers of a language supposedly agree.

How, then, do I interpret another speaker? It is clear, first of all, that speakers of a language will not use expressions in just the same manner. The point is especially evident in discussions of philosophy, where it may take us considerable reading, and considerable attention to the inferential structure of a text, to determine just how a writer is using 'realism,' 'sense,' or 'subjectivity,' or other expressions of similar abstraction. Speakers may, in addition, make consistent errors in their use of a word. So on an actual occasion of interpreting another, my theory of the language he is using must account for his precise usage and his errors, or else we shall not be able to hope for a fully successful communication. When I encounter another speaker of my language community, of course, I do not have to begin my interpretation, as with strangers, in the dark. I shall already have strategies to make sense of someone who speaks English, and if I have a history of interpreting a particular person as well, the theory I bring to our encounters will be far more an individualized one; and what I know about the other's occupation, class, and area of residence will also influence the theory I am ready to apply when I am making sense of his words.

Let us call the theory I have in advance of interpreting John my *prior theory* of John's language.[36] As I engage in actual interpretation of his sayings, I shall make adjustments in my theory to account for his precise usage and errors. Communication will succeed fully if I come up with a theory of his language that matches the theory that he himself employs in producing his utterances. We may call the theory I come up with during actual interpretation my *passing theory* of John's language. Some features of the short-term passing theory I shall incorporate into the long-term prior theory of his language that I shall have at the ready when I encounter John on another occasion.

If we accept that description that Davidson thus urges upon us, we must try to locate just where in the foregoing transactions we have what we can properly call a language, whose literal meanings, as Davidson has listed the conditions, are systematic, shared, and known in advance. The first of those three conditions is easy to satisfy, but problems arise

[35] Ibid., p. 436.   [36] Ibid., p. 442.

when we look for something that can satisfy simultaneously the second and the third. The passing theory is systematic and shared, but it is not known in advance; we work it out during the act of interpreting. The prior theory is systematic and known in advance, but it is not shared; my theory for interpreting a speaker's words will have to be adjusted to match his behavior. Davidson concludes that there is no such thing as a language, not if a language "is anything like what many philosophers and linguists have supposed."[37] Even speakers of the "same language" share much less in advance of interpretation than most theoreticians of language believe. In fact, says Davidson, "we have erased the boundary between knowing a language and knowing our way around in the world generally."[38] The full range of our cognitive skills and strategies is put to work in the interpretation of another, and it is the employment of those skills, rather than the sharing of conventions, that makes communication successful. To say that two people share a language is just to say that "they tend to converge on passing theories."[39]

Has Davidson's argument succeeded here? Too much of the weight of the argument is perhaps borne by the condition attached to the conclusion: that there is no such thing as a language, if a language "is anything like what many philosophers and linguists have supposed." For there will be the ready reply that natural languages are not much like that, because those philosophers and linguists have been too influenced by models of what a theory of meaning is like for a formal language. Davidson sets an absurdly high standard for what a theory of language would have to be that would justify our belief that there are such things as languages. He says that none of the candidates he considers "satisfies the demand for a description of an ability that speaker and interpreter share and that is adequate to interpretation."[40] Then again: "We have discovered no learnable common core of consistent behavior, no shared grammar or rules, no portable interpreting machine set to grind out the meaning of an arbitrary utterance."[41] The mention of the machine grinding out the meaning, and of a shared ability "adequate" to interpretation, suggests that if there is such a thing as a shared language determining literal meaning, then a theory for that language must be *fully* adequate to the task of interpretation. It must be able to take any utterance of a speaker and generate a statement giving the truth conditions for that utterance, without need for any further application of our general cognitive skills.

Now perhaps that was indeed the proposed outcome of a Davidsonian semantic theory, but that outcome was, I think, hopeless from the start. To learn that a language does not have a set of rules and conventions of

---

[37] Ibid., p. 446.   [38] Ibid., pp. 445–6.   [39] Ibid., p. 445.   [40] Ibid., p. 444.   [41] Ibid., p. 445.

that sort, with the power to generate literal meanings in that fashion, should not make us conclude that we have no shared languages, and no conventions that underlie them. The conventionality of a language is linked to a looser sort of semantic stability, and to a looser connection between mental states and utterances. It is not that everyone who speaks English must, in following its semantic conventions, express precisely the same belief with the utterance 'A socialist economic program is unpatriotic.' We would have to listen further, and attend to the speaker's examples and conceptual oppositions and patterns of inference, to see just what he means by 'socialism' and 'patriotism.' But it is hardly as if the speaker could have associated any belief at all with those sounds or shapes, and still have counted as one who was following the rules of English. The conventions under which we operate as speakers of a natural language specify a certain range of maneuver beyond which we shall count as being in violation of the rules. (That is not to deny that we can sometimes make interesting and informative moves by violating the conventions of language use, provided enough of the rest of what we say adheres to the rules.)

While an economist might find it interesting to make a precise model of a single individual's economic behavior at a single point in time, that project would never replace the attempt to discover patterns and regularities that belong to the economic system as a whole. It is likely, in an analogous way, that we shall not try, in semantic theory, to give a perfect model of a single individual's linguistic behavior on a single occasion of usage. We shall choose instead to locate whatever structures account not only for the holistic semantic stability that is consistent with individual differences, but also for the pressure that taking someone to speak a shared language places on what we take him to mean, and on what should count as a misapplication of a term. We might consider here an analogy with styles in clothing. Some clothing, such as military uniforms and judges' robes, is determined by conventions to which those in certain positions are expected to conform. Then there are other occasions when there may be a great deal of conformity not because of conventions but because of a common socialization, as when college students going to a basketball game may end up dressed very much alike. Davidson seems to regard the similarities among speakers of the same language as more like the latter sort of conformity than like the former. He consistently underplays, in his philosophy, the significance of belonging to a shared practice, and of being in the wrong when one fails to follow its rules. So he likes to focus on situations where usage is odd, as with malapropisms, rather than on the situation, for example, of reading the daily newspaper, where one can depend on a close adherence to conventions associating certain strings of shapes with specific meanings.

I have suggested that Davidson may now overemphasize the to some degree anarchic character of ordinary communication because his previous model of what a language is owed far too much to an analogy with the semantics of formal languages, and to his conception that the user of a language is producing his utterances by applying a theory about the language. The criteria for identity of formal languages, and for theory-identity as well, are very strict, and it should be clear that what two English-speakers share will not be of that sort. (We should be wary of the notion that speaking a language is very much like activating a theory about the language.) In that respect, it is something of an advance for Davidson to make the almost Derridean move of claiming that a natural language is not like a conventional game, because there are no rules that can determine in advance what are the allowable and nonallowable moves for speakers, no conventions that can establish a firm boundary for what is within the game and what is outside it. A move will always come along that might have seemed in advance to be a breaking of the rules, and thus to fall outside the "proper" sphere determined by the language's conventions, but that still manages to bring about a successful communication with other speakers of the language. Davidson is correct in making that claim, but in making it, he should not go on to undervalue the ways in which ordinary communication is deeply conventional, provided we have a more relaxed notion of what those conventions require than is the case with a semantic interpretation of a formal language.

At a rougher level of resolution, we can make out the institutional reality of a language, and the kind of conventional associations between utterances and meaning that keep it distinguishable from other languages around it. For Davidson, who pays little attention to that stable institutional reality, sharing a language comes down to being able to converge on passing theories. But we should note that two speakers bilingual in French and English will converge very readily on passing theories even if one is speaking English and the other French. The Davidsonian criterion, then, is not sensitive to the difference between monolingual speakers who converge on passing theories and bilingual speakers who do so just as effectively even while speaking different languages. Davidson seemingly cannot find a happy middle ground for his account of semantics. Earlier he said a semantic theory would uncover only the recursive logical structures of a language. Now he tells us one's semantic theory for another's language must include the vast amount of background information one uses in making sense of his utterances. He recognizes that such "theories" hardly deserve the name anymore, since they arise and then pass from existence so quickly, on each occasion that we interpret another speaker.

Let us grant that conventions and linguistic identity are theoretical abstractions that arise over the course of theory construction, rather than givens that constrain such theory construction right from the start. It still remains an open question at what point they will be brought in as useful abstractions. My own claim has been that taking different speakers to be speaking the same language will occur at an earlier point than Davidson supposes. Some of the trade-offs we make as interpreters will involve counting a speaker as part of a community, even when this means ascribing to him a greater number of beliefs that are false. There was no reified language to start with, but the demand of being faithful to the full range of evidence made it necessary that a shared language enter as an abstraction at this point in developing the theory.

Perhaps we could say that Davidson has an insufficient appreciation of what we might call the Hegelian middle realm: the cultural world that mediates between the particular features of an individual and the universal principles that apply to all in the same manner. (We might claim that Davidson, so careful about rejecting the habits of empiricism in so many areas, retains its deep preference, in philosophical investigations, for what individuals do as they confront their surroundings.) An underappreciation of that middle realm is shown in a different manner in Kantian ethics, where universal principles of reason confront every rational thinker in just the same fashion. In Hegel's account, we do not face those universal principles as naked individuals, but through the mediation of a particular community, with its rich ethical life that shapes our intentional activity and trains us in how to live, through its habit-forming institutions. The Davidsonian linguist has a universal principle of determinacy, in that all speakers must be taken as talking about the same world of entities. But then each individual speaker is fitted to that world as a naked individual, and a theory of meaning will be valid only for a single speaker on a single occasion. Speakers are not seen as being related to that universal horizon of sameness through the mediation of particular linguistic communities whose institutions impress their meanings upon a speaker's mental states and utterances.

It is central, of course, to Davidson's entire project that meaning and intentionality are social. There is no more to mental and semantic facts than can be made manifest, in principle, to an interpreter. And Davidson recognizes that socialization shapes how we speak, and makes those in a community rough copies of one another in how they use language. Most importantly, he thinks the very notion of intentionality is such that only communicators could have belief states; it is only by recognizing that others express beliefs from a different perspective, different beliefs about the same world that I do, that I can have sufficient purchase on the notion of objectivity to count as a believer. But Davidson does not grant enough weight to the pressures of a common cultural world on our activity of interpreting, as we are now in position to see, when we consider one of the principal arguments that has been raised against Davidson's stance on this issue.

Meaning and the Linguistic Community

Tyler Burge opposes Davidson on the issue of how a communal language might help to fix the semantic content of what an individual means and believes.[42] Davidson will not, of course, deny all such influence. I have good reason to make the expressions in my own idiolect match public usage, since I want to make myself understood, and the cultural environment will shape individuals whose idiolects are similar. But he denies (while Burge affirms) the following claim: that what an utterance means in the linguistic practices of the community is a factor that will lead an interpreter to assign a *different* meaning to someone's utterances and beliefs, different from what would be assigned just on the basis of an interpretation of the individual himself, considering his behavior, linguistic and otherwise. Consider then the belief expressed by a speaker of English who says "Carl has arthritis" and believes (incorrectly) that 'arthritis' applies to an inflammation of the joints only if it is caused by calcium deposits.[43] (Davidson is here adapting an example of Burge's.) That utterance is interpreted by Davidson as expressing the belief that Carl has an inflammation of the joints caused by calcium deposits, while it is interpreted by Burge as the belief simply that Carl has an inflammation of the joints, since that is what 'arthritis' *means* in the language of the community to which the speaker belongs. Roughly speaking, Burge is a socialist about belief content and Davidson an individualist (though Davidson, we have seen, strongly supports the notion of meaning as social, in the sense of being public and available to an interpreter).

I shall be considering what can be said in support of their positions. The debate has become an important one, as it seems to collect around itself a number of issues that are important in philosophy and central to our self-conceptions. There is, for one issue, the general matter of how to play off individual responsibility against membership in a community. On the one hand, individuals count rather little in the long relay race of cultural evolution, as cultural ideas and skills and forms of life use individuals to propagate themselves into generations to come. On the

---

[42] See Burge's "Individualism and the Mental," in *Midwest Studies in Philosophy*, IV, Peter French, Theodore Uehling, and Howard Wettstein, eds. (Morris: University of Minnesota Press, 1979), pp. 73–121; "Individualism and Psychology," *Philosophical Review* 95 (1986), pp. 3–45; and "Other Bodies," in *Thought and Object*, Andrew Woodfield, ed. (Oxford: Clarendon Press, 1982), pp. 97–120.

[43] Davidson, "Knowing One's Own Mind," *Proceedings and Addresses of the American Philosophical Association* 60, no. 3 (1987): 449.

other hand, my words mean what they do because of the life that I breathe into them through using them a certain way and through expressing myself in their patterns. Recall Hegel's Protestant distaste for the Catholic's "merely external" use of indulgences; others, it seems, can do the work that makes me sanctified. The more socialist accounts of meaning and belief will perhaps seem, to many thinkers, closer to the case of indulgences than is philosophically hygienic. (Davidson's individualist position also has the virtue of resisting the postmodern critic's too easy move of taking for granted the death of the subject, the death of the author, the death of the individual meaner.)

The issue of how belief content is fixed is also important for Davidson's own philosophical work. For it has been one of his purposes to show how the alienated subject of modern philosophy arises from a misunderstanding of how it is that thought is about the world, and he wants as well to give a convincing response to the claims of the skeptic. His strategy is to get rid of any distorting medium that could be used in an argument that we might be very much out of touch with things as they really are. The views he opposes typically present the linkage between beliefs and the world as passing through intermediaries that make that linkage indirect, with sense data being the most obvious case of such a structure of indirection. The epistemic problem is that one can think of a process by which those intermediaries would be produced, even without the world being at all the way it is supposed to be when they come to be present. Davidson's response is that while there may be *causal* intermediaries between one's beliefs and the world, these will not play any threatening epistemic role.[44] For when I am concerned about what makes beliefs mean what they do, and about the conditions that make them, finally, true or false, the causal story about steps along the chain of belief formation is inessential. The interpreter must consider only the end points of the chain, namely, the beliefs themselves and the things that ultimately cause them and that they are about. Those end points are then described so that at least a rough fit between them is guaranteed, no matter what may be happening along the causal route that links them. Only after that has been done globally is there a sufficiently stable background to allow that the chain of belief formation might bring with it some significant degree of distortion. But there can be no systematically distorting medium that pulls apart one's beliefs and what they aim at being about.

---

[44] "Since we can't swear intermediaries to truthfulness, we should allow no intermediaries between our beliefs and their objects in the world. Of course there are causal intermediaries. What we must guard against are epistemic intermediaries." Davidson, "A Coherence Theory of Truth and Knowledge," p. 312.

But now a communal language, it seems, will be a medium that allows at least very considerable distortion. If the interpreter's connecting of beliefs and world must accommodate a linkage that passes through the possibly diffracting medium of communal meaning, then that interpreter will not have the freedom to interpret in a way that makes a believer have generally accurate beliefs. If someone says, "The sun is not a star," I may interpret the meaning that he assigns to 'star' in a way that makes his belief a true one. But once I am under the pressure of matching his usage with that of the linguistic community in which I find him, then I shall assign the meaning of 'star' to him in a way that allows his belief to be false. The deference to the public language will be responsible, then, for a far higher percentage of false beliefs in my assignment. But Davidson has hoped that his account of meaning and belief would show that a general skepticism about belief is misguided. It seems that his answer to the skeptic is under much greater threat from Burge's "socialist" arguments than from Putnam's Twin Earth experiments that we considered earlier.

How should we come down on this issue? There are ways of making the contrast between the two sides less severe. We could make a distinction between what someone believes and what belief his utterance expresses. Consider someone who says, "Carl has arthritis" and who believes that arthritis must be an inflammation of the joints caused by calcium deposits. How would he react upon discovering the proper meaning of 'arthritis'? He might well say that while he *expressed* the belief that Carl has arthritis, the same one that other members of the community would express by those words, still that was not quite his belief, since once he discovered what the word really meant, he felt that he needed a different statement to express the belief that he had tried on the previous occasion to put forward. Another compromise is to bring the socialist considerations into the heart of the individualist account itself. Thus I might say that for many expressions, the meaning that I myself assign to them will contain a reference to what experts in the community mean in using them. My utterances still mean what I make them mean, but what I make them mean has a built-in reference to the understanding of others.

There is something right about these responses, but they do not go deeply enough into the complexity of our notions of belief and meaning, a complexity that itself encourages the conflict between the individualist and the socialist. While I am like others in preferring, in philosophy, a good fight to an easy compromise, I think that both sides here pick out factors that an adequate account of belief will want to retain. There is no inconsistency in that result; it is a matter just of honoring the diverse functions for which our psychological vocabulary developed. What are some of the contexts in which our intuitions in favor of the individualist seem to win out?[45] One case will be when our principal interest is in the prediction of the other's behavior. Then we are trying to make a mapping of his mental space, as it were, and are less concerned with the way that his belief gets its life from a public practice shared by others. A similar result will occur in cases where we are more interested in someone's private stances than we are in his work as a transmitter of cultural belief. Suppose Tom finds out that Martha said his presentation at a political rally was "terse." But he also knows that she incorrectly understands 'terse' to mean not just concise and polished but also cold and unemotional. The belief he takes her to have expressed by her words will surely be the one that is fixed by what *she* takes the word to mean and not by what it means in communal usage.

It is also true that we give experts more leeway to set their own meanings. If a well-known philosopher has a somewhat idiosyncratic usage of 'antirealism,' we assign semantic content to his utterances on the basis of that usage and not on the basis of what others may mean by the term. When an undergraduate philosophy student, in contrast, writes on an exam: "Fodor is an antirealist about mental states," we take him to be expressing the same belief that those in the field would express by those words, and thus to be demonstrating his assent to a false belief. There are some expressions where all of us are given considerable liberty of application. We allow others to make their own usage more precise and so our debates often include statements such as, "If that's what you mean by 'courage', then...," and we try to see the exact inferential structure in which the speaker places sentences that contain the word 'courage.'

Our individualist intuitions will also be fostered by cases where someone is so way off in his use of an expression that we cannot properly take him to be using our term. Suppose that Nguyen is studying English in a refugee camp and his ruler slips so that for 'philodendron' he reads the definition of 'philosopher.' If later he says, "Aristotle is a philodendron," it would be absurd to assign him, for socialist considerations, the belief that Aristotle is a type of plant. That was certainly not the belief expressed in the sentence he produced. His causal link to correct usage was too thin to support the claim that it is our concept that he has learned and is now employing. With others as well much will depend on how proper it seems to insert their utterances into our sort of practices. The child who says that the sun is not a star is being trained in our concepts and has a false belief, while the Brazilian tribesman whose utterance we best translate as "The sun is not a star" may well be

---

[45] A detailed defense of the individualist position, one very much influenced by Davidson, is in Akeel Bilgrami, *Belief and Meaning: The Unity and Locality of Mental Content* (Oxford: Blackwell, 1992), pp. 64–129. I have found Bilgrami's treatment helpful in considering what can be said for the individualist position.

counted as employing his own concept and thus as believing truly. Sometimes we want to emphasize the notion of the believer as taking a stand in what he believes, as putting himself forward in his words and abiding by them, as in statements in court. Here too we tend to be individualists. We want to know just what the believer thinks of himself as saying, with just the inferences he would accept.

All of these are cases where our intuitions make us side more with Davidson than with Burge. Yet we have another set of intuitions as well. There is a cultural process of *objectification* by which beliefs are constituted as public entities that are the same from speaker to speaker, in spite of differences in understanding on the part of those involved. Such beliefs are public not just in the Wittgensteinian sense that they are in principle interpretable by others, but in the sense in which a production process makes a certain performance more readily repeatable and interchangeable, even as different agents occupy the site of production. This will happen most often, of course, where there is a public body of knowledge that is grounded in the work of experts and that is transmitted across generations. The natural sciences are the most advanced form of this sort of knowledge that we know. (It is not that we manage to hook up to an already formed Platonic world of objects of belief. Our practices of training speakers and of counting sayings as the same gradually form such a world of ideal objects that have a certain independence of the particular qualities of those who are taking a stance in relation to them.)

From considering that sort of objectification of beliefs, we can begin to get a grip on the cases where Burge's intuitions seem more persuasive than Davidson's. Where precise replication by others is important, as with experiments in the sciences, we must count various practitioners as saying the same thing, and as expressing the same beliefs, when they use certain expressions important to a discipline. Often transmission of beliefs over many transmitters is important, and then we must be able to discount for the idiosyncracies of transmitters who may be, to a very considerable degree, imperfect. I may tell you, based on my haphazard reading, that "superconductivity now is known to occur at much higher temperatures," and in telling you that I shall properly be taken as expressing the same belief content that a scientist would by those words, even if I have several misconceptions about what superconductivity is to begin with.

If we turn again to the 'arthritis' case mentioned by Burge and Davidson, then this concern about transmission across many transmitters, often with different and incorrect associated information, will be evident. Let us suppose it is Arthur who thinks that 'arthritis' applies to an inflammation of the joints only if it is caused by calcium deposits. Davidson points out that if Arthur were to tell a doctor that "Carl has arthritis," it would be important that the doctor understand just what Arthur means by that belief; he should not be taken as expressing the belief that the medically better-educated would express by just those words.[46] But that assumes (perhaps Davidson still has an empiricist bias) that Arthur's belief was formed by direct causal contact with the circumstances of the world that his belief is about. Yet it is very often the case that we are transmitting beliefs that we have learned from others. Perhaps Arthur heard from Carl himself about the disease, or perhaps he heard from Carl's doctor or from his friends. Then it would be wrong to do as Davidson suggests, namely, to suppose that Arthur's mistaken views about arthritis determine what belief he is expressing, and what belief he assents to, when he makes that statement to others. He would surely be passing along the belief that he had taken over from the earlier believer. (It would likely be true, as the individualist will insist, that Arthur will in this case take himself to be expressing that transmitted belief.)

Our socialist intuitions are also animated when there is, whether for an individual or for a culture, an implicit teleology of development. We shall see the process of education differently depending on how *local* meaning is taken to be. Meaning is local when the determination of what it is to mean the same thing considers only local facts about a speaker over a modest period of time. On a nonlocal view of meaning, there is a much wider range over which *meaning the same thing* will extend, so that what other speakers mean now or later, or what I mean at a later time, can affect what I mean on a present occasion. Now suppose that a child is coming gradually through education to make his beliefs more accurate and his meanings more precise. A ready answer is that the utterances used by him mean the same thing that they did when he understood them less well, and express the same beliefs as before, only now he has replaced many false beliefs by true ones. Once he said, "The sun is not a star," and now he would express the same belief by those words while recognizing it to be false. We define some activities in terms of a certain kind of completion that they aim at, even if the young or the unreflective do not understand their aim in that fashion. (On the other hand, merely producing an utterance is not enough to enter this sort of game. The child must have an understanding of a relevant set of associated beliefs before we even count him as engaging in our practice, and as having at least some of his beliefs defined by what that practice is about.)

But the localist about meaning, it seems, will not allow our determination of sameness of meaning to extend over that educational period. If we keep meaning local, then we have far more leeway to adjust the assignment of meaning to make it depend only on the speaker's own

---

[46] Davidson, "Knowing One's Own Mind," p. 449.

understanding of what he is saying. Perhaps ten years ago I said, "Superconductivity can occur only close to absolute zero," and today I say, "Superconductivity can occur at relatively high temperatures." The normal and appropriate response will be that 'superconductivity' means the same thing in both statements, and that the truth of the second statement makes the first one turn out to be false. But the localist can now say that it is the meaning of 'superconductivity' that has changed, since the pressure of a more global determination of sameness is no longer valid. In the first statement I can be said to be using 'superconductivity' to refer to only a subclass of the cases that fall under the more general notion of the second statement, namely the subclass that includes only cases that occur close to absolute zero, because (we are supposing) that is part of what I understood 'superconductivity' to mean. Then both statements can be true, without any inconsistency. But if that is the direction that the Davidsonian account of interpretation and meaning moves in, then it has done its job too well, so well that we can no longer find it acceptable. Error will be reduced to a minimum; any change in belief will not be a change from a false belief to a true belief but a change in meaning, so that both the former and the latter belief can count as true ones. (Recall how Davidson, on the issue of ontological relativity, wants to let substantive differences collapse into linguistic ones.) But that result shows how the localist position at least presses toward, perhaps without being finally committed to, an absurd conclusion. (There is something very odd in the notion that what ought to be controversial empirical beliefs become true because an interpreter must assign a meaning to my statements that is based on my lack of knowledge regarding what I am talking about.)

It is not the case that the localist cannot account for error at all. Perhaps a longer time-slice of the individual's behavior would allow a determination of sameness of meaning that would make some beliefs false when seen against the background of later beliefs, even if we consider only the speaker's understanding of what he is saying. But there remains the problem that even extended that way, meaning remains too local. We want to be able to talk not only about the education of individuals, as they weed out false beliefs in favor of true ones, but also about the education of a community as it evolves, and even about larger communities across history. And here the situation reappears that we have seen already in the case of the individual. The analogue of the localist position in the history of science is the view that the meaning of statements in a theory depends on two factors: the intratheoretic structure of inference into which those statements are fitted, and the causal ties of those statements to experience. But then any time we change the beliefs and accepted inferences in a theory, we change that intratheoretic structure and thus the meaning of all the statements that the theory expresses. So it will be very difficult to marshal any notion of sameness of meaning such that when one theory is rejected and replaced by another, we can say that false beliefs are being replaced by true ones. Then we shall have Feyerabend's conclusion that different theories do not share enough for us to say that they are talking about the same things, or that one has succeeded better than another in describing what the world is like.

I think that concept of education, where the young are gradually trained in the use of *our* concepts, and are interpreted as aiming at expressing them even when their information is faulty, comes out (unintentionally) in some of Davidson's own arguments. He says, for example, that when he uses 'porcupine,' he is talking about porcupines, rather than about a class made up of entities that are either porcupines or echidnas, even if he cannot himself tell the difference between the two animals.[47] His reason is that he learned the use of 'porcupine' in a situation where there were porcupines in the environment, so that porcupines, and not echidnas, were at the other end of the causal chain that formed his beliefs. But is the presence of porcupines in the learning situation enough to fix what he means? Suppose that a young child of American consular officials in Australia happened to learn 'porcupine' by having her father point to echidnas and, through his lack of expertise, say 'porcupine.' The father's own learning of English and his connections to the community of English-speakers is such that the meaning of the child's term 'porcupine,' as she learns it, is fixed by those connections rather than by the presence of echidnas in the learning environment. The child would have learned some false beliefs about the fauna in her immediate neighborhood. It is true that we could tell some kind of story by which 'porcupine' becomes part of a dialect shared only by the consul's family and is used actually to refer to echidnas. But that is not the normal case. It seems that the practices of the linguistic community sometimes fix the meaning of a term being learned, even so as to override the causal role of that which in the environment is producing the relevant occurrent beliefs.

Our ordinary language does not have to match the articulations of scientific language. Porcupines and echidnas are of different species (indeed one is a rodent, the other a mammal), but a cultural history was possible in which early settlers in Australia called the echidna a porcupine and the name stuck in English, so that the correct use of 'porcupine,' as used by Davidson himself, would have included reference both to porcupines and to echidnas, even if zoological language was careful

[47] Davidson, "Myth of the Subjective," in *Relativism: Interpretation and Confrontation*, Michael Krausz, ed. (Notre Dame, Ind.: University of Notre Dame Press, 1988), pp. 168–9.

about the distinction. Again, that which determines that there is one classification to be picked out of the environment rather than another will depend on communal practice, and that will be an essential factor in determining just what concept the child of the consul in Australia can be said to be learning.

One who favors individualism about belief content and localism about meaning may still want to account for the pressure of communal practices on meaning. It is often the case that when someone is corrected, as Arthur may be in the 'arthritis' case, he considers himself to have been in error, and so he changes his behavior to make it match public usage. He himself, then, seems to employ standards of individuation that make him count his earlier employment of 'arthritis' as aimed at expressing the same beliefs that others would express when they used statements containing that term. That is precisely why he changes, why he readjusts the connections in his system of semantic representations. But Akeel Bilgrami, for one, says that this deference to communal usage is a move whose significance is only pragmatic.[48] Arthur makes the adjustments since life will be easier for himself and others if he makes what *he* means by an utterance match as closely as possible with what they do. But it is not the case that the meanings of others contributed to fixing the earlier content of Arthur's statements containing 'arthritis,' or weaken the claim that those statements meant no more than what *he* meant by them when uttering them.

Again, the individualist can give a different account of education and of theory change.[49] What Bilgrami wants to protect is the notion that a person's utterances mean what he understands them to mean. He can be speaking about *x* only because he has at least some beliefs whose content directs his utterances *x*-ward. The position Bilgrami most strongly opposes (he thinks it is present in Kripke) is one for which what *x* is, and the causal relations between *x* and the believer, can determine the content of the believer's sayings, independently of any understanding or associated beliefs on his part. The only basis for holding different believers to mean the same thing and to refer to the same thing is, for Bilgrami, a set of shared beliefs that in each of them is fixing meaning and reference. But those shared beliefs can be a small subset of one's total relevant beliefs about the object in question. So Bilgrami can make the following reply on the issue of whether it is belief or meaning that has changed over time. After we accept Davidson's attack on reified meanings, there will be no principled distinction between those two kinds of change. But when in a particular context we are convinced that a false belief has been replaced by a true one rather than that meaning

---

[48] Bilgrami, *Belief and Meaning*, pp. 78–81.   [49] Ibid., pp. 122–9.

has changed, the individualist will be able to point to a set of shared beliefs at least rich enough to back that claim, without giving up his more basic claim that it is what an individual understands himself to be saying that determines what he is indeed saying.

Bilgrami is willing to include, in that set of shared beliefs, such other-including beliefs as 'what the guy in the plant store was pointing to when he was discussing yuccas with me.' And we have just seen that not all of the believer's relevant background beliefs must be taken into consideration when we ask what he understands himself to mean. Those two admissions leave more room for socialist factors to enter into fixing the semantic content of belief. (The reference to what others know and believe is inherently social, and our choice about which subset of beliefs to consider most crucial in fixing meaning will likely be guided by an attempt to achieve a considerable sameness of meaning across different speakers.) What seems right about the individualist account is that we as speakers do not get dragooned over our objections into the service of semantic institutions that brutally override our intentions and our understanding when we speak. We are free to make words mean what we want them to mean; I might for the fun of it use the utterance 'apple' to refer to lamps and see how long it takes others to catch on.

But what we typically intend to mean by our words is what others in our linguistic community do. That is what we take ourselves to be saying, even if there is no explicit belief to that effect represented within us. We accept such a commitment as part of our implicit social contract as speakers, though our obligation may easily be overridden by other interests and goals. That usually implicit self-understanding is often more important, as the interpreter tries to fix content, than are the other beliefs associated by the speaker with an utterance. In that sense, it is something about the individual that determines what he means, as the individualist has insisted all along. But it is difficult to see how the socialist about meaning will be upset with that result. Sometimes a person may intend us to understand his 'arthritis' in the idiosyncratic way he uses it, given his deviant beliefs. But more often his implicit self-understanding is that he intends 'arthritis' to mean what English-speakers mean by it, and he takes himself to be governed by those common norms. The claim made by Davidson and Bilgrami that such deference to social usage is merely pragmatic seems not at all to give sufficient weight to our understanding of our "contractual" relationship with others in our linguistic community, and to our very clear sense of having failed to meet a standard when we go wrong. If the individualist wishes to honor the individual's self-understanding, them he should grant that we do not look upon such errors as merely pragmatic ones that have made it harder for us to achieve our ends.

Bilgrami himself is worried about another sort of attack on individualism.[50] Some may use Wittgenstein on rule following (we looked at the argument earlier) to establish that only where there is communal usage do we have a standard of correctness; without such a standard, there is no rule following and no meaning, only noises. But I think the Wittgensteinian argument is an attack not on individualism but on nonrepeatability by others. To have semantic content at all, someone's utterances must be capable in principle of insertion into a chain of repeatings that others may take up, such that how the others must go on to do the same thing has not been completely fixed in advance by any content-determining activity on the part of the individual speaker. But an individualist of Davidson's sort can easily grant that account of semantic content. The fact that belief content is interpretable by others does not make it the case that interpreters must impose the *communal* meaning on the individual's belief. So the Wittgensteinian considerations cannot decide the debate between the individualist and the socialist; they work at a different level, against a different sort of position.

Davidson and Skepticism

One of the reasons for getting into this debate in the first place was its relevance for Davidson's argument against the skeptic. What strategies are available to the skeptic against the Davidsonian claim that most of any believer's beliefs must be true, even if the believer cannot be sure of the truth of any particular one of them? One debate goes like this. The skeptic claims that most of our beliefs might be false because our mental states could remain the same while the world they are about was made to vary, so that it became profoundly different while appearing as the same. The Davidsonian replies that the skeptic has not been skeptical enough. For he has taken it for granted that mental states have the character they do independently of how matters stand in the world. It is true that in a different possible world where we had the same mental states that we do now in this one, most of our beliefs might be false. But the question is whether we would have the same mental states in that different possible world. For world and mind are internally related in such a way that in a very different world one would interpret the mental states differently by making them about whatever in that world is causing them. So there would be a change not only in the character of the world, but in the correct description of how that world is *appearing*. Appearances would not have remained the same while the world varied.

The skeptic hopes to reply here by making the link between belief content and world more indirect than that picture suggests, through

---

[50] For Bilgrami's discussion of possible Wittgensteinian objections to individualism, see *Belief and Meaning*, pp. 84–122.

bringing in the notion of what semantic content is shared among members of a community. So we need to ask, in considering Davidson's reply to the skeptic, what is the upper limit on the extent to which what I mean may depend on what others mean, in such a way that the direct Davidsonian linkage between beliefs and causes of belief is circuited instead through an intermediary, with the result that many more beliefs will turn out to be false.

Imagine that Maud has been hired as nanny for a wealthy infant. She is an anarchist who wants to bring down the ruling class, so she sets out to miseducate the child so that he will get around poorly in the world he will be entering. First of all, she will teach him the wrong meanings of words so that he will consistently have false beliefs. She points to trees over and over using the term 'gorilla,' and also points to the color green many times while using the word 'pink.' The child catches on and eventually will make, when looking at green trees, statements such as "There is a pink gorilla." Now suppose that process to go on generally in the language instruction. Has Maud taught the boy a language that he will misapply most of the time?

It seems rather that if he is consistent in how he applies terms, we would say not that she has miseducated him in English but that she has educated him in a new language that only the two of them speak. He surely does not have the belief that gorillas are pink. Suppose we consider instead a process of inducing misleading sensory experience in another. If we keep the interpretive framework stable, it will be proper to find him believing very many falsehoods. But as the total pattern of experience comes to be seen as falsehood-inducing, then we shall want to say, the Davidsonian will claim, that the interpretive framework has become too unstable, and we have to develop a different assignment. Our reading even of what experiences the subject is having may change. When we consider nonlinguistic behavior as well, our finding of another to be a believer in falsehoods will reach a point where he is no longer a defective believer but a producer of subintentional motions.

The skeptic, if he is to make the believer's error more global, might try to following strategy. Perhaps the stable semantic and worldly background used in the assignment of content to a speaker's utterances is *different* from the actual environment that is presently causing belief. Here we are likely to come upon the sort of thought experiments that many readers dislike. A favorite one is the brain-in-the-vat. Your brain has been removed and hooked up to a computer that feeds it impulses causing the sort of perceptions you previously had when perceiving the world. Now Davidson can say that once in the vat your beliefs start to be about the new causes of them, namely, the computer stimulations, and thus turn out to be true.

But it seems important that there would be a lag time in that situation. If Oscar, in Putnam's experiment, is transported to Twin Earth, it would be odd to suppose that his thoughts stop being about his wife back on earth and become about her twin on the new planet. Someone's *earlier* causal history will have connected his thoughts and beliefs to the world in a way that remains decisive in the present causal environment, for at least a very considerable period. So perhaps we are ourselves (says the skeptic) in such a transitional period where our beliefs have their semantic content determined by their earlier causal history but are made false by their present causal surroundings. (Davidson again seems influenced still by empiricism in stressing so much the present causal influences.) As we enrich a causal theory of belief such as Davidson's with considerations of teleology and of prior causation, including perhaps the causation of belief in others who may be absent, we show how error is possible (it was an objection against a very strict causal theory of belief that it seemed not to be able to). But we also begin to show how very much error is possible as well.

Or suppose that a culture of the future actually uses something like the brain-in-the-vat situation to train its young, and to give them through the computer the kinds of experiences that will best suit them for the world they are about to enter. Then the meanings of the community's utterances, and of the utterances of the vat-brains in the future when they have been attached to bodies and live in the environment they were trained for, will provide the stable semantic background needed to support a claim of systematically distorted beliefs while in the vat.

I share the reader's distaste for the use of such experiments, and I shall not continue examining them, but I do think they show that the skeptic has extensive resources if one wishes to push them hard enough. There will always be space for the skeptic to maneuver in; we just cannot be sure enough about the world or about the character of our mechanisms for knowing it to reduce that space to zero. Davidson's work is important not because it can evict the skeptic from all the territory he has claimed but because it gives us a better way generally of thinking about how mind and world are related, a picture that shows that our stark alienation from the world, while not impossible, should not be thought of as supported by our philosophical pictures.

But now we should note that even without the strange thought experiments the skeptic may not feel that he ends up all that badly on the Davidsonian reading of matters.[51] All he has to grant to Davidson is that after the percentage of false beliefs in an assignment gets to be very high,

---

[51] For an account of Davidson and the skeptic, see Peter Klein, "Radical Interpretation and Global Skepticism," in *Truth and Interpretation*, LePore, ed., pp. 369–86. Part of my discussion is shaped by ideas he raises in that essay.

the conditions for counting the other as using the same language as a linguistic community, as part of a strategy to show how assigning him a greater percentage of false beliefs can be proper, are undermined. But this conclusion does not bring along with it much epistemic solace. There is, first of all, a very noticeable vagueness about what has been shown. Davidson says in the same essay that "most of a person's beliefs must be true," that "it becomes impossible correctly to hold that anyone could be mostly wrong about how things are," and that "it is impossible for all our beliefs to be false together."[52] What percentage do we mean here by 'most'? It is probably true that only a fairly low percentage of our beliefs must be false for us to be wildly wrong in our dealings with the world.

And even the Davidsonian response in the vat-brain case, that we have mostly true beliefs about the computer stimulations, seems to strengthen, rather than remove, the worries of a skeptic. For having mostly true beliefs is not the only goal that I set for myself as a believer. I want to have beliefs about a reasonably generous portion of the things that it is possible to have beliefs about. If the range of my beliefs is restricted to a ridiculously small portion of the beliefs worth having, then my worries about my weaknesses as a knower will hardly be lessened. We can see another problem with (what I take to be) the Davidsonian solution to the case of the vat-brains. Suppose I know, for Davidsonian reasons, that most of my beliefs must be true, and suppose I know that the words I use in saying what beliefs I have must generally capture which beliefs they are (since the interpretation context will affect interpretation all the way in). Still there will be no difference at all, so far as anything I can tell, between stating such true beliefs as a brain in a vat, or stating them as a person moving through this world of real bodies. The skeptic will have little reason to be dissatisfied with that outcome. (Again, I think the time we ought to spend worrying about whether we might be brains in a vat is zero, but that sort of argument is one that we cannot fairly strip away from a very determined skeptic.)

The skeptic will surely make us draw one further conclusion from Davidson's work. The claim that Davidson argues for, that if an entity is a believer, then most of its beliefs must be true, will lead not to the conclusion that most of our beliefs must be true, but to a disjunctive conclusion: Either most of our beliefs are true or the happenings in us cannot qualify as beliefs but only as semantically empty firings. And how do we know that the second half of the disjunct is not the one that in our case makes the Davidsonian claim true? Again the skeptic will try to present us with something like the case of the brains in the vat. The best account of what is happening there is not that there are beliefs and

---

[52] Davidson, "A Coherence Theory of Truth and Knowledge," p. 314, 317, 319.

intentions having to do with the computer stimulations, but that there are just meaningless neuronal firings. There is no well-formed, self-maintaining individual here with sufficiently rich causal connections to a world to count as having things matter to it, so there are no intentional states at all. How, then, are we supposed to know that that is not the case with us? Is our experience of regularity of patterns enough? If it is only a regularity of formal patterns, of course, then it will be wrong to say there is even an experience here; there is not even a way things *seem*, only a syntactic engine chugging away. The skeptic will surely claim that this case is a possible one, though I shall not pursue the issue further.

Davidson's arguments are sometimes seen as exalting our knowing faculty. Most of our beliefs must be true; any other knower would have to share something like our logic and our metaphysical categories. But the disenchantment of subjectivity actually brings rather weak conclusions. Except in very unusual circumstances (we cannot guarantee, against the skeptic, that these are not present) the believer will properly be taken as at home in the world, as having beliefs generally suitable to the causal environment around him. But our categories and our sciences may compare very badly when set over against those of beings far more intelligent. (Note that as soon as the neanderthals qualified as having beliefs at all, Davidson's argument guarantees that they had mostly true beliefs. But how pleased can we be as knowers to have passed a standard so easily passed as that?) We may not be intelligent enough to come to a satisfying account of the universe or of ourselves. Nothing in the findings about the disenchantment of subjectivity shrinks the world to make it fit what we are capable of grasping. Our utterances may aim at situations that we ourselves could never recognize as making the utterances true or false. And much of what a very intelligent understander of the universe may find worth saying about it we might not even begin to say or to think.

I have spoken of Davidson as encouraging a recovery of the world, and thus as giving support for positions that are at least weakly realist. Yet it is also true that he would be uneasy with that classification. He resists accounts that would take beliefs to be made true by a mirroring of already determinate worldly features that have a sentencelike structure and that can, by having it, determine in advance the truth status of the beliefs we generate. And he resists accounts that would use a causal hookup to an already determinate world of units and sorts as the basis for a "building-block" approach to explaining the semantic determinacy of our mental states and our utterances.

Davidson's work suggests, though it would perhaps be going too far to say that it endorses, the following picture. Consider a triangular space whose sides are the world; the intentional life of subjects, including their own self-understanding; and the cultural realm in which our semantic production is repeated and interpreted and shaped. We might give a simplistic picture of the history of philosophy according to which there are attempts to ground ontological and semantic determinacy successively on each of the three sides, with the most recent project being that in which interpreters or cultural practices are supposed to do the trick of fixing what subjects take the world to be, so that what they take the world to be can determine what it is like, at least relatively. The failure experienced at the second and third stages of this circulation may encourage a return to the first one. One then becomes a "new realist" and hopes one can find in the world itself the determinate structure that we need.

But Davidson, if I have him right, rejects that sort of return. The historical circulation in question has not been a wasted one. There is something right about the modern turn to the conditions we set for what the world can be, and something right about Quine's claims that what an interpreter takes a believer to be saying helps to fix what that believer means and believes. But it is important to resist, at all levels here, a theological architectonic that would locate the determinacy-conferring power in just one side of our triangular space. Recall that for the late medievals, the migration of that sort of power to God's position could not be a partial one. As there could be no limit on God's power and freedom, the world had to be emptied out as an independent source of determinacy.

We repeat that sort of thinking when we suppose that a discovery of a certain role for subjectivity in fixing the correct picture of the world, or of a similar role for interpretation or for cultural practices, will bring along with it a necessary emptying out of the other sides. It is important rather to work against the inertia leading us toward that sort of structure, and to acknowledge a space of mutual determinations in which there remains very considerable pressure from all three sides on fixing truth and meaning. To make that claim is, of course, not to give a finished theory, but to make an initial gesture toward one still to be developed. But it is important that Davidson can accept the various sorts of underdetermination that allow for the influence of the second and third positions in our triangle, while still adhering to the belief that it is a holistic pressure from the way the world is that makes our beliefs what they are and makes them true or false.

In talking about the truth conditions of sentences then, rather than simply about their assertability conditions, we are doing more than accepting the very much deflated claim that is embodied in the Tarskian statement that " 'Snow is white' is true in English if and only if snow is white." We are acknowledging the need for a holistic accommodation of our belief systems to how matters stand, and we are supposing that an ideally successful practice of making beliefs coherent, and of adjusting our beliefs in accord with what our practices let us get away with, will automatically have brought about the holistic correspondence between beliefs and world. We shall have properly honored the worldly pressure on our belief system, even if the structure of mutual determination is such that we cannot separate out that pressure as a neutral input to the other two sides. (Nor can we separate out a scheme that has its world-determining character independently of what that world is.)

There is a certain graceful twist to Davidson's attack on the patterns of thought in earlier philosophy. He sets up pairings in which the second member has been taken by earlier thinkers to be the means by which the status of the first member is secured. Then he undermines that second member while showing that all along it made that which it was supposed to make secure far less so, with the result that its defeat actually makes possible the more reliable security that we were looking for in the first place. One tries to guarantee self-knowledge, for example, by supposing that we have a special ability to read off our internal entities. But that route to self-knowledge will fail, as the arguments for externalism regarding mental content show. However, by getting rid of the notion of such internal entities that are immediately available for our reading, we gain a greater assurance that we understand what we mean and believe. (That argument was given in Chapter 2.) Or we suppose that an appeal to determinate referential hookups will show how we are in touch with the world, when actually that appeal will make our grasp of the world more open to charges of relativism. It is rather by getting rid of that notion of reference that we make our beliefs reliably about the world as it is. And so on with epistemic intermediaries and linguistic conventions. (Such conventions are supposed to show how communication is possible, but the greater the status we give to them, the more we open up the possibility of different conventional schemes that separate us.) A similar case can be made regarding Davidson's realism. He will remove from the picture any already determinate truth conferrers such as atomic facts, and he will disallow determinate routes of reference. But the loss of these would-be supports for the realist position actually makes it clearer why our beliefs generally capture the world as it is and, at least holistically, are made true or false by it.

Davidson's attack on various reifications exhibits an important move in our ongoing reflection on the legacy of modern philosophy. Once one no longer accepts the answer that mind and meaning can get their determinacy through a parasitic hooking up to, or actualization of, an ontologically determinate world, then the question arises as to how to make determinate what objects one is talking about. The obvious answer for a number of thinkers was that this would have to be deter-mined from within the resources of subjectivity, through the subject's ability to specify an ontological scheme or through an interpreter's ability to specify one for him. Davidson, we saw, has argued that we cannot make sense of either one of these determinations from the subjective side. There are no resources there that could specify one set of objects of reference from among competing alternatives. But it is precisely that lack of power that allows us to be confident that we are referring successfully to the world. The result is not, as with many postmodern thinkers, that we give up the notion of reference to objects in the world. We just give up the notion of reference and ontology as having a certain metaphysical depth, of a sort mandating that the results of our intratheoretic manipulations must be contrasted with what a *real* relation of reference or a *real* ontology would have given us. When you retain the strong metaphysical notions, you think of the internal logical work of assigning structure to sentences, and the consequent ontological commitments, as something one does *instead of* understanding the metaphysical character of the world. But with Davidson you understand that doing the internal work is just what it is to understand that character, because of the role that the world has played all along in displaying itself in our utterances.

Davidson is with Hegel in rejecting Kantian and empiricist strategies for linking up beliefs to the world. There is no layer of evidentiary givenness waiting to be organized; there are no schemes waiting to organize it; no anchorage points from words or ideas to things; no worlds constructed by a subjective apparatus and distinct from things as they are; no truth-conferring moments of confrontation with things; no reified subjectivity separable from the activity by which individuals involve themselves as knowers and willers in the world. Instead, both Davidson and Hegel argue that if we understand the realm of thought properly, we can see that just by maneuvering around within it, by making various internal connections, by aiming at coherence, by setting concepts and beliefs in relation to one another instead of looking for word-to-world confrontations, we can be sure that we are generally in touch with things as they are:

What is needed to answer the skeptic is to show that someone with a (more or less) coherent set of beliefs has a reason to suppose his beliefs are not mistaken in the main. What we have shown is that it is absurd to look for a justifying ground for the totality of beliefs, something outside this totality which we can use to test or compare with our beliefs. The answer to our problem must then be to find a *reason* for supposing most of our beliefs are true that is not a form of *evidence*.[53]

The Hegelian might well not be unhappy with that project description, though his strategy for carrying it out was quite a different one from Davidson's.

---

[53] Ibid., pp. 314.

4

Rorty and Antirealism

Rorty and Davidson

Richard Rorty has written an influential narrative about the dismantling of the modern notion of subjectivity.[1] I think he is wrong in his claims concerning the stance that we are supposedly led to as a result of that history. To show that he is wrong, however, I need to wedge him apart from one whom he takes to be his most natural ally, Davidson, since I find many of Davidson's positions persuasive, whereas I am generally in disagreement with the picture offered by Rorty. The attempted link with Davidson is not an incidental one. It is part of Rorty's overall strategy to show that his position, radical though it may seem, is largely motivated by considerations that come out of the work of one of the most honored of contemporary analytic philosophers. But I think this strategy is unsuccessful; there are profound differences between the two thinkers.

When Rorty is trying to defeat his opponents, he describes them as holding a radical position virtually no one holds, and opposes it to the position he claims to share with Davidson. But then when he describes the position he thinks he has established as a result of defeating those opponents, he describes not what he supposedly has in common with Davidson but a more controversial antirealist position. So the frequent misreading of Davidson serves a purpose; it makes an argument appear to go through that really does not, and enlists Davidson's support for an account that he would not, or should not, endorse. There is a deeper basis, I think, for the manner in which Rorty sets up the alternatives we are to consider. I shall argue that his work is embedded in patterns of thought that we have already traced when reviewing religious influences on our metaphysical and epistemic pictures. He presents himself as rejecting such pictures, and in some respects he certainly does so, but without them one would have far less motivation to develop his account, or to accept it once it is developed.

Let me begin by comparing an image of Davidson's with one from Rorty. Davidson speaks of a process of "triangulation":

If I were bolted to the earth I would have no way of determining the distance from me of many objects. I would only know they were on some line drawn from

---

[1] Richard Rorty, *Philosophy and the Mirror of Nature* (Princeton, N.J.: Princeton University Press, 1979).

me toward them. I might interact successfully with objects, but I could have no way of giving content to the question where they were. Not being bolted down, I am free to triangulate. Our sense of objectivity is the consequence of another sort of triangulation, one that requires two creatures. Each interacts with an object, but what gives each the concept of the way things are objectively is the base line formed between the creatures by language. The fact the they share a concept of truth alone makes sense of the claim that they have beliefs, that they are able to assign objects a place in the public world.[2]

I can recognize myself to be a believer, to have a point of view on the world, only through being able to recognize others as having possibly different points of view on that same reality. So only communicators, says Davidson, can have a sense of an objective world, and only they can have beliefs. Rorty says that "in the end, the pragmatists tell us, what matters is our loyalty to other human beings clinging together against the dark, not our hope of getting things right."[3] The two images are similar in their attention to our relations to other believers. But one corner of the Davidsonian triangle is missing in Rorty's picture: the world itself. As we shall see, its disappearance is characteristic of his philosophy; we need to examine why it so readily disappears.

I do not wish to underplay the very considerable agreement between the two thinkers. Rorty happily accepts the Davidsonian attacks on various psychological and semantic reifications: on our notions of meaning, reference, subjectivity, and language. Both reject accounts that would join language to the world through discovering some relation of reference between individual words and things in the world, or some relation of mirroring between representations and sentencelike entities such as facts. Davidson, we saw, also suggests that we give up the notion of subjective representations that stand as epistemic intermediaries between our beliefs and what they are about. So mental states, we may conclude, do not represent the world in either of those two senses (either by mirroring sentencelike worldly entities or by serving as epistemic intermediaries). Therefore there are no representations, at least as far as many traditional uses of 'representation' are concerned. (There will remain senses in which we do have representations.)

Rorty agrees with all this, but his conclusion is that without any representing going on, there is no longer any sense to our notion of getting matters right.[4] So we must then be pragmatists and grant that

---

[2] Donald Davidson, "Rational Animals," in *Actions and Events*, Ernest LePore and Brian McLaughlin, eds. (Oxford: Basil Blackwell, 1985), p. 480.

[3] Richard Rorty, *Consequences of Pragmatism* (Minneapolis: University of Minnesota Press, 1982), p. 166.

[4] Rorty favors the view that "great scientists invent descriptions of the world which are useful for purposes of predicting and controlling what happens, just as poets and political thinkers invent other descriptions of it for other purposes. But there is no sense in which any of these descriptions is an accurate representation of the way the world is in itself."

our symbol sequences are meaningful only insofar as they help bring about habits of action that turn out to be useful; to give up reference and representation is to give up the "aboutness" of our statements in any sense richer than that. Davidson's response to the claim that there are no representations is rather different. Beliefs remain for him *about* the world and it is important to him to show, against the skeptic, that they are, very generally, getting matters right. Whereas Rorty says there is no such thing as a language-to-world relationship to worry about, Davidson sees that relationship as a holistic one that cannot be built up out of linkages or isomorphisms at the word or sentence level. Because there is that holistic portrayal of the world roughly as it is, we can understand the large features of reality by studying our ways of talking about it.[5]

Rorty holds, as Davidson does, that our beliefs must generally be correct, but his reasoning is very different. For Davidson the fit is world-driven; it is because of the role the world plays both in causing beliefs and in guiding the identification of beliefs by the interpreter that we are sure of a rough match. For Rorty, in contrast, that matching is guaranteed because the world is little more than a reflection cast by our generally accepted beliefs:

To sum up this point, I want to claim that 'the world' is either the purely vacuous notion of the ineffable cause of sense and goal of intellect, or else a name for the objects that inquiry at the moment is leaving alone; those planks in the boat which are at the moment not being moved about.[6]

Now, to put my cards on the table, I think that the realistic true believer's notion of the world is an obsession rather than an intuition. I also think that Dewey was right in thinking that the only intuition we have of the world as determining truth is just the intuition that we must make our new beliefs conform to a vast body of platitudes, unquestioned perceptual reports, and the like.[7]

Rorty also defines pragmatism as the view that "there are no constraints on inquiry save conversational ones," no wholesale constraints "derived from the nature of the objects."[8] And he says that "our inheritance from, and our conversation with, our fellow-humans" is "our only source of guidance."[9] In all these quotations the only direction of fit at issue is between one's beliefs and the unquestioned beliefs of one's time and place. The "world" is nothing more than the planks on the boat that we are leaving alone for the moment. If the world is defined so as to have its character given by what we believe about it, it will hardly be surprising that our beliefs must be generally true. Rorty will then be

Rorty, *Contingency, Irony, and Solidarity* (Cambridge: Cambridge University Press, 1989), p. 4.

[5] Davidson, *Inquiries into Truth and Interpretation* (Oxford: Clarendon Press, 1984), p. 199.
[6] Rorty, *Consequences of Pragmatism*, p. 15.
[7] Ibid., pp. 13–14.
[8] Ibid., p. 165.
[9] Ibid., p. 166.

correct that 'true' is nothing more than an empty compliment that we give to those sentences that are paying their way, that we do not for now see any reason to question. But that is hardly Davidson's position. His triangular picture has us attending to the beliefs of others so that we may have a sense of an objective world that transcends our beliefs about it, and toward which the beliefs of different believers can be thought of as directed. We retain, even in so attending to others, our attentiveness to a world about which we are trying to gain a better picture, and we put ourselves into the sort of relation to that world that will make us more likely to understand what it is like. For Davidson, the world cannot be a criterion of our belief in the sense of providing sentencelike entities that have already conferred truth in advance on some beliefs and not others; the world, on its own, cannot make our beliefs true. But it remains a criterion in the sense of being that to which our beliefs attempt holistically to accommodate themselves, and taking it as a criterion in that sense affects our practices. Rorty will not allow the world to be any sort of criterion at all for belief; it collapses into that for which it was supposed to be providing the standard. For Rorty the world is just a shadow of our discourse while for Davidson language can be meaningful because of the shadow cast upon it by the "antics" of what is real.

We can see that difference between the two thinkers in the way they reject the empiricist picture of bringing a statement into a confrontation with the world that makes it either true or false. Both hold that there can be no such confrontation; beliefs can be compared only with other beliefs. Davidson expresses the agreement between the two thinkers as follows:

As Rorty has put it, "nothing counts as justification unless by reference to what we already accept, and there is no way to get outside our beliefs and our language so as to find some test other than coherence." About this I am, as you see, in agreement with Rorty.[10]

But again they draw different conclusions. Once we give up the notion of a confrontation with the world, believes Rorty, there is no place at all for distinguishing among beliefs on the basis of their responsiveness to the causal pressure of the world. Beliefs just pop up in our belief systems like bubbles and survive or die through a kind of Darwinism of the epistemic realm. But Davidson thinks the empiricists were on to something with their notion of protocol sentences.[11] It may seem that Neurath thought of belief regulation as a matter simply of coherence, with any belief at all a candidate to be thrown into the "machine" to be tested for

[10] Davidson, "A Coherence Theory of Truth and Knowledge," in *Truth and Interpretation*, Ernest LePore, ed. (Oxford: Basil Blackwell, 1986), p. 310. His citation of Rorty is from Rorty, *Philosophy and the Mirror of Nature*, p. 178.
[11] Davidson, "Empirical Content," in *Truth and Interpretation*, LePore, ed., pp. 320–32.

its coherence with other sentences already in there. But that would be chaotic; every sentence and its negation would thus be candidates. What would be thrown in rather are sentences believed true by scientists. And the training of scientists is aimed precisely at conditioning them to register true beliefs in the presence of situations that cause other scientists to register them; scientists learn what many of their sentences mean in such situations. They are habituated to form sentences in circumstances that make them true because of the very role of those circumstances in making the sentences mean what they do.[12] No belief thus becomes self-certifying, but the scientist does give a certain privilege to shared observation statements, and she learns to position herself, through experiments, in situations in which the causal pressure of the world will cause her to register its features in her beliefs.

Perception plays a similar role in Davidson's account of interpretation. Whereas Rorty gives our direction of attentiveness as a sideways one, as we take others' utterances in and interpret them by the pragmatic criterion of helping us get what we want, Davidson says that interpretation cannot even get underway unless we attend to the world and assign the other speaker beliefs on the basis of what in the world occasions his various utterances. Both in the case of the scientist and her training and in the case of interpretation, the world's position in the Davidsonian triangulation, and in the Davidsonian account of belief, disappears for Rorty's analysis. He says, for example that what makes science different from other fields is just that agreement is easier in science, that more background truths are accepted in advance by its participants.[13] The virtues of science thus have nothing at all to do with the way they bring us into relation to reality's way of doing things; the gulf between the views of Davidson and Rorty remains wide.

It is easy to miss here just what Davidson is objecting to in empiricist philosophies. The empiricist has a strong notion of what it is to bring at least base-level statements into confrontation with truth-conferring circumstances; Davidson clearly believes that that kind of confrontation cannot occur. But he can give up that strong notion of letting experience decide matters for us, and yet still hold that our beliefs direct themselves toward the world and aim at getting things right. From the fact that there is no *naked* confrontation, that a sentencelike entity such as a belief can be compared only with information already in the form of sentences or beliefs, it does not follow that what makes a belief true is that coherence itself. Davidson rather shows us why we should understand, given how the world itself comes into play in the very determination of belief content, that coherence must yield at least a rough correspon-

---

[12] Ibid., pp. 331–2.   [13] Rorty, *Consequences of Pragmatism*, p. 141.

dence. It is not that lining beliefs up with other beliefs is the end of the story, as it is for Rorty.

Rorty has to skip over much of what Davidson says in order to take him to be in agreement. He says that "for Davidson, Quine's idea of 'ontological commitment' and Dummett's idea of 'matter of fact' are both unfortunate relics of metaphysical thought."[14] But Davidson spends most of the essay "The Method of Truth in Metaphysics" discussing the ontological commitments that arise when one develops a truth theory in the manner that he suggests. He says that "if the truth conditions of sentences are placed in the context of a comprehensive theory, the linguistic structure that emerges will reflect large features of reality," that "postulating needed structure in a language can bring ontology in its wake," that "for large stretches of language, anyway, variables, quantifiers, and singular terms must be construed as referential in function," and that "apparently we are committed to the existence of times if we accept any such sentence as true."[15] The question of ontological commitments is at the basis of much of his work in suggesting translations of natural language sentences into the first-order predicate calculus, such as sentences containing adverbs. (What Davidson attacks, we saw, is not the notion of ontological commitment, but the claim that there are ontological schemes and that statements about what there is in the world must be made relative to them.)

Rorty and the Loss of the World

My claim about Rorty and the disappearance of the world may appear too strong if we see what he says elsewhere. He accepts that "the world is out there," and that "most things in space and time are the effects of causes which do not include human mental states."[16] He holds that there is an objective world that is causing our beliefs and says that he is not a linguistic idealist, that is, one who holds that everything is language or that objects are only linguistic constructs. But we have to consider these claims, and the sense that he can give to them, in the light of his version of pragmatism. All true claims are for him just symbol sequences that are useful in leading to actions and habits that get us what we want; we should not suppose that they represent anything or correspond to anything or refer to anything, as the realist believes. Their significance for him is causal rather than semantic; they are like the animal's horns that help it get what it wants but that represent nothing hornlike in the world.

---

[14] Rorty, "Pragmatism, Davidson and Truth," in *Truth and Interpretation*, LePore, ed., p. 353.
[15] Davidson, *Inquiries*, pp. 201, 207, 210, 211.
[16] Rorty, *Contingency, Irony, and Solidarity*, p. 5.

So when he claims that there is an objective world causing our beliefs, we should not take that statement itself referentially or suppose that he is committing himself ontologically to such a world. What happens rather is that a certain sequence with the words 'objective world' and 'causing beliefs' appears in his belief space and contributes (or does not) to useful behavior. Whatever we might say in everyday discourse, Rorty's pragmatist will not allow claims about the objective world and its causal powers to be interpreted realistically, as founded on a certain relation of aboutness between those claims themselves and the world. Objectivity and language independence are what we constitute as such from within conversations that should not be thought of as constrained by a reality independent of them. We linguistically project, as the mere shadow of our useful expressions, a world that the very projection allows us to count as independent, and as giving rise to the beliefs that come to appear in us.

Why shouldn't we conclude then that Rorty's pragmatism has collapsed into some form of linguistic idealism? The resistance of the world to thought is simply what thought or our conversational habits count as resistance; there is no further causal independence that is forcing us to accommodate ourselves to its working. There is a difference between the world itself making us think a certain way about it and the appearance of the syntactic shapes 'the world's causal power' in a useful statement that cannot be taken referentially, and it seems that Rorty can make sense only of the latter. There is little, then, to make us resist the temptation to think of him as suggesting not a thinking mind but a speaking voice (in his case a communal one) that produces all determinations out of itself, as in Samuel Beckett's novels. (And there is the question as well of why we should call anything that appears in that space a belief.)

Rorty makes it very clear where the determining power is supposed to be coming from and where it is not. He criticizes those who want to see cultural conversation "*guided*, constrained, not left to its own devices."[17] When some vocabularies are claimed to be better than other ones, they are "just better in the sense that they come to *seem* clearly better than their predecessors."[18] We, or at least our ways of talking, are setting the standard defining the objectivity that is their supposed measure. When we speak of standards or criteria that our cultural conversations must meet, these are temporary ones that the conversations impose on themselves, for reasons the sociologist rather than the metaphysician can explore. For the pragmatist, he says, "a criterion ... *is* a criterion because some particular social practice needs to block the road of inquiry, halt the progress of interpretations, in order to get something

[17] Rorty, *Consequences of Pragmatism*, p. xxxix.   [18] Ibid., p. xxxvii.

done."[19] There is no constraint of objectivity that we do not raise up for ourselves. So objectivity is simply a projection of our practice, what we count as such given our present interests and the inertia of our conversations. The world, as before, has little role to play in such an account. When we are considering "the jargon of Newton versus that of Aristotle . . . it is difficult to think of the world as making one of these better than another. . . ."[20] I am reminded here of the idealist Fichte, for whom the objectivity and resistance of the world to the ego are themselves set forth in an infinite self-positing activity of mind; that has become, in Rorty, an infinite self-positing activity of discourse.

It may be suggested here that we should read Rorty as ending up with something of a Kantian position. There is an internal pragmatic stance from which we happily use and accept realist-sounding sentences, with their commitment to objectivity and world guidance and language transcendence. But then there is an external stance from which we recognize the "merely" pragmatic function of all such sentences as we use them. Through understanding that function, we recognize that objectivity cannot be understood in the realist way, but is a projection of our practices. So we become internal pragmatic realists and "transcendental" linguistic idealists.

But Rorty will surely claim that the genuine pragmatist will not allow himself to be forced into that twofold Kantian stance. He will hold that all claims are internal ones, to be judged for their usefulness in our conversations, and that we cannot, nor should we want to, step outside our practices to make overall claims about the status of our claims themselves. But then where has Rorty himself been speaking from in condemning the realist? He will want to say that he has been making one more internal statement concerning the usefulness of a kind of talk. Like a good banker he has examined the statements in use and has recommended that we cut off those "investments" that are not paying their way; the realist statements fall into that category. So the realist cannot be accused of making a general *philosophical* error; he must be shown to be recommending the use of lots of useless sentences.

But if that is Rorty's strategy, his way of carrying it out seems very odd. Suppose we do consider sentences as tools that are useful or not. Tools are useful in some circumstances and not others, for some purposes and not for others. Realist discourse is embedded in very many of our practices, and it is highly unlikely that there will be a general uselessness of such notions that can be decided without a detailed cost/benefit investigation of the particular practices. But Rorty does not even suggest that such an investigation is in order. The pragmatist web of belief ought to be a complex interweave whose threads must be added or

[19] Ibid., p. xli.   [20] Rorty, *Contingency, Irony, and Solidarity*, p. 5.

removed in a piecemeal fashion. Yet in Rorty there is the sense of a crucial boundary being crossed whenever we get to sentences with an implicit realist commitment. For a genuine pragmatist the classifications into useful and useless concepts will not take place at such a global level; that is where philosophers tend to do their work. There will be no clear boundary that will exhibit itself from that height.

In making global classifications into good and bad sentences from the overall perspective of the philosophical pragmatist, Rorty seems to be accusing his realist opponent of a philosophical error, not a pragmatic one, of not seeing correctly the relation between language and reality that Rorty, from his own external stance, can see correctly. But if he has been right, that stance ought not to be available to him. There is the general Kantian problem here of holding that we can never achieve a stance from which we can talk about the relation between language and reality, while holding (in claiming that objectivity is *merely* phenomenal or *merely* pragmatic, in contrast to a more full-bodied realism) that we can present a version of that relation showing our opponents to be wrong about it. The further problem for Rorty is that he seems to need such a (for him) impossible stance to defeat his opponents. For when we examine our discourse in detail according to the criterion of usefulness, the everyday realist vocabulary seems very useful indeed, useful enough to have survived very well the Darwinian clash of vocabularies in history. So as a nonphilosophical pragmatist, he ought to be a realist without qualms. It is true, surely, that certain large metaphysical pictures, with their theological underpinnings, are no longer of much use. But Rorty's quarry all along has not so much been those (we should be in agreement with him if it were), but rather the very idea of the world as that against which our beliefs are ultimately measured.

How Rorty Exploits the Alliance with Davidson

I hope it is clear now that Davidson and Rorty are philosophers with quite different beliefs, even if the latter expends a good deal of energy trying to make those differences less visible. He says that Davidson gives us "the first systematic treatment of language which breaks *completely* with the notion of language as something that can be adequate or inadequate to the world or to the self."[21] Yet Davidson, we saw, finds it important to argue, against the skeptic, that our beliefs are indeed adequate in that regard. Rorty, in contrast, is happy with the "world well lost."[22]

Rorty says as well that if we adopt Davidson's account of language, we

[21] Ibid., p. 10.
[22] Rorty, "The World Well Lost," *Journal of Philosophy* 69 (1972): 649–65.

shall not be tempted to ask about the place of intentionality in a world of causation or about the relation of language and thought.[23] Either Rorty is wrong here or he is making his claim very carelessly. For while Davidson says that there will be no reduction of psychological talk to physicalist talk, and that there can be no strict causal laws picked out at the psychological level of description, he does find it important to show that mental events, under other descriptions, are situated in a determinist causal order.[24] (Rorty pays attention to the adjective but not to the noun in Davidson's "anomalous monism.") Davidson also asks, in an article that is even entitled "Thought and Talk," whether entities have to have a language in order to count as having thoughts and beliefs, whereas Rorty, we have just seen, says that Davidson will not ask about the relation between language and thought.[25] Rorty believes as well that Davidson has an instrumentalist theory of mental states. Talk about beliefs and intentions, on this view, is an invented vocabulary that has turned out to be rather useful in making sense of the marks and sounds that others produce.[26] Davidson, in contrast, seems to believe that mental states are real states of the individual that our ordinary mentalist vocabulary is able to capture rather well.

Why then does Rorty insist on their similarity? It is true that in some respects they are quite similar, and that Rorty can make good use of Davidson's attacks on traditional conceptions of mind and meaning. But there are two other reasons as well for that insistence. First, it makes it easier for him to appear to be holding a moderate position. He needs so to appear since he criticizes his opponents not by taking them to be defending the negation of the position he has recommended but by taking them to be defending more radical positions that few thinkers hold and that are the negation rather of the more moderate position that he presents himself as sharing with Davidson. Second, he thinks he can enlist Davidson as a supporter of what we might call a "causal-mutational" account of large changes in the picture we have of the world. Let me look at each of these now.

[23] Rorty, *Contingency, Irony, and Solidarity*, pp. 11–12.
[24] For Davidson's view that reasons are causes, see the essays "Actions, Reasons, and Causes," and "How Is Weakness of the Will Possible?" in Davidson, *Essays on Actions and Events* (Oxford: Clarendon Press, 1980). For his view that the mental is irreducible to the physical, even if all mental events are physical ones, see the essays "Mental Events," "The Material Mind," and "Psychology as Philosophy" in the same volume. Very helpful is the summary by Ernest LePore and Brian McLaughlin in *Actions and Events*, LePore and McLaughlin, eds., pp. 3–13 and the essay by McLaughlin, pp. 331–68 in the same volume.
[25] Davidson, "Thought and Talk," *Inquiries*, pp. 155–70.
[26] "To say that it is a language user is just to say that pairing off the marks and noises it makes with those we make will prove a useful tactic in predicting and controlling its future behavior." Rorty, *Contingency, Irony, and Solidarity*, p. 15.

One quickly becomes familiar with a certain pattern of argument in Rorty. It is suggested that we have a choice of accepting either his position or an outlandish one that few, and certainly not most of those who are disturbed by Rorty's account, will want to support. Let me begin with a quotation given earlier:

To sum up this point, I want to claim that 'the world' is either the purely vacuous notion of the ineffable cause of sense and goal of intellect, or else a name for the objects that inquiry at the moment is leaving alone; those planks in the boat which are at the moment not being moved about.[27]

If we do not accept Rorty's account of the world, according to which it is a projection of our currently accepted practices, then our alternative is to conceive of it as an ineffable noumenal source in the manner of Kant.

But this trivial sense in whick 'truth' is 'correspondence to reality' and 'depends on a reality independent of our knowledge' is, of course, not enough for the realist. What he wants is . . . the notion of a world so 'independent of our knowledge' that it might, for all we know, prove to contain none of the things we have always thought we were talking about.[28]

The opponent is again presented as accepting, insofar as he is uneasy with Rorty's position, something like a Kantian noumenal world. But consider a modest realism of the following sort. (I shall, in future chapters, be making more careful distinctions about sorts of realism, but I need here just to show that there is considerable space to occupy between Rorty's position and the position he assigns to his opponents.) Suppose our beliefs are about a world that transcends what they take it to be. That world conditions our beliefs so that over time they adjust themselves to its own articulations. Perhaps the manner in which the world's way of determining itself emerges for us will depend to some degree on the sort of subjective apparatus we have, and on the interests that make us find some possible boundaries to be more important than others. But even if our subjective apparatus thus plays a role in how the world appears, it is the world itself that is appearing to us, not some substitute realm of appearances. How reality is and how we take it to be cannot vary independently in the Kantian fashion, not because we determine what reality is, but because it determines how an interpreter will fix the semantic content of our statements. Our abilities are limited, and perhaps there are very many features of the universe that are worth having beliefs about and about which we are not able to have any beliefs at all. But the beliefs we do have are largely about features that are really there, and we can hope to extend gradually our conceptual reach so that our picture of how things are becomes more adequate.

Let us grant that considerable work will have to go into filling in that sketch, and in making contrasts with other views more precise. But surely it is an intelligible and stable position that can take its place as one candidate for describing the relation between language and the world. It is also the case that such a position differs, very clearly, both from Rorty's own position and from the position he assigns to his opponents. (Against his position there is regulation of belief by the world; against the other position, there is no commitment to a noumenal world that might be not at all like what we take it to be.) So making those opponents appear to hold unacceptable claims will go no way at all toward making Rorty's own conception more plausible.

Indeed, he maneuvers between his view and the modest realism I have just described when he feels himself vulnerable. He does appear vulnerable, for example, when he says that Davidson "does not want to view sentences as 'made true' by anything," whereas Davidson says that he aims to reestablish our "unmediated touch with the familiar objects whose antics make our sentences and opinions true or false."[29] But he brushes off the apparent inconsistency by claiming that his realist opponent must be making a stronger claim than Davidson's, must indeed be committing himself to a world "which could vary independently of the antics of the familiar objects . . . something rather like the thing-in-itself."[30] But the modest realist would be a fool to accept that redescription of his position. Only Rorty's sliding between Davidson's account and his own makes the more modest response seem unavailable.

A similar sliding occurs when Rorty describes his own position as the generally accepted one that we have access to reality only as already conceptualized, and describes his opponent as one who "thinks that, deep down beneath all the texts, there is something which is not just one more text but that to which various texts are trying to be 'adequate'."[31] Now we ought to be careful here about making a certain distinction. To say that we do not encounter a bare, unconceptualized reality is not to say that we encounter only texts. Even if the world appears according to the character of our conceptual apparatus, it is the nonconceptual world that is appearing, not the conceptual apparatus itself or one of its cultural artifacts. (The idea that we might be confronting only our own constructions, only texts, again reflects the influence of the theological, self-relational, and demiurgic picture of subjectivity that I have been trying to defeat.) So it is a very modest claim indeed to say that there is something to which our various accounts are trying to be adequate, and that is not itself just another account.

Of course, we do not bring about that adequacy by comparing our

---

[29] Rorty, "Pragmatism, Davidson and Truth," p. 333; Davidson, *Inquiries*, p. 198.
[30] Rorty, "Pragmatism, Davidson and Truth," p. 354, n. 58.
[31] Rorty, *Consequences of Pragmatism*, pp. 154, xxxvii.

account to a reality not yet touched by the character of any conceptual apparatus at all; but we often do succeed in bringing it about nonetheless. Is it some inscrutable world toward which we have thus aimed? No, we go ahead and use our own best picture in describing reality as it is in itself. That is the reality we have been aiming toward, even if other intelligences might describe the same world somewhat differently. So again Rorty has tried to take over a relatively noncontroversial view, that we do not have access to an unconceptualized reality, and to push his opponent into an acceptance of inscrutable noumena. But defeating such an opponent will then be useless when Rorty slides back to his own more radically antirealist stance, for the position of the modest realist still remains on the field.

That pressing of opponents into untenable positions they would be foolish to endorse is ubiquitous. He suggests that his opponents are working out of a legacy of an age for which God's language has already determined truth for the world.[32] They are searching "for some final vocabulary, which can somehow be known in advance to be the common core, the truth of, all the other vocabularies which might be advanced in its place."[33] But I do not know of many thinkers today who expect such a vocabulary to be known in advance or to be final. And the modest realist can easily grant that we need a pluralism of vocabularies in order to give an adequate account of how matters stand, and that there may be different acceptable ways of using such basic terms as 'object' and 'individual.' In criticizing those who disagree with his "liberal ironism" and who suppose that there are good justifications for our moral values and decisions, Rorty describes such an opponent as believing there are "algorithms" for solving moral dilemmas.[34] But again, no good Aristotelian, and few moral philosophers at all, would hold that there are such algorithms, or that the adjustment of our ethical beliefs to the world would require that sort of outcome. He also says that those who are afraid of abandoning the language of respect for fact and objectivity believe in science as having a "priestly function" that puts us in touch with a realm that transcends the human.[35] There is, of course, an obvious sense in which the realm of galaxies and quasars and subatomic particles and rain forest flora transcends what is human. But that sense would hardly encourage a belief in any kind of priestly other world. We have seen why he needs this strategy, but we should not be convinced by an argument that is based upon it.

There is a second reason, I said, why Rorty exaggerates his closeness to Davidson. A clear hint of this motivation for distorting Davidson's

[32] Rorty, *Contingency, Irony, and Solidarity*, p. 5.
[33] Rorty, *Consequences of Pragmatism*, p. xlii.
[34] Rorty, *Contingency, Irony, and Solidarity*, p. xv.
[35] Ibid., p. 21.

views comes from his use of Davidson's treatment of metaphor. I need to set the stage for the discussion here by describing Rorty's picture of how our accounts of the world change. He says that the relation between our vocabularies and the world is causal rather than epistemic. Darwin's account of the emergence and decline of species is a causal explanation of that sort:

> Davidson lets us think of the history of language, and thus of culture, as Darwin taught us to think of the history of a coral reef. Old metaphors are constantly dying off into literalness.... Our language and our culture are as much a contingency, as much a result of thousands of small mutations finding niches (and millions of others finding no niches), as are the orchids and the anthropoids.[36]

Species emerge when conditions are favorable, but there is no rightness as to which ones emerge, and the strategies of the successful ones (horns, speed, mass reproduction, and so forth) do not work because they somehow mirror the built-in metaphysical contours of the world; they just increase the likelihood that the species will propagate. Or we might think of a similar causal explanation of the emergence and decline of geological features and of stable climatic environments. The causal story doesn't need any norms of rightness or of matching already present contours.

Rorty believes that human vocabularies replace one another and then die off in a similar fashion. Once one is in place, it will fix what is the right thing to say in various circumstances, but in the transition from one vocabulary to the other, there can be no rightness, only the causal story. The distinction between rational and irrational persuasion, between reason and power, breaks down for his account. So when we are dealing with the questions of relations among competing vocabularies, or of historical transitions from one to another, the philosopher has little to say. The literary critic who is sensitive to rhetorical strategies and ambiguities, and who can play off dissimilar texts against one another in interesting ways, will be far more helpful, and is coming today to have more power as his abilities in this regard are recognized.

What can Davidson's position on metaphor have to do with that conception? He holds that metaphorical statements have no semantic value as metaphorical.[37] Their meaning is the same meaning they have when taken literally, but such statements also have the pragmatic function of suggesting that we think of matters in new ways. (I think he is wrong on this issue.) Davidson's treatment seems to have the purpose of specifying just what falls within the range of semantic theory and what does not, so as to define the range of phenomena to which semantic

---

[36] Ibid., p. 16.
[37] That is his conclusion in "What Metaphors Mean," in *Inquiries*, pp. 245–64.

theories of the sort he proposes must be sensitive. So Davidson's interest is mainly in keeping the field of semantic investigation free of infiltration by metaphor.

But Rorty thinks he can enlist Davidson as a supporter of the picture of language just given. He says that there are no rational standards of change. We do not get a better picture of the world; some habits of speaking give way to others. So when Davidson makes metaphor nonsemantic, Rorty sees that position as favoring what we might call a mutational view of changes in our dominant vocabularies. Metaphors causally bring about change in such vocabularies, but since they are nonsemantic, there can be no question of truth or inference in the process of adopting them; that process does not occur in accord with rational standards, nor on the basis of an accommodation to the world. Metaphors are literally meaningless, but they are able to cause changes in usage so that once the new vocabulary has taken hold, sentences formed with it can be true or false, according to the rules that the new vocabulary is then in a position to determine.

Now in some respects, to be sure, Rorty gets Davidson right on metaphor. There is that image in Davidson of metaphorical speech dying off into literalness. But I do not see much support in Davidson for transforming that conception of metaphor into a full-scale picture of changes of vocabulary in history, and it seems unlikely that he would agree with Rorty's claim that there are no rational standards being applied when one large theoretical apparatus replaces another. Rorty's picture of changes in our large cultural conversations ignores, as before, the role of the world, while for Davidson, it is the fact that different conversations or theories are interpretable as being about the same world that guarantees that they are commensurable. Rorty makes a similar use of Davidson's treatment of changes of character, as when a person chooses to remake himself into a different sort of person, with different characteristic desires. In such cases, says Davidson, when the new way of looking at one's life is not yet fully integrated into the rest of one's existence, there may be incompatible belief-desire systems residing within the same person, so that from the point of view of the established belief-desire system, the change to the new one must be irrational; there is no motivation from within the old one to bring about the change, which must appear relative to the old one as the result of causation from outside.[38]

It will be no surprise that Rorty leaps to make use of that account. He sees Davidson as favoring, as he himself does, the view that historical change from one vocabulary to the next is nonrational. But again

---

[38] See Davidson, "Paradoxes of Irrationality," in *Philosophical Essays on Freud*, R. Wollheim and J. Hopkins, eds. (Cambridge: Cambridge University Press, 1982), p. 305.

Davidson nowhere indicates that he is sympathetic to such an extrapolation from the individual mind to historical change, and in the psychological case he mentions, the overall change may well be rational even if it is not so from those standards available from within the belief-desire system being called into question. Then, too, the case of theory change is one of the replacement of some beliefs by other ones, while the Davidsonian analysis cited by Rorty concerns the replacement of some desires by other ones, and that appears to be a case of a rather different sort. (This is not to deny, of course, that many changes in intellectual history take place through causal processes that have little to do with rational thought.)

If Davidson is a poor supporter of Rorty's picture, we can still ask whether that picture is itself plausible. When we look at the analogy between Darwinian evolution and large-scale changes of belief or vocabulary, it seems to break down right at the start. The standard of success in the rise and fall of species is survival, the increase of one's species at the expense of other ones. By analogy, then, the only measure of success for a set of beliefs is its increased distribution in the total "belief population." But there may well be more believers in astrology today than there are in evolutionary theory, and we shall not take the reproductive success of the former as granting it the privilege that, on Rorty's view, it ought to receive. We go on to ask which of the two theories, if either, is true. If Rorty then switches the relevant field to the total belief population among natural scientists, so that the belief in astrology does much less well, then we need to ask why there should be this sort of preference. Darwinian survival is survival; we do not suppose that survival in, say, England has an automatic privilege in terms of biological distribution. But of course the reason why distribution of beliefs among scientists has greater value is that their belief-formation methods, at least in their fields, are generally reliable ways of coming to understand how matters really are.

If Rorty is right, then a scientist, rather than learning proper laboratory techniques, would be better rewarded if he studied the sociology of belief fixation in the scientific community. Adopting a scientific theory is, for Rorty, like adopting a fashionable way of speaking or dressing; one wants to be the sort of person who comes up with new fashions that others will copy. There are academic fields for which that analogy may unfortunately be valid, and one may find even in the natural sciences a willingness to believe what is fashionable. But in the long run the best strategy for getting one's theory generally accepted is to attend to the world, and to discover something about how it works, rather than to attend to strategies of sociological manipulation. There is a very good reason why that is the best strategy. Future scientists will be attending to the same world and will have their beliefs caused by its happenings, so that the more one's beliefs are sensitive to how matters stand in the world, the more likely it is that future scientists will adopt the same beliefs and will give one credit for one's discoveries. The interest in explaining why the universe operates the way it does is continuous across many different vocabularies over centuries. That interest allows the world itself to be a measure of those vocabularies' rightness in a way that the world cannot be a measure of the "rightness" of the horns of an animal.

Rorty, Davidson, Heidegger

Rorty's allying of himself with Davidson is, we have seen, deeply suspect. Whatever the legitimate points of comparison, the two part company on the basic issue of whether the world disappears as something substantial and independent over against the momentum of our ongoing conversations. Once we have seen that point, then we may become suspicious as well of another alliance that Rorty has claimed: that with Heidegger. I do not want to compare their work in any detail, but it is worth noting that something of the Davidson–Rorty contrast reappears.

Heidegger, like Davidson, is trying to rethink the structure of subjectivity that led to the problems of modern philosophy.[39] He rejects the picture of a subjective determining power that, from a position of independence, constructs or orders or projects its patterns upon a world of objects. Thinking is what it is only through already "belonging to" the world and through letting it manifest its character. It is only in "being toward" the world, in being situated in its surroundings, that I as thinker or experiencer have any real content to my activity; and language, rather than being the embodiment of some conceptual scheme or other, is an "openness" in which things themselves are making their appearance. We do not have to work to bring an alienated subjectivity back in touch with things, because it is by its very nature as subjectivity always in touch with them. The Davidsonian will be uncomfortable perhaps with the language, but should nonetheless recognize genuine analogies there with his own work.

(I should perhaps emphasize that we do not have a simple contrast here but a triangulation. Davidson and Heidegger will also differ in important ways. To take just one case: Although both reject a correspondence between sentences and sentencelike entities in the world, they give different accounts of what it means for us to be already in touch with worldly things. For Davidson we are situated within the world's

[39] A similar contrast between Rorty and Heidegger is given in John Caputo, "The Thought of Being and the Conversation of Mankind: The Case of Heidegger and Rorty," in *Hermeneutics and Praxis*, Robert Hollinger, ed. (Notre Dame: University of Notre Dame Press, 1985), pp. 248–71.

causal processes and it is generating beliefs in us, so that an interpreter will properly interpret those beliefs by relating them back to their causes. Heidegger describes rather what he calls our "preunderstanding" of things, our nonconceptual manner of being among things through being open to their contexts of significance. Those contexts are neither given to us nor made by us but are what both we and things find ourselves within as a condition for our encounter. We must avoid the one-sidedness that would take them to be no more than projections of a communal subjectivity, yet we must work within our historical preunderstanding in letting what is there to be encountered take hold of us.)

Rorty's use of Heidegger is very much like his use of Davidson. He ignores the way that thinking and speaking are for Heidegger under the sway of Being; the lesson he learns is rather that once correspondence is dismissed as the basis for connecting thought or language to the world, then we are left with the discourses themselves, with linguistic sequences that generate other ones without the world being there to constrain the process. But that disappearance of the world is the most reliable sign we have that one is working within, rather than genuinely transforming, the patterns of the modern picture of subjectivity. Discourses come to occupy the position of the modern thinker or determiner. They make their own objects and transform the world into a reflection of their patterns.

There is a conflict here between different accusations of going theological. For Rorty, the Heideggerian is like the religious thinker who, having given up God, still needs to feel under the sway of something Godlike. (It is clear that Rorty would make much the same accusation against my own work in this book.) The Heideggerian may say in response that Rorty is employing a theological structure of subjectivity that diminishes the world and makes us lose sight of the way we are at home in it, so that there seems to be an unconstrained self-positing by discourse. Perhaps there is a trace of the search for the divine in Heidegger's rather mystical appeal to Language and Being. But what he has in common with Davidson, as they challenge our picture of subjectivity, stands independently of that sort of language. Rorty is quintessentially and "religiously" modern in holding that if we open ourselves to any constraint at all from the world, we are submitting ourselves to an unacceptable authority that limits the free, self-relating play of subjectivity. Let me develop this notion of Rorty as a "religious" thinker.

Religious Structures in Rorty's Thought

Many of Rorty's arguments, I think I have shown, do not stand up well to analysis. But something else is going on in his work that is worth examining. There are recurring patterns of thought in it that repeat either some of the patterns we described earlier as religious or theological in origin, or some of the characteristic structures of modern philosophy. (The presence of those patterns is not unrelated to the failure of the arguments.) Or so I shall now argue.

Let us begin by noting again Rorty's propensity to see just two alternatives for explaining the success of our beliefs. Either our statements must make themselves adequate to a bare noumenal world, or the only measure of utterances succeeding in what they set out to do is their coherence with the background of accepted beliefs at the time of utterance, the planks in the boat that for the moment we are not trying to change. We saw that there was another candidate, a modest realism, that Rorty habitually ignores. It is as if that stable middle position cannot be achieved in his thinking. Once we turn away from a commitment to a Kantian noumenal world, there seems to be, in Rorty's description of affairs, an irresistible momentum that leads directly to Rorty's version of pragmatism. If we reject that version, he sees us as unable to find a stable position until we arrive at a belief in regulation by an inscrutable thing-in-itself. But why should there be this instability in the middle? Why should the world's ontological order and character collapse so readily into one of the two sides: into an unreachable, unconceptualizable noumenon or into an objectivity projected as the shadow of our practices? What is wrong with the world of the modest realist, as described in an earlier section of this chapter?

One will be reminded here of the picture suggested by late medieval nominalism. The Aristotelian natural world is dissolved in the face of the infinite power of God's free willing; we cannot know things as they are, but we can produce pictures of the world that help us cope with it successfully. There too the middle collapses. Ontological determinacy must either be a feature of the world as God determines it, inscrutable to us, or it must characterize our useful pictures of the world rather than the world itself. There will be a migration of features either to a noumenal world fixed by God's determinative power or to a subjectivized world fixed by our own, and the world must be regarded by us as a blank and indeterminate realm that is the testing ground for whether our pictures help us to cope or do not. It is important, then, that we not claim too much for our accounts. When we move over the line to realist talk, we are violating our proper limits; we are trying to be divine. Rorty's space of possible explanations seems to repeat that late medieval one.

It is true, of course, that Rorty rejects the commitment to noumena; he correctly sees that commitment as an outcome of theological thinking. But once that part of the structure is gone, then our motivation becomes very much unclear for supposing that our conceptions of the world are merely good for coping with it. It is not that one can just remove the noumena and keep the rest of the structure; the two sides went together and were defined by their opposition. Without the pressure of God's omnipotent determining of the world, there will be no demand that the world's own character be eroded until it is an indeterminate realm onto which we project pictures in order to cope. Then our conceptions of the world can properly count as world-guided; how we take matters to be will be not an instrument for producing useful predictions but an approximate exhibiting of at least some of the world's own features. The middle ground will hold stably against Rorty's bidirectional momentum. When merely coping is contrasted with seeing the world as God does, it makes sense to restrict our capacities to the former. When a realist's claim about an account's getting matters right rather than just helping us to cope is made in the context of theological intentionality, it makes sense to condemn him as violating his proper limits. But if coping is not defined by such a contrast, then why should we continue to define it as "merely" coping? Without the earlier picture, it is no longer tempting to think that there are only the two competing candidates; it was only the notion of a theological intentionality that made the middle position of the modest realist seem to disappear, as he had to appeal to a realm whose determinacy had supposedly been eroded by God's unlimited power, or by the power of human subjectivity, as it takes over God's position in the field.

Rorty supposes that the realist is claiming to be able to describe the world as it is prior to any contact with our perceptual or conceptual apparatus. But again, the modest realist who opposes Rorty will not be fool enough to make any claim of that sort. I may well believe that there might be more sophisticated knowers than human ones who may find my picture of the world a crude one. But what appeal can there be in the notion of a world that might be *completely* different from how it appears to me, and that must be describable apart from the resources of any conceptual apparatus whatever? The strongest motivation, if not the only one, is that there is a kind of knowing, a divine one, completely different from our own, even to the extent that we and God are really knowing different worlds, not just the same world with different degrees of accuracy.

So the late medieval theological positions put in place a structure with characteristic patterns and with built-in directions of force: the eroding of the world's own determinacy; the migration of features to subjectivity; the notion of a noumenal realm that might differ completely from how things appear; the belief that unless we are knowing such a noumenal realm, apart from the working of our own subjectivity, we are not in touch with things as they really are; the restriction of our conceptions to aids for coping with the world; the instability of the middle as the momentum of the structure pushes one either toward a commitment to the noumenal or toward the merely subjective; the notion that what is not immediately given in experience must be something that the mind adds for instrumental reasons. That structure continues in a more secularized form in much of modern philosophy, and Rorty chops off a considerable part of it while assuming that the rest is unchanged.

Note how Rorty makes the same move when he rejects the account given by the logical positivists. They see the world as providing us with an empirical given; that is its contribution to our beliefs. Then we add schemes of linguistic ordering that process the data so as to yield correct predictions about future experiences. We do not suppose that the features present in such schemes pick out features in the world as it really is; they help us to predict and to cope. Rorty acknowledges that attacks on the notion of the empirical given have been successful; *that* side of the picture will then be seen to drop off. But then he retains the other side of the picture as it was:

One difficulty the pragmatist has in making his position clear, therefore, is that he must struggle with the positivist for the position of radical anti-Platonist. He wants to attack Plato with different weapons from those of the positivist, but at first glance he looks like just another variety of positivist. He shares with the positivist the Baconian and Hobbesian notion that knowledge is power, a tool for coping with reality. But he carries this Baconian point through to its extreme, as the positivist does not. He drops the notion of truth as correspondence with reality altogether, and says that modern science does not enable us to cope because it corresponds, it just plain enables us to cope.[40]

We have the construction of ways of talking that help us to manage but nothing is given to such ways of talking, from the direction of the world, that constrains how they are to develop. On Rorty's account, the world may help to cause changes in vocabularies, by analogy with the way it causes changes in geological formations, but it is an empty world that falls into insignificance in favor of the momentum of the vocabularies themselves.

But as before, we want to ask how *half* the positivist structure can remain as it was when its correlate, the empirical given, has disappeared. In Davidson, by way of contrast, the attack on the given is accompanied by a rethinking of the relation of subjectivity to the world. If we do not split up experience into a sensory given and what we then add, we can consider the entire belief-regulation apparatus, as a holistic system, to be sensitive to how matters really are, so that the success of our accounts is not limited to mere coping. While Rorty applauds Davidson's attacks on semantic and mental reifications, he remains committed in a significant way to a reified (linguistic) subjectivity that is

---

[40] Rorty, *Consequences of Pragmatism*, p. xvii.

positioned over against an emptied-out realm, and that now can go on autonomously, with little or no regulation by that extremely thin world. That is a result one reaches through taking over the modern picture (earlier a theological one), and through naming the positions in it somewhat differently, rather than by rethinking the entire subject–world structure. (Rorty describes a two-step process by which we first "program" ourselves with a language and then let the world cause us to hold beliefs in that language.[41] But isn't that a Kantian picture? Are we cut off from the world's guidance during the first "programming" step?)

Fichte claimed that the goal of the self is to see the world as embodying one's own activity; his account continued the theological tradition that I described in Chapter 1. God's activity must ultimately be a self-willing and the Fichtean subject will in some sense imitate the divine self-knowing and self-willing; the world will be a shadow cast by the self as a field for its activity. In Rorty, likewise, the defeat of the myth of the given is accompanied not by the Davidsonian reaffirmation of the world's causal sway over our entire belief system, but by an unconstrained self-relating (of discourses one to another) for which the world is an empty reflection. He complains that "positivism preserved a god in its notion of Science . . . the notion of a portion of culture where we touched something not ourselves."[42] And he makes the following claim:

The wonder in which Aristotle believed philosophy to begin was wonder at finding oneself in a world larger, stronger, nobler than oneself. The fear in which Bloom's poets begin is the fear the one might end one's days in such a world, a world one never made, an inherited world. The hope of such a poet is that what the past tried to do to her she will succeed in doing to the past: to make the past itself . . . bear *her* impress.[43]

We have here the hope of one strand of German idealism, and of the romantic movement that is often associated with it. Rorty, of course, favors Bloom's poet rather than the Aristotelian sage. But Rorty, avowed defender of the disenchantment of subjectivity, has thus turned religious himself. He accuses his opponent of theological yearnings in holding that in thinking about the world we "touch something not ourselves." But my thinking does not have to be taken up into any religious context at all for it to make sense to me that the world I dwell in extends well beyond what my own small purposes make of its arrangements. The universe had gone on for billions of years before we emerged on this planet and will likely go on for billions more if an asteroid should wipe us out. On the other hand, there is a yearning for divinity in Rorty's hope that I shall encounter only myself in everything I touch. (That was the

[41] Rorty, *Contingency, Irony, and Solidarity*, p. 6.
[42] Rorty, *Consequences of Pragmatism*, p. xliii.
[43] Rorty, *Contingency, Irony, and Solidarity*, p. 29.

structure, we saw, of the self-relational activity of Aquinas's God.) One is hoping for a divine way of being in supposing that all determination will be a self-determining, and that the boundaries a human discourse runs up against will be boundaries that it has set for itself. (It may seem inconsistent to attribute to Rorty both a leftover part of a picture that emphasized our weakness over against God, so that our beliefs are a matter of coping, and a picture that divinizes subjectivity through exalting its self-relational powers. But it seems to me that such a combination of modesty and ambition is what is most characteristic of modern philosophy. To take over the religious structure means either that the subject ambitiously takes on a divinized role or that it modestly projects its schemes upon a world it cannot hope to understand in itself.)

Hegel's version of the idealist program tried to restore the ontological solidity of the world through a rethinking of that structure of self-relating. But Rorty gives us the more narcissistic version of encountering only ourselves when we think and talk. To come to grips with the world is just to encounter our own present cultural artifacts. Instead of the Hegelian expansion of the understanding of self-relating-in-relating-to-otherness, Rorty gives us a picture of otherness collapsing into the self-relational activity of conversations feeding off other conversations, so that we never encounter anything but what we have made. Rorty often seems profoundly a part of (one strand of) the German romantic tradition. We can see a version of Fichtean self-positing in his talk of "the sense that there is nothing deep down inside us except what we have put there ourselves, no criterion that we have not created in the course of creating a practice, no standard of rationality that is not an appeal to such a criterion, no rigorous argumentation that is not obedience to our own conventions."[44]

Rorty's pragmatism also continues another structure with religious connotations. One of the chief Protestant impulses (at least as Hegel set matters out) is the demand that we not accept what is simply given, from the world or from tradition or from authorities, but that our own activity of taking-to-be must be the condition for securing matters as objective and legitimate. Our labor and our making must transform what we encounter into what we can recognize as our own. (After being cast out of the garden, the simple enjoyment of what is real cannot be ours; we must make ourselves real through laboring upon the world.) Since God's presence to us will be inward, at the basis of our making and self-making activities, the role of a noumenal world, as an external realm guaranteed by God's knowing, will become otiose. Our relation with the real will then be understood in terms of work, constitution,

---

[44] Rorty, *Consequences of Pragmatism*, p. xlii.

transformation, the production of artifacts, insofar as these express our interiority and our personal "calling." Indeed things can be secured as real only through our labor. Now I think pragmatism in general, and especially Rorty's form of it, retains significant traces of that conception. Sentences are helps to making and changing things in desirable ways; it is our labor that makes matters what they are.

But Rorty, it appears, will have difficulty stating exactly what his position is supposed to be. On his account statements will not have their meaning through the way they are *about* the world, but through the causal interrelations by which they contribute to producing successful or unsuccessful bodily interactions with the environment. The weight of the account comes down on the moment of intervention and reinforcement, and on the moment of perception by which some statements rather mysteriously appear in the system of one's beliefs. But at this point we may repeat an argument given earlier in the chapter. Given the extremely weak sense of the external world that emerges in Rorty's version of pragmatism, we cannot give much weight at all to the notion of genuine causal interventions in the world, and of reinforcements by its causal activity. The world is not sufficiently other; it will be just a projection of our practices themselves, not that which can be genuinely guiding them. The causal interaction with the world is not *real* causal interaction; it is rather that Rorty in his own speaking finds the production of the sounds 'causal interaction' to be useful and interesting in the ways they connect to other sounds and to behavior.

What Rorty needs here, it seems, is to be able to stand outside his strict pragmatist posture just long enough to make some general realist claims about the causal interactions between linguistic strings, on the one side, and a world substantial enough and independent enough to contribute to conferring a semantic content upon them. Only after having done so will he have given sufficient sense to the world and its causal power to make the further pragmatic account intelligible. There is a parallel here, I think, with what we concluded in Chapter 2: that when you try to separate off a realm of subjectivity and ask what character it has apart from a relationship to a particular world, you get the empty running of a syntactic engine. At least on Rorty's account of pragmatism, that realm of subjectivity becomes a network of communal conversations that are supposed to be constituting their referents from out of their own intertextual patterns. But if we have no world with the determinate character that at least a modest realism would grant it, there is nothing substantial enough to cast its shadow on those conversations and make them meaningful. They become patterns of noise in a vacuum.

Now the loss of the world as meaning-conferring is no difficulty if it is God whose presence to and lighting up of the subjective shapes makes them meaningful. Or there will not be a problem if we have divinized subjectivity or Language so that they have on their own, independently of the world, a self-determining power. But the medieval and modern structure of subjectivity comes under enormous pressure that it simply cannot handle when God and his divinized substitutes are removed from it. Rorty continues that structure and we might say that for him the background platitudes and practices of the culture are supposed to take over the divine role of assuring the meaningfulness of the utterances and thoughts of the individual, since the world has been reduced to an empty frame. But if the foregoing argument is correct, there is nothing to keep them from being meaningless in their turn. The antirealist's erosion of the world, at least in Rorty's version, turns out to erode as well the semantic content of his sayings. (A partial antirealism, concerning ethical beliefs, for example, would not suffer from the same defect.)

Let us return to the "Protestant" emphasis on labor, making, and constituting, on our securing the real as such through our working upon it. Rorty's pragmatism, we suggested, continues that emphasis; sentences must pay their way in the work they accomplish. To say that they mirror the world is, for Rorty, to take the determinacy of the world as already given, as another external "authority" to be obeyed instead of what we ourselves, from the inside, take to be worth obeying. (The realist is then, for Rorty, like the Catholic who wants to be under the authority of the Pope instead of taking responsibility for his own epistemic projects.) In the earlier religious model there is an assimilation of knowing and making. Something is determinate either because God has made it so or because we have; God knows the world as it is because he made it, while we know the substitute world that we have constructed through the application of our labor to the raw material of experience. As before, Rorty removes half of the picture and keeps the rest as it was. There is no noumenal world that God has created, and no raw material that we are given to work upon as demiurges, but still we ourselves know only what we have made, the cultural artifacts upon which we have labored. But once we remove the religious and theological incentives for that conception, once we no longer take the model of God's creation as a metaphor for the relation of thought and reality, then we shall not so readily accept that relation of knowing and making. The removal of God from the scene, and the consequent demotion of the model of divine creation, will cause us to rethink the entire picture of the relation of subjectivity to the world. Then we shall not be left with our making, coping, and laboring as what remains after God's laboring disappears. We can instead think of our knowing as allowing the world to display its own character, even if our ways of thinking and seeing let the world become visible in some ways rather than others. Perhaps the articulations of the world need to be actualized in our thinking, or in the thinking of other sorts of believers, in order to count as genuine articulations. But they are features of a world whose self-exhibiting we may enjoy as thinkers.

If Rorty does appeal to the pragmatist notions of labor and economy, of making sentences pay their way, he also transforms the structure that supported that manner of thought. There is no longer the "calling" from God that sets up a proper field for our labor, and there is no longer the raw material of "givenness" that constrains what that labor will be able to accomplish. Without those two constraints the Protestant work ethic turns into textual play, as (in America) the search for a religious justification has turned for many into a search for a sexual or therapeutic one.

Rorty, Disenchantment, and Modern Institutions

As we remove the various effects of religious and theological ideas on thinking about the self, there will be a temptation to see our political and epistemic institutions as no longer having a kind of basis that once was available. It will be said that these institutions that developed in the modern era did so in tandem with practices of self-formation, and with conceptions of selfhood and subjectivity, that can no longer be honored. Rorty himself believes strongly in the virtues of our modern liberal political and ethical institutions.[45] He believes that the support seemingly given once by philosophers' arguments to these institutions was illusory, but he also thinks that it does not matter. Philosophical thinking does not make much of a difference to practice anyway, and humans can learn to live very well with the notion that their institutions have no deeper support or justification than their own habits of commitment to them. (Sometimes he is less sure that such a society will do well.)

We may see this case as parallel to the loss of divine support for our forms of ethical life. It is worth noting, of course, that for hundreds of millions of individuals it is still religion that forms the strongest basis for moral beliefs, and surely there are many instances where a lessening of religious influence has led to a weakening of habits of living morally. But one of the great modern projects was to give a new basis for ethical life by appealing to various conceptions of subjectivity. It is an important fact of recent history that this new basis, expressed especially in appeals to human rights, equal treatment, civil and political liberties, and democracy, has been able to ground firm commitments to at least some ethical institutions even in those who are not at all religious. It is perhaps unsurprising that these conceptions of subjectivity retained aspects of the earlier religious and theological forms of thought. There

---

[45] See his essays "The Contingency of a Liberal Community" and "Private Irony and Liberal Hope" in Rorty, *Contingency, Irony, and Solidarity*, pp. 44–95.

was, for example, the Kantian notion of a self that determines rational principles for its life from a stance outside of space and time; and there are Kantian accounts that retain that sort of stance without the metaphysics. The question now is whether our practices can endure the loss of such religious pictures of the self and its activity, as they once endured the loss of religion itself as a support.

Now I think Rorty is correct that the disenchantment of subjectivity does not have to be threatening to such institutions. (In my way of seeing matters, our Enlightenment practices were not simply creatures of those metaphysical pictures and can thus survive their disappearance.) But I think, in contrast, that Rorty's version of pragmatism can be dangerous in regard to them. The problem is a double one: the dissolving of the world as that to which our practices must accommodate themselves in order to get matters right, and the dissolving of the self-relating subject into a mere construction of social practices and linguistic codes. (For Rorty, "the human self is created by the use of a vocabulary."[46]) Rorty believes that either we must make a very controversial metaphysical commitment to a noumenal world and a noumenal self-willing, or we must accept, as he does, that there is no further support for our practices beyond the fact that we support them.

But again Rorty seems not radical enough in rethinking the structures of modern thought. One modern idea, we said, was to try to derive from the resources of subjectivity itself the standards that reality and rational practice, as well as political and ethical life, must satisfy. Now as the disenchantment of subjectivity undermines that project, there are two responses available. One, Rorty's, is to retain the modern picture of an impoverished world whose determinacy must come from the self-relational structure of subjectivity, while granting that what comes from the subjective side must be, after disenchantment, a mere preference for some fashions over others. Rules of argument, human rights, liberal institutions, ethical habits will, like fashions in clothing, have their only backing in our activity of backing them, an activity that could just as well have settled on many other preferences. (It should be said, however, that in at least one sense, Rorty is not a relativist about such matters. Even if our commitment to our institutions has no deeper grounding than that, we shall quite properly take for granted the shape that such a commitment gives to our lives and our communities.)

The other response is that we need to rethink the picture of subjectivity as projecting its determinations on the real. Rorty goes only part way in his process of disenchantment. A more fully naturalized subjectivity will be one whose identity we will be able to specify only by seeing it as accommodating itself to real features of the world. Rather

---

[46] Rorty, *Contingency, Irony, and Solidarity*, p. 7.

than being a result of habits or fashions we just *happen* to accept, or being derivable from the very nature of subjectivity, our epistemic and ethical practices can be seen as part of a holistically adjusted process of gradually getting things right. So an alternative to trying to find support in an increasingly less potent and less divine subjectivity is to return to the world, though in a more sophisticated fashion than in traditional realism. It will take considerable work in the coming chapters to show that this alternative is a plausible one, and that the world can thus regulate our ethical beliefs. But if we can make that conception plausible, then Rorty's position will become much less so.

I think Rorty is wrong in supposing that we could accept the fashion analogy and still have the kind of commitment we need to our epistemic and ethical and political institutions. It is hardly the case that we must discover Platonic or Kantian foundations for them, nor do we have to suppose that there is no place for invention on our part, for our interests to give some degree of shaping to what we may take getting things right to be. But I think we need also the sense that epistemic goodness and ethical goodness are at least as much discovered as made, that they transcend the peculiarities of our practices and regulate to an important degree the adjusting of those practices to what is epistemically or ethically the case.

It is true, I grant, that the issue of whether Rorty's "fashion" model of our ethical and epistemic practices will undermine them is an empirical question about what human beings are like. We do not know now what attitudes those in the future must have toward their practices if they are to have the needed commitment to them to keep them going. It will be said that the English have a passionate commitment to the practices and the exact rules of cricket, even if cricket has no basis other than their own setting of the rules. But we need to ask whether our engagement in a communal ethical life could be of this sort, whether we could accept the analogy that our commitment to human rights follows just from the rules we happen to play by and happen to like very much, since they help give a sense to our Westernness, in the way that cricket helps give a sense to Englishness. I think we shall demand that some deeper basis remain after reflection, and that we understand our ethical thought to be a responding to ethical considerations that are only partly constituted by what we do. And there is the question of whether, even if we could succeed with an understanding of our commitment as cricketlike, our understanding of what we are about as ethical individuals will have been impoverished. For we shall have failed to grasp in just what the importance of being ethical lies. It is not just an interesting game that we have happened to invent. (I shall be defending a version of moral realism in Chapter 6.)

The success of the institutions of the West can be measured for Rorty only by subjective criteria. Western science and political forms of life do not have their prestige because they have discovered more about how nature is articulated and about what forms of community best suit human beings. Europeans rather have been very good at changing their vocabularies and reinventing themselves rapidly.[47] Presumably Europe became a fashion leader in such vocabularies, and so managed to keep its cultural hegemony, because it could keep coming up with new vocabularies faster than those in the rest of the world could copy them. But surely there is a large difference between Eastern Europeans' adoption of the Western legal system and democratic institutions, and, on the other hand, their copying of Western clothing and rock music. It is true that within the fashion model we might decide to make our commitment to some fashions much more important than our commitments to others. But how would we thereby have made it comprehensible that others must, in order to get matters at least roughly right, follow us in making those same fashions (human rights, for example, and greater equality of opportunity) more important? Why is there that limitation on their freedom? Could it really be the case that there is no deeper rightness here than that the trend-setting West has happened to make those fashions extremely important for joining "our" club?

Rorty favors a "poeticized" culture, in which there is a split between a privatized Nietzschean self-inventing and a public world characterized by the liberal institutions of the modern West.[48] But that split between private and public worlds is again a staple of modern thought. It is true that the emphasis on an active interiority that sets the standard for how reality can or should appear often leads, among modern thinkers, to vigorous demands on the political order. But it is also likely that there will be a separating out of this private self-relating from the world. As an early modern self, an individual will not want the public life of the ancient polis; his concern will be rather to have political institutions that do a good job of preserving the sphere of private self-making, so that he can carry out the calling that is his through his being open to God's presence to his interiority, and for which inner attitude is more important than public status. Kierkegaard expresses a later version of this outcome. My public performances as a member of an institution seem to count very little for him. What matters is my inner choosing to be a self, to take myself as a choosing self seriously. That sort of attentiveness to the self will not be immune to narcissism; but the Kierkegaardian self avoids that outcome because in taking over one's subjectivity, one's self-relating, in the most serious possible way, one automatically becomes closer to God and thus gains a career for the self that is grounded in an other.

---

[47] Ibid., p. 78.   [48] Ibid., pp. 65–6.

In Rorty we seem to have something like the Kierkegaardian structure without the saving relationship to an eternal divinity. There are the public liberal institutions that one favors but a participation in which is not assigned a very high value. Then there is the private Nietzschean self-inventing, the production of interesting and novel vocabularies that may or may not find successful replication in the culture. As in Locke's notion of a calling, Rorty praises bourgeois liberal society precisely because without it, "people will be less able to work out their private salvations."[49] Participation in public life does not seem to have any value in itself. Rorty praises Derrida for having been the first to recognize that philosophy can only be private ironic play rather than the carrying out of a public responsibility; Derrida has given up even the appearance of giving arguments, of trying to get matters right, of discovering foundations for the institutions we believe in.[50] But then there is little to stop that play from turning into an empty narcissism. (As we shall see in Chapter 8, that is also not a very accurate picture of what Derrida is about.)

Rorty, while speaking favorably of utopian politics, has little to say about the normal processes of self-revision that have become embodied in Western societies. On his view, as self-invention becomes private, we simply accept our liberal institutions without trying to justify their character. Since what is moral is defined by our practices, it is impossible to ask whether ours is a moral society,[51] and our allegiance to liberal institutions is like our allegiance to friends or heroes in that it does not require, and cannot have, justification in a common language.[52] But allegiance to a friend may require such a justification (if he becomes a neo-Nazi, for example) and allegiance to a hero may as well (if he turns out to be a vicious racist). In Hegel the self-relational structure of subjectivity becomes a demand placed on political institutions, that they develop until their own structure is suitable for forming a community of citizens who can be both rational and free. But in Rorty the activity of the self-inventing, self-determining self has become cut off from that relation to political life (a familiar pattern by now). So institutions become inert, simply accepted, divorced from that which needs to ground the self-revising processes of the modern order. And while he speaks of Nietzschean self-making, the self-determining activity of the modern self seems to become in Rorty a playful, ironic consumption of linguistic codes, more passive than active in relation to the world. There is a split-off, self-relational activity that has little to do with the public order except insofar as, by accident, it happens to throw up a new vocabulary into the ongoing conversation. As the subjective world becomes a realm for an empty sort of play, there is a withering not only of

[49] Ibid., pp. 84–5.   [50] Ibid., p. 125.   [51] Ibid., p. 59.   [52] Ibid., p. 54.

public life but of the very notion that we might improve our lot through rational self-reflection regarding our institutions.

So I think that Rorty continues modern structures more than he subverts them. Simply to show that Rorty gives us a later version of modern philosophy instead of rethinking it is not to show thereby that he is wrong. It is to show only that he fails by his own standards; he is trapped within an older fashion, an older vocabulary, as the narrative has moved on. But if my arguments have been valid, it is by more than his own standards that he fails. Rorty is missing what is significant about recent work in philosophy and has learned the wrong lessons. When we apply ourselves thoroughly to rethinking the subject–world structure of modern philosophy, we end up not losing the world but recovering it, not in narcissistic play but in a project of increasing our sensitivity to what the world is like and to what is right and wrong.

5

Realism

There are two rather different reactions to what I have been calling the disenchantment of subjectivity. We might see it as pushing even further the relativist tendencies of the earlier disenchantment of the world. As the metaphysical depth of various features is challenged, as semantic and ontological reifications are deposed, as the realm of subjectivity takes on, relative to the interpreter, the thinness the world took on relative to the subject, there are fewer stabilities left to prevent interpretation and discourse from developing as they will. (We might call that reaction the postmodern one.) The other reaction is to see the disenchantment of subjectivity as removing the principal obstacle to finding ourselves in the solid world of the realist. Subjectivity was exalted to a stance in some respects divine, and that produced an economy encouraging qualities to migrate from the world to the subject. With that condition no longer present, we are now free to move toward bringing about a restoration of the world. How well is this latter project likely to succeed? In the next chapter I shall make a defense of a version of realism in one area, that of moral judgments, because that seems an area in which the turn toward realism will be most controversial. In the present chapter I want to look more generally at issues that come into play when we try to defend realist accounts.

Antirealism, Religious Conceptions, and Modern Thought

There are many realisms and antirealisms. I am interested here in two issues that become prominent with the modern turn to subjectivity, as one grants increasing power to thought or language to set conditions for what passes as real. One of these issues concerns the thinning out of the world relative to the subject, the other its contraction. Very many features once seen as due to the world's own determinations are instead seen as projections upon a much thinner world by the powers of the subject, or as fictions produced to make the prediction of experience more reliable. As well as losing its determinacy to thought or to language, the world also suffers a contraction, as the epistemic or semantic powers of the human mind are said to limit in advance the extent of reality. It might be claimed, for example, that we could not make 'reality' have a meaning that allowed its application to extend beyond what human investigatory powers could reach out to; or we might say that it is nonsense to think of the world as transcending what our own experiences can show to be the case. A satisfactory realism for a certain class of judgments, as I shall understand it, will resist both those movements, toward thinning out the world and toward contracting it. It will hold, regarding those judgments, that our beliefs must accommodate themselves to, or "track," the contours of the world, and that even with the full exercise of our abilities we might fall short of grasping what is the case. The important idea here is that reality is not the child of our abilities for organizing, meaning, and evidence gathering, but is an independent measure of how good those abilities get to be. The notion of a resistance to those two ways in which the world becomes impoverished gives some flesh to the barer claim by the realist that the direction of fit is mind-to-world rather than world-to-mind. (One may be a realist regarding a set of judgments in one area and an antirealist regarding another set.)

Now there will, of course, be occasions, even for the realist, when we want to say that what we took to be a feature of the world is a creature of our own projections. A man may have naturalized certain aspects of the structure of his society and may on that basis believe that certain relations between men and women are dictated by the facts of nature. But I am interested here in positions where the antirealist tendency is both more general and more radical. There will be, in these positions, an "energy system" in which there is a strong momentum to enhance the determinacy-conferring power of thought (or of language or of practice). So there will be a pressure toward having an ever thinner world confronted by a subjectivity that is itself ever richer, and toward collapsing reality into what can be secured by the experiential and conceptual powers of the self. That will still leave us with a considerable range of views, from the various phenomenalisms and positivisms of the empiricist to Fichte's idealism (and, in some respects, Kant's), and from the antirealism of Dummett to Rorty's conversational idealism and to various positions considered postmodern.

Given so many different accounts, there will be a wide range of motivations for adopting them, and a study of influences in intellectual history will give a complex picture of why various kinds of antirealism came to thrive at certain times. I have no intention of attempting such a history in this book, and yet I do want to make a suggestion about one factor in the appeal of the various antirealisms. (I should grant that what I am suggesting is speculative, and I shall be satisfied if it seems more plausible to you upon finishing this section than upon beginning it.) What I want to do is to generalize on the sort of claims I made regarding Rorty in the preceding chapter, so that I can present a challenge to a wider range of antirealisms. Some may, for example, be rather well persuaded that Rorty remains in the grip of a theological, self-relational notion of subjectivity, but may believe that result has little to do with antirealisms that have their basis in empiricism and in positivist philosophy of science. So I want to give an historical account that puts quite different antirealisms under pressure.

We might think of a field of thought in which certain habits of thinking and certain structures of opposition become strongly reinforced. Then aspects of that field are gradually removed as new systems of thought are constructed over the earlier architecture. But those aspects, in being removed, are not quite fully erased. For what remains continues to show the effects of its situation in that earlier field, as if some of the original patterns and oppositions were still in place and were still offering support for the remainder. The inertia of that way of setting things up makes it retain an appeal for later philosophers, even when the now truncated field thus taken over is actually a poor candidate for doing what those philosophers need it to do. The earlier architecture I am thinking of here (it will be no surprise) is that of late medieval and early modern philosophy, when the religious and theological background for thinking about metaphysics and epistemology was still clearly evident.

Take the case of the logical positivist who wants to defend science against what he sees as the nonsense of the philosophers. That motivation, by itself, ought to have led to a general, and on the whole realist, account of the ways in which the statements of science are public and repeatable, and of the ways in which they are sensitive to evidence and to the demands of making good inferences. That account would be joined with a demonstration that many of the statements made by philosophers are not of that admirable character.

But instead we get the activation of a model, that of Hume's empiricism, that must in the end cause the project to fail quite badly. One believes that the privacy of one's experiencing is the proper basis for justifying the statements of science, but then the whole idea of science as an ongoing public enterprise will collapse. One also adopts a criterion of meaningfulness that rests on the character of one's experiential and investigatory powers. By that very criterion, the statement that there is an external world becomes meaningless, so we have the contraction of reality back into the realm of private experience. But if these private happenings can no longer be thought of as experiencings *of* such an external world, in what sense can they have *intentional* content or aboutness at all, and if they cannot, what would be their content? I have argued in Chapter 2 that the inner world would go dark if there were that contraction into a private space cut off from its connections to the world and to a possible repetition by others, and I shall not repeat the arguments here. When you collapse enough of the system *around* it, the claim that I am having an experience of 'red here now' becomes meaningless, becomes no longer a claim but an empty production of shapes. The point is that the Humean model is a terrible one for the logical positivists, given their aim of defending science, and their choice of it is evidence far more of the inertial power of philosophical pictures than of the pressure of direct philosophical needs.

The Humean stage-setting for thinking about statements and their justification owes much to that of Locke, though important aspects of the latter's picture have been removed. An historical investigation might find with Locke, whose upbringing was Puritan and whose university training was scholastic, some connections to the earlier religious and theological models of which I have spoken. There would be the sense of the reality and depth of the subjective realm that Hegel, for one, sees as the emphasis of Protestant thought, so that there is an immediate relation to the divine in one's "infinite subjectivity." There would also be the contrast between what we build up out of the material we are given and things as they are knowable by God, so that it makes sense to think of an "I know not what" substrate of appearances, and of a fundamental distinction between nominal essences and real ones. One sees as well the Protestant sense of responsibility for the contents of consciousness, the preference for what we can construct through our labor over an acceptance of the authority of the world or of ideas innately present, as we imitate God through a demiurgic activity that has a much reduced scale for its application. (Things become real for the Protestant, says Hegel, insofar as he can *make them his own* through his activity as a subject, through mixing his labor with them.)

What is worth noting here is that the thought space in which the empiricist operates makes considerably more sense when the surrounding religious and theological background is in place than when it has been removed in an attempt at being more rigorous. The idea of a subjective realm secured in the character of its contents no matter how the external world might go, and even if there should be no external world at all, is more persuasive when we still have a picture of inwardness and immediacy that is supported by our religious conceptions. Then the inner region seems to have a depth and evidence that, due to the directness of the relationship to God, could survive even if what is beyond the mind were to drop out of existence. God's operation on the soul can be immediate, without the mediation of Aristotelian spheres or of the Church's bureaucratic system. In that sense Berkeley is just purifying the structure in claiming that God might produce sensations directly, without any need for an external material world (in the way in which the believing individual is directly illumined by God when reading the Bible rather than needing the priestly tradition of the Church). God seems easily to have the kind of power that would enable him to produce sensations without there being anything at all like that of which they are supposed to be the experiences. Since he is the primary cause of all activity in the world anyway, it is no large step to suppose that he might skip the causal detour through created entities and cause our experiences directly. But once we remove that surrounding structure, then empiricism is at least threatened by an internal collapse, as we saw in Chapter 2.

What seems to have happened is what we described earlier in this section. A certain conception develops that is located in a rich context of thought. Then its more objectionable metaphysical (theological and religious) aspects are removed, and one believes one can keep the structure that remains, without that structure being affected by the loss of much of the larger system to which it belonged. One does not properly think through the problems that arise for that remainder, once it is thus isolated. And the very inertia of the surviving structure, as it continues to be attractive due to the supposed backing it gives to the sciences, makes certain philosophical pictures appear to be successful, even when they do a very poor job of handling the tasks they are assigned.

Let me examine another case of how recent philosophy might depend on the "space" for thought carved out by late medieval and early modern work. Blumenberg argues (I mentioned his work in Chapter 1) that the stance of early modern philosophy is a reaction to the status of the world, and to the situation of man, that are an outcome of the theological absolutism of the late medieval period.[1] In attempting to give the Christian God the perfect self-sufficiency of the Greek one, the medievals worked through an inner logic such that God's absolute power and freedom eventually had to swallow up all other determinacy. God can will at any moment that the world become different from what it is, so that it can have no metaphysical depth of its own that might be a check on his freedom. It becomes radically contingent, with a kind of minimal determinacy that offers the least limitation on the power of God's willing.

God's absolute self-sufficiency demanded that his relations to what is other be understood as a species of self-relating. None of God's actions can be determined by the characteristics of other entities but must occur within that structure of self-relation. As the inner logic of that notion is worked out, there is less of a place for humankind in the plan of the universe. One of the themes of patristic Christianity was that God's becoming man, for the sake of man, was the central story of history. But if theological absolutism is taken seriously, then salvation can have

---

[1] Hans Blumenberg, *The Legitimacy of the Modern Age*, Robert Wallace, trans. (Cambridge, Mass.: MIT Press, 1983), pp. 125–226. My picture of late medieval philosophy and of early modern self-assertion is taken from Blumenberg's discussion. I shall be summarizing some of his positions in what follows; then I shall be drawing my own conclusions regarding recent philosophy.

nothing at all to do with what the human race is like or what it needs; the Incarnation results from a pure act of divine will that could just as well have been directed at another species. Man is no longer at home in a meaningful universe in which he has a proper place, in which it is something about him and what he is that gives him a role in God's dealings with creatures. The radical contingency of the world is matched by a radical insecurity of the self.

Now that logic was so inexorable, says Blumenberg, and the new sort of insecurity it introduced so complete, that it eventually brings about in humans an attitude of self-assertion. Instead of trying for a theoretical understanding of the metaphysical character of the universe (an understanding that has become impossible), we shall instead turn to what we can take reality to be through our own labor and construction, to the ways we make it our own through the working upon it we accomplish. Given the dependence of the world on God's willing, we must take it to have, for all we can know, just a minimum of determinacy. (It has only that minimum on its own, and that which God gives to it through his willing is inscrutable.) But that conception also opens a space for human demiurgic activity, as the world becomes the barest substrate and is characterized in a mathematical and mechanical way that might apply to any world at all. It provides us with a basic material, a basic givenness, to be worked over by schemes that we construct in the interest of prediction and control. We recognize that our concepts and reasoning powers have no ultimate fitness for the world as it is, and are not at home in the universe in a way that transcends our needs. Their status is instrumental, as we use them to get what we want.

The world that has become metaphysically thinned out in relation to the absoluteness of God can no longer provide a basis for thought and action. The self must discover a new ground within itself, must find its principal metaphysical and ethical determinations to be produced out of itself, as it projects determinacy upon the austerely given world. It must discover a foundation for thought in its own internal states, in an immanence that remains reliably its own no matter how affairs might be arranged in the world. One might ask why the absolute power and freedom of God will not have its effects all the way in to the deepest interiority of humans, so that even what goes on in that interior no longer gives us a secure stance for opposing the radically contingent world. But the late medieval and early modern response (I am over-generalizing) is to claim that God, whatever his power, will not erode the autonomy and determinacy of our inner acts of willing, since freedom of the will is the fundamental characteristic he has given to us as humans. In addition, man's freedom in that internal world is necessary to avoid finding God guilty of error when we make poor choices, since he will be charged with having designed our mental apparatus badly. Error arises

from the use of our free will in making judgments that go beyond what
the evidence presents, and God is not wrong to give us that freedom,
since it is our highest glory, even if we should misuse it. So a certain
internal space remains truly our own, and we can rely on our knowing
apparatus if we are careful about reducing our claims to what we can
have immediate evidence for, and to what we can construct out of that
through careful method. Our constructions must be carefully performed
because our concepts are not properly fit for the world as it is and their
only validity lies in those constructible links to immediate experience.

So a rich constellation emerges joining together the following themes:
modern self-consciousness; the metaphysically thinned-out world; the
emphasis on human construction, on what we can make of things through
our labor; a refusal to let what we construct through our schemes be
taken to reflect the metaphysical character of the world; the emphasis on
foundations in sense experience and on careful methods of construction;
the grounding in human subjectivity and in the determinations it can
produce out of its own resources. Sometimes in the working out of that
constellation, there will be clear reference to the theological determination
of real essences or noumena against which our human constructions
must be contrasted. At other times the relation of the metaphysically
indeterminate world to God is erased and there is a collapsing of the real
into what subjectivity can produce and secure. But the subjective side
then retains the character it had in the earlier structure.

That constellation is a powerful one and it is tempting to see it
still ordering the field in many contemporary debates about realism
and antirealism generally, about realism in ethics, about the basis for
what words mean and refer to, and about realism and instrumentalism
regarding unobservable entities. We may ask, then, about the degree to
which that large framework of ideas still reflects its situation of origin, its
role as a reaction formation against the radical contingency of the world,
and the radical insecurity of the self, that had been constituted in
relation to the absoluteness of divine power.

Perhaps we might see matters in the following way. The constellation
of ideas we are considering still displays the working through of Christian
theological and religious notions in the history of thought. It gets a good
deal of its energy and persuasiveness from the relation between the
process that shaped modern self-consciousness and the kind of world
formed by theological absolutism. The conditions of the formation of the
modern self were bound to favor antirealist and constructivist accounts
that turned on the capacity of subjectivity to generate determinacy out of
its own resources. But now, this story will go on, we are coming to the
end of what may properly be termed the religious era of philosophy.
(Williams says that with the passing of the Christian era we are now
closer to the Greeks in ethics than Western culture has been since the

triumph of Christianity.[2]) We are gradually giving up even the more secularized versions of the structures formed in accordance with, or in reaction to, the Christianized philosophical picture. And without the stripping away of the world's own character that was required by the freedom of God, there is no longer the thinned-out world, the almost indeterminate substrate, that was the occasion for the stance of self-assertion, and for the constellation of ideas that went along with it. So now we are free to discover a richer and more solid world that is the scene for our thinking and willing, even if we do not wish to restore the same metaphysical depth that many premodern philosophers had found in reality. Our conceptual networks and our moral values will not be imposed on a featureless substrate but will be due to a very considerable extent to our sensitivity to the real contours of the world. (It is compatible with that claim that much might still be up to us.)

A key to the change will be that subjectivity no longer has the same radical anxiety and radical responsibility from facing an emptied-out world that offers no support for the self's activity. As the world itself is allowed to be richer in its determinations, there is less pressure on subjectivity to produce all determinacy out of itself. The character of what is out there in the world can play a role in fixing what we mean and refer to so that our own labor does not have to do all the work of setting the conditions for our engagement with reality. That was a lesson we learned in considering the topic of externalism regarding mental content in Chapter 2, but the lesson applies across a wide range of cases. Two scientists can speak about the same thing even when their beliefs and semantic constructions relative to it are different, because of the presence in the causal environment of the same object that contributes to determining what their beliefs are about. And (another case) since we interpret a network of concepts by seeing how the conceptual discriminations are fit for the surrounding world, we have little incentive for supposing that there could be genuinely alternative conceptual schemes. The role of the world itself in fixing the content of those schemes eliminates the possibility of radical difference. To give up the architecture of the late medieval and early modern period is to reject the idea of an indeterminate given that is then worked over and structured by our schemes of thought. We do not have to do all the work anymore if we let the world take up its proper share of the burden.

For the way of looking at matters now under consideration, the world's entry into our belief system does not stop with an austerely described sensory given upon which we then build fictional constructions for instrumental purposes. That belief system instead reflects a holistic sen-

---

[2] Bernard Williams, *Ethics and the Limits of Philosophy* (Cambridge, Mass.: Harvard University Press, 1985), p. 198.

sitivity to the world, so we may have good reasons for commitments to unobservable entities. The contract at the basis of self-assertion was that we would give up trying to understand the world in its possible metaphysical depth and would gain greater power to alter and control its appearances. But that contract is no longer in effect, since the pressure of theological absolutism is gone, and there is no longer the sense of trespassing on forbidden territory if we take a wider range of our thought determinations to have a real basis in the way that the world articulates itself. It will not follow that we shall take all aspects of our conceptual machinery to have such a basis. But there will not be the same pressure as before to describe the world's character in the thinnest manner possible.

Once the self no longer has the task of founding epistemic and moral systems on its own internal states and activities (it had that task only in the context of the late medieval thinning out of the world relative to God), then there will be far less appeal in foundational epistemologies based on our sensory experience. Certainly we shall not make a fetish about drawing a strict line in our metaphysical commitments between what our sensory apparatus has access to and what it does not. That apparatus is, after all, a quite accidental feature of evolution on this planet. Our intelligence is active and flexible enough to allow us to recognize the limits of our sensory abilities; to be sensitive to features of the world those abilities were not designed to capture; to produce technological developments that improve those abilities well beyond what evolution designed into us; and to use abstract systems of thought and our own imaginations to understand what matters might be like for which we have very little in the way of direct sensory information, even if we must rely ultimately on observations in justifying our beliefs. The stance of self-assertion that we described made it important to mark off a properly human sphere for our activity and so gave a privileged status to the sort of sensory mechanisms that we have. But suppose that a richer world is restored as the focus of our engagement, rather than a substitute world constructed in the interests of prediction and control in a universe where our concepts can never be truly at home. Then we shall try to establish an account limited as little as possible by the happenstances of how evolution designed the human access to the world. In that context the evidence and arguments used in defending judgments about unobservable entities will be on a continuum with those used in defending claims about observable entities, and it will also be true that 'reality,' as we use it, can reach out toward being about features that our own conceptual apparatus may never be adequate to understand.

Richard Boyd talks about a number of changes in recent philosophy of science that he says encourage a conception of what he calls "the primacy of reality" (what I would in my account attribute to the restoration of the world that is possible once we give up the constellation of ideas that emerged in response to theological absolutism).[3] He says that the ways we change our instruments of detection and measurement in response to what our theories say will be good ways to change them show that we are allowing the world itself, as those theories present it as being, to guide our practice. We thus take our own theories in a realist rather than instrumentalist manner. Boyd speaks in favor of theories of reference, meaning, and knowledge that allow the world to play a role, in an a posteriori manner, in contrast to constructivist and conventionalist accounts that find certain features to be determined in advance by what subjects, through their labor, take them to be. (Reference to natural kinds, for example, can be determined in part by what natural kind is out there to be talked about, and not just by the information possessed by the speakers.) At the same time he argues against verificationist accounts that would shrink reality to fit what thinkers are able to make of it. If my reading is correct, then the "new realism" that Boyd is endorsing in the philosophy of science is a sign of the weakening of the "Christian" architecture of a thinned-out world requiring the projection of determinacy from the side of the subject.

Many antirealists will want to resist the historical narrative I have put forward here, and I should perhaps be clearer about its status. Understanding the long-term causation of ideas in history is difficult, and I have not looked in any detail at what the causal routes of transmission might have been. I wanted to emphasize a persistence over many centuries of certain patterns of thought, and to call attention to a number of parallels that would encourage the reader to acknowledge that persistence. Habits of making some connections rather than other ones, and of setting questions in some contexts rather than other ones, build up in a cultural system and can become self-replicating. Now in explaining the persistence of some such habits, we may find ourselves placing the burden of explanation either on the subject matter itself or on the inertia of patterns of thinking in the culture. Take, for example, the antirealist picture that I have tried to associate with the space of human self-assertion over against theological absolutism. One might take that picture's appeal to some philosophers today to be due principally to the metaphysical problem itself, and to the sensitivity of certain thinkers to where arguments concerning that problem will lead us. Or one might attribute its appeal more to the way present habits of doing philosophy may be written over an earlier space of thought carved out for a different purpose, but still acting as a scaffolding that makes us

[3] Richard Boyd, "How To Be a Moral Realist," in *Essays on Moral Realism*, Geoffrey Sayre-McCord, ed. (Ithaca, N.Y.: Cornell University Press, 1988), pp. 188–99.

readier to find some accounts preferable to others, as they seem to click into place more naturally.

I have been encouraging a greater openness to accepting the latter sort of story. The model of a (to us) thin world upon which the self-assertive mind makes its projections made more sense in its earlier incarnation than it does today. It was useful then to support the new science against Aristotelianism and to mark out a space over which individuals could take responsibility for their beliefs. But there are no longer those propaganda advantages and indeed the models of early modern philosophy actually make science incomprehensible as a genuinely public and communal enterprise. The religious and theological structures that we have examined lead, through their cultural self-replication, to different strains of antirealism. On the one hand, the structure of self-assertion favors accounts of a construction or projection by mind upon a world that we must consider as in itself indeterminate. On the other hand, the European tradition keeps alive the model of a divine activity that relates to itself in any relating to what is other. So we are not at all surprised when we see, in literary criticism that comes out of that tradition, claims that in literature Language is relating to itself, in such a way that the world and even texts themselves seem virtually to disappear. Different kinds of training keep persistent the rather different patterns of thought, but the general tendency of the religious and theological models of subjectivity is antirealist. At least that is what I believe is the case, though I confess I have not done the sort of work on historical causation that would be needed to persuade someone skeptical about that claim.

I should acknowledge here, and give consideration to, another source of a thinning out of the world. It is the tendency to define what is really there in terms of what could be accepted by any believer of sufficient intelligence, once the features peculiar to his subjectivity have been factored out. In other words we define reality by what we arrive at as we move toward a stance of greater objectivity. But should we restrict our designation 'real world' to features that remain in such a picture and call all other features subjective? Suppose that the following is a correct account of the articulation of the mental realm into units and sorts. (I am not arguing for a psychological position here, merely trying to specify a certain kind of explanation.) There are very complex interactions among physical states in the brain and nervous system, and these are causally productive of behaviors that are also of great complexity. We need to pick out patterns in the behavior of others and to make them more predictable; the assignment of mental states is part of that enterprise. But there are, let us suppose, very many patterns that might be picked out. Just as numerologists can find a virtually unlimited total of number patterns in the Bible, so too, let us say, a superintelligent onlooker would have the problem of finding too many, rather than not enough, patterns in human behavior.

We are, to our good fortune, not in the position of that onlooker. Part of being human is that we have brains engineered by evolution to be sensitive to some patterns and to filter out others; the inertia of human culture, through what is stored in cultural knowledge, has supplemented that engineering. We have propensities to find some patterns relevant and others not, and specific interests that pattern recognition must serve. There are also considerations of complexity of information processing, memory capacity, and so forth, that affect what we might call the level of resolution at which we are picking out relevant configurations. At different heights above the city of New York, different configurations will appear among its features; there is a trade-off between how much detail we get and the degree to which global structures are allowed to emerge. So too in picking out mental states, it will be said. A rough articulation into kinds may have the advantage of efficiency, given our limited abilities, and may make certain important patterned relations (say, between certain beliefs and certain desires) come out very clearly. Choosing a less global level of resolution may help us specify detailed differences better. Let us suppose that evolution, again, has done much of the work of choosing the level of resolution at which we shall find behavior patterns significant, for the purpose of attributing mental states.

Now if that story is true (I am not claiming that it is), are the mental states we talk about there in reality, or do we project an articulating scheme upon what we experience? Well, the patterns we thus pick out are indeed there in the world to be perceived. But they emerge as patterns (from all the other possible ones) only for those who share, at least roughly, our propensities favoring some of them over others. One unexpected outcome of that picture is that as we move to a neutral and universal stance, one that can be shared by all subjects, we experience a loss rather than an increase in one kind of understanding of reality. Only from a stance internal to the practice, a stance taken by one who shared the habits and propensities of the participants, would there be a determinate way of picking out the right configurations from the range of those that are really there. There are, then, real features of the world that we do not have access to from a more universal stance. (That story about mental states was a speculative one, but I wanted to question our habit of supposing that only that can be real which can be accepted by any possible subject of sufficient intelligence. For that habit provides an important motivation for thinning out the world.)

That discussion suggests that we may want to strike a balance in our accounts between what the world contributes and what we do, between discovery and invention, between what the world determines us to believe and what we take it to be. I shall now be turning to two recent accounts that attempt to strike such a balance. Then I shall consider, and try to defeat, a range of arguments that would encourage the world's contraction for epistemic or semantic reasons.

Parochial Realism and Wiggins

A metaphysician might find aspects of both Kant's philosophy and
Aristotle's appealing. He might wish to acknowledge the Kantian turn to
subjectivity by showing how the way we set ourselves in relation to the
world as thinkers helps determine the sort of world we can have. But he
might want to do this in a way that allowed for a solid Aristotelian world
to whose own self-articulating our thought must accommodate itself; and
so he would acknowledge the realist turn in recent philosophy, and the
richer status the world gets as a result of that turn. The problem
will be to find a way of stopping the momentum that seems to move
any account, once it has acknowledged some degree of subjective determination of the real, from pressing toward an ever more radical antirealism for which the world virtually disappears as something that could
genuinely regulate our beliefs. Let us say that someone might be a
parochial realist regarding a certain feature. The realism of the position
consists in the claim that regarding the feature in question we are
dealing with a tracking of some real aspect of the universe. Yet the
position is a parochial one in making the further claim that a certain
sensibility not shared by all thinkers or experiencers, or a particular way
of engaging the world, is a condition for letting that feature emerge as
determinate.

David Wiggins, in presenting a version of this sort of realism (he calls
it "conceptual realism"), uses the metaphor of a "lighting up."[4] Our
interests and values and propensities light up the world in a particular
fashion and so make certain features of the world emerge rather than
others. He gives us another metaphor as well: "The size and mesh of a
net determine not what fish are in the sea but which ones we shall
catch."[5] And he says that we construct objects "no more than the
focusing of a camera fixed in a certain spot creates that which it records
when set at that focus."[6] These metaphors are intended to underscore
the realist aspect of his position. But Wiggins also says that "there are
no 'lines' in nature," that an object "does not simply individuate itself
or, in and of itself, differentiate itself from other things," that we impose
the lines or boundaries on nature "in ways that are determined for us by
our constitution and ecology, by the scale appropriate to our physical
size in relation to the rest of the world, and by our intellectual and
practical concerns," and that "individuation is the mind's work."[7]

---

[4] "But the object is there anyway, even if it took a particular sort of empirically and
logically constrained looking to light it up there." David Wiggins, "On Singling Out an
Object Determinately," in *Subject, Thought, and Context*, Philip Pettit and John McDowell,
eds. (Oxford: Clarendon Press, 1986), p. 180.
[5] Ibid., p. 171.
[6] Ibid., p. 180.
[7] Ibid., p. 170; ibid.; ibid.; ibid., p. 179.

It is not clear how we are to bring these two groups of sayings together into a single conception. The references to focusing, lighting up, and the fishnet suggest a world where the lines are already clearly drawn, and we just determine which objects we let appear. But then it is difficult to see how is it the case that there are no lines in nature itself. Fish out there beyond our nets (to look at the literal side of the metaphor) surely are to a considerable extent self-maintaining and self-differentiating. They maintain their boundaries against the world, take in nutrients and transform them into their own sort of stuff, and struggle against other organisms to reproduce their own kind. Does it make sense to say, then, that they do not differentiate themselves from other things and that individuation is simply the work of the mind? Even if individuation is to some degree left up to us (that is surely the case in many areas), that is a very different claim from the position that there are no lines in nature.

Wiggins has already argued that there are no bare individuals. To be an individual is to fall under some sortal concept that specifies the conditions for remaining the same individual.[8] 'Being human' is such a concept for Caesar. Since it specifies what makes him the individual he is, with the boundaries he has, then he could not lose the property of being human and still remain the same individual. Being human is then a necessary property for Caesar, not because of some mysterious essence he possesses but because without it he could no longer be singled out as the very individual he is; he would stop being Caesar. Now the question is: Where do we get these sortal concepts, the ones that are essential for individuation? Do we just discover them by learning more about the world or do they depend on us? Wiggins says that individuation is our work, based on our interests and circumstances and capabilities, so that the individuative scheme we bring to bear upon the world is in some sense a matter of invention. But once the features of our interest in the world have focused our attention upon it in a certain manner, then it is a matter of *discovery* what individuals we find there; we have no further freedom in our articulation of reality.

We may ask whether Wiggins has thus arrived at a way of bringing his realist and antirealist intuitions into a satisfying harmony. While we should perhaps not put too much pressure on the metaphors, still his image of the fishnet creates problems depending on whether we stress its Kantian or its Aristotelian aspect. The Kantian side makes us think of ourselves as making the fishnet, and so as setting the standards, through the size of the mesh, that anything must meet if it is to count as really present. The Aristotelian side makes us focus upon the fish in the sea that are what they are, and are individuated as such, independently of

---

[8] See Wiggins, *Sameness and Substance* (Cambridge, Mass.: Harvard University Press, 1980), pp. 47–126.

what net gets dropped into the ocean (or of what kind of lighting up is employed or of what direction of focus we choose in thus lighting up an area). We might then, because of the mesh we have chosen or been given, have no contact with features crucial to our understanding of how things really are. Either we have a filter that cuts us off from reality as much as it helps to capture it, or we have a cutting up of the world in a way that Carnap, for one, would easily find acceptable. Yet it seems clear that Wiggins wants to avoid both of those disjuncts.

He is unlike Rorty in refusing to let the world's position in the Davidsonian triangulation disappear. It remains the verdict-giver after we have made our sentences say what they do, and so have determined what such a verdict-giving can mean. But the antircalist aspect of Wiggins's position threatens to undermine the world, to make its character too thin. For it is not clear how it places much constraint on what we in our inventiveness might bring to it in the way of indi-viduative schemes. We seem to have appearing here a successor to the problem of the substratum. There is a world fertile with the potential for exhibiting articulations, but these can come forward as such only for particular subjective mechanisms that light the world up in various ways. How many of these various ways of lighting up will be available? If many options are possible, then the world will come to seem more abstract and indeterminate, and the articulations will be seen to depend more on the character of the subjective mechanisms and their lighting-up capacities. If the world is so promiscuous in the candidates it presents to be lit up that almost any way of lighting up the world will bring forward *some* acceptable boundaries for individuals and sorts, then it is in a weak and empty way that the world is self-articulating. There will then be an understandable temptation to count the features lit up as merely subjective, as owing their status to the way that our scheme has "cut up" a much thinner world.

One source of the difficulty is Wiggins's willingness to divide up the contributions of the subject and those of the world in what is perhaps an oversimple fashion. He seems to describe a two-step process by which our engagement with the world is supposed to occur.[9] In the first one, we have considerable freedom to fashion concepts, and to fix upon a set of concerns and interests, and that activity enables our sentences to set themselves a goal. But then our freedom is exhausted. Once our conceptual activity has made us arrive at a certain place, as it were, the world then determines what is found there and what satisfies a given concept.[10]

[9] See Wiggins, *Sameness and Substance*, p. 142; also Wiggins, "On Singling Out an Object Determinately." p. 180.
[10] Wiggins, *Sameness and Substance*, p. 142.

That may be a harmless way of putting the matter, but it runs very close to ways of putting it that are not so harmless. It may at least appear to deny a more intimate connection in both directions. We do not want the world to be just a potential and indeterminate measure of truth that comes into play once our activity of individuation has marked off lines in it. A realism robust enough to deserve the name should specify more of a back-and-forth process through which our way of articulating the world accommodates itself to the world's way of doing things. Reality must be to an important extent self-articulating so that even if it offers more than one option as to how we might raise some of its articulations to metaphysical prominence, depending on our interests, still it must impose a significant discipline on our work of individuation. There must be a world guidance that does not become effective only after we have set forth our individuating schemes upon reality, but that helps to shape what ways of individuating and sorting will let the world display what it is like. If we are to be realists about natural kinds, for example, then we do not want the delineation into kinds to be like cutting up reality into units of measure, into pounds or kilograms, for example. That sort of case does not leave enough work for the world's regulation of our schemes themselves, and I do not see that Wiggins has a developed account of that in which such regulation would consist.

His two-step process seems to face difficulties concerning the other step as well. It is not true that once we have fashioned our sentences, the world then has the power to confer truth or falsity on them without any further contribution of our practice. For just what the sentence means depends on how a practice of saying the same thing goes on to new cases of application. Our taking it to mean what it does remains necessary to that continuing, and is exhibited in what we take to be evidence for its justification. So while we may properly say that it is the world that renders the verdict on whether the sentence has attained success, still what we *take* to be a verdict in our ongoing practice seems to contribute to determining precisely what sentence is there upon which a verdict can be rendered.

Putnam's Internal Realism

Hilary Putnam's internal realism is the best known of the group of positions I have been calling parochial realisms, but we have to be careful in specifying what sense to give to the 'internal' in that designation. Putnam himself talks of objects being internal to a scheme and of schemes cutting up the world into objects:

'Objects' do not exist independently of conceptual schemes. *We* cut up the world into objects when we introduce one or another scheme of description. Since the objects *and* the signs are alike *internal* to the scheme of description, it is possible to say what matches what.[11]

A very natural way of reading that passage is to see Putnam as a modern or Kantian thinker. We know what we have made, what we have mixed our labor with, and our referential powers will range as far as our capacity to construct. On that reading, Putnam retains the essential aspects of the space of thought that, as I have claimed, we have inherited from late medieval and early modern philosophy. The human speaker is able to refer successfully to the world because it is a constructed world given its forms by our own conceptual activity. Putnam speaks about a "human kind of realism," about rationality for us, about "what is rightly assertible for us, as opposed to what is rightly assertible from the God's eye view. . . ."[12] Science, says Putnam, does not aim at a "description of metaphysically ultimate fact," but its strategy has been to "confine" itself to claims with a clear empirical significance.[13] And he says that he is "not inclined to scoff at the idea of a noumenal ground behind the dualities of experience," and that "because one cannot talk about the transcendent or even deny its existence without paradox, one's attitude to it must, perhaps, be the concern of religion rather than of rational philosophy."[14] Even when he says firmly that his position excludes the notion of noumena or of a God's-eye point of view, he may resemble the atheist who in giving up a belief in God still orders his conceptual field in terms of the oppositions set up by religion and theology. As he denies any commitment to noumena Putnam seems to retain the other half of the Kantian opposition as if it could remain unaffected by the removal of its partner from the field. There is still the "human," constructed world whose objects are "internal" to a conceptual scheme. That use of 'internal' seems the residuum of the earlier model for which the constructions could indeed take place internally to the mind. But just where would the objects be located that are internal to a *scheme*?

That reading of Putnam, however, ignores a different direction of thought in his writings. He seems in various places in his work to be struggling to free himself from the habits of thought shaped by late medieval and early modern philosophy. One of those habits, we saw, led to the picture of a minimally determinate world upon which the speaker projects a richer set of characteristics. Putnam strongly rejects that picture. He says that we have to give up the set of oppositions that leads

---

[11] Putnam, *Reason, Truth, and History* (Cambridge: Cambridge University Press, 1981), p. 52.

[12] Putnam, *Realism and Reason*, Philosophical Papers, Vol. 3 (Cambridge: Cambridge University Press, 1983), p. xviii.

[13] Ibid., pp. 227–8.

[14] Ibid., p. 226.

to it: between objective and subjective, between what is really there and what we project upon it, between properties that objects have intrinsically and properties that they have due to the way that we take them to be.[15] And in giving up those oppositions, he claims, we also reject invidious distinctions between first-class conceptual systems (the ones that capture how things really are) and second-class ones that may be useful but that are not registering the world as it is.[16] There will not, then, be the modern thinning out of the world. A discourse that does not have the precision of the natural sciences, and that may not offer much hope for universal agreement regarding the judgments peculiar to it, may still count as exhibiting a sensitivity to what is really the case. So ethics, for one example, may make valid use of a notion of moral objectivity. Putnam says that if we find that we *must* use a certain conceptual system, then "we must not simultaneously advance the claim that it is not really 'the way things are in themselves.' "[17]

Perhaps matters will be clearer if we consider one of the principal examples Putnam offers in support of his position. He describes a minimal world and asks how many objects we should say it contains.[18] The answer, he says, will be different depending on whether we are using 'object' as Carnap did or in the manner of the Polish logicians. (The latter hold that for every two particulars there is an object that is their sum.) The same world might be said to have three objects in it (for Carnap) or seven (for the Polish logicians). There is no right answer here, says Putnam, so the individuation of the world is internal to a scheme. But there should be little surprise here for anyone, internal realist or not, in that result. Imagine a group a member of which may sometimes count as exercising the vote of a given constituency as well as his own. An individual may be allotted a vote for himself and, because of his title, may have another vote that represents, say, the members of the town fire department. One person, seeing a meeting of this group, reports that there are seventeen voters present, meaning distinct individuals who are voting, while another reports that there are twenty-seven voters, indicating the total number of votes to be cast. Surely there is no problem here of interpretation and no problem at all that will concern the metaphysician. We can count differently if our rules for counting are different; Carnap and the Polish logicians will understand one another easily to be talking about the same world. If accepting Putnam's internal realism involves no more than accepting such relativity as that, one can sign up for it without qualms.

Note that the voters themselves are not in any way *internal* to a scheme. There really are twenty-seven voters if we choose to count one

---

[15] Putnam, *The Many Faces of Realism* (LaSalle, Ill.: Open Court, 1987), pp. 26–32.
[16] Ibid., p. 37.   [17] Ibid., p. 70.   [18] Ibid., p. 32–6.

way and seventeen if we choose to count another. We do not need to describe a noumenal world whose description is neutral as between those two ways of counting and that generates different appearances to distinct conceptual schemes. To describe the situation as one in which there are twenty-seven voters is to describe it as it is in itself; likewise with a description of it as one in which there are seventeen voters. The difference is a semantic one that turns on what meaning our language is assigning to 'voter' in the particular situation. We can hardly be surprised that such semantic differences will allow for different equally correct answers. But then it is unclear in what sense objects are for Putnam *internal* to anything at all.

Putnam does claim, perhaps more controversially, that such conceptual relativity goes all the way down. Even our notions of 'object,' 'exist,' 'real,' 'thing,' 'individual,' and the like will be defined relative to some conceptual system that has been developed on the basis of our interests and propensities. There can be, then, no very thinly described substratum upon which other languages project their conceptual structures; there is no privileged language that captures such a minimal metaphysical determinacy. We must be already working within some conceptual system or other, with its way of using the basic metaphysical vocabulary, in order to talk about the world at all. Yet we may still count as talking about things as they are when we put such a conceptual system to use. Reality does not have a preference for a unique way of determining what an object is, over all the others; nor does it have a preference for a unique way of describing it, such as that of the natural sciences. (Perhaps we shall want to hold, for Davidsonian reasons, that these different ways of using 'object' and 'real' and so forth must already have very much in common in order that the differences themselves can be determinate.)

So Putnam does end up attacking, especially in *The Many Faces of Realism*, crucial aspects of the field of thought established by the modern philosophers in the context of the earlier theological absolutism. He resists the "energy system" that requires a thinning out and a contracting of the world as we try to separate out the contribution of subjectivity. Yet even in that recent work he still makes claims such as the following:

If Kant was saying that truth must not be thought of as correspondence to a pre-structured or self-structured Reality; if he was saying that our conceptual contribution cannot be factored out and that the 'makers-true' and the 'makers-verified' of our beliefs lie *within* and not *outside* our conceptual system; then Kant may properly be called the first 'internal realist'.[19]

Again there is the odd usage that what makes our beliefs true lies inside the conceptual system. What he ought to be saying, given his own

[19] Ibid., p. 43.

more recent picture, is that objects, while they are not internal to a conceptual system, can emerge as determinate only when we put a particular set of concepts to work in talking about reality. But then there is a problem for someone who says, as we have just seen Putnam saying, that we cannot have a correspondence to a prestructured or a self-structured reality. Just what does he mean by that denial? What a modest realist wants to say, it seems, is that reality is to a very considerable degree self-structuring, but in most cases not to the degree that it imposes a unique scheme of individuation and sorting upon us. Animals are self-differentiating more than mountain chains are, but even with the latter, we are hardly free to impose boundaries anywhere we wish. Putnam's references to Kant suggest a world that must be considered as *undifferentiated* prior to our application of a scheme. But the world cannot be as indifferent as that to our various descriptions of it. It must, *on its own*, make some boundaries more salient than others, more appropriate to those who wish to describe it and explain its changes, even if it does not single out a unique way of marking off individuals and sorts. (I argued in Chapter 3 that our speech sounds and brain activity can be counted as meaningful only in the context of a world at least some of whose contours are such that they can be taken for granted for purposes of interpretation.)

We can see here a danger for any project of the sort attempted by Putnam. He wants to encourage a pluralism of vocabularies and to avoid the picture of a thin world upon which certain conceptual networks are merely projected. But he wants also to be a realist for whom there is a genuine world guidance of our beliefs. The danger is that after giving up a privileged sense of objectivity that science provided us with, he is left with any number of vocabularies all of which count as objective by their own standards. Then we have so weak a sense of world guidance that it will be hard to differentiate our position from that of Rorty with his cultural conversations and disappearing world. What has happened to Putnam the realist as his pluralism regarding different vocabularies has become more prominent?

He will claim, first of all, that once we have settled upon the conceptual system we are going to apply to the world, then there is a fact of the matter as to which of our statements or beliefs the world makes true. But realism seems to demand more than this in regard to regulation by the world. If just about any way of articulating the world into units and sorts will do the trick, then we are back with the undifferentiated substratum that does not seem to regulate our conceptual networks until we are ready to apply them. It is not as if any interest at all on our part will do if we are investigating what reality is like. The world and our ways of thinking about it evolve in tandem and it helps to select in us the kinds of interests, and the kind of subjective apparatus, that when brought to bear upon it, will make it exhibit what it is like. As we are engaged in the world on the basis of our interests and values and standards, we learn more about what interests and values and standards are worth having if we want the satisfaction of understanding how things really are. Putnam's schemes, in contrast, seem to spring full blown from the richness of subjectivity, and then to lay out for themselves conditions of objectivity.

Putnam may here reply as follows. That picture of an undifferentiated world that seems to offer very little constraint on the schemes we apply to it becomes a worry only if we are still trying to divide up matters into what the world contributes to our accounts and what we contribute. If we have that goal, then as we discover that we are unable to specify what the world is like apart from any contribution by subjectivity, we shall come to think of the world as, on its own, undifferentiated. But Putnam has rejected from the start the notion that we could divide up matters in that fashion. He might support that rejection by claiming that we could never succeed in *adding* together those two contributing factors as if they were independently definable, since their relationship is such that each side has the determinacy it does only when the other side is already taken into consideration. What I am taking the world to be has a definite content only insofar as it is already in relation to a particular world. And any description of what reality is like requires a particular way of lighting up the world, of making some of its contours more prominent than others. We can often, Putnam assures us, distinguish between accounts that allow more or less of a role for the working of subjectivity. In making such distinctions of degree, we must evidently bring to bear at least a rough, holistic sense of what it is for beliefs to be world-guided. But the plan of a separating out of subjective from objective factors is a hopeless one. We shall not, then, be able to give an account of world guidance by first specifying what the world is like apart from subjectivity and by then seeing how *that* world guides the development of the concepts that apply to it.

Let us grant the soundness of that argument. Still, one cannot rest one's case with the bare claim that it is useless to try to distinguish what is projected from what is really there. For we often make that distinction successfully in discourse. Some of our beliefs about gender and race are merely projections of arrangements in the social order and are not a registering of what is really the case. Very many of the beliefs of astrologers involve a projection onto nature of patterns that have no basis in the way it is. Putnam does not wish to draw the relevant boundary such that the natural sciences fall on one side of the line and everything else on the other. Still, he must draw the boundary *somewhere*, however rich he allows our conception of reality to be. If our realism is to have any force to it, then it is insufficient to say, as Putnam does, that once a particular conceptual system has constituted its own objects, then its rules determine what counts as a sentence's being true. There must be a regulation of those conceptual systems themselves by the world, as, over time, they have to accommodate their articulations to *its* way of doing things. Reality itself "educates" our sensibility toward it so that we come to recognize, for example, that an interest in the mechanical operations of very tiny particles will let us understand nature's articulations better than an interest in the magical control of substances. I would even argue (and do indeed argue in the next chapter) that there is some such education by the world in the development of our moral sensibility, as we come to understand that some things have an intrinsic worth independently of our habits of finding them valuable. On the other hand, there is no similar education by the world in the meanings we assign to certain patterns of figures on a chess board. Can Putnam's position distinguish adequately between patterns that are world-guided and those that are mere projections, once he has brought that basic distinction into question?

Putnam certainly has room in his account for such a notion of a gradual adjustment to reality. He defines truth by appealing to the notion of *idealized* rational acceptability,[20] and he says as well that the notion of a rational belief-forming process requires the submitting of beliefs to communal practices of criticism, practices that, as we may suppose, go on into the future and join us with future communities. So he can make sense of the notion of a progress toward greater objectivity, even if he holds that there can be no unique end point of inquiry, since even there interests would play some role in determining what counts as a good reason for belief, and how we are to use such concepts as 'object' and 'real.' But while Putnam can thus make sense of a movement toward greater objectivity as putting pressure on our conceptual systems, so that they must adjust themselves to how reality is arranged, he says very little about what such an accommodation might be. What we need is an account that shows why as we move toward a more objective stance, we may continue endorsing some of our more local ways of seeing while we have to abandon others. As we come to have a better understanding of those boundaries and classifications that the world makes more salient than others, we see that some of our ways of talking develop through a sensitivity to how matters really stand. We shall follow Putnam and refuse to assume that what is truly objective is what can be endorsed by any rational believer at all; beliefs may be objective and world-guided even when the interests that activate them are to some degree local. But we need a better understanding of how the world constrains and regulates our conceptual schemes themselves, instead of just providing

[20] Putnam, *Reason, Truth, and History*, p. 55.

answers once such a scheme has appeared on the scene with its own rules for constructing objects. And I do not see that Putnam gives us much to advance that sort of understanding, though his work is not without hints as to how we might begin to look at the issue.

The problem for Putnam is to find, once he has begun his recoil from a strongly realist position, a stopping point that prevents his momentum from taking him to positions more relativist than he finds attractive. But then very much will depend on how rich a notion of objectivity he wants to build into his reference to an idealizing of "our" practices. Let us grant him that we cannot make much sense of what it would be to measure our practices against what is available from a God's-eye point of view. To be a believer at all is to occupy some particular stance, to find some patterns rather than others as significant. And some ways of being engaged with the world might be so different from ours that we could not properly think of them as relevant to the doing well or badly of what *we* do. Instead of the comparison to God's-eye account, we need a notion of what it is gradually to extend our practices, and to extend the 'we' whose abilities count as relevant to the success or failure of those practices, so that we have a robust notion of objectivity and world guidance.

On this issue Putnam is quite vague. He says that our beliefs must match up with evidence as that evidence is represented within our conceptual systems. But he thereby seems to freeze into place, even with his mention of idealization, a conceptual framework that may be bound up with a limited and inadequate way of looking at the world. The pressure of the world on beliefs will be exhausted by what that framework takes that pressure to be, through the way it structures the evidence that is available. But the pressure of the world ought to be such, for a realist, that it forces us to bring about changes in that framework. (Along with Davidson, we do not wish to reify such a thing as a conceptual scheme.) An accommodation to that pressure will not require that we make sense of a naked confrontation with the world, but will demand instead the recognition that the *same* world may appear both to us and to others more advanced, so that what these others take that world to be can be a measure for the meaning of our utterances and the truth of our beliefs. Sometimes Putnam suggests that the relevant 'we' is a narrow one, marked off by cultural interests that may be rather parochial. At other times he talks of a "human" sort of realism, of an objectivity relevant to us as human. But it is unclear why we should put our epistemic seal of approval on our human abilities, so that the scientific knowledge of nonhumans much superior to us will not count as significant for the success of "our" practices, as an extension of the projects in which *we* are engaged. It is on just this issue of the extension of the 'we' that Putnam must be clear if we are to make sense of his internal realism, and to decide just how realist a position it is. But I do not see that he offers us that needed clarity. (I develop that issue in the next section, independently of Putnam's work.)

There is a way in which Putnam's stance is, and ought to be, an internal one. We can understand that way if we look at a treatment Putnam offers on the topic of reference.[21] He first suggests that we may not know what objects others are talking about, and may not even know what we ourselves are talking about, and says that his result is more radical than Quine's account of the inscrutability of reference. He uses model theory and certain transformations familiar from mathematics to show that two interpreters might assign to our speech very different interpretations, or models, with each interpretation accounting perfectly well for our speech behavior, and especially for our attitudes of holding sentences to be true or false. One model takes our word 'cat' to refer to cats, and the other takes it to refer in many cases to cherries. (The story is obviously very complicated. My interest here is not in whether model theory is properly employed in that argument but in Putnam's response to it, so I ask the reader to take for granted that the possibility Putnam describes is a genuine one. We are not going to do the logic here.) So it appears there is no fact of the matter as to whether we are really referring to cats or to cherries when we use 'cat,' since there seems to be no basis for choosing one interpreter's assignment of a model to our language over another's, if both capture our attitudes toward our sentences equally well. But then I cannot be sure what my words are referring to.

But that difficulty arises, says Putnam, only for a strong realist (Putnam's "metaphysical realist") who has a wrong notion of how reference works, and of how we identify the model that tells us how our words hook up to the world. Such a realist assumes there is a stance from which we can inspect, from above as it were, a set of expressions and a set of things, not yet linguistically identified, while we examine various ways of tying the members of one set to the members of the other. From this stance, reference must appear as indeterminate, for there are too many ways to draw the linkages while still accounting for the speaker's behavior.

However, there is no such stance, Putnam asserts, for we can only identify *from within* the things that our words refer to. The only grasp we have at all on things is by taking the referring powers of our own language for granted while we use it. (It is not that some interpretation then has to be added from the outside to give my words a grasp on

---

[21] I am considering here an argument in Putnam, *Reason, Truth, and History*, pp. 32–8, and the kind of solution Putnam offers to the problem raised by that argument, in *Realism and Reason*, pp. 1–25, esp. 21–5.

reality.[22]) Thus I have no stance from which I might independently identify things in the words and then ask which of my words refer to them, and no stance from which I might put my finger on possible lines of reference between my words and those worldly objects. The way I pick out the referent of 'cat' is just by using the word itself, so that it is a necessary truth that 'cat' refers to cats and not to cherries. It is no mystery, says Putnam, which model adequately captures the reference of my expressions. For models themselves are not "lost noumenal waifs" that need to be identified from a stance external to any particular practice of using language.[23] They have their names from birth, says Putnam. In other words, I can automatically identify the model that captures the reference of my speech as the one in which 'cat' refers to cats, 'dog' to dogs, 'cherry' to cherries, and so forth. The condition for identifying the appropriate model is that I identify it that way.

Putnam's "internal" position here is another way of saying that language-to-world relations do not have the metaphysical depth that some have taken them to have. When we take them to have that depth, we expand the envelope, as it were, beyond what ordinary practices of usage and interpretation can give us, and then we look for something to fill the gap, or note that there are lots of ways of filling it. Reference would not, then, be like a natural kind that has its determinacy independently enough of how we take it to be that we might be very wrong about it. We do not have to keep reconciling our accounts to the world as we "discover" that 'cat' refers to cats and not to cherries. We know what our words refer to in the fairly trivial sense we saw earlier in Davidson.

How Well Do Our Concepts and Practices Travel?

One way in which our practices might be considered local rather than universal ones will likely be a threat to a realist position. Let me introduce this issue by considering how a parochial realist might respond to a claim that she has a relativist attitude toward truth. It is not the case, she may say in denying that claim, that the same sentence gets a value of true relative to one way of seeing and of false relative to another. The explanation is that sentences, like some wines, do not travel well, so that they are not available to be uttered by those whose form of life is very different from our own. So if a sentence is true from our perspective, it is true *simpliciter*. As one moves toward a rather different stance, or toward a universal one, one leaves behind (so the argument will go) the set of values, interests, and propensities that were necessary to give a determinate shape to what one was about. Utterances

---

[22] Putnam, *Realism and Reason*, p. 24.   [23] Ibid., p. 25.

cannot be torn from their intimacy with our practices and recognitional abilities and then placed in radically different circumstances that we could not reach, such that they could, even in those circumstances, still be made true or false by them. For they would thereby lose the very conditions that give them a determinate content.

But now consider what happens when that sort of parochialism is applied to our rational and epistemic practices, to our ways of using 'true' and 'rational' and 'real.' Those expressions gain their meaning, it will be said, from the intricate patterns relating the sentences they appear in to other sentences and to evidence from the world. But then it is impossible that what the world really is like, or what is objectively the case, could be all that different from what we take it to be. For our taking it to be a certain way is what in part fixes what we mean by 'real' and 'true' and 'world.' Expressions with such terms will not be able to attach themselves to the world at all, or to other sentences, if they are removed from our everyday capacities of recognizing truth to obtain and are given ambitious metaphysical tasks, as in claims about what is really the case beyond all our capacities to recognize it to be so.[24]

One sign of this pattern of argument is a claim that "we would not *call* it *x* if it did not have such-and-such properties." We may ask, for example, whether others could have beliefs so different from ours that we could not even begin to translate them. But a parochialist might claim that if they were so different from us, then we would (properly) not call them believers at all. To have beliefs is to belong to a practice of forming and testing perceptual reports, of drawing inferences, of aiming for coherence, of adapting reasonably to recalcitrant information. If we cannot recognize the others as doing roughly those things, with roughly our logic, then they are not believers at all. This is not a verificationist point about our recognitional abilities. It is about the conditions for being a believer in the first place.

But if truth and rationality are relatively local phenomena, then it will be difficult to make sense of a notion of objective reality as a common realm toward which we and believers very different from us are directed. For the notion of belief, as intimately linked as it is to our notions of truth and rationality, becomes local as well, and then we do not have the sense of objectivity that derives from the thought of there being very different perspectives on a world that remains, for the different thinkers, the same. The realist, we said earlier, should resist the temptation to contract reality so that it fits the range of our investigative abilities. But

---

[24] This issue is nicely set out in Thomas Nagel, *The View form Nowhere* (New York: Oxford University Press, 1986), pp. 90–109. His own view is not at all sympathetic to these localist considerations that would set semantic or epistemological limits on what reality can be.

he should also resist the related sort of contraction whereby our actual abilities to produce concepts and to investigate are so honored that we can no longer make sense of transcending them to any great degree. If we cannot make sense of doing what we do but of doing it rather differently, and perhaps quite a lot better, then we lose our hold on a notion of objectivity rich enough to support the conception of the realist.

One way of accounting for that possible transcendence of our actual practices is to follow a suggestion made earlier in the chapter: that once we allow the world itself to play a role in fixing the content of our practices, it will no longer be the case that such content must be given to those practices just by what we understand them to be. The practice of referring to natural kinds, for example, may be given its sense in part by what is out there in the world to be known, even for speakers who have a rather poor understanding of the basis for those natural kinds. And that direction of thought may provide part of an answer in the case now under discussion. The world that we aim at through our epistemic practices helps to define what those practices are and what it would be for them to improve, in the sense that what counts as improvement will be what would help us come to understand that very world better. Yet that answer can only provide a limited part of the story. For the world's fixing of content does not simply happen to our practices from without, as if what they are did not have all that much to do with what we take them to be, through their relations to our other practices and to our own understanding of them. Engaging in rational investigation is at least partly like doing philosophy or being ethical. It is not that there is some natural kind *philosophy* whose character has a metaphysical depth determined by how the world is, apart from how our cultural practices develop. If a practice is different enough from what we do, then it just is not a doing of philosophy. Yet at the same time we recognize that future members of our culture may end up continuing our practice of doing philosophy in ways that we could not, for what we know now, very well conceive. The issue is how far the practice could get from what we recognize as such and still count as a doing of philosophy. The same issue will arise in the case of our rational practices, only here more is at stake. What it is to be a rational practice is at least in part constituted by what we do, and by what we take ourselves to be doing. Yet it is also important for the strong sense of objectivity needed by the realist that our network of concepts having to do with rationality, belief, truth, and reality be not too strongly limited in its application by what we are like, by the abilities that biological and cultural evolution happened to design into the human species.

In trying to come up with the right thing to say here, we might profit by actually looking at some of the arguments that would make our truth-telling and reason-giving practices a provincial phenomenon. Brian Ellis says that our concepts of truth and reality derive from our human epistemic perspective, which is based on our biology.[25] Truth is a matter of rightness of belief, which is defined in terms of the maximizing of epistemic value. (So science is more like ethics than we might assume.) The principal epistemic values are consistency, empirical certification, and corroboration; we should see how these values have their origin in a need for cooperative action. Therefore truth, and the notion of reality that accompanies it, has its home in the practices of humans whose biology has built certain values into them, especially the value of co-operating to get what they want; it is neither universal nor value-free.

Stephen Stich also looks at the issue of truth from within an investigation of human epistemic practices.[26] He accepts what he calls "cognitive pluralism": The biological and cultural evolution of practices of reasoning and methods of cognitive storage may lead to rather different such practices and methods in different thinkers. The only measure of these can be a pragmatic one; there are no intrinsic epistemic virtues.[27] Now it will appear to many that such a claim must be wrong, for being rational and generating truths are surely virtues in any epistemic apparatus worthy of the name.

But Stich argues against that claim by examining how we give content to a notion of truth or to one of rationality. Another cognitive system will count as rational only insofar as the employer of it can be seen as doing something mostly like what we do (forming beliefs mostly like ours, drawing inferences mostly in the way that we do, and so forth). We make sense of another through making use of a "principle of humanity" by which we interpret others so as to make them rational by our standards. Indeed the only way we can succeed in interpreting is to make others and their practices rough models of ourselves and of the ways in which we reason. But our ways of reasoning and our systems of cognitive storage are provincial; they show the constraining limits of our biological and cultural evolution. So the very meaning of 'rational,' as we employ that expression, will be local; it will apply to a very narrow range of practices that happened to evolve in us, or to practices recognizably like them. There might, then, be many other epistemic practices in the universe, including some that would be useful to us, that would be properly called "irrational." So rationality, given how parochial a feature it is, can hardly be a measure of the goodness of all cognitive practices.

There is a similar outcome with the notion of truth: "Neither being rational nor generating truth would turn out to be an intrinsically

---

[25] I am giving an extremely brief summary of a view that Ellis develops in detail in *Truth and Objectivity* (Oxford: Basil Blackwell, 1990).

[26] Stephen Stich, *The Fragmentation of Reason* (Cambridge, Mass.: MIT Press, 1990).

[27] Ibid., p. 24.

valuable feature for cognitive processes to have."[28] Truth is defined, in the typical theories that define it, in such a manner that beliefs or sentences can be true only if we can set them up in a theory that gives truth conditions through using our own language as a metalanguage. (Stich is following Davidson's line here.) So true beliefs must be translatable into our language. But again such translation can work only by finding in the other roughly our own logic and our rational practices. Since these have been shown to be local, the notion of truth dependent on them will be local as well. As with rationality, truth cannot then be a general epistemic virtue. Stich says that for many philosophers,

the fact that true beliefs must lie within the range of the interpretation function, the fact that the domain of the interpretation function is limited to systems of cognitive storage similar to our own, and the realization that the function is an idiosyncratic hodgepodge bequeathed to us by our cultural and/or biological heritage may well be reason enough to decide that they do not value true beliefs intrinsically.[29]

Note how Davidson and Stich use a similar argument to very different effect. Davidson agrees with Stich that a condition of interpretation is that the interpreter take the other to share, roughly, his rational practices, and to have a roughly similar set of beliefs. But he adds that this condition would apply to an omniscient interpreter as well, one that would have, by hypothesis, perfectly developed rational practices.[30] That omniscient interpreter would interpret us, and any believer, as being at least very roughly like it in rational practices and in beliefs. So our reason and logic are in the end not local phenomena. Stich, in contrast, says that those conditions of interpretation make rationality and truth so local as to be unimportant to epistemology. (Philosophical analysis of our notions of knowledge and justification will not do us much good either, since those notions themselves have emerged from such a parochial and limited evolution.) Davidson thinks it is good news that his analysis of interpretation shows that there are sharp limits to how irrational we could be; any interpreter would have to take us as generally rational. Stich thinks that if there are such limits on how irrational we could be, that is because rationality has been shown to mean so little to epistemology.

Note that we could go on to apply Stich's argument to other areas. We might say that if aliens we encountered were profoundly different from us in their social behavior, they would not have a different ethical system; they would have no ethical system at all. A practice must be

---

[28] Ibid., p. 21.
[29] Ibid., p. 120.
[30] Davidson, "A Coherence Theory of Truth and Knowledge," in *Truth and Interpretation*, Ernest LePore, ed. (Oxford: Basil Blackwell, 1986), p. 317.

very roughly like our own to count in the first place as an ethical practice, so our ethical practices must be, on the whole, correct. But the follower of Stich might add that we have thereby made ethics so local a practice, so linked to the contingencies of our evolution, that having morally correct practices by such a criterion cannot be worth very much. There may be other ways of acting that would be far superior, but that would not be "ethical," in the local sense we are able to give to that term.

How seriously should we take those arguments? I think Stich is motivated to take our epistemic notions to be more local than they are because he has too much confidence in the forms that theories of meaning and truth have assumed in contemporary philosophy. (Note that for him the notion of being an epistemic practice seems to have a much wider range than the notions of being true or of being rational.) There is much to agree with, first of all, in Stich's pluralism about cognitive techniques.[31] I think, for example, that the inferential rules of our various formal logics often miss successful cognitive forms that are important in everyday life. We learn, for example, to fit things into narrative patterns so that the future behavior of others becomes more predictable. Evolution has likely favored quick and dirty heuristic techniques that may fail in very abstract settings. We are probably better at finding analogies to earlier patterns than at formal inference, and the mistakes that subjects make in experiments testing reasoning skills are often due to the application of techniques that work well in the contexts most important to the subject, but that may lead him astray in the more abstract situations of testing.

But I think that Stich is too ready to accept the way that truth and rationality get defined by the theories now available. The Davidsonian theory of meaning, for example, does make translatability into our language a condition for counting sentences as true, and his account is supposed to show us what our theoretical grasp of truth is about. (Stich needs that Davidsonian position in order to argue that the notion of truth is limited to those practices we can see as very like our own.) But we should not be quick to base our arguments on semantic theories that are, I believe, in a primitive stage of development. Our pretheoretic notion of truth is wider than the more technical notion articulated by theories such as Davidson's. Truth is a property that some utterances and beliefs have because of their success in being about the world they aim at. With that pretheoretical notion, we can easily imagine utterances being possibly true that are produced by exotic believers, those whose intelligence is so much greater than our own that we could not even translate what they are saying. With rationality as well, our pretheoretic

[31] See Stich, *Fragmentation of Reason*, pp. 13–15.

notion of what it is to be sensitive to good reasons can easily be thought of as applying to such far more intelligent beings, even if they have rather different kinds of "cognitive storage."

Stich's strategy is to make truth seem a local and not very important notion by looking at contemporary semantic theories and then asking us: If that is what truth is, does it matter all that much in the long run? But I think that as we build better accounts of truth, that strategy will seem less attractive. Consider also Ellis's claim that our epistemic values are merely human ones that are based on biological selection for practices helpful in cooperative effort. Even if that is the way our notions of truth and rationality developed, still it would be odd to limit such cooperation to the human species when we engage in practices that have their basis in such notions. If selection works to enhance the individual's capacity to pass on his genes, it is true that cooperation may make this more likely. But it is unclear why should we limit the range of those cooperation with whom will enhance this capacity. The epistemic virtues described by Ellis will still be in play if some of us, in the future, come to learn from a superior alien species. In those circumstances, a *transhuman* sense of collaboration will have adaptive value. And mechanisms that evolution designs for narrow purposes may come to have uses well beyond the functions that caused the original design to emerge. So an evolutionary account of our epistemic practices will hardly be enough to make rationality and truth into local, merely human phenomena.

Against Stich also we want to say that rationality is not limited to, and defined by, the actual causal operations of the machinery that evolution has designed for the human species. Evolution may have produced a species whose members can sometimes approximate the activity of a being that is ideally sensitive to good reasons for belief, but it has also made us intelligent enough to know that the very circumstances of our development, given the conditions of selection, must have introduced a range of biases even into the basic machinery with which we reason. That is the truth in our pictures of God as a perfect reasoner, as capable of doing better than any human what we do when we reason. Our goal of being good reasoners requires that we not think of reason as a local phenomenon, one that is closely linked to the design of human biology, but as an ideal a striving for which may make us compensate for, rather than rely upon, certain design features of the human brain. The capacity of our intelligence to do much more than it was designed for, especially as it is assisted by our cultural accomplishments, makes us capable of bringing even our own reasoning processes up for critical review, as we try for a more objective account of what makes for a sensitivity to good reasons.

It is, of course, not the case that some Platonic standard of rationality is used as an external measure of our rational practices, in a way that respects not at all what we take those practices to be. But in our own self-understanding of what we are doing when we think and reason and justify our beliefs and aim at a true account of the world, we take ourselves to be doing something that others might do much better. Our practices themselves help determine the degree to which others perhaps quite different from us might contribute to setting the standard against which what we ourselves do should be measured. With some concepts we shall not allow much transcendence of our own way of doing things. Playing cricket well, with the full range of qualities of competence, sportsmanship, and character that this involves, is a local cultural phenomenon that does not look to be corrected by some future and better understanding. But the attempt to understand superconductivity or to control viruses is part of a practice that others might extend in ways we could not at present conceive. A deference to experts is built into the practice. And the same will apply with our practices of reasoning, truth-telling, justifying beliefs, and capturing what reality is like. Here also there is a deference to future experts, as we recognize that our practices aim at a completion that may transcend our present abilities to a very considerable degree. There is no reason to limit those future experts to human ones. The reach of our concepts may go well beyond their grasp, especially concepts such as the more global ones by which we try to talk about reality itself as it might exceed our comprehension.

There is an important point to be made here about how it is that utterances are meaningful. I have earlier spoken about the distribution across a system of items of the power to confer semantic or metaphysical determinacy. In the energy system set up by theology or by accounts of modern subjectivity, that power is more and more drawn to a single point from which all determinacy is said to derive. Then it seems that whatever a speaker's utterances mean, that meaning must be conferred on them by the speaker's own abilities, by what he has constructed through his own workmanship. So it is not at all clear how his utterances could come to be about a reality that transcends his ways of using and of testing them, and not at all clear how our practices could be projectible onto situations that transcend our powers of investigation.

But in my treatment of mental content, of Davidson, and of Rorty, I have argued against that move toward a single point from which determinacy is projected, and in favor of a distribution of meaning-conferring power across a triangular structure whose points are the world, the speaker's activity (including his self-understanding of that activity), and cultural practices of interpreting statements and of repeating previous statements. Utterances would be the meaningless production of noise if we could not already take into consideration the world and its contours as the context in which sounds and shapes are to be interpreted. And utterances can mean what they do only if they can at least in principle be determined as objective from an interpreter's standpoint, and only if they can in principle be taken up into a chain of further repetitions and interpretations and determinations of truth value. Wrench the speaker loose from that triangular context and nothing is said at all.

But now that different way of distributing the meaning-conferring power (different, that is, from the modern account of what the subject can produce out of its own resources) shows how we can speak about a reality that transcends our own practices of use and investigation. The secret is that we do not have to do all the semantic work anymore; the other two aspects of the triangular system are making their contributions beyond what I might understand those contributions to be. So when I use 'reality as it extends beyond our abilities to investigate it,' I can confidently project that expression toward circumstances whose obtaining I might not be able to detect. Its meaning and application are determined both by what I make of it and by *what comes upon it* through its residence in the world as it is and through its insertion in chains of usage extending before and after its occurrence. The utterance cannot go forth on its own, as it were, to a realm undetectable by us and be made true or false by the circumstances there, independently of how any future practices should go. For Wittgensteinian reasons, there can be no undetectable truth conferrers that grant determinate truth values independently of such a practice; what ongoing practices take to be a justification will be part of what gives the utterances the semantic content they have. But if we understand the triangular space of meaning conferral that we spoke of, and understand how that space opens out to include future practitioners who may be continuers of what we do, and even perhaps continuers with far greater abilities than our own, then we shall not have a problem with understanding how our notions of objectivity, reality, and reason can easily transcend our own abilities and practices, so as to support the strong sense of objectivity that the realist needs for his position.

Again we see what some may find to be an odd dialectic. The reduction of the subject's power to confer determinacy on its statements may be useful in strengthening a commitment to realism. For one way of attacking the realist is to use the localist claims about how it is that our statements are meaningful, and then to argue that the realist cannot confer on his own statements, through his own powers, the kind of meaning that his metaphysical position supposedly demands for the very stating of it. It seems that the realist would somehow have to transcend his own practices and take up a God's-eye stance; otherwise he would not have a perspective from which his statements could be about the world as it extends beyond human capacities for investigation. Absent the requirement that he must confer meaning on his statements simply by his own powers (or by those of his immediate community), the realist is well able to state what he means by his realist claims even without taking on any God's-eye stance.

Antirealism in Dummett and Wright

The antirealist program of Michael Dummett and Crispin Wright arrives at quite different conclusions from my own in the preceding section, and we ought to have at least a brief look at their arguments. I am not claiming that the two agree on all relevant issues, and I shall focus more on Wright's exposition of the program than on Dummett's, though the latter is more prominently identified with it. I am also looking at a specific project that appears in certain of their writings and am not giving consideration to their more recent work.

What was wrong with empiricism, it might be suggested, was its reliance on introspection and privacy. But we can reclaim many of its features even as we grant the effectiveness of Wittgenstein's antiempiricist attacks. Meaning, we shall say, must be understood in terms of a public display instead of in terms of an internal construction from sensory experiences. What I mean and believe is what can be made manifest to an interpreter who is trying to make sense of what I am doing. But after accepting that proposal, one may then try to bring back, under a new guise, certain modern features associated with empiricism. (Examples include accounting for meaning by focusing on the individual's own abilities for proof and construction; building up the system of knowledge upon foundational sentences made true by a truth-conferring confrontation with the world; believing that the world's objectivity must be a construction out of the individual's recognitional capacities.) Let us see how such a program might develop.

Dummett says that we can make the notion of meaning clearer by asking what someone understands who understands the meaning of a sentence, so that a theory of meaning will start with a theory of understanding.[32] Now an understanding of linguistic meaning will consist, says Dummett, in an ability to recognize when certain conditions obtain that would justify one's asserting a statement.[33] And that recognition

---

[32] Dummett presents his account in "What Is a Theory of Meaning?" in *Mind and Language*, S. Guttenplan, ed. (Oxford: Clarendon Press, 1975), pp. 97–138; and "What Is a Theory of Meaning? (II)" in *Truth and Meaning*, G. Evans and J. McDowell, eds. (Oxford: Clarendon Press, 1976), pp. 67–137.

[33] I have benefited greatly here from Crispin Wright's presentation of the antirealist program in Wright, *Realism, Meaning and Truth* (Oxford: Basil Blackwell, 1987), pp. 1–43. He acknowledges his debt to Dummett, and presents arguments that Dummett developed, but he is looking toward the strongest way to put those arguments, rather than toward giving an exposition of Dummett's work. So what I have taken from him should not be taken as an account on all the details of which Dummett would be in agreement.

cannot be a matter of luck; knowing what a statement means will mean having procedures to follow that will culminate in one's being in a position to make such a recognition. Additionally, the recognition, rather than being an inner act of consciousness, must itself be publicly displayable.

But then any realist claim about what reality is like beyond what we can have evidence for is in trouble. For it does not seem that any behavior we could ever produce would display our understanding of conditions obtaining that transcend all the evidence we could have for their obtaining. The problem is a simple one. We could not present ourselves to another as recognizing conditions that exceed our ability to recognize them. But by the Wittgensteinian demand for publicness, we cannot mean by our statements more than we can manifest ourselves as understanding them to mean.

Besides that difficulty in manifestation, there is a parallel difficulty in acquisition. (I am indebted here to Wright's presentation of the issue.[34]) How could we ever acquire an understanding of meaning if what we must come to understand is evidence-transcendent truth conditions? We shall be trying to learn the proper correlations between the making of various statements and the obtaining of various conditions in the world. There might be conditions that we could not recognize as obtaining, but these could obviously never figure in our learning to make correlations between statements and evidence. So the nature of our language acquisition is such that we could never properly deploy a notion of evidence-transcendent truth conditions as a feature of our understanding of the language.

We shall therefore have come up against limits on what we can mean, and shall be in a position parallel to that of (some of) the empiricists. An analysis of meaning could for them appeal only to two sources, sensory impressions from the world and the interior operations that manipulated them into complex ideas. Statements about a noumenal world cannot have their meaning in that fashion and become, for that program, without meaning. Now the antirealist in the manner of Dummett and Wright will press a similar outcome. Our statements can mean only what we can manifest them as meaning through our behavior of asserting them or not asserting them in the face of various sorts of evidence (or through the pattern of inferences by which we build up a network of meaningful statements from those base-level ones). But then my statements cannot succeed in being about a reality that transcends what I can have evidence for and that can on its own make statements true or false. It is not that I succeed in speaking about such an investigation-transcendent world but then can never be sure if what I say about it is

---

[34] See Wright, *Realism, Meaning and Truth*, pp. 13–23.

true. I cannot even make sense of what it would be for me to speak about it. The realist cannot even put his conception of things on the table as a candidate for our approval. Even the realist's own statements concerning realism cannot reach out and refer to an undetectable world so as to make the claim that *it* might make our statements true or false beyond what we can determine to be so. So the realist is speaking nonsense. The modern thinker's epistemological objections to things in themselves have been replaced by semantic ones.

Others at this point might suggest that the extent of reality is determined by the evidence available to an interpreter who has no limits on his investigative powers. But Dummett says that this strategy would try to explain *our* understanding of expressions by appealing to how those expressions might be used by beings very unlike ourselves, and so "fails to answer the question how we come to be able to assign to our sentences a meaning which is dependent upon a use to which we are unable to put them."[35] We could not genuinely explain our own practices by referring to practices that we could not even recognize as extensions of them. On the other hand, Dummett will not object if we, in considering the evidence-gathering and recognitional abilities that are in principle available to a speaker, think of an investigator whose abilities are a modest but recognizable idealization of our own. (I might think of myself as having much better memory, faster processing time, and so forth.)

Dummett and Wright's antirealism, we said, is supposed to be different from empiricism in that they take a third-person view rather than a first-person one. They ask how various recognitional abilities could be displayed to an interpreter, rather than about introspective abilities. Now it seems clear that I could display my understanding of evidence-transcendent truth conditions just by my behavior of connecting some sentences appropriately with others. From knowing the truth of 'It is raining in Central Park on April 1, 1989' I shall accept as an inference that 'It was raining in Central Park on April 1, 1989' will be true when spoken in the year 2001, even if no one then has evidence to prove it. My engaging in argument with those very differently situated in terms of their investigative abilities, and my willingness to be corrected by them, show that I take the semantic content of utterances to be separable from the evidence available to those who utter them. Even my willingness to say things such as "It is either true or false that it rained on a certain day ten thousand years ago even if we are unable to prove that it did or that it did not" will support the same conclusion.

To one who has genuinely taken up the stance of the interpreter, it seems that such a display of my understanding and abilities is all that could be asked. The interpreter will have every reason, faced with

[35] Dummett, "What Is a Theory of Meaning? (II)," p. 100.

that evidence, to suppose that I understand my statements to have investigation-transcendent truth conditions. But that display will not be enough for Dummett and Wright. Their empiricist model is shown in their demanding that my recognition be of a certain kind. Wright says, for example, that the ability to use sentences with 'salt' must be supplemented by a further ability to recognize and respond properly to salt itself when it is placed immediately before me.[36] All meaningful claims must be grounded in experiences of having-in-evidence, that is, in experiences of confrontation. That was, of course, a principal empiricist dogma, and it enables the antirealist argument to move forward with great dispatch. For the antirealist demand will now be that a speaker must display to the interpreter not the abilities listed earlier, but a special kind of recognition that occurs in those confrontational situations with objects.

That demand will thus be that to exhibit an understanding that truth conditions can be evidence-transcendent, the speaker must display his recognitional confrontation with such evidence-transcendent conditions. But it will be very clear that no one can display his confrontation with circumstances that by definition transcend any confrontation of which he is capable. There will be nothing in this case analogous to one's ability to recognize and handle salt. But if we get rid of the empiricist premise that recognition must consist in something like a direct confrontation with truth-conferring circumstances, then there are many ways I may display to an interpreter my understanding of investigation-transcendent truth conditions, as we have already seen.

Antirealism of the sort under discussion also appeals, we saw, to an argument about how we acquire language. We were asked to consider the conditions for someone's learning of a concept, and to conclude that no concept of evidence-transcendent conditions could ever be learned. But we ought to reject outright such an account of the conditions for acquiring a language. Our resources for concept-formation are hardly as passive as the antirealist arguments would suggest. We expand concepts by extending them to cases that are newly encountered. We form metaphorical projections of concepts to new realms entirely, or let the sense of certain concepts gradually become more abstract. We are good at developing our conceptual worlds through analogy. Some concepts we form will be at rather a remove from the evidence the world impresses upon us, and will have their determinacy more through intralinguistic hookup, and through the effects that some beliefs have on the formation of other ones, than through a relation that sentences containing expressions for the concept have to a particular set of truth-conferring circumstances. (And the basis for connecting some sentences with other ones will not

---

[36] Wright, *Realism, Meaning and Truth*, p. 17.

just be logical deduction, as my mention of metaphor and analogy suggests.)

We will also use concepts in a Kantian manner, as guiding our way of ordering experience. The concepts that I employ are those that have emerged through creative trial-and-error as being helpful in forming beliefs that guide actions successfully, and I do not have to justify my use of a concept by tracing it to episodes where the world impinges on my consciousness in a direct manner. (As speakers, we are like nature in the way that its living organisms keep producing novel structures to test against the world; there is much more autonomy on our side than the empiricist admits.) When I see that through learning I come to have evidence for claims that I made, but did not have evidence for, previously, I can form the analogous notion that the evidence making some claims of mine true or false might not be available to someone with human mental capacities.

Quite generally, the antirealist program under consideration begins from an unacceptable picture of how it is that utterances come to mean what they do. One adopts the picture of meaning as what gets conferred on strings of symbols through the determinacy-producing abilities of individual speakers or believers. These abilities no longer consist in private constructions in an interior space, but the rest of the picture remains. My suggestion earlier was that if we understand the significance of certain findings concerning externalism about mental content and the disenchantment of subjectivity, then we shall see that the power to determine meaning is distributed across a triangular structure, so that expressions can mean more than what we make them mean strictly through our own abilities of meaning conferral. Dummett and Wright do not go deep enough in rethinking the conceptions of modern subjectivity; instead of letting the epistemic capacities of our knowing structure set limits on what reality can be, they let the semantic capacities of our linguistic apparatus set those limits. We might say that they engage in the disenchantment of subjectivity while at the same time retaining the picture of reality as what we can secure through our determinacy-conferring labor. But that picture arose out of the special circumstances of the late medieval situation and belongs together with a divinized conception of subjectivity. A more thorough reflection on the consequences of a disenchantment of subjectivity would bring into question not just the philosophical role of an introspective privacy but also the notion of a thinned-out world whose character must be grounded in our powers to confer determinacy upon it through our labor.

I want to pursue now a direction of thought that may be reading too much into the Dummett–Wright program, and that may be trying for more than I can establish. The idea is that a certain modern structure has in it a tendency toward self-collapse, and that the program now under review shows again that it does so. We are familiar with the modern turn away from the world and toward the subject. The more we understand how the structures of subjectivity determine the character of our access to the world, the more we are tempted to take that limitation as, instead, a source of power. Reality can be no more than what we can take it to be; it must fit the conditions laid out by our constructive or investigatory abilities. But then there is at least the threat of a collapse of the world back into subjectivity. Why not get rid of the material objects out there, for example, and say that our sensory impressions and the patterns we make of them are all that we need? A genuine subject–world opposition is given up and we are left with just the former side of that divide, with the latter remaining as a mere shadow cast by subjectivity.

So far the story is familiar, but now comes a further step in the progression. Let me give it a Hegelian tone by taking a quotation from Stanley Rosen:

> But it is a crucial premise in Hegel's teaching that a genuine rejection of the world is impossible. In attempting to reject the world, we define ourselves in terms of the world. We carry the world with us as a shadow-image or *Vorstellung* which is our only real substance, and which, because it is reduced to the status of a shadow, desubstantializes the self as subjectivity as well.[37]

The modern thinning out of the world thins out the self as well, making it more abstract and emptier as it loses the rich set of worldly involvements in which it could see itself mirrored. Consider the type of empiricist who says that our sensory impressions and the constructions we make of them are the only things that are real. We appear to have a realm of determinate subjectivity over against a disappearing world. But then the question emerges of just why we should still count these as sensory *impressions*. To do so assumes they still carry a semantic content, that they remain intentional, as if they were presenting information about the world. But without that world, why should we not say instead that this is now the meaningless running of a syntactic engine, and that no subject at all remains that is setting itself in relation to anything? What I want to do now is to show how the progression of that turn away from the world to subjectivity is repeated in the program of Dummett and Wright. We shall try to see both the collapsing of the world into our ways of being directed toward it, and then the self-collapse of subjectivity. (What is "subjective" for those two thinkers, of course, is nothing interior and hidden but the speaking and recognitional practices of the individual.)

One problem acknowledged by Wright is that the arguments presented against the realist are so strong that it seems they will under-

---

[37] Rosen, *G. W. F. Hegel* (New Haven, Conn.: Yale University Press, 1974), pp. 202–3.

mine any sort of evidence transcendence whatever.[38] For let us suppose that what someone understands, in understanding sentence meaning, is Dummett's somewhat idealized assertability conditions that would include evidence he could *in principle* gather, even if his actual situation and abilities restrict him from doing so. But how could such an understanding be manifested to an interpreter? The speaker's practical abilities will include an ability to demonstrate recognition of conditions that actually obtain, but he cannot demonstrate recognition of conditions that he in principle would recognize with increased abilities, but that he, with his own abilities, is unable to detect. And it is unclear how the speaker could ever *acquire* an understanding of such evidence-transcendent conditions, even a transcendence of Dummett's modest sort, since all the conditions he has actually encountered in learning the language are conditions that he could actually recognize as obtaining.

So the antirealist arguments have a momentum that, it seems, will not come to rest until a speaker's semantic reach cannot exceed the immediate grasp of his actual evidence-gathering abilities at the time of his speaking. His world will have fallen back into what is specified by that grasp. (There is a similar momentum with phenomenalist accounts.) But now we have to ask whether what we are left with on the side of the subject are activities that can still be classified as the production of meaningful speech. We are back in familiar territory. Meaning intrinsically requires for its constitution the possibility of *absence* and *error*, of a doing the same thing elsewhere and later, and of a doing the same thing badly rather than well. It is not that we can keep reducing the range of relevant evidence until we arrive at the situation of the individual's present assertions in reaction to causal conditions; we would have removed the possibility of his utterances being meaningful, the possibility of their reaching out to an elsewhere in which they can be repeated. Every time the immediately available evidence changes in the slightest, one's statements change their meaning as well. But if meaning is as volatile as that, it is not clear how anything at all is being said.

Dummett and Wright ask how we might acquire an understanding of past-tense statements, as they are about conditions that are no longer present and cannot be experienced as conferring truth upon our statements.[39] My training in the use of past-tense statements will always concern evidence available *now*, at the time of my making the statement, that justifies my making it, and that can be exploited in correcting my errors. That training cannot (so their argument goes) involve my re-

[38] Wright raises this issue in the essay "Strict Finitism," in *Realism, Meaning and Truth*, pp. 107–75.

[39] Wright considers this issue in "Realism, Truth-Value Links, Other Minds and the Past," and "Anti-Realism, Timeless Truth and *Nineteen Eighty-Four*," both in *Realism, Meaning and Truth*, pp. 85–106 and pp. 176–203.

cognition of the conditions that made the statement true at the time that the statement is supposedly about. My understanding, then, of the meaning of past-tense statements will be in terms of assertability conditions that obtain at the time of utterance, and that offer themselves for my inspection, so that if memory is called upon, it is the present memory that serves as evidence, and not the conditions that may once have caused it. So my successful use of the past tense does not warrant my belief in the past as having, on its own, the sort of reality that makes a past-tense statement true.

Wright suggests that we think of a moving train and the view we have from one of its windows.[40] (He is not persuading us to adopt this conception, but he does think the antirealist gives strong arguments to make it plausible.) Reality for a speaker will be defined by the sum total of statements that she can determine to be true or false. Like the view from the train, that reality will change as she moves forward in time, and as evidence for some statements disappears and evidence for other statements becomes available. Therefore, says Wright, I cannot know, just by knowing now that 'It is raining' is true, that 'It was raining' *will be true* at some time in the future. What I can know, by knowing that the former sentence is true, is that what someone will assert by saying 'It was raining' at some point in the future is true *now*, at the time of my speaking. But I cannot know that it will be true *then*. (It is unclear how someone could be asserting the *same* thing then.)

So the past collapses into the present. But here again we see the structure that I have been investigating. Suppose that I am looking at dinosaur bones in Montana and making inferences about what dinosaurs must be like. If the arguments about the semantics of statements of the distant past are correct, then *what* I am asserting is fully captured just by noting the kinds of situations in which I am willing to assent to or dissent from utterances with the sound 'dinosaur.' That is all that reference to dinosaurs consists in; the evidence for dinosaurs does not push me toward absent entities whose antics in the past make my present statements true or false. There is no reference to *dinosaurs*, in the realist's way, and the commonsense way, of understanding what such reference would have to be. (That does not mean that I am thereby talking about dinosaur bones and the like when I use 'dinosaur.' Presumably the evidentiary situations in which I assent to utterances with 'dinosaur bones' will be different from those in which I assent to utterances with 'dinosaur.')

Now consider what happens as (following the argument tentatively presented by Wright) we let meaning collapse into what is fixed by immediately present evidence at the time of utterance. But evidence is

---

[40] Wright, *Realism, Meaning and Truth*, pp. 183–4 and pp. 192–3.

what points me to what is absent and elsewhere, and as the elsewhere disappears, we are not left with a different sort of collapsed evidence, but with something that it is hard to call evidence at all. (Recall on this issue our earlier result with 'impression.') As is often the case, Dummett and Wright give up the empiricist focus on interiority, but what they replace it with leads to a similar result. As the world collapses into being congruent with the space of my evidence-gathering abilities, then on what basis shall I say that it is still *evidence* gathering that I am doing? What meaning can now be given to that practice? The very notion of an aboutness that structures our conception of evidence seems to disappear. I cannot make any sense of evidence transcendence, cannot comprehend what it would be to form causal hypotheses about an absent world that has left its traces around me, and that, to be the world it is, must make true or false not only the statements I can have evidence for, but very many other statements besides.

It is not that we can accept the antirealist reduction and then have what remains to us retain just the same status and content as it did before the more extensive world was stripped away from it. For the now reduced realm needed the relation to the more extensive world in order to be constituted as a determinate realm. Making sense of the interpreter's stance is essential to the third-person, Wittgensteinian sort of antirealism that Dummett and Wright would promote. But as we pursue the antirealist arguments to their end, there does not seem to remain enough semantic stability and repeatability, and enough of a shared world, to allow us to get a grasp on just what an *interpreter* is supposed to be doing. It is unclear what can any longer pass as interpretation. Of course, we have already encountered reasons to reject the arguments that begin this whole progression, as well as the picture of subjectivity and the world that motivates them.

What is right about the antirealist program just considered is its refusal to allow that the world on its own makes our utterances mean what they do and makes them true or false. In talking about truth and objectivity we must already be considering the triangular situation mentioned earlier. Our utterances mean what they do through the uses to which *we* can put them, and those uses must be publicly displayable to an interpreter; thus the second and third sides of the triangle have been properly brought into play. But the empiricist lineage of Dummett's program is shown perhaps in the tendency for two of the sides, the world and cultural practices, to threaten a collapse into the other one: into what an individual can make his sentences mean by his actual abilities. Dummett, it is true, allows for some idealization of those abilities, so that a more extensive evidence can be considered when we ask about the investigatory abilities that we could bring to bear upon our utterances. Yet Dummett, I think, would still hold in too high a regard, for questions of truth and objectivity, the limited abilities of human speakers. The 'we' that begins to open out a sphere of repetitions and evidence transcendence for our utterances ought not to be so quickly reduced to a rather local 'we' and its powers. That 'we' whose practices will extend our own may have abilities that we could not now recognize as extensions of them. And the world continues to have its irreducible place in the triangle, rather than being a construct of the investigatory abilities of speakers, even if it does not have the truth-conferring powers that some realists have taken it to have. It is in letting those two sides of the triangle have a substantial character that we are granted a rich and proper notion of objectivity. Wittgenstein on rule following shows us that utterances cannot be straightforwardly made true or false by the world because they are the utterances they are only through practices of repetition, interpretation, investigation, and use. But he does not have to encourage, as he seems to encourage in Dummett and Wright, the collapse of the world into what some rather local practices can take it to be.

Our notions of objectivity and of the guidance of our beliefs by reality are themselves world guided. Over time we develop a better conception of what it is for the world to guide our conceptions. It is not that the world's regulation of our beliefs uniquely fixes an account of that in which such regulation consists, or of what the world is like that is doing the guiding. The triangular structure that we have investigated will remain in play, and so there may be some room for maneuver regarding precisely what account we come to of objectivity, and of exactly where the boundary will be set between beliefs that are world guided and beliefs that are not. It may happen then that what counts as an idealization of our practice of adjusting beliefs to reality will depend in some measure on what practices ours develop into in history, and so on the conceptions of future communities. But that fact, if it is one, gives no justification for Rorty's claim that our notions of objectivity and reality are simply projections of our practices. Those notions develop within the holistic process by which we adjust our beliefs to how matters really stand, and they are part of that adjustment, instead of being aspects of a framework that sets a discourse in motion, and that, as such, is immune to revision until another such framework replaces it.

6

Moral Realism

Moral Value and the Character of the World

The modern project, put one way, is to reproduce a world of natural and ethical determinacy out of the resources of subjectivity. But then we have the question of what within subjectivity can replace the constraints of the natural order. The situation is ripe for an imitation of the medieval God. God's thinking and willing can have a proper completeness, even if they are not given such by any natural order external to him, because his activity has *itself* as a goal, and so is self-relating and self-determining. In a similar way, it will be suggested, one's willing can have a proper end, without its autonomy being weakened, if the will aims, as in Kant's picture, at fully willing itself as a rational will. In so doing it imposes a rational form upon itself, as defined in the categorical imperative. Then there are the less rational forms of this reflective structure: the Nietzschean self-creating self that values itself as a valuer; the Kierkegaardian self whose aim is an act of willing willed with the full anxiety of itself as subject; the existentialist self willing to go on willing in a meaningless world.

Many modern thinkers will not subscribe to Kant's project, and so will not try to generate a determinate moral order out of a theological structure of subjectivity. But there will be, generally, an increasing subjectivization of ethics. The only things valuable in themselves will be subjective states of willing or feeling, and a stable moral order will have to be due to a stability in the character of human passions or attitudes. And I think that Williams is correct that the Kantian program most clearly displays the salient aspects of what he calls "morality, the peculiar institution," the form of ethical life especially associated with the modern world.[1] He claims that this typically modern institution weakens traditional ethical distinctions in favor of highly abstract notions of obligation, right, and formal procedures. It threatens to colonize all other ethical goods by granting them status only if they can be understood in terms of the notions of obligation and right. It lets the structure of morality expand, Williams continues, until it takes over the entire sphere of

---

[1] Bernard Williams, *Ethics and the Limits of Philosophy* (Cambridge, Mass.: Harvard University Press, 1985), pp. 174–96.

practical reason, and so threatens the integrity of individual lives and the role of nonethical goods in the shaping of such lives, if they are to be happy and well lived. Finally, it focuses so exclusively on will and intention that the practices of habituation that surround those acts of willing, and that make responsible choices possible, appear as coercive, as imposed by what is merely external.

I think these features can be seen as attaching naturally to a picture of the subject in which a divinelike activity of self-willing must generate the structures of moral objectivity out of itself. Such a picture will lead to the theological field with which we have become familiar. There is a moment of autonomous self-relating (the rational self willing itself as rational) that gathers value into itself, and then the rest of the field loses its pluralist contours and collapses into an otherness of mere inclination, mere compulsion, and irrational power. That otherness must then be worked upon, must be subjugated, so that the self-relational structure of subjectivity can make itself real in the world.

Now a theme of my investigation is the recovery of the world. It will be important to what I am aiming at that I defend a more realist account of moral beliefs than modern philosophies seem to allow. One suggestion is that we repeat in regard to ethics the story I put forward earlier concerning determinacy generally. It would go something like this. The world can be disenchanted of all value, can become ethically empty, only because subjectivity remains "divinized," as it takes up the divine role of determining a moral universe out of its own activity. Perhaps if we disenchant subjectivity fully, and make it a natural phenomenon at home in a world that engenders and shapes it, then we are free to recognize that most of what we take to have value really does. We might try, then, to employ some of Davidson's moves in order to come up with an argument against projectivist accounts in ethics, that is, against those that take moral determinacy to derive from what moral selves project upon a thinner world.[2]

In the Davidsonian account of interpretation, the interpreter is simultaneously assigning beliefs, meanings, and preferences to a believer, by taking such internal states to have been conditioned by the world. Now Davidson claims that to be a believer at all, one's beliefs have to count as mostly true. We can then make a parallel case for the will, concerning intention and preference. I shall be able to give content to the other's preferences and value claims only by taking him to have formed the sort of values that at least a moderately rational person would have formed in his circumstances. Those will be values defined relative to what is worth valuing in the surrounding world and in the believer's life, given the sort

[2] For a more detailed account of the factors that come into play in such an argument the reader will find it useful to consult Susan Hurley, *Natural Reasons: Personality and Polity* (Oxford: Oxford University Press, 1989), pp. 56–113.

of being he is. But then a condition for there being determinate preferences and values in the subject is that the world already be seen as having features worth valuing. So it will make no sense to analyze values as projected upon a world that in itself has nothing in the way of value. We do not have one determinate side, the subjective, first, and then a projection of its features upon the other side. Except where the latter already has ethically relevant content, we cannot begin to make a determinate assignment to the former. So ethical values cannot properly be taken to be projections upon the world.

But consider that a scientist might condition a group of rats to demonstrate preferences for arbitrary features of the environment; we could explain the rat's behavior on the basis of those preferences without supposing that what was preferred had intrinsic value. Conditioning might also be done to a human community, in a much more complex way and with much more complex properties, so that we came to prefer some arbitrary features of the environment to other ones. We would still find it easy to interpret others' preferences; we would just take our own preferences for granted in trying to make theirs comprehensible. But no role would have to be played in the interpretation by the real worth of the things in the environment.

It seems clear, on the other hand, that not all preferences could be of this sort. Some coherent pattern of preferences relative to what is worth preferring in the given environment would have to be present before we could count the other as engaging in intentional activity at all. (Our training of the rat must assume some preferences on its part as well.) So not everything that is an objective reason for acting could be a matter of projection. We must at least start off by taking the other to be not only a believer in what is true (very roughly), but also a preferrer of what is good (very roughly).[3] But that minimal basis needed to make any coherent interpretation at all might take us very little way toward assigning well-developed ethical attitudes to an agent. So the projectivist will need to offer only minor qualifications to his story in the face of that objection; he has, of course, not claimed that humans have no natural preferences. We need a stronger argument.

If we wish to make a case against the antirealist, in favor of a more realist conception of ethical goodness, then we need to develop a picture in which ethical beliefs are guided by the world. I think that one factor making it appear difficult to establish such world guidance for moral beliefs is an inappropriate picture of what that sort of guidance would have to be. The world, it has seemed to many, would have to contain propositionlike entities, moral facts, that moral beliefs succeed in mirroring,

[3] Davidson makes this point in "Expressing Evaluations," The Lindley Lecture, The University of Kansas, 1982.

in the way that mathematical beliefs seem to be sensitive to the facts of mathematics. And there do not appear to be such facts around, given how deeply our moral disagreements seem to go. But I think that the strategy of the moral realist ought to be different. We need to ask whether there are aspects of reality that are in themselves worth valuing, whose value does not derive from the acts by which conscious beings take them to be valuable. Even if there are such, it may remain a very complicated story how, and to what degree, that pressure from the world on our acts of valuing will determine the rightness of our moral beliefs. Perhaps there is much that we as individual subjects or as moral communities contribute to determining just what sort of attention and respect needs to be paid, when we engage in moral deliberation, to those aspects of reality that count as having some degree of intrinsic worth.

Let me begin with a claim that will be controversial to some, though not, I expect, to many others. I am convinced that a highly developed planetary ecosystem does have an intrinsic worth of the sort we are discussing. Suppose we discovered in another galaxy a planet with no intelligent life but with an ecosystem of marvelous complexity. It has an astonishing variety of living things, though no examples of a well-developed conscious life, and what is more, there is an intricate inter-dependence among the various species and between living things and nonliving; and within the system itself there are complex adjustments that allow it to maintain itself as having an overall character. Now some scientists decide, for a test or perhaps for the fun of it, to see if they can destroy the planet by bombarding it with atomic weapons. I think that act would be a serious moral wrong. Its wrongness would be grounded not simply in our conventions and contracts and attitudes, such as a feeling of horror we might have at the idea. The act would be wrong in itself because it would destroy something that has intrinsic worth. (I am not claiming that there could never be a good moral reason to destroy anything that has intrinsic worth.)

I have picked that example because I want to resist right off the modern tendency to find value only on the side of subjectivity, in conscious states, in certain kinds of willing, and the like. The worth of the planetary ecosystem would depend at least in part on what we might call Aristotelian–Hegelian considerations rather than Kantian or empiricist ones: the degree of self-maintaining unity in a system with great diversity and differentiation; the degree to which changes are internally regulated rather than externally caused; the degree to which there is a distinctive character to the system's patterns of self-unifying and self-differentiating as it orders itself as a well-formed whole. We would not thereby be claiming that those dimensions are the only ones that count in determining what has worth; it is clear that they would be insufficient as criteria for making our moral distinctions precise. And we may well follow out this Aristotelian–Hegelian line of thought by claiming that we find those dimensions most fully developed in the thinking and willing of self-conscious selves, so that these have the highest level of intrinsic worth. But at least our account would have ample room for acknowledging that what is both nonhuman and nonconscious may still have an intrinsic worth, in such a way as to demand a measure of respect from those who are capable of ethical deliberation.

Suppose we could give a defense of an account roughly like that one. Then we would be able to show that it is something about the way the world is that constrains how at least some of our ethical beliefs must develop, if they are to be correct.[4] My defense is going to be an indirect one. I want to do some work to clear away the philosophical habits of mind that would, from the start, make realism in ethics seem naive, and I shall spend the majority of the chapter in that work of clearing away. If these habits are removed, then I think we shall find it quite natural to accept the claim that aspects of reality have an intrinsic worth that we have to respect.

Now I do not want to argue that the constraints placed by the world itself on our ethical considerations will leave no room for what we make of our own lives through living them. To say that moral beliefs are world-guided is not yet to decide just how much constraint the moral believer will be under. Wiggins, for one, believes it is true, as the antirealist argues, that there is a certain "cognitive underdetermination" of a life that is worth living.[5] A straightforward sensitivity to the world, and only that, will leave us too open-minded to discover how we shall live. One discovers certain meaningful projects and values only by bringing some conception to bear that enables one to shape a life that is meaningful for himself. But it does not follow that we have here a case simply of invention or projection. Life's having a point "may depend on what the owner of the life brings to the world in order to see the world in such a way as to discover meaning."[6] We must have developed and focused a certain way of seeing in order to discover what is, objectively, a better life than others we might lead. Wiggins's position, he says, is one "which allows the world to impinge upon but not to determine the point possessed by individual lives, and which sees value properties not as

---

[4] While I was thinking of Hegel and Aristotle in reflecting on the view under consideration, it is interesting that Robert Nozick gives a defense of a somewhat similar view. See his discussion of intrinsic value as degree of organic unity in Nozick, *Philosophical Explanations* (Cambridge, Mass.: Harvard University Press, 1981), pp. 413–22.

[5] Wiggins, "Truth, Invention, and the Meaning of Life," in *Essays on Moral Realism*, Geoffrey Sayre-McCord, ed. (Ithaca, N.Y.: Cornell University Press, 1988), pp. 127–65. On the issue of cognitive underdetermination, see pp. 154–65.

[6] Ibid., p. 160.

created but as lit up by the focus that the man who lives the life brings to the world."[7]

I think this is right, if incomplete. (Some things have worth no matter what kind of focus we bring to them, but Wiggins is making a somewhat different point about what makes a human life meaningful.) The world offers us a plurality of goods, and it presents itself as having a plurality of features that deserve to be valued. So an individual will face possibilities of different lives that embody different sorts of goods, and that raise to a greater level of importance, than do other lives, a consideration for certain features of the universe that are worth respecting. Even if I acknowledge that the world makes some things have more intrinsic worth than others, it may still be partly up to me to determine what sort of respect is owed to them, and just how the range of them will be honored in an ethical life. I do not see why we should expect that there will be a theory that systematically weights the various goods, or the features of intrinsic worth, and that determines what is the right action to perform in a given case. It is not theory but my leading of a certain life that brings out some goods, of the many available, and gives them a more intimate relation to my activity. The narrative of my life, which will be different from that of other lives, gives a particular focus to my moral engagement with the world, a focus that allows some patterns of ethical concern rather than others, and some ethical observations rather than others, to emerge. Some constraints that the world places on my valuing will be absolute; but there also will be a very considerable sphere in which I am actively letting emerge some values rather than others, in living a life that takes those values seriously. (One might be reminded here of the Hegelian claim that the ethical universal demands to be embodied in a *particular* life, so that its taking on of a more parochial content is not alien to it but is part of its own unfolding as what it is.)

A similar point may be made, I think, about the narratives of historical communities. We are constrained to discover some things as having worth if we want our ethical development as a community to go properly. But considerable room will be left for our history to fix a relative weighting of different goods, and to make our ethical lives embody in themselves some goods more than others. There is not, for example, some answer built into the nature of ethical value and ethical reflection that fixes the precise relation between individuality and community as goods in human lives. Our own historical narrative has gone so as to give the separating out of individuals, and their autonomy over their lives, a central place in those communities thought capable of producing worthwhile lives. Perhaps a different history would have brought other goods more visibly to the fore, and would have "lit up" with a different

[7] Ibid., p. 165.

focus the realm of what is there to be valued. But it is our task to move the narrative forward, not to begin it again from scratch.

That narrative supplies us with a range of competing paradigms of what a well-lived life might be like and somehow, from a holistic taking into consideration of those different paradigms and from our powers of analogy, we must project that narrative (it may be of an individual or of a communal life) toward new cases. By learning more about what is there to be valued, we learn more about what it is to be a valuer. One's activity of taking a life to be meaningful is needed to shape a particular life that has meaning in a world that, while not without meaning or worth, does not of itself give sufficient shape to the character of a life, and does not on its own fix just what a sensitivity to moral worth must uncover. So our ethical beliefs cannot be world-guided to the full extent that beliefs in the natural sciences are. But all I am claiming is that ethical beliefs are to an important extent world guided and that what is there anyway in the world offers a strong constraint on how belief formation must go in ethics if it is to be correct.

Harman's Argument

There is a well-known argument by Gilbert Harman against the claim that the world regulates our moral beliefs.[8] He sees a link between what we can properly take as real and what we need to appeal to in forming explanations. When a scientist sees a certain path in an cloud chamber, the best explanation of his seeing it, barring problems with the instrument, is to suppose that a certain subatomic particle played a causal role in his coming to have that experience. The explanation may include as well reference to his training, to his psychological states, and to his perceptual mechanisms. But these others cannot replace the explanatory role of reference to the particle itself. On the other hand, when I perceive a certain act as morally wrong, it seems that the explanation need only refer to my psychology and to my training, and to the event neutrally described. I do not need to assign to the wrongness of the act a causal role in my coming to have that perception, and we should not, therefore, take that wrongness to be a feature of the world.

A first reaction to that argument may be that Harman has here stacked the deck, so that his conclusion was built in from the start. He has begun with notions of cause and explanation such that only entities and properties picked out by the natural sciences have any chance from the beginning of passing muster as causes. But let us grant that the argument's power is not due to that limitation, and that Harman is genuinely open, in setting the conditions of the argument, to whatever sorts of explanations we will need to give a thorough account of ourselves and of the world. Now imagine that Julia, in writing a biography about her uncle's experiences as a soldier in World War II, states that it was the evil of what he discovered, as a camp liberator, that caused his perception of it as evil, a perception so strong that it changed his life. Her friend John does not doubt the strength of that feeling, but says that he can explain it more efficiently, without making any metaphysical commitment to moral badness as itself a property of actions able to play a causal role. John's explanation describes the upbringing of Julia's uncle and his training in having reactions to certain kinds of events. The uncle had learned to play the human valuing game very well, and deserves to be valued by others for doing so.

Julia will feel that something crucial to her explanation has been lost in John's submitting it to a psychological reduction. The full explanation of her uncle's observations and his later actions seems to require assigning a causal role to the moral badness of what he saw. The explanation of his decision to enter a monastery, for example, will be impoverished (we will truly *not* understand it as the human action it is) if it can be fully explained by a training in producing moral reactions, a training that is not itself guided by the moral character of the events, and that does not consist in making the trainee sensitive to that moral character. Julia wants to claim, instead, that his training produced someone with the capacity to be open to moral aspects of the world around him. Our explanatory repertoire will be incomplete, she says, if we are unable to appeal to moral goodness and moral badness as causes of our observations and of our ethical beliefs.

One way to understand experience (we looked at this model in the last chapter) is to take the world that is the object of our observations to be extremely thin, and to suppose that a relatively rich subjectivity works up that thin input into a thicker picture of what is real. The pressures of that modern conception can be expected to have their effects on our account of moral kinds. Harman, we have seen, says that we do not need to grant that moral qualities are really there because we can explain someone's moral observations just by supposing that he has nonmoral facts as input and then reacts to them in a particular way because of his "psychological set."

But consider, for comparison, what happens with an expert chess player. We say that she is sensitive to complex patterns that form as the game advances, and that a particular pattern, defined by strength of position on the board, caused her to make a move with her knight. Now along comes Harman and says that no such chess patterns are really there to be perceived, and no such chess patterns can be a causal factor in the expert's perceiving them. For another explanation of her behavior is perfectly adequate. In this explanation, the input to the expert is physical shapes and visual patterns, not chess patterns, and she has been programmed (her psychological set) to respond to these by counting them as patterns of chess. But why should the availability of that explanation make us deny that the expert is sensitive to chess patterns and that a particular chess pattern is *causing* her moves? Her mind has developed so that in being sensitive to certain physical patterns, she is automatically being sensitive to configurations of chess. Only that level of explanation shows what is going on here; the relevant affairs here are patternless and meaningless until that level of articulation is introduced. Only here do we bring out the focus and point of the explanation, that is, whether her moves are truly being caused by a perception of that pattern or whether other factors have led to a lucky and unforeseen outcome. To learn the detailed engineering arrangements of how she does things does not compete with the original claim that a chess pattern caused her perception of it as a chess pattern.

What we need to claim here is that the natural world can arrange itself into configurations that cannot be picked out as such at the physicalist level of description, but that can be recognized through a sophisticated psychological set whose input is the (in principle) physically definable information from the world. And we may apply that sort of account to the case of ethics. The development of our subjective apparatus has come about so as to make us sensitive to the thicker features *in* being sensitive to the thinner ones. So it is not all that helpful to know that an explanation appealing to two factors, nonmoral facts plus psychological set, can account for our moral observations. We need to know just *how* the psychological set comes into the account that we are willing finally to endorse. It is still an open issue whether that which was produced by biology and psychological training is a sensitivity to morally salient patterns that one sees in looking at the world from a morally interested standpoint, or is, in contrast, a projective mechanism guided only by subjective criteria that we raise for ourselves when encountering the world.

Now I think the account just given is a correct one regarding the character of at least many moral properties. But the analogy with the expert sensitive to chess patterns will have, it is clear, a significant weakness for the moral realist. Chess is a game invented by humans, and chess patterns would be nothing at all without our invention. We might grant that there are valid explanations appealing to chess patterns that cause our perceptions, but it was a prior communal decision to adopt certain rules that constituted the patterns as such to begin with. Then we have a moral realism hardly worth fighting for, if the same is true in the case of ethics.

So the focus of the debate can now turn to the issue of how the psychological set that plays a role in explanations of moral perceptions and beliefs can itself come to be what it is, can itself be either recognizing the significance of patterns or imposing that significance upon them. And that question will be an historical one as well. Perhaps it is a satisfactory explanation of a particular individual's moral perceptions that he sees the patterns his community has trained him to see. But then there is the question as well about the community's "communal set" that it employs in his training, and about how that set came to be what is now taken for granted.

We should, in investigating this issue, not be misled by Harman's comparison with how matters go in the sciences. I want to show that there are important disanalogies between how world guidance works in ethics and how it works when we produce theories in the natural sciences. These disanalogies, I shall claim, are relevant to making Harman's argument far less threatening, through showing that we should never expect ethical properties to play the explanatory role of the sub-atomic particles in Harman. The world's guidance of scientific beliefs may be thought to proceed in the following manner. The world is like a behavioral psychologist that rewards and punishes our hypotheses by letting us get more or less of what we want from it. True beliefs are selected because those who have them are more likely to manipulate things to their benefit. But it is difficult to see that there is any comparable reward-and-punishment mechanism that selects for true ethical beliefs. We do not get more of what we want by adjusting such beliefs to make them more accurate. There is, to be sure, the satisfaction of comprehending the universe, of rising above the interests of our own lives in order that those lives may accommodate themselves to a larger order. But there will be nothing comparable to the way that having false scientific beliefs may make a rocket fail to achieve lift-off.

There is not in ethics the kind of interplay between theory and perception, and between explanation and prediction, that we find in the natural sciences. We do not generally test moral beliefs against the world by developing them into a theory and by then deducing from that theory observations that it predicts will occur, after which we put ourselves in position to have such observations or to discover that they do not take place as predicted. Consider, for example, a change that some have made very recently: toward a belief that very many of our institutions that make use of animals for the benefit of humans are immoral. It is not that one forms some hypothesis about animal rights and then intervenes in the world in a way that will produce certain observations if the hypothesis is correct and other observations if it is wrong. There is not that sort of distance in ethics between believing in a theory and having particular observations. (Even in the sciences there is of course no absolute independence of theory and observation, but there is enough distance between the two so that one can be very much surprised by how one's observations turn out.) One's coming to believe that the treatment of animals is wrong is due to a more holistic process that gradually produces changes both in one's beliefs and in one's observations.

There is another disanalogy between science and ethics that should also influence our evaluation of Harman's argument. It is important that in the case of the particle in the cloud chamber, we are dealing with theoretical entities that are supposed to be operating beneath the level of what appears. We hypothesize that certain invisible entities are causing the changes that we have observed. In such a case, it will of course be crucial that we suppose there to be no more of such entities than we need to explain the occurrence of our observations. For the only motivation we have to commit ourselves to unobservable entities is that our explanations cannot be fully satisfactory without them. In the case of ethics, on the other hand, we are not dealing with unobservable entities that are supposedly operating behind the scenes to make the world have a certain appearance. We are concerned instead with configurations available *in what appears*, but available only to a subject with an apparatus for picking them out, for recognizing patterns at that level of resolution.

But if that is the case, there will not be the same pressure, as in the cloud chamber example, to describe the world as thinly as possible. Our metaphysical commitment here is of a different sort, not to hidden entities known through their causal power, but to stable configurations that emerge in the visible world when we arrive at a level of description sophisticated enough to make them stand out. It is very much unclear why there should be a strong bias toward saying that we impose such patterns instead of finding them. (Whereas it is not unclear why there should be a parallel bias when we are committing ourselves to unobservable entities.)

A more comparable case would be the apparatus through which we find the world to contain individuals and sorts. It is a reasonable claim that when we pick out individual zebras or cockroaches, or when we divide up natural kinds according to the periodic table of the elements, we are being sensitive to boundaries that are really there in nature, even if not every knower has to give those boundaries the same significance that we do. Animals and elements are in important respects self-differentiating. Now suppose that an explanation is possible that takes those individuals and kinds to be impositions by us on a continuous stream of sensory data. One side says the patterns are there to be picked out, the other that we project them. I do not see that the latter account, the thinner-world-plus-richer-subjectivity one, has any advantage here, for reasons of economy, in the way that a more economical account of subatomic particles does. We look at our accounts holistically and make an all-things-considered judgment about which one is ultimately more attractive. And from that point of view we recognize that it is just very odd to say that the cat or the dog we see in front of us is not self-individuating. Similarly with the patterns that the ethically sensitive person is able to pick out. Our all-things-considered judgment, once bad philosophical habits are removed, is that we can be sensitive to ethical value that is genuinely real, even if a thinner account of the world is also available. And unlike the case with the chess player, it does not seem up to us to lay out the rules.

We might consider a further analogy as well. Suppose it is claimed that my belief that another has a certain belief or intention is caused by such a belief or intention that he actually has. There may well be another explanation that counts the causal input to me as much thinner and considers the psychological vocabulary a projection by me on the thinner world. But my ability to pick out those psychologically relevant patterns in and through the more thinly describable stream of data is a genuine sensitivity to what is there; the simple availability of the thinner explanation will not make me withdraw that claim. (To take still another case that I mentioned earlier in a different context: The patterns in the carpet are really there even if there is an explanation that takes the carpet more thinly, as a grid of colored knots, and then claims that the patterns are only our projection onto the grid. There is not a built-in preference for the thinner account; it would very often be wrong.) Harman's argument relies on taking cases as analogous, in science and in ethics, that are not analogous at all.

We may properly ask why we should expect that moral beliefs must belong to moral *theories*, as Harman's analogy would suggest. It is unclear why the moral agent should have to arrange his beliefs into the form of a systematic theory from which predictions about observations can be drawn, or a conclusion about what action is proper to perform. One might be very successful as a moral agent through a well-developed ability to draw analogies between familiar cases and unfamiliar ones, and to be sensitive to ethically relevant patterns in the information available, without having that ability mediated by an ethical theory of any complexity. Of course, it would not be necessary that every agent must construct such a theory; perhaps the theory must only be constructible by some if ethical beliefs are to be world-guided in the way that theoretical beliefs are. But why should ethical knowledge generally be thought of as fitting the models of theory testing that are more familiar in the natural sciences?

Our predictions have to be rather of the following sort. As individuals become more intellectually and ethically mature, as they belong to cultures that themselves encourage the maturing of ethical sensibilities and reflection and debate about what is worth valuing, as they put their well-developed ethical sensibilities to work making sense of the world, their exposure to the world will gradually produce in them converging ethical beliefs. There is no special faculty of moral perception; the holistic operation of the full range of our ordinary belief-forming capacities is required. There will not be an interesting *particular* story about the causal mechanisms that come into play in the formation of our ethical beliefs. There will be rather the general story about how people develop their capacities for making good judgments, and the claim that such people, exposed to the world and interested in what might make things worthy of ethical consideration, will eventually come to see in it the intrinsic worth that some things have, and the moral badness of not respecting that worth. The psychological set that is sensitive to ethical value is formed at least partly in response to the world itself. We no longer have Harman's reasons for favoring the thinner world, and we can then follow our intuition that we are discovering ethically relevant patterns as much as inventing them.

Realism and Antirealism in Ethics

But even if those differences make Harman's argument less threatening, there remains a general antirealist strategy that merits our attention. It offers a powerful way of challenging claims that a given set of beliefs is guided by the world. We can come at that strategy by first looking at an argument that might be made against the antirealist. Many will feel that there is something deeply unsatisfying about the projectivist explanation of what happens when we come to believe that human slavery or the present treatment of animals is morally bad. We want to know that the causal chain leading to the changed beliefs includes the slave himself as having a certain intrinsic worth that must be respected, or the animal itself as having sufficient biological development that we must at least give consideration to it in our ethical choices. (I am not speaking of animal rights here, and if the whole notion of an ethically required respect for animals is unacceptable to you, you may choose a different example. I have used it because I have seen it frequently used in recent ethical discussions.) There is something ethically undeveloped in those for whom that sort of causal chain has not figured in the formation of their moral beliefs.

Now the projectivist has a reply here; one version is given, for example, by Simon Blackburn.[9] Our acts of valuing may be directed not only toward objects but toward other acts of valuing. Thus I may find more valuable a world in which people do not mistreat animals because of

[9] Blackburn, "Errors and the Phenomenology of Value," in *Morality and Objectivity*, Ted Honderich, ed. (London: Routledge and Kegan Paul, 1985), pp. 4–11. Blackburn gives an argument of the general sort that I shall be presenting (and challenging). I am not claming that he would endorse all aspects of the version I consider.

what happens to the animal itself, in comparison to a world in which people think it is their own attitudes that make the cruel treatment wrong. My attitude that I project upon the world finds certain attitudes and ethical beliefs and ways of being morally engaged with the world to be better than others, to be worth endorsing. This is a very powerful move. Take any ethical determinacy that the realist claims to discover in the world. The projectivist simply appends an "I will that such be valuable" to the attitudes that endorse that ethical determinacy, and so ends up with a projectivist account able to support the realist-sounding discourse without making a metaphysical commitment to the presence of values in the world.

Such a move at least resembles one in the standard repertoire of modern philosophy. Take the Kantian reconstruction of the way we distinguish objective reality from what is merely subjective. A realist account would have it that the objective determinations are those that we get from understanding how the world is, while subjective determinations are those due to the ways that experience is ordered by the mind. But Kant tries to retain that distinction, and to support it, by reinstating it *within* the sphere of subjectivity. We then have objective features due to the necessary rules that subjectivity imposes in order to have experience of objects, and subjective features due to the way that matters appear in the experiencing consciousness.

Now an antirealist in ethics may adopt a strategy something like that one in order to refashion, within the realm of the subject's projections, certain distinctions that, as the moral realist will claim, are more naturally supported by his position. In the Kantian structure there are two stances for the self, an empirical stance for which the world is given as having an objective character, and a stance of transcendental idealism from which it is understood that the objective character in question is due to the subject's rules of ordering. The antirealist may propose, in a way roughly similar, that two stances are available in ethical valuations. On the one hand, there is the self having moral perceptions as it encounters the world and comes to understand the ethical character of what it perceives. On the other hand, there is the stance by which the self directs its attitudes and ethical endorsements toward itself and others as relating to the world ethically, and by which it imposes its "rules" for moral objectivity. It might endorse at that level the sort of ethical engagement with the world that many will think of as more typically that of the realist. It might value, for example, the acts of valuing generated by those who look to the world rather than to themselves in developing their ethical beliefs, and who hold that it is something about slaves or animals that makes our historical treatment of them wrong, and not something about our own attitudes. An antirealist of this sort can say that one whose ethical beliefs are formed by his perceiving various circumstance as morally bad is superior to someone whose moral beliefs are formed by copying those of others in the society.

Now the higher-level act of valuing may come to us with our training in a form of life, and may change slowly and without much reflection, or it may be a more reflective activity of individuals. But it allows there to be in ethics something analogous to the Kantian combination of empirical realism and transcendental idealism. Any claim by the realist that x is good in itself can be reparsed as the antirealist claim that my "deep" act of valuing takes the act of valuing x for its own sake to be good. In everyday practice I perceive x as objectively good, as having a character to which I am responding. But the ultimate support of those perceptions is not goodness itself as a feature of reality, but my own acts of valuing directed toward ways of being engaged with the world. (I value the sort of ethical attitudes that lead one to perceive x as good.)

We can see the power of this two-level account of moral projectivism if we consider how it gives us a reply to a case introduced by Nicholas Sturgeon against Harman's argument. Sturgeon says that we typically appeal to moral facts in our explanations of events.[10] One of his examples is the historian DeVoto's claim that the leader of an expedition to rescue the Donner party botched the attempt because of his bad character. But a projectivist such as Blackburn can be content with such explanations. There are the deeply ingrained moral projections that help to constitute our form of life, and these will include our endorsement of attitudes toward certain kinds of character. Then there are the everyday judgments we make that take for granted those constitutive projections, and so we can say that someone's bad character caused him to act as he did. (I do not see that Blackburn has to join Harman in resisting that sort of causal claim, provided we grasp the projectivist's understanding of what we are committed to in endorsing it.)

But I do not find this repetition of the modern strategy satisfactory. It still leaves too much to subjectivity and not enough to the features of the world themselves. Suppose that Blackburn and others like him (the example is his) do have preferences that take world A, where people treat animals well because of something about the animals themselves, to be better than world B, where such treatment is seen to have its basis only in our feelings. Still the animals themselves have not been brought into the causation of moral beliefs in the right manner. It is still ultimately our deep subjective act of valuing certain attitudes that brings the animals into the realm of things requiring ethical consideration. We should not be satisfied until their entry into that realm is shown to be due more to pressures that they themselves bring to bear on us to come

---

[10] Sturgeon, "Moral Explanations," in *Essays on Moral Realism*, Geoffrey Sayre-McCord, ed., pp. 243–55.

up with the right sorts of valuation. There is a weak sense of 'discover' such that for the projectivist we can discover more about the application of our deep projections to particular cases. If we have an attitude that takes wanton cruelty to be wrong, we may discover that we ought to treat animals differently from the ways we now treat them. But again, this does not seem a strong enough sense of 'discover.' The wrongness of that treatment of animals was there to be discovered whether or not we had made that original projection of value.

There is also the question of just how stable that sort of antirealism will be. It is true that one's everyday moral judgments will not be a matter of arbitrary projections. For one's higher-level act of valuing will presumably have valued a stable set of ethical attitudes. But there will be the realization that those higher-level acts are themselves ultimately arbitrary, in the sense that the world itself cannot make some of them better than other ones and the only support for them can be other acts of willing or valuing. Then that realization, once we take hold of it and focus upon it, will threaten the stable attitudes that we have supposedly endorsed. For there will be the understandable temptation to take advantage of the freedom of that powerful stance and to be more creative in valuing quite different kinds of attitudes. In practice, it is true, antirealists will usually cling to a set of very decent moral beliefs and refuse to give them up. But that outcome shows, I think, that those beliefs reflect a sensitivity to the actual ethical character of persons and actions, so that the antirealist's own behavior is best explained by the account of the moral realist.

There will be a further reflection of the arbitrariness of our value-conferring powers for the antirealist.[11] He typically proposes to explain moral judgments as a result of a two-step process: the input to one's belief system that is described in nonmoral language, and the additions made by attitudes that are not to be taken as being sensitive to moral features in the world. The problem is that the failure of various programs to define moral properties in terms of nonmoral ones makes it appear that the input from the first step just described will not give us the classifications we need upon which to project our moral valuing. There will not be well-ordered kinds that we then may *take* to have value. So our projection of value from one individual case to the next will be arbitrary.

Simon Backburn, in pleading the antirealist case, readily grants the possibility of that outcome: The world may indeed be "shapeless" regarding the classifications that our moral projections engender.[12] He

[11] On this issue, see John McDowell, "Non-Cognitivism and Rule-Following," in *Wittgenstein: To Follow a Rule*, S. Holtzman and C. Leich, eds. (London: Routledge and Kegan Paul, 1981), pp. 141–62.

[12] See Blackburn's "Reply: Rule-Following and Moral Realism," in *Wittgenstein: To Follow a Rule*, S. Holtzman and C. Leich, eds., pp. 163–87.

introduces a provocative analogy with things that are funny. If we found different things to be funny, that would be for the extension of 'funny' to have changed; there is not an already articulated extension that is causing us to accommodate ourselves to its contours. In each individual case there is some factor that motivates our taking it to be funny, yet we do not suppose that there must be a way of describing matters, apart from any consideration of their being funny, which will articulate things into the same classifications that we will articulate when we apply our attitudes of taking things to be funny.

But suppose someone says that he just happens to find certain individual lives or actions or traits morally admirable, and that in each case he can find some objective feature that makes him find them so, but that there is no thread of sameness that connects them, other than the bare fact that he finds them admirable. Could we consider him to have a genuine moral sensibility? Concerning what is of moral worth, in contrast with the case of what is funny, it is important to our counting someone as making moral judgments that what is taken to be of worth has, on its own, a certain coherence. What is wrong with the antirealist's picture here, I think, is the way of dividing up matters so that there is an input very thinly described and then, in a second step, projections by subjectivity onto that thinly described world. What happens instead is that in the second step, as our ethical interest is activated, we increase our observational powers and become capable of picking out ethically relevant patterns that were not available to us when our stance toward the world did not yet include any such interest. In some cases the ethical stance that makes those patterns visible will belong to a parochial practice, a particular way of lighting up the world (though what is thus lit up is truly present). But I think there are some ethical features that will be available to any observer at all who cares about what the world is like, ethically speaking.

The realist and his opponent give different accounts of just where the ultimate power is located for conferring an ethically determinate character on traits and actions and institutions. Does it lie with the world or with subjectivity? One way to look at this question is to ask at what points that process of conferring determinacy is open to a variability such that if things had gone differently, a different set of ethical beliefs would have been correct. If the projectivist is right, then if our deep ethical projections had been different, torturing children or animals might have been morally admirable. We would have constituted a different moral universe, with different ethical attitudes seen as worth endorsing. That point brings to mind the late medieval suggestion that if God's free willing, undetermined by anything outside of it, is the source if moral rightness, then his willing that murder is right would have made it morally unobjectionable. Once more we have the modern subject taking over the earlier theological role. But isn't it clear that a divinelike role of determining any ethical objectivity whatever simply is not available to us, even when we consider the race as a whole and not just the powers of our present moral community? There just is not variability where the projectivist says it ought to appear. (Again, I think the notion of turning to higher-level acts of willing or determining, instead of to the world, owes some of its appeal to the fact that God once occupied a position in that structure, and so provided a reason to believe that such acts could be determinate and effective without reference to a world that had been thinned out.)

The move I am making here is, of course, a fairly standard one. I am trying to induce the intuition that at some point our moral beliefs run up against a bedrock objectivity to which they must conform themselves, if they are to be correct. As before, the antirealist is not driven from the field by this move. He will say that the experience of that bedrock objectivity is the experience of coming up against the boundaries of what we ourselves have placed out there to be bounded by. But I do not think we have failed if we are unable to make that move no longer even available to the antirealist. It remains a move in the game, but an unconvincing one, when we consider issues such as that of torturing children and even, I would add, when we consider issues such as respect for an intricate ecosystem. (Provided I can show that the philosopical arguments in favor of moral antirealism are actually much weaker than is typically supposed, then we can open up a space for letting our naturally realist intuitions about ethics be philosophically respectable.)

Now the projectivist may try to turn the tables here by noting a parallel obligation on the part of the realist. We have been considering a demand that an ethical account ought to yield counterfactual truths. If x is genuinely the ground of ethical rightness, then if x were different, ethical rightness would be different as well. (That is part of what we mean by beliefs *tracking* a certain feature; they should vary along with it.) I have claimed that the projectivist does not fare well at satisfying that demand. But how does the realist fare in turn? Can we make sense of the notion that if the world had been different, ethically speaking, then our moral beliefs would have been different also? Harman believes that we cannot. There is no ethical goodness or badness in the world, he thinks, whose varying would cause our moral beliefs to vary along with it.[13]

Now I think that Harman is wrong here. Someone with a mature ethical sensibility, including a well-developed apparatus of belief formation in regard to ethics, will develop the ethical beliefs she does because of the way the world is, ethically. We shall be careful to distin-

---

[13] There is a discussion of this issue of counterfactuals and ethical claims in Sturgeon, "Moral Explanations," pp. 243–55.

guish‏ her from those whose correct ethical beliefs are due more to indoctrination than to the development of an acute sensibility. Consider a case where she takes a particular action to be unethical. If it were not unethical, that is, if it differed slightly but significantly from the unethical action in ways likely to be picked up only by the morally acute, she would not have developed the belief that the action was unethical. There we have a counterfactual whose truth shows that her belief is world-guided. A change in the world would have brought about a change in her belief.

But the antirealist, it seems, would challenge the realist to establish a stronger counterfactual than one of the sort just presented. For the antirealist is happy to acknowledge that once it is given that our "background" ethical projections are the way they are, the morally acute individual would not have had a certain moral perception if the world differed in an ethically significant manner. Genuine world guidance would have to support counterfactuals more like the following. If the universe were different so that its contribution to the articulation of moral kinds were different, then our moral beliefs would have varied as well. If the world had made alternative patterns have positive moral value, then we would have come in the long run to have corresponding beliefs. The model here is that of the natural sciences. We can easily suppose that there could have been an alternative universe in which subatomic particles and scientific laws were different from what they are here, and in that universe, the beliefs of the best scientists would have tracked those objects and laws rather than our own. So it is clear that how the universe actually is helps make our scientific beliefs the ones they are.

But that seems an improper demand to make of ethical beliefs. Ethical practices are different from scientific practices in still another important respect. The interest behind the latter is simply in explaining why certain events occur as they do. So the natural scientist would retain the same interest even in a universe whose principles of operation were very different. But the interest guiding our ethical practices seems more intimately linked to having content be one way rather than another. It does not strain the imagination to suppose that the universe might have been such that certain particles moved in exactly opposite ways from the ways they move in our own. But could there be a universe in which it was ethical to torture and mutilate small children and kill whole populations in gas chambers? That would simply not be an ethical practice, we shall readily and correctly assert. The way the world is, ethically speaking, is such that ethical worth could not vary freely in the way that the behavior of the physical world might vary in a different universe. An ethical interest seems to put far stronger constraints on what an alternative universe could be like than a scientific interest does; it couldn't be all that much different from our own. But that those two interests are unalike in that respect does not force us to reject a claim that in forming our ethical beliefs, we are being sensitive to the world.

Yet we may still want to ask if we can make sense at all of the claim that if the universe were different in its articulation of ethical kinds, then we would have different ethical beliefs. I think that we can. There is something of empirical discovery in our coming to understand what it is to have intrinsic worth, such that if we lived in a different universe from the actual one with its contingencies, the correct ethical account for us might be different. (I am saying more, of course, than that we would have different moral beliefs in the sense that in a universe without race, our moral beliefs about racial equality would be absent.) I suggested earlier (without developing any detailed picture or argument) that an important component in what we find to have intrinsic worth is a well-formedness and self-unifying maintained along with a complementary differentiation and richness; and that by developing our understanding of that component we would come to see that a planetary ecosystem that maintains itself while allowing for very diverse forms of life has value in itself and is deserving of a certain respect.

But I also believe that contingent features of our universe and of the chemical and biological evolution within it are to some degree at the basis of such intrinsic worth. For one thing, being well formed and well functioning, and being able to hold together a complex organization in a unified self-maintaining, will clearly have special worth in a world in which there is natural selection of biological entities capable of surviving a very heated competition to reproduce. For another, the difficulty of such complex and stable unities forming in a universe of chance, and their comparative rarity, make them more valuable than they would be in circumstances rather different. Imagine a universe in which planetary ecosystems, even if destroyed completely, would come back exactly as before within a day of their destruction. Imagine that every planet has billions of duplicates. Imagine that all intelligent beings are easily cloned and their memories easily stored, so that the individuality an entity has in its particular body comes to seem quite unimportant. In such a universe, perhaps, the deepest basis for our notion of intrinsic worth might be different. So our moral beliefs are guided by the world in the sense that we would not have them if the universe were a very different one.

One claim of the projectivist is that he can at least gain a tie on the issue of explanatory power and then win through doing better on the issue of metaphysical parsimony. But just what status ought we grant to his victory in the latter area? A realist *might* make a strong and controversial commitment to a well-articulated ethical universe that stands, like the mathematical one for many theorists, over against happenings of the natural world. Or he might make a commitment to hidden and exotic entities that are supposedly causing our ethical beliefs. But all I have claimed is that a purely physical universe might come to arrange itself, by chance, in certain stable configurations, and that some of these will have a worth that must be respected by individuals who are ethically sensitive. (Much of the more precise determination into ethical kinds comes "from us.") I think the required metaphysical commitment is a rather weak one, and I do not see that a desire for even greater parsimony than that ought to be given much weight in our theorizing about ethics. We are hardly dealing here with anything like a commitment to disease-causing demons in an explanation of disease; we are saying only that some natural arrangements that the universe assumes have an intrinsic worthiness that is a basis for our valuing. We should ask rather just what is behind the desire to make the world extremely thin, so that as many of its determinations as possible will count as up to us.

What I have been proposing, as one explanation of that desire, is that the inertia of the medieval-modern picture of subjectivity retains a considerable power. I described in Chapter 5 how a certain structure emerged in response to the theological absolutism of the late medieval period. That structure included the notion of a self-assertive subject that, in facing a world that could no longer be depended on for metaphysical support, had to generate metaphysical and ethical determinacy from out of its own resources. (Our philosophical training, I claimed, often endorses that conception of the "modern" self imposing its schemes or its ethical determinations upon a much thinner world.) As that conception weakens its hold on us, and as there is no longer the automatic preference for taking the world to be as thin as possible, we shall be much readier to accept that our ethical judgments depend at least in part on a sensitivity to real features of the world.

Perhaps we shall not find a conclusive argument that forces the antirealist to admit defeat. But I hope it is also clear that neither Harman's argument nor the other antirealist arguments considered are strong enough to make us give up realism in ethics. Moral properties are not some *additional* sort of properties at the same level as natural ones. Rather, they are what a morally sensitive person perceives *through* perceiving the nonmoral facts about the world. (Mark Platts has made a similar argument.[14]) We do not have some further kind of evidence to give after we have described the sort of facts about the situation that are available to the sciences. (That is why we can describe the input thinly.) What we are concerned with is the way such facts will *appear* to a moral judger whose moral sensitivity to the world is sufficiently well developed

[14] Mark Platts, *Ways of Meaning* (London: Routledge and Kegan Paul, 1979), pp. 243–7.

to enable him to extract morally relevant patterns from the more thinly described picture of the world.

These debates between realist and antirealist seem interminable because there is always a move available to the other side. Some hold, because of how these debates go on, that it must finally be a matter of one's overall psychological set whether one finds realist or antirealist accounts more satisfying. That would make the issue between the two sorts of accounts turn ultimately on antirealist considerations, as to whether one is projecting an overall preference on the world that will make either realist or antirealist explanations come off as satisfying our deepest criteria for explanations. I think the realist should not accept that final, deep antirealism. It is our overall engagement with the world that helps form in us a way of looking at the world that makes realist accounts in the end preferable both in science and in ethics.

We have been considering philosophical accounts of what it is generally to make moral claims. But an antirealist might try a different sort of strategy and claim that his position does not strive for such a general validity, but rather shows what has become true about our ethical stance as a result of modernization. He might follow Williams in holding that there is a local sort of ethical objectivity that derives from the rich vocabularies that particular communities, especially premodern ones, employ, and that enable them to be sensitive to real features of the local environment.[15] But the introduction of more reflective practices, and encounters with other communities, ultimately lead to communities whose basis for living together must be much thinner and more abstract, and in these communities ethical objectivity will be lost. The question about what ethical beliefs are sensitive to is not so much a timeless metaphysical one. In becoming modern we change our ethical worlds so that we can no longer be taken to be responding to something objective when we express our moral beliefs.

But Williams is, I think, too ready to accept the modern picture of how ethics must go about replacing the more substantial Aristotelian world of good and bad. He thinks that reflection must undermine objectivity because he sees only one way that reflection can go. It must take an account based on what the world can tell us about what is worth valuing, and, in the modern fashion, replace it with an account based on what an abstractly defined subjectivity can generate out of its own structures. So Kantian notions of will and obligation must become the ground of modern moral life, and these notions will be colonialist in their effects of transforming the sphere of practical reason in their image.

But there is another path that reflection might follow. Let us grant that it was the cultural task of modern philosophy to press to the greatest

---

[15] See Williams, *Ethics and the Limits of Philosophy*, pp. 132–73.

extent possible the project of coming to grips with the enriched subjectivity of the modern world, and of seeing to what degree our accounts of
the world could be generated out of the subjective realm. We have seen
that this overall project fails, though parts of it remain important. So
now we are free to ask whether a return to the world, abetted by our
increased powers of reflection and supported by our rejection of the
modern theological pictures of subjectivity, can give us a subtler account
of ethical determinacy.

Moral Realism, Theory, Virtue

There are recent accounts different from my own that seek to overcome
the ways that modern moral theory leaves us with highly formal and
projectivist conceptions. One version of moral realism claims that ethical
investigation is more like ordinary scientific investigation than we might
suppose. A way of defending that claim is to develop a naturalized,
empirical account of ethics in which 'good' means what is good for humans in the sense of satisfying their needs or developing their capacities.
Richard Boyd produces such a theory; he calls his version "homeostatic
consequentialism."[16] What he means is that there is a range of goods
that satisfy human needs, and that these tend to be arranged so that they
are mutually supporting; they form a cluster such that increases in some
contribute to increases in the others. Moral goodness is defined by that
cluster of human goods and the psychological and sociological mechanisms that tend both to increase them and to increase the degree of
cohesion among them. A fair number of our ethical beliefs must be true
if there is to be *epistemic access* of our theories to that homeostatic cluster
(that is, our beliefs can count as genuinely about it) and if it can regulate
the beliefs we have concerning it.[17] The history of the last few centuries,
says Boyd, shows that we do have that sort of epistemic access; our
moral theories are improving pictures guided by empirical features of the
world, even if they have rather far to go.

Peter Railton also wishes to show how there could be a long-term
process by which what is morally good can regulate our moral theories.[18]
He identifies the good with "social rationality" (such as legal and institutional procedures that apply equally to all and practices that give
all interested parties participation in the activities leading to policies).
When the level of social rationality is low in a society, various groups are
treated badly or are left out of decision-making processes, and their
discontent makes the societies unstable. The only historical direction

[16] Richard Boyd, "How To Be a Moral Realist," in *Essays on Moral Realism*, Geoffrey Sayre-
McCord, ed., pp. 181–228.
[17] Ibid., pp. 207–9.
[18] Peter Railton, "Moral Realism," *Philosophical Review* 95 (1986): 163–207.

that will make societies more stable, in the long run, is one that increases the degree of social rationality. So moral beliefs endorsing social rationality, and thus (for Railton) true moral theories, will be selected for by historical development. Railton thinks that the best explanation of certain historical trends will appeal to a causal feedback mechanism in which the objective rightness or wrongness of social institutions will figure essentially.

Now I am not going to investigate those positions here, but I do want to mention what I think will be difficulties for those who wish to defend them. First of all, it seems that a projectivist would have an easy way with Railton's causal mechanism. What is causing the change is social instability, and not whatever moral qualities are possessed by the social order. The projectivist is perfectly willing to grant the existence of mechanisms that may favor more stable societies, and thus societies where fewer people are resentful about how they are treated relative to others. But he does not see anywhere in the process where moral badness or goodness has to come in as a cause. The projectivist will be sure that the kind of self who becomes upset at certain inequalities is one that is itself formed by modern culture. The feedback mechanism does not involve a causal shaping by the moral properties of the social order, but an interplay between a society and the sort of selves that it forms. And there will be, of course, the Nietzschean questions about whether a society that produces selves who are satisfied when they are not being treated unequally is a society that produces morally admirable beings; it is unclear how Railton could even raise this question.

Second, one will be uneasy with how briskly Boyd and Railton assume that what we are looking for in our reflection on ethical life is a systematic theory that will parallel in very many respects the sorts of theories we find in the natural sciences. Why should I suppose that the range of things I discover to have worth will have that degree of theoretical coherence? While we expect theories in science to include what was true in past theories, and suppose indeed that all true statements in a science can be put together into a systematic and consistent account, we cannot expect anything analogous when one form of life, even one we recognize to be on the whole better, takes over from others. We should not look to remove competing conceptions of the good life from political debate, and we do not want to undermine the ways in which our self-shaping is a political process, one in which we choose to weight various goods in part by what we choose to make of ourselves, individually and communally. It is important to see that moral realism requires only the sort of causal power on the part of moral features that we needed to defeat Harman. We do not have to conceive of that causal power as regulating our beliefs in a way as to generate a unified, systematic theory of the good.

Boyd says that the good society will support social mechanisms that contribute to bringing about greater "homeostasis" among the various human goods. But it is by no means clear that such conflict reduction among things that have worth should always be the goal of a society. That project will encourage us too readily to abandon ways of doing things that have an intrinsic and uncommon worth, but that are less easily assimilable than other practices to the cluster of goods in modern society. One social mechanism that will increase homeostasis among human goods is to find a set of goods that do cohere well, and then to use education to encourage self-making processes that form individuals whose preference is for that set of goods rather than for others. But it ought to be evident that there are serious dangers in such methods of achieving homeostasis.

Then there is perhaps the most important objection we can make to theories of the sort put forward by Boyd and Railton. They take as their basis the question about what kind of life would be one that allowed humans to flourish, that satisfied human needs. But then one has decided from the start that only the human good can be ethically significant. But that is, I believe, a fundamentally wrong assumption. We are one species on one planet whose environment has been evolving for billions of years. Like relay runners, we have been able to take advantage of astonishing advances made by other species, and perhaps there will be further species to which we pass the baton. We must ask what has sufficient intrinsic worth to deserve our ethical consideration, in a way that does not take human flourishing to be all that counts, and there may come a time when we must ask which of the natural and cultural goods the planet has so far produced we need to hand onto others, whether human or not.

Another response to the problems of modern moral theory is to return to a more Aristotelian account of ethics, one based on the notions of virtue, character, and habit. Alasdair MacIntyre claims that the life of the virtuous individual requires a community with a clear conception of what is the good for human life; practices that cultivate the virtues needed to develop the self and the community so that living that good life is possible; and a more narrative-oriented (rather than punctual) notion of the self so that it makes sense to ask about the shape aimed at by a whole life.[19]

Now MacIntyre might have gone on to say the following. Modern forms of life have ethically admirable strengths. They promote, for example, social rationality, equality, social justice, and individual self-making. But they tend to weaken other aspects of human living that are also admirable: the "Aristotelian" character-forming institutions, excellence, honor, and the like. So our task is to try to build a way of life that

---

[19] Alasdair MacIntyre, *After Virtue* (Notre Dame, Ind.: Notre Dame Press, 1984).

finds some kind of balance among the strengths of the ancient and modern conceptions. We have no reason to believe that there is a systematic way of bringing the various goods together, in order to weight them against one another in a scientific manner. Our goal instead is to test various social forms that seem appropriately to respect the various kinds of goods that human individuals and communities can achieve.

But MacIntyre does not say that. He thinks we must turn away from the modern forms of life because they are, at their basis, nihilistic. But we need to ask whether they are inherently so or whether the problem is rather with a particular way of understanding the relations of self and world, and their relation to ethical value. The problem, I believe, is not with modernity itself, but with the theological conception of subjectivity that is behind may modern positions, and that must lead to highly formal or to projectivist accounts, and to the thinned-out ethical world. But the recovery of the world that I have been arguing for, with its rethinking of the role of subjectivity, allows us to reject the nihilistic reading of the modern.

I am sure it is worthwhile to contribute to the revival of the vocabulary of character, virtue, habit, honor, excellence, citizenship, civility, stoicism, self-control, endurance, and moral heroism. Its replacement by a psychological and sociological vocabulary, and by the therapeutic vocabulary of subjective feeling and self-expression, has hardly been to our advantage. There are very genuine problems about how to balance, on the one hand, the good of living in an ethical community with well-formed habits of character formation and interaction, and, on the other, the goods of freedom, self-making, and reflection. But it ought to be clear that a rejection of the Kantian institutions of the modern world is not the way to go on this issue. On the other hand, there is a need to keep a wide range of vocabularies and ethical conceptions in play against the homogenizing tendencies of culture, and to pay more attention to those goods that modern forms of life, insofar as they operate blindly, tend both to underestimate and to weaken.

7

Self-relating Selves

In Chapter 2 we looked at intentional states and their place in the causal order. One strategy for giving them a place, we saw, was to account for the intentional in terms of nonintentional causal processes. Such accounts, insofar as they attempt to replace the one sort of explanation by the other, came off as unpromising. Now we need to look at subjectivity in a more general manner, and to consider some of the features of entities that possess it. If earlier I have given arguments in favor of a disenchantment of subjectivity, I shall be resisting in this chapter what seems to me a too easy and too radical acceptance of that outcome. For some in cognitive science, the issue of intentional content is easily separable from any question about the *experiences* of subjects; the first-person standpoint of the conscious experiencer may seem little more than a nuisance for a theory of intentionality. Then there are the thinkers who claim that subjectivity is a social invention aimed at increasing control over individuals, and that we ought to proclaim that subjectivity is dead, in the sense and tone in which Nietzsche proclaimed the death of God. What is common here is the belief that the important phenomena and powers that earlier philosophers ascribed to subjectivity not only have no special status but are marginal or illusory, or even dangerous. An idea rather prevalent in work called postmodern is that once we claim that the subject is just a product of cultural discourses, a fiction encouraged by them in the interests of power, then there are no further problems regarding how subjectivity is possible. There are no further issues regarding the nature of consciousness, or regarding what it means to *take* the world to be a certain way; no unanswered questions about what it is like to be an experiencer of a particular kind, about the conditions for having something *matter* to an entity, or about what it is for a self to be concerned with itself. But these questions and many others like them remain, and at this stage we are not very good at answering them.

In resisting the outcome that flattens out the subjective realm until it is insignificant, I want to ask whether there are certain features of the modern notion of subjectivity that "disenchanted" accounts explain rather poorly. I shall not question the resolution to reject those pictures that gave metaphysical depth and power to the modern self by taking over models from theology and religion. But perhaps many features integral to the modern conception, and investigated by modern philosophers, remain of importance even after those models are rejected. Perhaps much more will survive the policy of disenchantment than more radical versions of it can allow.

Ways of Being Self-relating

Often we think of subjectivity in an impoverished way, as if it were just the "how it feels" that most inquiries into the nature of intentionality can ignore, or as if it had to do with the empiricist's cataloguing of internal objects. But I think we shall have better luck if at least to begin with, we briefly consider some investigations of the character of subjectivity that can be found in German idealism and in phenomenology. I shall not focus upon metaphysical or epistemological issues here, and I am by no means attempting a systematic treatment of the topic. As my purpose is not historical, I shall not worry overmuch about attribution to, and distinctions among, individual philosophers. I want instead to set up a context for discussing a range of issues concerning subjectivity, and I shall be trying just to put on the table, uncritically at first, various ways we might think about the capacities that arise from, or are a condition of, the occupation of a subjective stance toward the world.

We saw that central to Hegel's notion of subjectivity, and ubiquitous in his work, was a structure of self-relating-in-relating-to-otherness. The very liberality of that notion may be helpful if it encourages us to think in less rigid ways, and with a considerably wider focus, about the sorts of things that might come into play in one's being a subject. So we want to look in a relaxed manner at how something might be self-relating; then we can use that discussion as a background for asking about the thresholds that an entity has to cross, and about the specific capacities it has to possess, in order to meet the standards for being a subject. I should note from the start that there is perhaps a bias built into our investigation by the decision to begin with the self-relational structure that thinkers such as Kant, Fichte, and Hegel were concerned with, instead of with sensations in primitive organisms. We can go rather far down the evolutionary ladder and still have forms of life that can taste and smell and the like. We are obviously at a higher level when we think of having sensations as involving an implicit reference to an 'I' that is having them, that is experiencing *itself* tasting and smelling and so forth. But I just do not know what is useful to say here about what it is for sensations suddenly to appear in the evolutionary scheme. There is much work in psychology today concerning perception and attention and consciousness, and those wanting to offer philosophical accounts of these matters have to be familiar with that material. But I am trying to do something less ambitious. I want to know whether looking at certain philosophical investigations of what it is to be self-relating can give us a useful perspective on some questions about the character of subjectivity.

We might ask, following Hegel, how something can be "for itself." For something to be self-relating (at least in the generous sense in which Hegel uses the notion) it must have, first of all, conditions of self-identity that to some degree it sets for itself; it must differentiate itself from what is around it. That capacity, of course, does not yet indicate the presence of subjective states, and it may seem an unacceptably loose playing with language to say that there is anything like a self-relating going on in such a case. But I think we often begin discussions about whether something could be a subject at too intellectualist a level of analysis (asking, for example, about the quality of logical powers of processing sentencelike units); we fail to ask to what degree having intentional states requires having a self-articulating *individuality*, such that how things turn out can *matter* for the entity in question. (Claims made about computers and intentional states often fail to consider this factor. That is one reason they often strike one as foolish from the start.)

The living organism is (in Hegel) more explicitly "for itself" because it more actively maintains itself as the same. It engages in behavior that fends off destruction and dissolution, its parts are ordered as members of a whole, and many of its changes are not determined from the outside but from its internal self-differentiation and self-development. It is not just that an onlooker may mark off organisms as individual units; they maintain themselves as such through a wide range of activities, and matters are in their interest or not depending on how they affect their self-maintenance and self-replication. (These, for Hegel, are again implicit forms of self-relatedness.[1])

The German idealists insist on seeing the subject's relation to the world as fundamentally active. It sets itself in relation to what is around it (that relation doesn't simply happen to it from without). It determines the conditions for its engagement with the things in its environment, and the character of that engagement becomes to a greater degree something for which it is responsible. We might ask in this regard (and I shall ask in this chapter) how something's relating to the world, its representing of it, can be something that it *does*. How active in this sense must something be before we count it as genuinely *representing* the world and not just as reacting to stimuli? When should we say that it not only responds to the world but also *takes* the world to be a certain way?

There is for these thinkers an implicit self-relatedness or *reflexivity* that is found generally in the various ways we encounter the world, and that is more evident when we come to the higher forms of mental activity.

---

[1] See, for example, the logical conception of the living organism in *Hegel's Logic*, William Wallace, trans. (Oxford: Clarendon Press, 1975), pp. 278–82.

Perhaps I can count as a believer or intender or rule follower only because I can implicitly take myself to be engaged in activities such as judging, representing, believing, rule following, and the like.[2] (It is not just that an interpreter finds it useful to assign me beliefs.) A child who understands herself to be following rules will behave differently from one who does not. She will be disturbed by certain challenges to her behavior, will offer some kinds of defenses for it rather than others, and will adapt her moves in relevant ways. Someone who takes herself to be a believer will be concerned with the status of her beliefs, and so with changes in evidence, and with the objections to those beliefs that others might raise. She may be disturbed in a situation not so much by a challenge to a particular belief she has put forward, but by the implicit challenge to herself as a believer. In claiming that someone did an action intentionally, I am not looking for a mysterious inner act of intending, but I do look for evidence that the other took himself at least implicitly to be engaged in that action as such. That structure of reflexivity (my being at least implicitly self-relating as a condition for my engagement with the world) is given a great deal of play by the philosophers we are considering, and it is important to see that the structure can be present before there are highly advanced states of self-consciousness and self-willing.

I can also be self-relating in being concerned with the sort of self I am and with its psychic integrity, and thus with the pattern of commitments and the characteristic way of being in the world that are important to its maintaining itself as the same. (It matters to me how things turn out for *me*.) There is a relation-to-self that occurs just by the fact that what sort of self I am to be is an issue for me, something still to be decided and decidable only by me, whether or not I come to think about the matter with full self-consciousness.[3] To be an 'I' at all is to have this self-concern, as Heidegger claims; it is present in my practical life even when I am not thinking about myself in the manner of Cartesian reflection. As I become more well-ordered and self-maintaining in regard to my psychic integrity, I shall become more clearly distinguished from others, and more able to expose myself to what is other without losing my identity, as my activities unfold from a more stable inner unity that I have to some degree brought about. The German idealists emphasize that I am

---

[2] There is a nice discussion of the importance of our taking of ourselves to be engaged with the world in a certain way in Robert Pippin, *Hegel's Idealism* (Cambridge: Cambridge University Press, 1989), pp. 3–59.

[3] This is the structure that was investigated by Heidegger in *Being and Time*. But one can also find such an investigation in earlier philosophy, in German idealism and in Kierkegaard, for example. For a good treatment of Heidegger on the relation of oneself to oneself, see Ernst Tugendhat, *Self-Consciousness and Self-Determination* (Cambridge, Mass.: MIT Press, 1986), pp. 144–218. Tugendhat's book is a study of the notion of the self-relating self.

freer, and more fully self-related, insofar as what I am and what I think become more a matter of my own doing, as I give a more determinate shape to my life and a more determinate order to my desires.

Hegel organizes his study of mental activity, what he calls the philosophy of subjective spirit, in order to show an increasing degree of active self-relating on the part of the self.[4] We relate to ourselves more in memory and imagination than in sensation or perception because in the former two we are freer to produce the material on our own, and so to encounter something of our own shape in what we are thinking about. In calling something a representation, says Hegel, we shift the explanatory burden from the object to the subjective apparatus; representing is something we do, and we might do it in the absence of what is supposedly being represented, so we are more actively present in the doing of it than in perception.[5] The mind gains a freer self-relating as its material becomes conceptual, that is, as it comes to share in the mind's own nature. The use of arbitrary signs is, for Hegel, a higher stage than the use of symbols because in the former the mind is freer to invest the sign with its own conceptual activity.

For certain thinkers in this tradition one's self-relating becomes more fully developed through an extensive set of relations to others. I come to recognize others as other, and to recognize myself as having one among competing perspectives on the world, and I recognize their recognizing of me as having a particular perspective, so that I see my way of seeing things *as* a way of seeing things, my way of being engaged with the world as just such a way of being engaged. In attending to the world, then, I am attending to something that has my mark upon it, that exhibits itself according to my perspective. And only in setting myself over against others do I have the kind of self-relatedness needed for my own individuality and self-recognition. There must be a structure by which an 'I' both differentiates itself from what is other and sets itself in relation to the other *as* other. (Compare that account to one that would reduce subjectivity to patterns of causal relations among internal entities.) The 'I', says Hegel, is an activity of *negation*, of opposing itself to what is objective, of calling into question any particular determinacy of the world or of the self.

My self-relating, says Hegel in the *Philosophy of Right* and elsewhere, aims at being objective. I try to carve out a sphere in which I can relate to something as mine, as that in which I can find myself to be invested.

---

[4] *Hegel's Philosophy of Mind*, W. Wallace and A. Miller, trans. (Oxford: Clarendon Press, 1971).

[5] See Willem DeVries, *Hegel's Theory of Mental Activity* (Ithaca, N.Y.: Cornell, 1988), p. 122. DeVries gives a summary of the developments in Hegel's philosophy of subjective spirit, and I have drawn upon that summary here.

That sphere will include not only personal property but actions and practices that I can take to be the embodiment of my willing, so that there can be a genuine sense to my claim that when I will, I am willing myself. Through labor I make my mark upon the world, I transform matters according to my conceptions, I compete with others to put my stamp on things, to claim things as my own. In coming to recognize myself out there in the world, through the ways I have transformed it and made it mine, I become capable of a more internal and reflective self-relating. It is crucial that others recognize me as someone capable of embodying my free activity in a sphere that is mine, and of willing actions in which I can recognize my willing. The institutions of developed modern societies, believes Hegel, include a rich set of such practices of mutual recognition, so that one's self-relating can be given objective form in those practices, and in societies of that sort.

In coming to grips with a world of objects, one is relating (say these thinkers) to that in which one's own conceptual life is invested. For the having of objects requires the employment of categories with which the subject "works over" what is given and transforms it into an objective world. (In knowing what is other, I am knowing in it the structures of my own knowing; in willing what is other, I am willing myself as a willer.) The forms of self-relatedness in one's subjective life are then quite varied in the tradition we are considering. I may explicitly turn toward myself in opposition to what is other. There is also an implicit reflexivity in my being directed toward the world while I am engaged within it. And I also discover myself mirrored in what is other so that my relating to otherness has, itself, a self-relational aspect.

I have so far not specifically addressed what is to many the most obvious case of being in a relation to oneself: the various capacities we include under sensation and consciousness. In what sense can I be said to be in relation to myself in being conscious? Perhaps I could develop a computer with sensors capable of analyzing the odors of various items, and of identifying them correctly as often as humans do. But the computer would not thereby be *smelling* anything. So if it is not just an episode of acquiring information about the world, what is an experience? How can matter organized a certain way produce the kind of self-presence that occurs when I have experiences, and that is not reducible to an acquiring of information about myself or the world by looking at internal objects or states? We need not suppose that whether something has sensations is simply inscrutable. Those who like wine can easily be seen as arranging matters so as to make certain taste *experiences* possible. But it surely remains true that the feature many recent accounts have most difficulty explaining is the having of experiences. Later in the chapter I am going to examine how Dennett attempts to explain this feature, and we shall need to ask whether the having of conscious states, including being in moods as well as having experiences, is a condition for having beliefs and intentions in the first place.

There is also an implicit self-relatedness in the way I am at home in my body in being at home in the world. Phenomenologists such as Merleau-Ponty in France tried to give a richer and more adequate analysis of our self-presence than that provided by empiricism or Cartesianism. They asked about the body's experience of itself as it moved through its surroundings. The "lived body" as I experience it is not an object about which I am learning facts, nor is it a barrier between me and the world, as if in experiencing its states I am acquainted with a class of inner items *instead* of with the world. It is my way of being present in the world itself. I am at least implicitly aware of myself as actively and purposefully projecting myself onto situations, and as called into question by their features.

Part of being a self, it seems, is having that implicitly reflexive, self-relational structure. One is somehow "with oneself," concerned with oneself, having an implicit attitude toward oneself, in being in relation to things and in making decisions about them. But how could my (even implicit) taking a stance toward myself be a condition for being a self? We seem to have an odd structure. It appears that what I am supposed to be setting myself in relation to comes into being only through my setting myself in relation to it. Only by having concern for myself and by recognizing myself as effective am I a self at all.

Our self-relational activity occurs in a developed form when we are free or self-determining. But in what sense can we have a genuine autonomy? Our activity will be the result of biological and cultural formation and will exhibit the limits of what that formation process has made of us. In addition, the selves that result will not be responsible for the processes that turned them into the self-relating selves they are. That will be an unacceptable outcome for a thinker such as Fichte. He claimed that there was an activity of synthesizing and taking-to-be that must be metaphysically more originative than, and not a product of, the world so taken. Even my desires must be taken to be such, must be made determinate and endorsed, for them to be effective.[6] We must not just be able to act upon principles or rules; we must be responsible for the adoption of those principles or rules in the first place. I must choose to be the very self that is choosing to lead a particular sort of life. If we are looking at the notion of self-relation in order to get a grip on what it is to be a subject, then a critical topic will be how much of these notions of self-determination and self-willing can survive the disenchantment of subjectivity.

---

[6] See the discussion of Fichte's practically self-determining self in Frederick Neuhouser, *Fichte's Theory of Subjectivity* (Cambridge: Cambridge University Press, 1990), pp. 117–66.

Individuality, Consciousness, and Representation

Let us see if we can reap any dividends from that investigation of German philosophy and its accounts of self-relating. We are trying to understand how the capacities that subjects possess might arise in a universe of physical stuff and its arrangements, and we want to see what some important thresholds might be in coming to have those capacities. I am going to look first at three issues: being an individual, being conscious, and being a representer. One question raised by the previous section is whether being a self-articulating, self-maintaining individual might be a condition for having intentional states. That question is an important one because of the direction of some recent discussions about the place of intentionality in the causal universe. One tries to show that there is nothing mysterious about intentional states by proposing that one can build a machine that has them, namely the computer. The best way to make sense of the chess-playing computer, it is said, is to attribute beliefs and intentions to it on the basis of its behavior. To have beliefs is just to have internal states that interact with one another, and with input from the world, in such a way as to produce the kind of complex behavior that is best understood by an interpreter as caused by beliefs. Many find this analysis to be foolish from the start. The chess-playing computer is just the wrong sort of thing to have beliefs and no matter how "intelligent" its behavior gets, it will never count as taking the world to be any way at all.

A computer scientist might reply that it is true that the syntactical operations of the computer, taken by themselves, do not mean anything. But they are given a meaning by their causal relations to things and by their insertion in public practices. But here again I think we see the sometimes unhelpful consequences of working with models taken from work in formal semantics. We suppose that the problem of meaning is simply a matter of how grammatically well-formed strings get assigned a semantic interpretation. So there seems no special problem in the case of computers.

But my mental states and utterances can mean something because the world can mean something to *me*. It *matters* that some things are present in the environment rather than others, and it does so because states of affairs are good or bad relative to my interests. And I can have these interests because I am a self-articulating and self-maintaining individual who aims at preserving both my physical and psychic integrity. So the objector here is correct to suppose that computers as we know them just are not proper candidates for the assignment of meaningful states. There are no processes by which they maintain and develop themselves as particular, well-differentiated individuals. They do not set off clear boundaries against what is other, nor do they transform what is other into something of their own. Their processes of development are not self-determined by the character of what they are. Perhaps they might be given the capacity to regulate and maintain themselves in the sense of monitoring and repairing problems with their chips, but that is not to maintain oneself as a self-determining *whole*. You can add peripherals to them and change software so that their "thoughts" are entirely different, and yet none of this makes any difference to the computer. Its boundaries are not in any sense boundaries *for it* that can be a matter of concern.

Now living things are, of course, the beings we know with the capacities just mentioned, and it might be easier to say that computers cannot have intentional states because they are not living. (Being alive would be a necessary but not sufficient condition for having such states.) But that is not quite right. There are things that living organisms *do* that make us ascribe to them the states we ascribe, and it should not simply be a matter of being made of protoplasm that does the trick. Perhaps we can understand intentionality better if we ask what it would be to grant computers something like the self-articulating and self-maintaining capacities that living things have.

That issue comes to the fore when we consider a well-known argument put forward by John Searle.[7] He develops a case against computational approaches to mind generally by asking us to imagine that he has been placed inside a box and given a series of charts. When certain written characters come in, he reads the charts and then sends forth other characters as output, using just his ability to recognize formal shapes. Now he does not know a word of Chinese, but to an outside observer the input–output relations are such, due to the high quality of the recipe charts that Searle has available, that Searle, or rather the box itself, seems to be speaking Chinese. But there is no understanding of Chinese here, says Searle; all understanding of the language rested with those who made the charts, analogous in this case to those who program a computer. No matter how good the formal program gets to be, following that program through manipulating syntactic shapes will never count as understanding. So computers do not, by instantiating a program, understand.

Now Searle has set up the experiment in a way that duplicates the two-step picture of subjectivity that we rejected in Chapter 2. First there are the internal happenings that are blind to the world and that are performed in this case by a homunculus (Searle). Then there is the step by which the sequences produced by those interior activities are given intentionality by the way that *external* observers link those sequences to the world. We are not at all tempted to think of the box-plus-Searle as having the self-maintaining unity that characterizes intentional agents. If

---

[7] Searle's thought experiment is in his essay "Minds, Brains, and Programs," in *Mind Design*, John Haugeland, ed. (Cambridge, Mass.: MIT Press, 1981), pp. 282–306.

there are such features as purpose, differentiation of self from what is other, and self-concern for psychic integrity, they reside in Searle and not in the whole. But only the whole is producing the Chinese-speaking behavior that might be considered intelligent. So the factors of self-individuation and world-directedness are just too dispersed to allow there to be intentional activity here. What he presents us with is a nonstarter; it never had a chance from the beginning of being a candidate for having a mental life. The experiment tries to put subjectivity together in the wrong way, as if you could break down the structure of self-relating-in-relating-to-otherness into two components that are then forced together in an arbitrary and external relationship, instead of being aspects of an overall structure that comes all at once. We should not be surprised, then, given the conclusions we reached earlier, that Searle is left with a blind internal manipulation of meaningless shapes.

Now Searle perhaps is only making an argument against those who hold that *just* by instantiating the formal program of something that has intentional states, an entity will count as itself having intentional states. On that point he is right; the position he is attacking gives a far too intellectualist picture of subjectivity, as if it were a matter of the processing of logically defined sequences. But Searle ought then to expand his story so as to bring into clearer focus just what computers are missing in not even being candidates for having a mind. To make his case more fairly, he would have to tell a science fiction story that allowed for a situation something like the following. Imagine a future world in which computerized robots are developed that have the ability to evolve on their own and that are capable of extremely sophisticated behavior. Both their internal engineering and their programs have some principle of mutation and adaptation to the environment, and there are different "races" of these robots that are made to compete with one another for access to the parts and the programming capacities that will allow them to replicate their kind. The robots are also made to have strong tendencies toward establishing themselves as individuals with clear self–other differentiation and with the goal of preserving themselves as individuals. I shall let the story go at this point; it would have to become much more sophisticated and perhaps it is already begging many questions. But couldn't some such story make sense? And would that kind of development make us more willing to say that these robots had beliefs and desires, or is the crucial factor that makes for intentionality still missing?

As I discussed earlier, many are put off by the use of these thought experiments in philosophy. But subjectivity is extremely difficult to think about and we need such stories, with their controlled variation of key features, to investigate what is necessary for intentionality, and what is an aspect merely of our human instantiation of it. We might even come up with a story that moved in the opposition direction. Perhaps taking away the self-maintaining individuality of humans would make them no longer count as having beliefs and intentions. Imagine that in the future there are huge computers built out of the same material and with the same engineering as human brains. These "brains" are lined up in a massive system for parallel processing, so that problem solving is made to work across the entire system, with no individual brain having any well-individuated function, and with the body of no individual person being guided by the system's operations. Would there be intentional states in that situation? Which is a more important feature for having them, being a self-maintaining individual or being made out of the right kind of brainstuff? What other features must one have to qualify? I think the questions are fair ones, even if I am not sure how to answer them, and some logical/computational investigations of computers and intentionality are fatally weakened right off by a failure to be sensitive to the issues they raise.

Another important threshold, of course, is that of consciousness. Colin McGinn points out that while we understand a lot about beliefs and about reasoning, consciousness still seems a complete mystery to us, even though its appearance in animal evolution is very early. He believes that the engineering of our brains is not designed so that we can form the concepts needed to understand the relation between subjectivity and the natural order. He thinks there is something principled about our inability to grasp that relation either by starting from physical stuff and its arrangements or by starting from conscious introspection. It is not that consciousness is mysterious in itself. Intelligent beings without the engineering biases of our brains might easily develop the concepts to understand it. But our own engineering gives us access only to the surface of what consciousness is.[8]

Now it could turn out that McGinn is right about this, but there is always something suspect in those arguments that set unsurpassable limits on what our concepts can grasp by looking at what they have been able to grasp to this point. It may be the case that just a revolution in our ways of thinking, and not a change in our brain engineering, is needed for us to think clearly about consciousness. There is a different argument to the effect that there is something wrong with the very idea of trying to fit subjectivity into our objective picture of the world. The kernel of the argument is that precisely by being subjective, by being a matter of how things *seem* to someone, subjective states will quite naturally fail to fit into what we determine as objectively present.[9] To

---

[8] That is the central argument put forward by McGinn in *The Problem of Consciousness* (Oxford: Blackwell, 1991).
[9] One version of this argument is in Bernard Williams, *Descartes: The Project of Pure Enquiry* (London: Penguin, 1990), pp. 295–7.

make the seemings objective, and thus to make them repeatably deter-minable from a stance that can be generally occupied, would be to detach them from the perspective that makes them what they are, that is, from how they seem to the one entertaining them. How matters seem is not one more item added on to how matters are, in an account that tries to list everything objective. But even if this claim is valid, we would not be right to rest with that bald conclusion about the unfitness of the subjective for inclusion in our picture of objectivity. We would still have to ask about what sorts of arrangements of physical stuff are able to sup-port these seemings. Perhaps the character of a subjective experience can be given a different sort of objectivity through an imaginative empathy that others can perform. Even if how something seems is not one more object in the universe, only an internal one, still we are not left with just a mute enjoyment of our own experiencings. We can still ask about the introduction of subjective experience in the chain of evolution, and about the kind of reasons we would give for saying that something was having experiences or was not. A great deal of investigation would be open that was not aimed at *reducing* the subjective to some objective arrangement.

So we need still to ask about how consciousness might emerge, and Dennett gives us perhaps the most developed story.[10] He asks, first, how the stream of consciousness comes about that introspection typically presents to us. His account is one that we might call "outside in," in that consciousness arises in part from once public practices that have become internalized. Early language-users could use sounds to warn one another, advise one another, scold one another, and so on. Gradually these self–other practices could be turned into practices in which the self communicated with itself. The production of sounds used to warn or advise could be given sotto voce and become a self-warning, a self-scolding, a self-advising. This would be especially valuable, says Dennett, when there is pertinent information stored somewhere in a speaker's brain, but he does not have the proper brain connections to link that information directly to action. But by hearing himself speak, he makes use of language-production and language-reception mechanisms that had developed to deal with other persons and their speech but that can now provide a new circuit, as it were, that gets the vital information to the instruments of agency. There is a very real sense, then, in which conscious thought is about hearing oneself speak in order to find out what one wants.

Some machines process information serially, with matters following one after another in one sequence or in one channel, while other machines are parallel processors, with many channels acting simultaneously and

---

[10] I shall be giving in the next few paragraphs just a brief account of the complex position put forward by Dennett in *Consciousness Explained* (Boston: Little, Brown, 1991).

exchanging information as they do. The human brain is the latter sort of machine, says Dennett, but the stream of consciousness is serial. Dennett's suggestion is that consciousness is a "virtual machine" pressed upon a more primitive brain architecture that operates quite differently. A virtual machine is a set of rules for moving from some machine states to other ones; it is expressed in software made to run on actual computing machines. The actual machine's hardware produces a programmed set of operations, but these can be made (through software) to mimic the operations of some *other* actual machine, which is then present in a *virtual* way when that machine is running with that software. (The Macintosh, for example, may be running a program that does word-processing. One might have designed an actual machine whose hardware was such as to be running that specific program, but it is usually far more efficient to design an actual machine flexible enough to be programmed to run many different machines virtually.) Consciousness is then for Dennett a "cobbled together" phenomenon in that the press of culture forces an actual machine, namely a brain designed for other purposes, to run a series of operations that are something like the running of a serial machine whose states can be fairly easily monitored by us. (Very much, of course, still takes place the old-fashioned way beneath the level of consciousness.)

Dennett is often persuasive in the ways that he shows how certain features of the stream of consciousness might arise. But the great difficulty for accounts of consciousness is not so much the talking to oneself that occurs when we deliberate, but the intrinsic aspects of our sensations that we call *qualia*, simply how they *feel*. (While the talking-to-oneself phenomenon may have occurred quite late in evolution, such qualia seem to have appeared early on in much more primitive animals. Dennett does have interesting things to say about how the phenomenon of attention might have developed from the usefulness early of an "all-hands-on-deck" monitoring of sensory information.) The taste of chocolate and the smell of garlic are very noticeable examples of qualia. We said earlier that if an extremely sophisticated computer were able to give an olfactory analysis of stimuli and could discriminate among the various smells that we can, still it would not be *smelling* anything. There are two factors, we might say, in our sensations. One is a set of causal powers to make discriminations about how the world is appearing and to dispose us toward certain other states and actions; the second factor is the experiential feel itself. The computer could have the former but not the latter, and that is why it cannot be conscious. But how can we find a place for such subjective sensations in our overall picture of the world? Dennett's answer is a very simple one. There are no qualia, he says.[11] There are

---

[11] Ibid., pp. 369–411.

only the dispositions to make discriminations and to affect other states.

The defender of qualia will want to say in reply that there really are two factors and that Dennett fails to collapse them into one. My experience just is not my experience without those intrinsic properties of my sensations. This claim can be supported if we can show that there is some experience that can remain the same, and can thus have its own identity, even as the discriminative and dispositional abilities attached to it are changed. People can be given image-reversing goggles, for example, that make everything appear upside down, and yet over time many learn to adapt their behavior so that they get about very well in the world while wearing the goggles. Now the question is whether there is an experience here that remains the same even as the behavior changes; if there is, then Dennett's one-factor account is wrong and there is more to qualia than he allows. And the natural reply is that one is having the same visual experience that one used to have when turned upside down. But Dennett says we will have a difficult time showing this. There will be no principled way of deciding whether we are having the same experience as we used to have upside down, and then are adapting our movements to the new feedback from the world, or whether we have adjusted rather for the different retinal input, so that we now are having the same experience of a right-side-up world that we used to have and are behaving accordingly. Given the way the brain works, with all its parallel tracks and with no central theater where the state of the processing is being *shown* to the self, even a god couldn't look inside and determine just where on the causal chain between input and action an adjustment has been made for the distortion. If there is no fact of the matter here, that is because there is nothing there for which there might be identity conditions; there are no qualia. There seem to be qualia but there are not. Seemings are not anything objective.

Now I cannot tell how people would characterize their experience with the reversing goggles, but I just am not persuaded by Dennett's argument. If something happened to my brain-wiring such that rotten eggs began to smell the way that chocolate does now, I think I would not have a difficult time deciding that there was an experience that had remained the same *as* an experience, but that now was attached to quite different discriminative abilities. How the world *seems* to me could have identity conditions apart from causal dispositions; there is at least that degree of objectivity to it.

So I think that Dennett has not shown that there are no intrinsic qualities of experiential states; that conclusion makes more questionable what our disenchantment of subjectivity has accomplished. If Dennett is correct, then there remains nothing in principle that is mysterious about having a subjective stance toward the world. If it is discriminative abilities and related dispositions that count, then computers, perhaps rather different from those now around, could easily count as being conscious. The experiential states that they supposedly would be missing would have been shown by Dennett to be nothing at all. But I am not persuaded that he is right. So the first-person stance of subjectivity will not surrender so easily to third-person reconstructions of it, and we shall have to acknowledge that the accounts we now have available just cannot explain what conscious experience is, so that our naturalization of it is so far unsuccessful. (It will still be true that we may profitably study how consciousness works in humans by studying the human brain and the various sorts of excitations and oscillations and wave patterns that occur in it when the individual's attention level is high. But those investigations cannot resolve the issue of the place of subjectivity in the universe. For we might take the patterns we thus uncover, reproduce them in a machine, and still wonder if what results should count as having experiences, so that there is something it is like to be a brain of that new sort.)

Another threshold important to subjectivity is that crossed when an entity can count as *representing* the world, but it is unclear what that activity would entail. In my look at German philosophy, I mentioned the claim that subjects are active in relating to the world, and that they set the conditions for their engagement with its features. Perhaps we can make use of that notion in asking about what it is to be a representer. Fodor and Dennett both give suggestions that are at least in the spirit of that claim. Fodor's suggestion goes like this.[12] He is worried that if we grant representational states to computers, then there is no stopping place that prevents someone from going all the way down and granting them to thermostats and to unicellular organisms. (The thermostat's internal states "represent" the room as being of a certain temperature.) Now we can say that an entity is registering some feature of the world if we can show it producing a behavioral response to that feature's presence. But let us make a distinction between two sorts of features that may be registered in that manner. Some of them are such that the story of the causal path from worldly feature to response needs to refer only to properties (in the thing whose feature is being registered and in the feature-registering mechanism of the behaver) that are specifiable by the causal laws of the natural sciences. That may seem a difficult way of setting off this category, but examples make it clearer. Magnitudes of light, of heat, and of electricity are of this sort, and an organism that responds to changes in light strength is responding to such a property. (Fodor calls the properties *nomic* ones.[13])

[12] Jerry Fodor, "Why Paramecia Don't Have Mental Representations," in *Midwest Studies in Philosophy*, Vol. X, Peter French, Theodore Uehling, and Howard Wettstein, eds. (Minneapolis: University of Minnesota Press, 1986), pp. 3–23.
[13] Ibid., pp. 8–11.

But humans may also register and respond to features such as what is fashionable to wear, what is dangerous to children, what is advantageous as a chess move. Such properties are not picked out by the causal laws of the natural sciences; and an explanation of someone's detecting of such properties, and of their responses to that detection, will not be able to work by appealing to how nomic properties in the objects affect the physical features of the detecting apparatus. It will be true that at some level we are sensitive to such properties by being sensitive to physical magnitudes; that is how we take in information after all. But our inner states are complex enough, and their interrelations sophisticated enough, that in sensing physical magnitudes in complicated patterns we can be sensitive to higher-level features and patterns. So the suggestion is that something passes over into the set of those things that have representations when it can take the world to have nonnomic properties. It is only such entities that take the world to be a certain way, that are capable of *seeing as*.[14] The causal chain from object to response must pass through a feature-registering apparatus whose internal complexity allows both inferences among internal states and the use of background knowledge in perceiving the world. A light-seeking organism will have no chance of making it.

Now imagine a case where a simple organism has three dangerous predators all of which are red. It evolves a red-detecting apparatus and flees whenever it sees that color. It makes a difference whether we say that behavior is a response to a nomic property (the wavelength of red) or to a nonnomic one (being a dangerous predator). Only in the latter case will we count the organism as having representations of the world, as having internal content. Suppose we assign content through determining that a sensitivity to which can explain the organism's success in replication. Its reproductive success occurs through being sensitive not to redness but to the dangerous predators. But the organism is being sensitive only to certain wavelengths of light, since it is only by matching that feature that the red predators make it into the range of what the organism takes its surroundings to contain. The content *for it*, we might say, is redness; fortunately for it, a sensitivity to that content is very often congruent with the more useful sensitivity to predators. Its success depends not on its representing of the world, but on the luck of an economy that nature has discovered by which a simple detecting of nomic qualities shields it from its dangerous enemies. Nature works by producing successful behavior, not by making the content that stimulates that behavior available to the organism under the description that indicates why the behavior is successful.

A genuine sensitivity to *x* must be such that there is at least a considerable degree of "tracking" of x; the inner states should change in response to changes in x, should take x to be such even as its appearances change. Suppose that being x and appearing under certain physical parameters should come apart, and an entity shows not the slightest ability to adapt its internal states so as to keep on tracking x. Then (we shall say if we follow the present suggestion) it is not representing x and is sensitive only to the nomic properties. The more the nomic properties can change, so that at that level of description matters are relatively "shapeless," the more the entity will be seen as tracking higher-level properties, though even advanced representers will have considerable limitation and rigidity in their capacity to go on tracking a feature as its appearances change. (Someone who represents the world as containing situations dangerous to children, and who is able to track that feature, will have to see it as instantiated in a great variety of physically different circumstances.) In representers, we said, the causal chain passing through the feature-detecting mechanism is affected by the complexity of organization of the internal states, and background information becomes important in determining just what will be detected. We shall have more reason to suppose that background information is being employed (and thus that representing is going on) when individuals of the same species make different responses to the same stimuli.[15]

Dennett makes another suggestion about what representing is.[16] He suggests that at least one factor in whether something is a representer is whether it has the ability to keep on registering and making appropriate responses to a relevant property even when that property is no longer immediately present in the environment. The thermostat and the primitive organism lose track of what they are registering when it is no longer present, while the wildebeest is still keeping track of the lion's position even when it turns its head and can no longer see the lion.

The capacities that both Fodor and Dennett pick out, in asking what representation is, fit in well with the notion of a subject as more active in setting the conditions for its engagement with the world. But we should note that those capacities could be possessed as well by the chess-playing computer. Its behavior can show a sensitivity to the property of being a dangerous chess position, and it will be the complexity of its own internal states that makes a sensitivity to that kind possible, and not a straightforward registering of physical stimuli.

Intentionality and Reflexivity

Yet we may be uneasy as to whether we have properly captured what it is to represent. Perhaps we can get a better hold on that uneasiness if we

[15] Ibid., p. 20.
[16] Dennett, *Consciousness Explained*, pp. 191–2.

recall the earlier unpacking of the notion of subjectivity as self-relating. There is an at least implicit reflexivity, we suggested, in my taking of the world to have a certain character. To have a belief or to follow a rule is at the same time to *take oneself* to be a believer or a rule follower. Having intentional states will be part of the larger complex of relationships by which I am self-concerned in being involved with the world. So now it will be suggested that representation is like that also. You cannot be representing anything unless you are capable of taking yourself to be a representer, unless you have at least an implicit understanding of yourself as representing, a concern with yourself as being successful in capturing how matters stand. There must be, on this view, a reference-to-self, a taking of your representations as *yours*, for there to be representing going on at all. (That is a Kantian point.) And perhaps a kind of implicit self-presence that is more like being in a mood than like being in a state of Cartesian reflection is a condition for having representations and intentional states. There will be, on the other hand, competing intuitions that we are setting up too strict a standard if we claim that such a reflexive stance is a condition for being a representer.

We are dealing with important distinctions here, but some of the difficulty may just be a matter of how we want to employ, and to make more precise, a psychological vocabulary that is itself rather vague. Perhaps you can have a fairly low standard for counting something as having content, a higher standard for having representations, and a still higher standard for having beliefs and intentions. It is with beliefs and similar states that we are most tempted to include an implicit self-relation as a condition. So let us look more closely at the sort of reflexivity that might be at work in the having of such intentional states.

The claim is that you cannot be a believer without taking yourself to be engaged in the practice of forming and testing beliefs. You will show this not so much by the way you use the word 'belief' (or its equivalents) as by what the pattern of your responses indicates about what implicit sense of yourself you have as you engage in the practice. An interpreter will consider whether you are bothered by discrepancies between what you believe and what others take to be true, and whether you recognize yourself as possessing a possibly incorrect point of view on a single world regarding which others may also have beliefs. You must do more than produce utterances that others can interpret as being about the world, and do more than pass the standard of having internal information-bearing states. You must show yourself as one capable of playing the belief game.

It seems to follow from the conditions just given that a dog could not have beliefs. But might not a dog believe that a cat is in the next room (when there is just a recording of cat sounds)? On the one hand, there is some level of internal content such that it seems right to say that the dog takes there to be a cat in the neighborhood even when he is unable to see it. On the other hand, there is the intuition that one cannot have a belief without having a sense of what it is to relate oneself to the world as a believer who aims at meeting a standard. There must be (for someone with that intuition) an understanding that one's beliefs are within the sphere of things that are one's own, so that one has a stake in how matters go for them as they turn out to be true or false. One decision will be to say that the dog has protobeliefs, but that we should not allow that usage to infect our more precise employment of the term.

Perhaps we have here a version of an issue raised by the German idealists, about how a reflexive, second-order structure of self-relation can be a condition for the appearance of that which is being related to at the first level. In other words, it seems that I must be capable of having beliefs about beliefs, about myself as a believer, in order to have beliefs at all. (I must take my beliefs *as* beliefs. It is one of those things I cannot do without understanding myself to be doing it.) And we may want to accept the more general claim that subjectivity generally requires such second-order intentional states: desires about desires, beliefs about intentions and desires, and so on.[17] We might then have to say that certain internal states (call them protobeliefs) do not become beliefs proper until the reflexive structure emerges. (Perhaps we shall allow that reflexive structure to be present in a primitive and implicit manner so that even very young children could count as believers.)

Davidson gives an argument to the effect that one must speak a language in order to have beliefs.[18] Only those who can interpret other speakers can understand the gap between how one takes the world to be and how it is; only such beings know what it is to be a believer; and only those who understand what it is to be a believer can have beliefs.[19] (There again is the reflexive structure; we have beliefs through understanding ourselves to have them.) Is Davidson right? The idea of falling short of a standard is important to the concept of a belief, as I have argued, but I do not think that one must have engaged in the actual practice of interpreting others in order to have the sense of such a standard. A Robinson Crusoe isolated from birth (perhaps with a different innate brain machinery from our own, with more knowledge built in) might well be able to understand himself as failing to meet some standard of accuracy. There would remain the Wittgensteinian reasons for holding that his belief game must at least in principle be playable by others, and his beliefs correctable by others as well.

[17] On second-order intentional states, see Harry Frankfurt, "Freedom of the Will and the Concept of a Person," *Journal of Philosophy* 68 (1971): 5–20, and Daniel Dennett, *Brainstorms* (Montgomery, Vt.: Bradford Books, 1978), pp. 267–85.
[18] Davidson, "Thought and Talk," in Davidson, *Inquiries into Truth and Interpretation* (Oxford: Clarendon Press, 1984), pp. 155–70.
[19] Ibid., p. 170.

I am less sure about a reflexive structure in the case of desire, as it does not seem necessary to take oneself to be a desirer in order to have desires. The dog has wants that can be frustrated or satisfied; its desires connect it to the world without its having to activate a more developed structure of self-relation. (But one may be tempted to form a notion of desiring as a higher-order state requiring more than just having urges; desires would have to belong to a larger and more coherent activity of setting oneself in relation to the world.) How would intentions fit this scheme? The cat watches a bird on the grass, ready to spring, and an observer may ask if it has the mental state of intending to catch the bird. There is some inner content here, to be sure, some processing of information about the bird, but I think the structure remains too primitive and automatic for us to say that the cat has intentions. In order to bring oneself into the class of intenders, one must have a sense of oneself as intending to do something. I must be able to recognize myself as putting myself forward in my actions, as making them my own. There must be a projecting of myself toward the future, so that my intending to do something can guide adjustments of my actions to future situations, as I try to realize the intentions I have. (The Heideggerian says that my self-relating is a "being-toward-the-future," toward future possibilities of myself, and perhaps that structure must be present in the background even when I am intentionally performing actions of so little import that I am not myself "at stake" in how they turn out.)

Davidson's popular account of acting intentionally (he has since modified it slightly) has it that an action is done with an intention when it is caused in a certain way by a pairing of a belief with a "pro-attitude" such as a desire.[20] If my action of eating a cookie is caused by a desire to eat a cookie and by a belief that what I am doing satisfies that desire, then I am eating the cookie intentionally. But that seems a picture of intention that (in the terms we have been using) does not make our intending sufficiently active and self-relating. It does not show my way of putting myself forward into possible futures, of investing myself in situations that I want to bear my stamp, of thus setting forth a context in which future adjustments can be made in the light of my self-concern, as I fit unimportant actions into that larger structure.

Suppose, then, that we accept the claim that one crosses over the threshold to having beliefs and intentions only when there is that implicit reflexivity. Still we have little sense of what it would be for that

---

[20] Davidson, "Actions, Reasons, and Causes," in Davidson, *Essays on Actions and Events* (Oxford: Clarendon Press, 1980), pp. 3–19. See also essays 2–5 in the same volume. A good discussion of Davidson on intention is by Ernest LePore and Brian McLaughlin in the introduction to their anthology *Actions and Events* (Oxford: Basil Blackwell, 1985), pp. 3–13. The claim that Davidson fails to give an adequate account of intentions directed toward the future is made by Michael Bratman in the same anthology, in the essay "Davidson's Theory of Intention," pp. 14–28.

sort of reflexivity to appear in the development of physical entities. What would you have to add to the chess-playing computer, for example, to make it count as self-relating? One philosopher who has investigated the implicit way we are in relation to ourselves in moving through the world is Heidegger.[21] A suggestion from his work is that we think about that sort of self-relatedness as like being in a mood. In a mood such as anxiety I am present to myself in a way very different from the Cartesian reflection on internal objects. (It is true that Heidegger is less interested in the psychological phenomenon of mood than in what he calls the ontological structure that supposedly underlies it.) Being in a mood is a state of consciousness, even if we may sometimes think of it as the sort of way I am "with myself" when I am moving through my actions "unconsciously." Instead of being an object within the stream of consciousness, the mood is what colors it as a whole and gives an overall feel to it.

Heidegger is especially interested in those moods (anxiety, depression, boredom, and the like) in which I am most clearly in relation to my own existing, in which how and what I am is an issue for me, something to be lived out and endured and chosen. There is not a theoretical relation to something objective, but a practical self-understanding that is present when I act and choose. Even before consciously deciding, I have already projected myself in a meaningful way toward future ways of being; I am always already "ahead of" myself in having the sort of self-relational structure that I do.

Now it will hardly be the case that we demand of all believers and intenders that they have the full structure of Heideggerian being-in-the-world. But his analysis will make us ask whether having the capacity for some such moods, and thus for consciousness, is a condition for the sort of self-relating that is itself a condition for having intentional states. One claim might be that there is no self-relatedness without the global sense of well-being or ill-being, of dread or calm or boredom, by which one has a vague sense of how things stand for oneself. But this kind of self-relatedness (the claim will go on) occurs only in biochemical entities that have something like the kind of chemical flows across the brain that we have, and that we have discovered to be mood producing or mood transforming. No chemistry, no moods. No global moods, no self-relatedness. No self-relatedness, no intentionality. Computers, since they have nothing like that chemistry, just couldn't have beliefs.

That conclusion raises the issue of just how far we ought to extend our psychological concepts to new cases. On the one hand, we do not wish to

---

[21] I shall speak only generally of Heidegger's work, but I am speaking here of his overall project in *Being and Time*, Edward Robinson and John Macquarrie, trans. (New York: Harper & Row, 1962). I have referred earlier to the discussion of Heidegger on self-relation in Tugendhat, *Self-Consciousness and Self-Determination*, pp. 144–218.

be too strongly influenced by the particular way that *we* manage to do things. Having a human brain and nervous system and biochemistry is only one possible engineering solution that supports being a self. On the other hand, we do want to look as carefully as we can at those features in us that seem most crucial to being a subject. It is not as if we have to make our concepts mirror a fully determined world of psychological kinds. There are real contours of the world that we have to adapt to in using these concepts, but it is likely that much is left up to us in determining how wide we ought to extend the net, or how precise we ought to be in our classifications, when we ask who should be counted as believers or representers or selves. All this talk about computers crossing some kind of threshold is meant only to make us think in less rigid ways about subjectivity. It is not as if there is some fixed mark that, could we only discover it, would tell us once and for all whether computers could have beliefs, and it is not as if whether they have them is all that important, at least as things presently stand. Our decision is a matter both of what we discover and of how it makes sense to extend our concept of belief.

Yet in the present case there does seem to be something to the claim that a certain kind of self-presence and self-experiencing, of the sort available only to conscious beings, is a condition for having the reflexivity that makes beliefs and intentions possible. In having pleasures, pains, moods, emotions, and especially a global feeling of well-being or ill-being or shame, and in experiencing ourselves as maneuvering through the world, we can have a sense of ourselves as at stake in how things are going around us. Without that way of being in the world, we cannot be sufficiently engaged in it to count as having mental states at all.

Yet we might also think of a machine without such an embodied consciousness whose behavior, at least, seems a sophisticated playing of the belief game. When told that some of its claims are false, it engages in sophisticated operations that work at making its "beliefs" more consistent, at gathering evidence, and so forth. Is it fair to say there can be no beliefs here because there is not any self-experiencing? Isn't the sophisticated behavior enough? (The computer may have feedback mechanisms that let it "read" some of its internal states, but that is not the same as having a self be in relation to itself through the special kind of self-presence that an embodied consciousness makes possible.) It is likely that our notion of belief encompasses several different and even competing aspects of how we make sense of others and of ourselves. Even if we chose to talk about belieflike states that entities could have just on the basis of their behavior, still there is an important place for the more restricted notion of belief applying to entities that have the implicit reflexivity we have been discussing. Only those entities will have enough of a self to support a genuinely intentional relation to the world, and not just a causal one. They can take the world to be a certain way through taking themselves to be thus engaged with it.

Earlier in the chapter we looked at quite a number of ways in which the German idealists thought of subjects as self-relating, and one may recall from that discussion the complex interaction of self-to-other and self-to-self relations that they described. I come to be a self-conscious subject through seeing my activity reflected in another subject as I struggle with him for recognition. My labor gives an external form to my conceptual life and so I can see myself out there in the world, and I am aware of others as other in the way that they frustrate my purposes and resist my attempts to put my mark on things. I invest myself in what is other by attempting to make it fit my plans, so that when things turn out badly for work I have done or decisions I have made or activities with which I identify, there is in some sense a loss of self for me. And so forth. The structure of self-relating-in-relating-to-otherness can become, we saw, rather complex.

But the computer does not make the sort of self–other differentiations that would allow for such investments in the other or for such frustrations. We may not wish to say that all of these features of human subjectivity, of the character of our self-relating, are necessary for there to be any subjectivity at all. Still, some range of these features seems important. Those complex differentiations, identifications, and investments are aspects of the way that one is, in being a self, related to things and to others, so that my self-presence does not mark off a boundary that keeps me apart from the world but is necessarily world-involved. Some of the relevant structures here may be specific to the human psychology and to how it develops. But others seem to have a deeper significance for how subjects can be such in the first place.

How could the self-reflexive activity by which the self brings itself into being emerge in the evolution of natural entities? What kind of explanation might we even hope for in answering this question? Instead of a determining from behind by an already existing self, it may be proposed that we have a situation that is in some ways analogous to the Darwinian one. Perhaps scattered information-bearing clusters and types of operations in the brain compete with one another to enforce a greater psychic unity, with the losing protoselves either becoming part of the new government or going underground. Perhaps in what results no unifying superpower emerges to give the mind its unity, but mental activity consists in the patterns that get put together through lots of smaller centers competing for influence. The patterns emerge without a central designer or central meaner or central unifier, as they do in the history of evolution.[22] Then that process comes under the increasing pressure of culture. Others treat a body as inhabited by a single self and one learns the first-person vocabulary by which one begins to order oneself as having a fundamental unity. There are also the hammer blows of culture, Nietzsche insists, by which we are trained to live up to promises and to take responsibility for ourselves, so that one understands oneself self-relationally as something that one *works on* and makes plans about. A certain inarticulate structure of self-concern, and certain ways of being attentive to others, may serve as the scaffolding upon which a more articulate self-concern and an attentiveness to self can emerge, as I learn to mark off the boundaries between self and other more precisely.

But it is amply evident how sketchy and speculative that story is, and how little it tells us about the character of subjectivity. However we come to develop such a narrative, it will be part of the larger project by which we ask about the place of self-relating subjects in an objective universe. Even if we accept the integrity of the subjective point of view, and hold that it is irreducible to what a more objective account might discover, there will remain that pressure of the objective. Once we begin to accept the dependence of subjectivity on the causal substrate that realizes it, for example, and once we accept what we have been calling the disenchantment of subjectivity, then the bearing of the objective way of thinking on how we think about subjectivity will be greater.[23] Individuation here will seem more a matter of what happens in the naturally describable world of divisible bodies in space, and less a matter of a "spiritual" continuity determined from within. Then there will no longer be a great metaphysical depth to that which makes a subjective point of view count as the *same* one, and there may be some degree of convention as to whether a subject has gone on experiencing or has ceased to exist. (Accepting that degree of insertion of subjectivity in the natural world will be consistent with holding that no account of processes in the objective world can capture what it feels like to be a subject. But could I accept an account by which my own continuing as an 'I' is not determined by how things feel to me from the inside, but rather by the history of the causal substrate that is realizing my basic psychological processes?)

We have been examining a number of strands that are connected to the notion of what it is to be self-relating, and I think it has proved useful to think of subjectivity in terms of that notion. I wish I could bring those strands together and make from them a coherent and per-

---

[22] For an argument against such a central meaner, see Daniel Dennett, *Consciousness Explained*, pp. 227–52.
[23] This theme is developed in great detail by Peter Unger, *Identity, Consciousness, and Value* (New York: Oxford University Press, 1990).

suasive theory, but I do not know how to do so. Perhaps we need both more sophisticated concepts and more in the way of empirical research.

Freedom and Self-willing

Among the German idealists, the highest stage for the individual in being a self-relating self lies in actualizing one's capacity to be self-determining and self-willing. But we might have different conceptions of the role of self-making in our lives. One view is that free active self-making is the highest form of human living, an end in itself. We gain pleasure from the exercise of human agency, and gain the highest pleasure from the exercise of that agency when it is focused on our own self-formation. But when one asks, at the end of a life, whether that life was worth living, having one's self-making capacity fully developed may not be the most important feature in making it so.

Suppose we were placed behind Rawls's veil of ignorance and asked to choose a life that will be our own when we pass back through the veil. One particular candidate for such a life is not, let us suppose, a very reflective one. The individual had good and loving parents who helped him be confident, competent, and loved. Without much choice on his part, he was very early given lessons on the cello, and after a few years came to like playing music very much. He became, as an adult, an internationally recognized cellist who found that playing the instrument well was the most fulfilling professional life he could think of. He also married for love, had an enduring and satisfying marriage relationship, and had four children who themselves came to lead very happy lives. Would we find something missing from that life if it is not in the highest degree a self-made one? (Surely he made the life what it is through his work, but let us suppose that he always took for granted most of the values by which his decisions were made and never asked in a radical way whether his life was worth choosing.) We may well believe that producing such satisfying lives in a society should not depend so much on luck, and that granting a more extensive role to reflection and self-criticism will be a more reliable route in the long run toward a more general production of worthwhile lives. But is there some intrinsic failure in a life in which self-making is not developed to the highest level?

Perhaps we need, first of all, to consider, and then remove from our conceptions, the religious and theological influences on our thinking about what self-willing is. One of these influences is that as with Cartesian self-knowing, one may take self-choosing to be an autonomous activity needing no links to the world to be what it is. The emptiness that evidently threatens such an activity will not be a difficulty if one believes, as Kierkegaard does, that in one's self-choosing, one is closest to God the more radically one does it. But without God in the picture, we have only an empty self-willing without links to public practices that could give it meaningful content and worth. Second, our model of self-willing may be itself a theological. one. We want our willing to be unconditioned, to enter the world of causes from outside, as an act of self-creating. Third, there is the medieval picture of God's autonomy as shown in that any willing of what is other is willed for the sake of himself, is a self-willing. The modern version of this picture is the Kantian claim that in a proper act of moral willing, I will myself as a rational agent rather than being moved by a content external to me, or the projectivist claim that when I encounter moral properties in the world, I am really encountering my own attitudes projected onto things. Both claims may be understood to deny a role for the world itself as helping to determine my choosing by the way it already articulates itself into features that have an intrinsic worth requiring my respect and features that do not. These religious and theological models only confuse an inquiry into what sort of free, active self-making is desirable in a human life.

Against the background of the theological model, it will appear that only an unconditioned willing could provide us the sort of freedom worth having. Then we shall be less likely to notice the all-important differences between some ways of being determined by the world to be self-making and other less desirable ways. Some may suppose that in a deterministic world the causal chains leading to actions bypass any sensitivity we have to good reasons for acting. But what we have been determined to be is machines whose running makes our overall activity one that is sensitive to reasons. It is that sensitivity that our biological and cultural evolution has tracked, and that we as individuals track to at least a modest degree, so what we do is properly described in that fashion, even if there is (in principle) a purely physicalist level of description as well. Even if that sensitivity operates in and through the determined actions of a physical system, it does not follow that we are not acting on the basis of good reasons, but are being driven by some low-level, nonrational causation.

Since we are physical organisms, there must be some rigidity and distortion in our operations; our machinery very imperfectly mimics the operations of a reasoner fully sensitive to reasons for acting in all their guises.[24] But an important part of what we want in being free is that our deliberations and intentional states have a causal effectiveness, so that things do not turn out as they do through bypassing our highest faculties. We want to be free also to develop those faculties, but it is a crazy dream to suppose that our freedom should require that we be fully

----

[24] I have found Daniel Dennett's work in *Elbow Room* (Cambridge, Mass.: MIT Press, 1985) helpful on this issue and, indeed, on this entire question of that in which freedom might consist.

the authors of ourselves. If the pressures of evolution have worked to produce an entity that is a good deliberator and chooser, and is such that its deliberations and choices are causally effective in bringing about what it chooses, then we are free, if we are such entities, in the only sense in which freedom can be had and is worth having.

We can give up the theological notions of autonomy and still have a very real and valuable portion of it. Autonomy is an achievement, not a metaphysical given, and postmodern claims about the death of subjectivity or the collapse of its autonomy are simply false. A certain kind of self-determination can no longer be a hope for us; we just cannot occupy the theological stance. But very much of what was important to the modern notion of autonomous, self-willing selves survives the disenchantment of subjectivity. The self is not reduced to simple passivity in the face of the determining power of what is external to it. It can come to achieve a degree of reflection and deliberative excellence and causal power such that it is in important respects self-making.

Perhaps it is the case that even from a God's-eye point of view, if there were such, we would choose a life that would not make its choices from a God's-eye point of view. Nor do I find appealing a life that makes becoming a free, self-choosing subject so central to itself that it cannot acknowledge the value of unquestioned commitments in the overall shape of one's history. When one looks back on a life from its end, what will stand out as having made it worth living are most likely the long-term commitments, to spouse and children and friends, that would not be what they are if they were frequently brought up for review. We may distinguish between what we make of a life and what happens to that life, but surely some of its beauty and worth will come from the latter. We may find happiness and even luck settling on a life beyond what we have made happen, a kind of grace from the world itself, as when a poem or painting seems caught up in patterns that take on a life of their own; it is an important fact about us as humans that we value such outcomes, even when our valuing them makes us assign somewhat less value to our self-determinative powers. We admire the life that is like the work of art in that a style and rhythm have taken up into themselves various raw materials and patterns that were simply given. Autobiographies will sometimes assert that a certain life chose the one living it as much as the other way around, that an unconscious shaping of choices worked out a destiny, say an artistic or literary one, that was poorly understood at, and even may have run counter to, the level of the individual's reflective deliberations. Yet that process may be seen as having given depth and worth to the life.

An instrumental reason for encouraging self-making selves is that the cultural process of making selves can so easily go wrong. By analogy we might say that if the production process of a factory is to a considerable degree defective, then in lieu of redesigning the production process so as to eliminate error (let us say this is not technologically feasible), we might produce machines that once in operation can monitor and correct for their defects. The most significant defects in the present case (human selves) would be those in the self-formation process that affect our ability to deliberate well, to reflect in an objective manner, to understand ourselves and our projects, and to be effective in satisfying our most important desires. Psychological and mental development may have introduced distorting mechanisms into our rational processes, frozen pathways that affect but are not accessible to our deliberating, rigid obsessions that contaminate rational thought, and so forth. So we want a society that not only gives us room to deploy our deliberative capacities, but also encourages processes that help us to monitor and repair defects even in the very mechanisms of our deliberation and choosing.

But is that instrumental reason for encouraging self-making selves the whole story? The thought of the German idealists was that a fully satisfying human life is one that is *conscious* of its freedom, that is aware of itself as freely willing in its activities. It is not enough that we simply have undistorted deliberating. We must, in order to be genuinely self-relating in the manner that autonomy requires, be able to take ourselves to be autonomous, and to be to a considerable degree responsible for being the sort of selves we are. There must be that measure of reflexivity in our freedom, not only because this is a good way to make us better deliberators but also because that kind of self-experiencing belongs intrinsically to what it is to be free. There is something right about that claim, even if we must be careful not to let this good overwhelm all other ones. The modern process of intensifying subjectivity, and of concentrating there all significant powers of determination, needs to be limited. But we are left with self-relating and self-determining selves with a surprisingly small loss of status. And attacks on metaphysical notions of interiority will not reduce the importance for us of a rich inner life, and of the commitments it makes possible.

8

Postmodernism

The Character of Postmodern Thought

Many positions may call themselves postmodern, or may be called so by others, and the modern period against which the postmodern is defined will depend on the subject matter one is treating. In what follows I shall make a type out of what is clearly a diverse group of individuals, with sometimes rather weak family resemblances. The postmodern thinker gains prestige through giving credit to, even if not through giving a proper account of, certain perceptions shared by many intellectuals today. There is the experience of living in a world in which television, advertising, and media manipulation seem to give reality itself the character of a manufactured image. One has the sense of the self as having lost a depth formerly attributed to it, so that it is now, as is the case with the world, a shallow artifact of cultural production. There is also a considerable disenchantment with the projects set in place by the Enlightenment. The emancipation of individuals through rational reflection has been accompanied in modern liberal democracies by subtler forms of coercion. And we are more fully aware of the ways that harmful biases can inhabit Enlightenment legal and political institutions, while claims to truth and objectivity are seen to mask relations of power. Recent culture also forms in us a highly developed self-consciousness concerning the contingency and artificiality of our systems of belief and of our forms of artistic production, so that an ironic play with conventions and vocabularies may become more appealing than using them to let the world display itself.

Postmodern thinkers will typically move on from those perceptions and habits of thought to radical conclusions that at least sound philosophical, though the intent behind them may be a rhetorical one. Where reality itself has become a manufactured image, it will be said, it can no longer make sense to measure our beliefs against how matters really stand. When selves are understood to be cultural artifacts, then the notion of self-discovery and self-emancipation is a delusion. If rational practices must occur within a nexus of power and taken-for-granted biases, then the goal of coming to have a more objective account of reality and of ethical relations is a foolish one.

So the postmodern thinker cannot criticize society in the way that, say, a Marxist can. The latter will claim, for example, that a late capitalist society distorts and conceals the real needs of individuals and the real social relations among them. But the postmodernist will claim that there are no such hidden needs and relations to be discovered; social construction is not imposed on a recalcitrant material but goes all the way down to generate reality, selves, and needs as artifacts of its working. If we have described a progression by which modern philosophy led to the picture of an ever thinner world, we have now reached, with the postmodern conception, a point at which the world has truly disappeared over against the machinery of cultural production. The modern notion of a representation or of a constructed objectivity retains its contrast with a world whose ultimate character is perhaps, to us, inscrutable. In Heidegger's history of Western thought, that sense of a representational objectivity is gradually replaced by a more technological mode of encountering the world, as reality becomes no more than a "stock in reserve," an inventory to be used up in order to keep the blind processes of modernity in operation.[1] But still here we have the suggestion of an absence, of a reality that has withdrawn itself from us and that might become available again to a different sort of attention. But with postmodern thought even the shadow of such a contrast is no longer present. We are dealing with simulations, artifacts, and signs all the way down. We can play with them cleverly or not, manipulate them self-consciously or with little awareness. But there is nothing missing here, no deeper reality that we might even want to strive for, no contrast with something that has a better sort of reality. So there is little point left in calling the view an antirealist one. The very distinctions have broken down between reality and a simulation of it, between truth and fiction, between objectivity and rhetorical manipulation.

(The reader may wonder here what is the significance of the claim that everything is a sign or a simulation once the implicitly contrastive content of those expressions has been removed. The claim that everything is a text is no longer very controversial if I have guaranteed its truth by expanding the sense of 'text' in such a manner that I am merely using that widened sense to redescribe ordinary beliefs. Hegel is again an instructive thinker here. On my reading of him, his claim to find the structure of subjectivity wherever there is any metaphysical determinacy belongs to a project of redescription, rather than to one whose outcome will be that the world is less substantial than we thought it was. So he does not fit the postmodern mold at all.)

It is often unclear how seriously one is expected to take the post-

[1] That history is summarized in Martin Heidegger, *The End of Philosophy*, Joan Stambaugh, trans. (New York: Harper & Row, 1973). Three of the four essays in that book are from the second volume of Heidegger's *Nietzsche*.

modern positions. Some groups use them as a tool against more en-
trenched opponents but then proceed quite earnestly to put forward
claims whose rightness and objectivity one is expected to acknowledge.
With some thinkers it seems that the universities can be a place for self-
indulgent play now that they are isolated from meaningful political
discussions, so that the play in question cannot have a damaging effect
on the Enlightenment political and legal institutions upon which everyone depends. What must be evident is that there is an enormous gap
between the evidence of the cultural experiences that the postmodernist
addresses, and the radical philosophical conclusions that are thought to
follow from them. Granted that the technological development of new
media may give us a changed sense of reality. Very little, if anything,
follows regarding how realist an account we ought to give of our success
in the natural sciences. Granted that we are more aware today of the
ways that our movement toward greater objectivity may hide new forms
of coercion and control. It certainly will not follow, from those considerations alone, that reason, truth, and objectivity become useless notions.

Insofar as arguments are given, they tend to be general indictments
of Enlightenment hopes that we can use metaphysical accounts to support modern forms of life. It will be said, for example, that we can no
longer believe in the sort of metaphysical self that can stand outside its
practices in order to criticize them; so our task of bringing about progress through self-critical reflection is in trouble. Nor can we have any
confidence in the great Enlightenment metanarratives about the triumph
of reason or of the proletariat. Such metanarratives are dangerous,
history has shown us, in the ways they excuse great suffering so that
their purposes can be accomplished. We are now better off, it will be
said, in a postmetaphysical age.

But just how much are we giving up in thus becoming postmetaphysical? It has been one of my claims throughout that we do not have to
give up all that much. Even if we join Davidson in his attack on
reifications, we can retain a robust sense of getting things right, of
having to accommodate our beliefs to a world that regulates our accounts of it. Even after we accept the disenchantment of subjectivity, and
no longer make any appeal to the powers of a numenal self, we can
have a satisfying sense of ourselves as self-relating and self-determining.
Even when we give up the belief that reason can guide history in the way
that divine providence was thought to guide it, and when we recognize
that universal laws of reason cannot be derived from the nature of a
pure subjectivity, still our practices of rational inference and evidence
gathering retain their importance and prestige, and have a very wide
scope of application instead of being either quite local phenomena
or fashions to which we are temporarily committed. In one sense of
the term, we are postmodern in having to face up to practices and

conceptions that have lost their deep metaphysical support. But it turns out that we remain modern in that these practices and conceptions can to a very considerable degree survive the changeover.

We shall be willing, then, to give up the metaphysical conceptions of the Enlightenment if by that is meant a giving up of a divinized model of subjectivity or of reason. The self cannot take up a God's-eye stance toward its own practices, nor can it confer determinacy upon the world or upon itself. And we should not see reason as occupying the available slot in the divine model we have described: that of a self-relating in relating to otherness. Reason, according to that model, appears as an imperialist power that seeks to have its own modes of articulation mirrored in everything it touches, so that all otherness is swallowed up into its working, as in certain conceptions of God. Then we have a dangerous notion of reason that is easily associated with violence and with a colonizing of the world and of the self. But it should be obvious that in giving up that metaphysical conception we are hardly giving up our faith in our everyday notions of truth, objectivity, and rational self-criticism. In earlier chapters I have defended just such notions while assenting to radical attacks on the divinized models of modernity.

What, then, can be behind the postmodern leap to a radical metaphysical account when the arguments that are available support a much smaller step away from the Enlightenment picture? My claim should not be a surprising one at this stage; I believe that even in supposedly ridding themselves of the metaphysical pictures of the modern period, the postmodernist retains a deep pattern of thought that we located both in late medieval and in modern philosophy. Let us reconsider the triangular structure whose sides are the world, the speaking or acting self, and cultural practices relevant to determining what selves and the world are like. We might talk of an energy system at work within that triangulation, and of how the power to generate determinacy is distributed across it. Earlier we examined, and resisted, a number of pressures that, in the relation of subject and world, would make all the determining power migrate from the latter to the former. Much of recent philosophy, we have said, can be seen as examining what happens when the third position (cultural practice, linguistic codes, the activity of interpretation) becomes more dominant in the triangle. One possibility (which I will persist in calling theological) is that all the determinative power will flow to the third position. Then the first two positions become too insubstantial to constrain that power significantly, and the projection of determinacy from the third must appear as external and arbitrary, as not made more or less fitting by what is the case in the world or in the self. The other possibility is the more balanced distribution I have argued for in previous chapters, with world, self, and cultural practice each helping to determine the content of the other two positions.

I take it to be typical of the postmodern thinker to adopt the first picture, that is, the one where all determinative power flows to the position of cultural practice and interpretation. There is a standard move that occurs in work that is called postmodern and that is frequent enough to be a signature. A claim is made that a set of beliefs is responsive to some independent givenness, to some independent determinacy; but then the postmodern thinker replies that what is thus being measured up to is itself an artifact produced by that which is supposedly being sensitive to it. Did the scientist match his beliefs with what reality is like? No, says Rorty. He made his beliefs conform with what conversational practices had frozen as the background that fixed what everyone would count as real. Did the study of madness or sexual deviancy produce a better understanding of these phenomena? No, says Foucault. The psychiatrist's beliefs were matched with objects that had been newly constructed by the psychiatrist's discourse: the madman and the sexual deviant. Does a particular form of political life fit the real needs of human individuals? No, it constructs humans with the sort of needs that will fit that form of political life. Do contemporary therapies help us to discover and to liberate ourselves? No, they teach us to form the kind of selves that will fit smoothly into contemporary modes of discourse, that will be just the sort of thing that therapeutic discourse will be well-poised to uncover. Did the canon of great works of literature arise because of a sensitivity to genuine quality in those works? No, those in power simply created and projected standards of quality that would enforce their own self-esteem. Does the careful study of a literary text help us to have a better sense of what *it* says? No, one learns to follow the construction codes of one's profession and so to generate a text out of fairly neutral raw material.

Now such claims may be persuasive in particular cases. But what interests me here is how dominant the move we are discussing becomes in postmodern thought. One is not just trying to show, as the parochial realist wants to show, that what one brings to the world in lighting it up will shape what is there to be found. Nor is one arguing that bias and power interests will distort the picture we arrive at of how things really are. One is instead inflating the role of cultural practices so radically that world and self virtually disappear as constraints on those practices or as measures of their success. And one tends to make that move across the board, in all areas, without qualification.

What could motivate one toward that very radical stance when there are many appealing compromise positions that fall well short of it? We are back to a familiar structure: There is an opposition between a determining power and that which is other to it, and gradually the latter is transformed into the merest reflection of the former. The world first becomes, for the moderns, an indeterminate sensory givenness, and then in Fichte even that givenness seems to disappear, as the finite ego and the world confronting it are both said to derive from a deeper subjective activity of self-positing, one that lays out a world as that against which the self's ethical activity needs to exert itself. The self-to-other structure is generated out of the self, so that the otherness of what is other becomes to a considerable degree illusory. And that pattern of thought goes back, we have seen, to earlier theological accounts. The world retains a weakened ontological stability in the subtle balances of Aquinas's picture, but it is further undermined in the thought of the later medievals. It is then difficult for theologians to give an account that prevents what is other from collapsing into God's own activity, that allows a genuine space for the metaphysical integrity and personal agency of created beings. A divine self-relational structure erodes the determinacy of everything else, so that the relation to otherness is itself generated out of that activity of self-relating.

It seems that the postmodern mode of thought retains the theological picture instead of rethinking it. Otherness is swallowed up into cultural and hermeneutic practices; self and world become no more independent and substantial than the world itself could be for the voluntarist God. It is as difficult to find a space for human activity over against the formative power of the cultural economy as it was to find a space of genuine human agency over against the absolute freedom and predestining power of the divine will. (Even if one turns against God, that turning has already, for the late medieval thinker, been given its place by God's creative power and foreknowledge. Even if we set ourselves over against the culture and demand that it recognize our reality, that stance has already, for the postmodernist, been constituted in advance by cultural institutions.) Codes of discourse, like the activity of divine knowing, find only reflections of themselves as they relate to the world, and selves are created by the discourses that purport to be about them. The distinction between thought and reality is itself set forth, as in Fichte, within a self-positing activity of discursive machineries. The enduring power of those earlier models makes the radical picture here more appealing, when what evidence we have warrants much more modest conclusions about the power of our cultural practices.

I have suggested that postmodern thought often employs a shift in the field marked out by modern philosophy, rather than a rethinking of it. Interpretation or cultural practices or criticism will do to the realm of semantic and psychological phenomena what the turn to the subject once did to the world itself. And we can see here a different way in which that pattern appears. Recall the description in Chapter 5 of the structure of modern self-assertion. The modern self may peculiarly combine modesty and passivity with ambition. That which thins out the world and makes it an appropriate realm for human construction and projection is precisely its relation to an absolute power that humans cannot hope to fathom, and that makes possible at every step of the way our working upon the world.

A space for postmodern self-assertion arises in a similar fashion. On the one hand, the self acknowledges that it is the artifact of cultural processes that it cannot hope to understand or control, and that are responsible for producing the self virtually out of nothing. But then the field of intentionality itself has been thinned out by those divinized cultural practices, and that very emptying out opens up a space upon which readers and critics, depending on the group they represent, can project whatever meanings and values they wish. One had to give the cultural practices a divinelike power of determination in order to thin out the space of semantic and mental phenomena in that fashion. The modern self acknowledges its humility over against God and then proceeds to become a demiurge constructing a substitute world of controllable appearances. The postmodern self acknowledges its humility as against cultural practices of production and then takes up a demiurgic role toward the minds and texts of others. The loss of the world gives the modern self a freedom it only gradually assumes, while the disenchantment of subjectivity, understood in the postmodern fashion, gives the postmodern critic or interpreter a freedom and power it assumes more readily. Whereas the freedom of the Hegelian self came not through a power to construct and project but through having genuinely comprehended the metaphysical character of the world, the postmodern self earns its freedom in the modern way, by the emptying out of that which opposes it.

Postmodern claims are often accompanied by generalizations far more sweeping, and from far less evidence, than the claims found in the supposedly dangerous metanarratives mentioned earlier. Here is a summary by Lyotard:

> The 'philosophies of history' that inspired the nineteenth and twentieth centuries claim to assure passages over the abyss of heterogeneity or the event. The names which are those of 'our history' oppose counterexamples to their claim.
> – Everything real is rational, everything rational is real: 'Auschwitz' refutes speculative doctrine. This crime at least, which is real... is not rational. – Everything proletarian is communist, everything communist is proletarian: 'Berlin 1953, Budapest 1956, Czechoslovakia 1968, Poland 1980'... refute the doctrine of historical materialism; the workers rose up against the Party. – Everything democratic is by and for the people and vice versa: 'May 1968' refutes the doctrine of parliamentary liberalism.[2]

That sort of thinking can hardly be expected to get us to pay more attention to the details of particular cases, to the ways they resist our

[2] Jean-Francois Lyotard, *The Differend: Phrases in Dispute*, Georges van den Abbeele, trans. (Minneapolis: University of Minnesota Press, 1988), p. 179.

large stories, to the differences between otherwise similar events. What can be more ludicrous than the claim that the events in Paris in May 1968 "refute" parliamentary liberalism? But the mention of such a refutation suggests the move that is at work here. Certain large meta-narratives were such as to have the theological tendency to colonize all otherness, to make themselves real by violently assimilating "hetero-geneous" events into the large machineries described by and embodied in those narratives. We shall, with Lyotard, not regret their loss of influence. But then he wants to describe the rational and political and legal practices fostered by the Enlightenment as if their support had to come from such a violent metanarrative.

What seems to happen in these discussions is that one accepts the field of conceptual play set up by the inertia of earlier theological patterns, and then proceeds to stigmatize reason in a global manner suitable for play only on that sort of field. The postmodern thinker will define the enemy, Enlightenment reason, as if it still occupied a position in the earlier structure, and therefore the sort of opposition that seems possible and necessary will be one determined through being set over against such a divinized opponent. But once we stop thinking about the institutions of the Enlightenment in those terms, then we can see that the practice of reasoning carefully and forming one's beliefs responsibly encourages a thinking that is pluralist, skeptical, critical, and attuned to particular contingencies. The destruction of the planetary environment is not due to the advance of Western reason across the globe, but to deeply irrational policy making. The swallowing up of difference and otherness may seem to be accomplished by Reason if one looks at the West with the earlier conceptual field in mind, and if one looks at the results of processes of social rationalization. But it is clear that a rational human would much prefer to live in a world that keeps alive very different ways of living as possibilities, even if not real possibilities for every individual, of what living a human life can be like, so that it is rational to oppose the erosion of difference. The cause of Auschwitz is surely not that there was too thorough a triumph of the Enlightenment legal and ethical and political institutions.

Our result here has analogies with the position found in Habermas.[3] Much of what he says about the structure of "subject-centered" reason in Hegel and Marx fits well with what I have been saying about the divinized self-relational structure that keeps appearing in different guises. Habermas feels that after we reject that way of understanding reason, we still have to recognize the not yet fully developed potential of Enlighten-ment thought to bring about emancipation, justice, and happiness.

---

[3] I am thinking especially of the set of lectures he has published as *The Philosophical Discourse of Modernity*, Frederick Lawrence, trans. (Cambridge, Mass.: MIT Press, 1987).

He mentions the virtues of our institutions of procedural justice, for example. I do not see any arguments on the postmodern side that would cause us to reject that conclusion.

One result of the postmodern turn will be a skepticism about the virtue of rational reflection on our forms of life, in any manner that might be thought to have practical effects, since reason is either theological and metaphysical or the artifact of practices of power. Lyotard wants, for example, to isolate large political ideas from those practices through which beliefs are typically formed and tested.[4] Such ideas and political revolutions as well are for him like Kantian Ideas of Reason or like the Kantian sublime: They may edify us in a way that promotes solidarity, but they cannot be tested against evidence and they offer us no help at all as we try to understand developments in history or to adjust our own institutions as we look to the future. Then there seems to be little room for anything but the most ad hoc reflection on and criticism of our forms of life. But that skepticism about reason has not been properly earned if the arguments for it still rely on attacking theological pictures that we are ready to do without. The larger stories are dangerous when they distort our rational practices and make them less rigorous. We have to distinguish between the falling away of Christianized models of how selves are related to the world, and, in contrast, the ongoing worth of the practices and values of the Enlightenment.

There is a result here something like one that we saw in Davidson's work. The defeat of the metaphysical reifications of modern thought does not, as Davidson understands that defeat, make us give up the claim that we refer successfully to the world and that our beliefs put us in touch with things as they are. Rather the loss of those reifications made it easier to establish the claim. In a similar way, the giving up of modernity's strong metaphysical accounts of world, self, and reason should not lead to a loss of faith in our Enlightenment practices. Rather we thereby remove the theological structures that in their contemporary form, as affecting how we think about reason, would undermine those practices.

It is typical of postmodern thought to suppose that once we see we cannot achieve a pure objectivity untainted by any bias at all, then we must assume that belief formation is a matter just of rhetoric and power. But we can very clearly make distinctions, as we examine the

---

[4] Lyotard, *The Differend*, pp. 166–70. There is a useful discussion of Lyotard in Christopher Norris, *What's Wrong with Postmodernism* (Baltimore: Johns Hopkins Press, 1990), pp. 6–15. I find many parallels between my own account of postmodern thinkers and that of Norris, and my reading of *The Differend* was influenced by his discussion of it. Norris's own interest is in resisting the way that various postmodern accounts would erode a space for a socialist political criticism.

development of natural science and of institutions to ensure social justice, between more objective and less objective ways of seeing. We can not only make sense of a point of view that has overcome, better than most others, the limitations built into it as a point of view; but can also see that some actual practices and institutions in our history help us in moving toward such a point of view. Perhaps we might usefully look at matters by asking about the pressures to which a belief-forming process in us will be sensitive. There will be pressure in this regard from four sources. It will come from the world, first of all, as we try to make our beliefs accommodate themselves to what is really the case, through putting ourselves in position to have the world generate beliefs in us and test the adequacy of those we already have. A second kind of pressure will come from the rational constraints on linking beliefs with other beliefs in chains of inference. Very many of our beliefs will not stand up to a rigorous evaluation of the inferential support we take them to have, as introductory classes in critical thinking quickly make evident. A third pressure on belief arises from our own interests and desires and prejudices. We shall prefer some beliefs to be true rather than others, and the acceptance of some may increase our power in dealing with those around us. A fourth pressure will be the inertia of previous beliefs and utterances. Our sayings echo, and are shaped by, many earlier ones, and we operate on the basis of discursive codes of which we may be very little aware.

Now we might express one disagreement between the postmodern thinker and a modest supporter of the Enlightenment in the following manner. The former holds that of those four pressures just listed, the first two collapse back into the second two; the world and our rational practices become the shadow of the inertia of discourse and of the play of prejudice and power. The Enlightenment supporter holds, in contrast, that the first two remain relatively independent pressures on the formation of our beliefs. The postmodern thinker performs a valuable service by showing us that when we think we are directly confronting reality and expressing things as they are, our beliefs are being very much shaped by intradiscursive factors that help to define what is sayable and what is not. And we are shown as well that when we think we are putting our arguments under the sway of reason, we are often working within practices that express our interest in power or that extend possibilities of coercion and control. But the demonstration of those results, worthwhile as it is, will hardly take us very far toward establishing that the pressures on belief from the world and from the constraints of good reasoning will collapse into the other two pressures defined above. A typical move is to give historical examples where power and interest have distorted belief formation, and then to draw such radical conclusions, unsupported by those examples, as the following: that the world is only what those in power, or discourses themselves, constitute it as being; that our categories did not arise at all from an accommodation to the world but are inventions for the sake of coercing those out of power; that rational justification reduces to what we are willing to count as such because of the inertia of discourse.

Why go for those more radical conclusions when more modest ones will do? My suggestion is that what these thinkers say is true of discourse is to a great extent true of their own discourse, even if it is not true of belief systems generally. The pressure of testing one's beliefs against the world, and the pressure of evaluating the validity of inferential connections, become very much diminished in their work, so that the inertia of discourse and the pull of interest can operate more freely. One feature of that inertia will be the appeal of the theological pictures that have remained, in various guises, in philosophical accounts, and that suggest the unconstrained operations of a privileged determining power over against a thinned-out universe.

Derrida, Language, and Philosophy

It is an embarrassment, perhaps, to my treatment of the postmodern that Derrida, whom some regard as the prototypical representative of the movement, does not fit my description at all well. I think that lack of fit says something about the character of his work, and it will turn out to be important to the claims I am making that Derrida is not a postmodern thinker in the sense I have been articulating. Some readers will be very familiar with Derrida's work, some not at all. Since I have proposed to give an account of what philosophy is like as it moves toward the century's end, let me give a brief description of what he is about, before I comment upon some outcomes of his work.

Suppose one accepts Wittgenstein's claims about meaning and rule following; that is, one accepts that the meaning of an utterance depends on what counts as saying the same thing on another occasion, and that all the facts about the utterance on the occasion of its use, including the mental states of the utterer, are insufficient to fix what other instances will properly be counted as the same. Suppose one also accepts the full range of Davidson's attacks on mental and semantic reifications. One endorses, then, what we called the disenchantment of subjectivity and the disenchantment of language, and one accepts a nominalist picture of the subjective realm. Then one will already have much of Derrida's philosophical position, though he is interested in having his work do other things besides stating philosophical claims.[5]

---

[5] I want to make clear from the start the limitations of my treatment of Derrida. I just want to give, especially for philosophers whose tradition makes them unfamiliar with his work, an overall account of some philosophically interesting positions Derrida seems to hold,

So we find in Derrida the claim that the *repeatability* of what is meant is not something that attaches to meaningful strings afterwards; only by being part of a chain of possible repeatings can an item have meaning at all. And there can be no closure such that a chain of signifiers can complete its repetitions and make semantic determinacy no longer deferred. Semantic determinacy always depends on sayings elsewhere and at other times, even in the future, that help fix sameness of meaning; there are no ideal semantic entities from which to derive this sameness. Derrida thus speaks of a movement of differing/deferring that is a condition for our meaningful utterances.[6] His early work rejected the Husserlian belief that at the ground of any sameness or determinacy or objectivity there is an activity of meaning conferral, or an immediate presence to self by which there is a "preexpressive" sense to one's mental intendings.[7] (We can see clear parallels between that work of Derrida and some of the topics we considered in earlier chapters, for example, in the treatment of externalism about mental content.)

If repeatability is a condition for meaning, then there must already be a possible field of difference against which the activity of counting as the same can occur.[8] Derrida tries to suggest what is at issue here, the structural relation to a presence that is always elsewhere, by using terms such as "trace," but we do not thereby have a trace of something that can itself appear on another occasion. Every trace, in the Derridean economy, can only be a trace of other traces, in an endless chain that does not stop by finally bringing the *real thing* into immediate presence. That vocabulary of traces and the like may seem odd to some readers, but what he means is a least similar to what is meant by more familiar claims. Recall that in Davidson, for example, there is no relation of

---

without trying to defend my reading by giving extensive textual citation. I should grant, then, that the reading I have done to develop this account tends toward that part of Derrida's work that can more easily be taken up by philosophers. Among the relevant readings: *Speech and Phenomena and Other Essays on Husserl's Theory of Signs*, D. Allison, trans. (Evanston, Ill.: Northwestern University Press, 1973); *Positions*, A. Bass, trans. (Chicago: University of Chicago Press, 1981); *Margins of Philosophy*, A. Bass, trans. (Chicago: University of Chicago Press, 1982); *Of Grammatology*, G. C. Spivak, trans. (Baltimore: Johns Hopkins Press, 1976); and the debate with John Searle in the pages of *Glyph*. See in regard to the last named my own analysis of that debate in Farrell, "Iterability and Meaning: The Searle–Derrida Debate," *Metaphilosophy* 19 (1988): 53–64. I have done no reading at all in some of Derrida's more playful works, such as *Glas* and *The Postcard*. I have also paid only a little attention to Derrida's own rhetorical stances in his work. Does he hold the positions that he seems to be holding or would a more complex rhetorical analysis of the work leave us in some doubt? I shall not consider that issue.

[6] See especially the essay "Différance" in *Margins of Philosophy*, pp. 1–27, but these ideas are found throughout Derrida's work.

[7] See Derrida, *Speech and Phenomena*, pp. 60–87.

[8] Rodolphe Gasché uses the "conditions of possibility" reading of Derrida in *The Tain of the Mirror* (Cambridge, Mass.: Harvard University Press, 1986).

reference that breaks us free of the holistic connections within language and anchors individual words to things in the world. There are no propositionlike entities that language mirrors, and we cannot steer individual sentences into confrontations with the world that make them, individually, true or false. There are no meanings a grasp of which allows a translator to come to rest at finally having brought the other language into contact with what is really meant. Since meanings and beliefs and intentions are assigned simultaneously by the Davidsonian interpreter, in a holistic account of the speaker, there are no mental states such as acts of intending that, if we could only uncover them accurately, would fix authorial meaning for us. I do not see that Derrida would have any disagreement with these findings.

Derrida refers frequently to what he calls the "written" character of semantic and mental items.[9] The traditional view is that meaning is somehow more fully present in the spoken word than in writing, since once's mental activity provides an ideal content that is immediately present in the case of speech, while written words are "dead" letters that usually become absent from the meaning-conferring activity of mind. Derrida holds that what we have taken to characterize the written word characterizes all meaningful activity. The semantic activity of the mind itself can be only an adding of "written" tokens to chains whose signifiers form systems of difference and repetition. We have a "nominalist," nonideal world of tokens spread out in space and time, with no set of tokens able to determine, in a final way, what another token must be if it is to count as an instantiation of the same content. Derrida's proposal that writing is prior to speech seems a strange one until we see that it is intended to attack semantic reifications that attempt to create ideal entities out of the chains of material signifiers. We find a similiar result when we look at another move in Derrida: the challenging of the distinction between use and mention and the distinction between original speech and citation.[10] But his point is that any use at all is already an implicit mentioning or citing of other uses elsewhere, not only the other texts that my own utterance can play off but even future utterances that will help determine what my own saying means right now, by contributing to the fixing of what is a saying of the same thing. So the "original" utterance implicitly makes reference to and depends upon (and thus in a sense "repeats") the repetitions of it – not the most common way of making the point but not an odd claim in itself.

---

[9] This theme is developed especially in *Of Grammatology*, but again one finds it throughout Derrida's writing.

[10] This is one of the themes of his debate with Searle. See his account of "citation" in "Signature Event Context," in *Margins of Philosophy*, pp. 307–30, and my analysis of his argument in my essay "Iterability and Meaning: the Searle–Derrida Debate."

Derrida's account provides him way of reading texts, especially the texts of philosophy. These will have contradictions in a special sense. They will explicitly make metaphysical claims about meaning and thought and determinacy, but the ·very machinery that is making it possible for the text to work shows these claims to be false. It is rather like the discourse presented to a psychiatrist. There is the explicit narrative that tells a certain story about an individual's life. But then there are the rhetorical gestures, the evasions, the marginalization of certain themes, all of which may be aspects of another, more fragmented discourse that is denying what the explicit narrative is saying. Similarly, Derrida looks for those moments (rhetorical usage, marginal comments, metaphors, the moves that set up a rhetorical context but disappear behind the main themes, the points that resist the logical shape and hierarchy of the text, the "fissures" that indicate, to the trained eye, where heterogeneous elements have been forced together like different geological plates) where the text itself shows the effects of the signifying machinery that makes meaning possible, but that is denied or "repressed" by the explicit claims being made.[11] (That is what we mean by 'deconstruction.')

In Hegel's logic, limitation and determination by what is external and arbitrary must eventually be understood as an internal self-limiting and self-determining. But Derrida is deeply skeptical of that move. There is no entity or utterance or text, he believes, whose internal self-articulation can limit in advance the power of further "merely" external and arbitrary features, things that get added on afterwards, as "supplements," to play a role in making it determinate. There can be no deep distinction available in advance between what is intrinsic and what is extrinsic to something's being what it is. In the case of meaning, each repeating as the same introduces elements of externality and arbitrariness, and yet the structure of repetition is basic to there being any meaning at all. No text can control which further sayings, and what about them, will be relevant to what it means.

Derrida is a sophisticated philosopher and his sophistication is such that it is difficult to see him as supporting the outcomes that I have been ascribing to postmodern thought. Unlike Rorty in his work of the past decade and a half, Derrida gives us a rich engagement with philosophical texts. He has a long essay, for example, in which he considers Hegel's treatment of the sign, and shows that it is important that Hegel places

---

[11] He makes much, for example, of where Searle's name and copyright notice appear on the draft of a manuscript. See "Limited Inc abc," *Glyph*, vol. II (Baltimore: Johns Hopkins University Press, 1977), pp. 162–254. Searle is supposedly, with his signature and copyright notice, claiming ownership over certain ideas, but Derrida suggests that the very claims Searle is making against him are (because he has misunderstood Derrida) claims that Derrida has himself already made.

that treatment under psychology in the philosophy of subjective spirit.[12] Representation and images and writing are treated in the context of the self-relating activity of mind. In representing or remembering something the mind is more at home with itself than when having things immediately present. And in putting itself forward into signs it is more at home with itself when using spoken signs than written ones, or when using a phonic alphabet as opposed to hieroglyphics. For it has a more plastic and "spiritual" medium in which it can express its movements.

So far that would be a traditional reading. But Derrida then looks at some of the metaphors in Hegel's writing on the topic, especially that of the pyramid, which can be both an image of the way in which spirit is entombed in a bodily form when we use signs, and (in another of Hegel's works) an example of how symbolic art is at a lower level than classical art, since spiritual ideas have not yet found an external vehicle for themselves that is adequate. It is a long essay, but what we gradually see happening is that within Hegel's texts the interconnectedness of various symbols and metaphors has begun to form a different chain of meaningful connections from the one being put forward by the progression of Hegel's argument. At the very same time that Hegel is telling us that the processing of Chinese characters or of a Leibnizian formal language cannot be an adequate vehicle (in the way that sounds can be) for spirit's generation of meaning, it is the "hieroglyphic" aspect of his text (the way that symbolic *shapes* such as the pyramid connect to one another) that is engendering meaning, a process that goes on linking the Hegelian texts to future ones such as Heidegger's. A textual machinery *external* to conscious mental life is setting up a space of meaning production, and that very machinery by its working shows Hegel's account of signs and meaning to be false.

Now I think that Derrida could be much clearer without loss of complexity. But one also has the sense that he is engaged in an important philosophical project of trying to understand the ways in which our discussions take for granted not so much premises of arguments, but the most fundamental background "scenes" that make a discourse possible and that already favor some ways of thinking rather than others. Even in his much-criticized encounter with John Searle, it seems clear that his play, if it may appear at times offensive, is intended to call attention to the *rhetorical* space that sets Searle's arguments in motion but that never appears explicitly in what he says. And doing that requires, Derrida believes, that he make visible the rhetorical moves by which Searle presents himself as a masculine analytic thinker able to take responsibility for, and indeed to have ownership over, what he means, and able

[12] Derrida, "The Pit and the Pyramid: Introduction to Hegel's Semiology," in *Margins of Philosophy*, pp. 69–108.

to defend, as the now mature son, the ideas of his symbolic father, J. L. Austin, who is no longer around to defend them.

In some respects Derrida extends Wittgenstein's notion of philosophy as therapy. Like a good theapist, he is more interested in setting up textual encounters that produce certain effects in the reader than he is in getting the reader to agree with his arguments. The philosophical analysand may accept arguments attacking metaphysical reifications, but his obsession is such that the symptoms keep appearing in other forms, in the less obvious ways that one takes for granted some notion that lets one bring a discussion to closure, by finally (one supposes) bringing matters to a confrontation with things as they are. So Derrida's task is to lead the analysand through so many different instances of these obsessive symptoms that we develop the habit of no longer looking for deeper metaphysical support for our practices. To take another example: Instead of just defending the claim that there are no ideal semantic entities that offer a constraint from without on how interpretation must go, only material signifiers in various sorts of intermeshing chains, Derrida keeps calling attention to their materiality by having his essays turn on puns, the way the words look on the page, the positioning of notes in the margin, and so forth.

On the other hand, I do not see how we can get from Derrida's careful investigations to large-scale postmodern claims about the end of the enlightenment, the death of the author, the death of the subject, the world as a postindustrial product, the freedom of the interpreter to impose meaning on an indeterminate text, and so forth. He seems to me more like Davidson and Wittgenstein in that he radically attacks certain metaphysical notions but in a way that leaves our ordinary practices relatively unchallenged. After deconstruction, with all our after-Derrida sophistication, we can reinscribe the distinctions important to our practices within the new account. If we consider authorial intentions to have a metaphysical independence and depth such that they control interpretation without being implicated in its chains of signification, then we shall be vulnerable to a deconstructive attack. But once we realize (with Davidson) that authorial intentions themselves are articulated within an overall interpretive practice, rather than having a deeper metaphysical authority, then we are free to go on appealing to the intentions of the author when we are asking about the meaning of a text.

To have attacked certain accounts of semantic determinacy is not at all to have professed a belief in some radical indeterminacy of meaning. It is quite clear that Derrida's own readings of texts pay very careful attention to what *they* do, to the operations that *they* engage in, rather than taking them to be thinned-out fields for critical play. (I hasten to say that to present Derrida as one who offers little support for radical postmodern claims about meaning is by now a relatively common move in the literature, even if it expresses thinking of mine that goes back to when it was not yet common.[13]) Derrida should be seen as encouraging a radical disenchantment of subjectivity and of language, but he does not reconstitute the modern theological structure with interpretation or cultural practices taking over the privileged position, as do many of those usually classified as postmodern. (There are passages in Derrida that might support placing him with the "loss of the world" philosophers such as Rorty. But I see him as more like Hegel, in the following respect. There is a sense in which Hegel makes the world "subjective," but then we see that he has reworked that notion so that self-articulating entities in the world can count as activating, in lesser fashion, the "logical" structure of subjectivity. He is redescribing the world in his vocabulary rather than supporting an undermining of its metaphysical character. Derrida, too, sees the structure of "textuality" at work wherever there is any determinacy, but again we should perhaps see his move rather as redescriptive than as reductive, so that he is not letting the world disappear over against the power of a linguistic subjectivity.)

Some may hope that the practice of deconstruction can play a needed antiauthoritarian role. But just the same moves of differing or deferring, exclusion, marginalization, and so forth, will occur in all texts. Why should deconstruction, any more than psychoanalysis, show favoritism for some texts over others? Perhaps the answer is that deconstruction reverses the relation between authoritative and marginal; it takes the "inferior" second member of an opposition and shows that it is more important for understanding the opposed pair and their relation. (We may properly see that as a move against Fichtean and theological notions of determination.) We saw that writing, instead of being seen as inferior to speech, is shown to control the opposition, so that speech becomes a form of writing. So deconstruction will favor the discourses of the marginalized. But just what will be the result of that favoritism? By showing that speech has features that philosophy would have assigned just to writing, we do not thereby make written work more important than spoken. Indeed the spoken-versus-written opposition recurs *within* the newly constituted "written" that now has a wider sense than before, and there will still be very many contexts in which the spoken form of written (wide sense) communication will be superior to the written (narrow sense) form.

The same goes for the relation of philosophy and literature. Derrida argues that the move by which philosophy distinguishes itself from literature (by contrasting its clarity of argument, for example, with

[13] Again, I would mention Christopher Norris's *What's Wrong with Postmodernism* as giving a similar account of Derrida's relation to postmodernism. See pp. 49–76 and 134–63.

the vagueness of literature) itself rests on a metaphorical system that associates reason with light and transparency. So philosophy uses metaphorical and rhetorical means to distinguish itself from the metaphorical and rhetorical.[14] Let us just suppose that Derrida is right in his claim. Should philosophers then start using more literary methods and be less attentive to the quality of arguments? Not at all. The philosophy-versus-literature distinction may have to be understood within an overall structure that has to some degree a literary constitution, but within that structure we can still distinguish clearly between the practice of philosophy and the practice of literature, and for many purposes we may find the former to be better suited. Certain metaphysical defenses of philosophy's status will have to be given up, but there will still be good reasons, in very many circumstances, to prefer clarity, tightness of argument, and the philosopher's sensitivity to subtle logical distinctions. Derrida is not arguing on that level but is asking about the constitution of the space in which we begin to think about the distinction between philosophy and literature.

I think that the task of supporting a more radical criticism owes much less to Derrida's actual work than to the theological picture we considered earlier of a thinned-out world or text upon which socially constructed readers or experiencers project determinacy, meaning, and value.[15] Derrida's own work, I am suggesting, does not support the account that encourages that outcome, but the work of another thinker popular in literary criticism attempts to do so, as we shall now see.

Fish and the Loss of the Text

Criticism is a wide-ranging field where trends change very rapidly; a set of essays by a single figure, and from more than a decade ago, will hardly be representative of that range, or of what is most contemporary. But Stanley Fish remains a figure of great influence, and I think that the essays collected in *Is There a Text in This Class?* make explicit a set of assumptions that are both widely shared and deeply suspect, and I do not see that his more recent work makes any very substantial revision of his views.[16]

[14] "Classical rhetoric, then, cannot dominate, being enmeshed within it, the mass out of which the philosophical text takes shape. Metaphor is less in the philosophical text (and in the rhetorical text coordinated with it) than the philosophical text is within metaphor." Derrida, "White Mythology: Metaphor in the Text of Philosophy," in *Margins of Philosophy*, p. 258.

[15] I have mentioned that while I have looked at much of Derrida's work, there is a considerable range of his texts that I have not consulted. Perhaps in some of those there is greater support for the "loss of the world" thesis.

[16] Fish, *Is There a Text in This Class?* (Cambridge, Mass.: Harvard University Press, 1980). As all my references in this section will be to that book, I shall from here on put page numbers in the body of the text.

Fish is arguing for a particular conception of what happens when we interpret. While his claims might be thought to have a special significance for the interpretation of poetry, he makes them such that he will be taken to be putting forward large assertions about language, meaning, and objectivity. In an often-mentioned essay, he notes that the utterance 'Is there a text in this class?' may have two meanings (303–21). It may be an inquiry into whether there is an assigned textbook, or it may have a more theoretical meaning familiar to most students today in literary criticism: It may be a shorthand way of asking whether the professor is committed to the view that the text has an objectivity that constrains what interpreters may properly take it to mean. To understand either of those meanings, one must be able to bring to bear a set of background beliefs and assumptions that help to fix, and to disambiguate, the move being made by someone producing the utterance in question.

Fish presents that conclusion with the air of someone who has proved something quite daring. But very few will disagree with a claim that on different occasions of utterance that appeal to different frameworks of interpretation, a particular sequence of linguistic shapes may be properly assigned distinct meanings. When I hear the statement "There is something wrong with the safety," it will make a considerable difference to my interpretation whether I am hearing the announcer of a football game or am with a group of hunters checking their guns. No linguist will find anything controversial there, and Fish must define an imaginary opponent who holds a much more extreme view. An utterance, he says,

does not have a literal meaning in the sense of some irreducible content that survives the sea change of situations; but in each of those situations one meaning (even if it is plural) will seem so obvious that one cannot see how it could be otherwise, and that meaning will be literal. (277)

Fish seems to be distinguishing himself from an opponent who is forced to hold that a sequence of linguistic shapes must have a determinate meaning independently of any context of utterance. He suggests that those who believe in determinate meanings are in trouble once they recognize that 'The air is crisp' might mean one thing when we are walking in autumn and another when we are listening to a musical piece (309–10). The idea is that once there is a need for introducing subjectivity at all, as in the need for an interpreter to bring to bear background beliefs and assumptions, then meaning cannot be objective. Fish's opponent is forced into the position of holding that where meaning is concerned, there is a "bedrock level of objectivity" that remains after all connection with interpretive contexts and interpretive practice has been severed. Such an opponent (who could he be?) believes that apart from any situations and from the frames of knowledge implicit in them, there is "some mechanical and algorithmic procedure by means of which meanings could be calculated" (318).

Perhaps he is making a different claim from the one he appears to be making by defining his opponent in that (absurd) fashion. Perhaps through his discussion of the student's question about whether there is a text in the class he is supporting the following Davidsonian theses: that we cannot specify conventions of a language that would reliably determine what an utterance means as used by a speaker; that there is no standard meaning that is agreed upon by speakers of the language in advance of interpretation; that the situation of normal interpretation has more of the character of the situation of radical interpretation than we might suspect; that the holism of interpretation makes beliefs comprehensible only against a background of other beliefs; and that the skills required to interpret a speaker, rather than being strictly linguistic skills, shade off into the general skills we employ for getting around in the world.

He would then be joining Davidson in attacking linguistic and semantic reifications, though he hardly makes any such claim very clearly. Both would then be interested in the way we can readily interpret others, even when they use a linguistic sequence in a manner rather different from what the dictionary meaning would give us. But it is important that Davidson sees the results of those attacks on standard notions of convention and language to be consistent with the view that the meaning of an utterance in a situation is to a very large extent objective, and that there is very much a matter of "getting it right" when encountering such an utterance. So by considering and accepting what Fish and Davidson have in common, we would not get far toward establishing the claim that texts are just shapes upon which interpreters, depending on their own social construction, project some meaning or other. In the case mentioned by Fish concerning 'The air is crisp,' it is clear that a dictionary with even a modest amount of semantic information about the expressions 'air' and 'crisp' would indicate how we are to distinguish the two meanings; there is no great challenge there to the semantic theorist. There is not even a need to go as far as Davidson's anticonventional account of language. There would just be two distinct conventional meanings for 'air.'

After vanquishing his imaginary opponent, Fish presents himself as having arrived at a controversial conclusion. He says that "the positing of context- or institution-specific norms surely rules out the possibility of a norm whose validity would be recognized by everyone, no matter what his situation" (319). What can Fish be suggesting here? He seems to be saying that if the standards for interpreting a statement are relative to the context of utterance and to an institutional community that uses the statement a certain way, then validity itself is relative. But that is not the case. It is a very common occurrence that a particular string of shapes or sounds can carry more than one meaning, and that I must settle what language is being spoken, and in what institutional setting, before I can determine what is meant. That sort of relativity is a natural feature of language, and has nothing to do with a more philosophically worrisome relativity regarding truth. For once the meaning of the utterance has been determined by the context, its truth conditions are fixed for any interpreter who interprets the sentence properly. There is no further relativity to differing standards of validity.

A stronger claim about indeterminacy of meaning is made in another essay (322–37). There he tells about a time when he left on the blackboard a list of authors for a class assignment, and then told his next class that it was a poem they had to interpret. It should be no surprise that they were able to discover a wealth of poetic meaning in the list. To Fish this result suggests that a text has no meaning on its own; it is a series of shapes for interpretation, and we *make* texts by what we as interpreters do with those shapes. Any interpretation is as acceptable as any other provided one can situate oneself in a community, however small, whose practices will count the interpretation as valid. The intentions of the producer of the shapes do not matter.

Yet in the previous essay discussed here Fish has argued for something quite different. The professor *misunderstood* the student who asked whether there was a text in his class. He was not getting matters right when he supposed the student to be asking whether there was an assigned textbook. Getting matters right involved understanding the student's intentions, as suggested by a disjunction offered ("Is there a text in this class, or is it just us?"), and Fish can make fun of a philosopher who was not smart enough to know what the student really meant. He will say that even those assigned intentions are a product of interpretation, but again we need to make a distinction that he himself fails to make. There is the Davidsonian claim that there is a holistic assignment of beliefs, intentions, desires, meanings, and so forth to the speaker; in that sense intentions emerge from an interpretation. But we do not thereby remove from consideration the careful scrutiny of others' intentions, and the use of that scrutiny in assigning meaning. Fish, with his example of the list on the board, seems to be suggesting a much stronger claim: that there is no such constraint on us imposed by the intentions of the producer of semantic shapes. But the fact that we might be able to do many things with a pattern of linguistic shapes if we see it out of context does not establish that stronger claim.

It soon becomes evident that what Fish is getting at is a full-scale philosophical conception of what objectivity is. It is not just that we have to appeal to different contexts of interpretation; no one denies that. But Fish transforms these contexts into something quite different:

into relativized Kantian schemes that construct their own objects and determine their own rules of validity. He says that "the entities that were once seen as competing for the right to constrain interpretation (text, reader, author) are now all seen to be the *products* of interpretation" (17). (That sort of antirealism should by now sound very familiar.) These schemes are very much reified in Fish. A believer inhabits one of them and takes its construction and validity-determining rules so much for granted that he accepts with certainty the beliefs they program into him. Then social programming may engender in him a different scheme, and he accepts without question its constructions and validity determinations, and the facts they make available. So Fish says that "one believes what one believes, and one does so without reservation" (361). Also:

> The fact that a standard of truth is never available independently of a set of beliefs does not mean that we can never know for certain what is true but that we *always* know for certain what is true (because we are always in the grip of some belief or other), even though what we certainly know may change if and when our beliefs change. (365)

> I may, in some sense, *know* that my present reading of *Paradise Lost* follows from assumptions that I did not always hold and may not hold in a year or so, but that "knowledge" does not prevent me from knowing that my present reading of *Paradise Lost* is the correct one. (359)

> It is always possible to entertain beliefs and opinions other than one's own; but that is precisely how they will be seen, as beliefs and opinions *other than one's own*, and therefore as beliefs and opinions that are false, or mistaken, or partial, or immature, or absurd. (361)

This is an extremely odd picture of the formation and regulation of beliefs. Virtually no room is left for rational deliberation about beliefs, for understanding and investigating beliefs without yet being committed to their truth or falsity. The interpretive rules of one's scheme (according to this picture) make one see the world in a way such that one takes a certain set of facts as facts, and without being programmed with those rules, those facts will be invisible. Fish complains that his opponent in a debate could only hear Fish's claims as wrong; he simply wasn't within the way of seeing that determined the truth-conferring and object-constructing rules of Fish's system (299). Anyone who disagrees with Fish simply hasn't accepted the rules of his game; that very disagreement shows that Fish is right in saying that we cannot see a claim as true unless we come to inhabit the game whose construction rules automatically make it true. I can communicate something, believes Fish, only to someone who already knows what I am trying to tell him, since he must already have my way of seeing the world to understand me. (We have seen that there are Wittgensteinian and Davidsonian reasons for supposing that we must take others whom we interpret to share very many of our beliefs, but it does not at all follow that quite novel beliefs cannot be communicated to others.)

Such a reification of ways of seeing is foolish. For Fish, the scheme programs beliefs into us that we accept absolutely and certainly, then we move into another way of seeing and accept just as certainly the beliefs that are determined by its programming. But of course we do not operate that way. We assign different degrees of acceptance to our beliefs. We can come to be familiar with the context that makes it possible to understand what a statement means without thereby accepting a scheme that makes us automatically accept a set of facts that its rules determine. (That is a distinction Fish very often fails to make.) We have more general skills of belief regulation that are common across many different contexts and interpretations, and we measure widely differing interpretations against one another when we are trying to determine what we should believe. We often hear others' beliefs not as false or absurd or partial, as Fish claims, but as likely candidates for acceptance on our part. (That is how we learn; it is typical of Fish to make learning come down to the programming of new construction rules that are neither better nor worse than the ones to which we were previously committed.) In accepting a way of conceptually lighting up the world, we are ready to be surprised by how the world presents itself to that sort of sensibility; it is not that objects and truths as well are simply determined by the conventions of a scheme.

Fish's position requires that he treat in the crudest fashion an issue treated with more subtlety by Quine and by Davidson. There is the metaphor Quine took from Neurath that a system of beliefs is like a boat whose planks must be changed in passage, so that we must hold most beliefs stable while bringing some of them up for review. Then there is Davidson's claim that to interpret others, we must take them not only to share a wide set of beliefs with us but also to be very roughly in agreement with us about what counts as good reasons for believing. Fish is obsessive in urging upon us his (obviously true) claim that no one can stand outside his beliefs in order to criticize them; we must take some of them for granted in order to have beliefs at all and in order to communicate with others. But in Fish this claim turns into the picture of interpretive communities as insulated sectors whose fixed background structures determine true beliefs almost all the way down, so that there is little room left over for genuine argument. It should be clear, however, that we can maneuver rather nimbly among different such communities, moving higher or lower depending on the context, so that more or fewer of our beliefs will come into question, even if not all of them can come into question at once. Working as a philosopher in semantics or in the philosophy of mind, I shall agree in advance with my colleagues on many points about what beliefs we may take for granted and about what kinds of arguments and thought experiments are presently most fertile. But I may also step outside that community to a larger one that I share with intellectuals more generally, and from that standpoint, with its more general conditions of good argument, I may wonder whether some of the work programs I engage in as a philosopher will have a long-term value or are rather like an intellectual chess game that seems important only because others at the moment are taking it to be important. Perhaps my moves toward objectivity will not take me as far as a Kantian community of noumenal reasoners, but they will surely take me much farther than Fish allows.

By now it should be evident that Fish exemplifies very well the patterns of thought that I discussed at the beginning of the chapter and that owed their power, I claimed, to the inertia of theological pictures. World and self and text are thinned out to the point of disappearance. They are then reconstituted as products of divinized cultural practices that create their own objects and that come upon the scene in an external and arbitrary fashion not itself under the world's epistemic regulation. Fish says that beliefs are not "subjective" because they are based on communal rather than individual practice (14). But he is just raising up a communal subjectivity that still inhabits the overall modern structure.

Note that Fish's account here will make an important difference to the practice of speaking to one's colleagues. The analytic philosopher tries to persuade his listeners to accept inferential connections they have not previously accepted. The follower of Derrida tries to get us to see what is invisibly at work in the setting up of a field that makes possible our ways of thinking about a topic. The encounters of Fish with his audience will be of two kinds. Either he will appeal to what his listeners already accept, so that there is a ritual celebration of what members of "our" group believe, with the familiar nods from the audience as the right words are said and the right enemies skewered. Or he will use rhetorical power, and not any rational persuasion, to get listeners to jump from one scheme of "facts" to the one that he (Fish) now favors.

It is the presence of the world in the Davidsonian triangulation that, in its constraining of proper interpretations of statements about it, makes us all count as having a wide range of beliefs in common, so that we could not be employing very different schemes of ordering the world. But as the world drops out of Fish's picture, that source of common belief is gone. So we shall think of change of belief not as an accommodation to a common world, but as a movement from one validity-determining scheme to another. Such schemes are then likely to appear as reified, so that there is something of a boundary crossing as one moves from one to another, and comparison of different ones is difficult or impossible, since each brings its own validity-determining rules to the debate.

Should we advocate a return to the text then? Fish is afraid that any restoration of integrity to the text, with its accompanying notion that the text is a source of constraint, will bring with it a "police state" mentality about interpretation (337). But if one considers the parochial realisms we described earlier, it will hardly be the case that a goal of attending to the text itself will produce a momentum for making a single reading authoritative, or for giving more credit to traditional readings than to those that have recently been popular. Still, the text will have sufficient objectivity to make very many readings of it wrong, indeed to make many of them hopelessly wrong. It is Fish's claim that the text cannot play even that role of regulating interpretations. It is not even substantial enough, he says, to make some readings "off the wall" (357). Given the right interpretive community, even the most "off the wall" reading can be valid, since there can be no further measure of rightness than what some community accepts as right. But even communal practices of interpreting can themselves be regulated by the world and by texts; some of them do a poor job of letting the text display its real articulations and possibilities. So the agreement among members of just any community at all cannot be an adequate criterion of rightness.

Some may say, in finding the work of Fish attractive, that a philosophy of the sort we saw earlier in Davidson is dangerous, because of its "conservative" tendencies. Compare the Davidsonian claim that most of our beliefs must be true with the notion that the text is an insubstantial pretext for a competition among different interest groups to make their way of projecting meaning onto the text predominant. Will not the former claim support the status quo? But it is of course true that only a small percentage of false beliefs is needed to produce a system of terrible injustice. One could be a Davidsonian and support extremely radical attacks on our various institutions. But Davidson makes us focus on the right issue. It is not that we must jump to a new scheme, but that we are unwilling to criticize our own beliefs rigorously enough, with all the means at our disposal.

World, Self, and Reason in Foucault

Michel Foucault is skeptical about the Enlightenment picture of self-knowing and self-determining selves. That picture has it that through individual and collective reflection, we shall transform ourselves and our institutions so as to allow for greater rationality and autonomy. But that interest in self-knowledge and freedom, says Foucault, may increase the power of coercive social forces. We are under the sway of a Christianity-shaped notion of a "deep" self whose truth must be discovered and expressed, so that happiness depends upon finding the vocabulary in which such expression can occur.[17] That deep self, says Foucault, is a cultural invention. Our need for self-discovery leads us into therapies and confessional practices that provide greater access into individual lives for our culture's ways of talking and its techniques of self-formation, and we become more easily subject to its management procedures and "normalizing" practices.[18]

Modern reflection will also be collective as we come to study ourselves scientifically, in the social or human sciences. Through a more scientific understanding of how humans develop and how various modifications of their behavior can be brought about, we can, it is hoped, make more rational, humane, and effective our institutions that concern education, criminal justice, social welfare, mental illness, juvenile delinquency, and the like. But here, too, says Foucault, the interest in knowledge and truth allows more coercive entry into individual lives. In the last two centuries the social sciences and public bureaucracies have greatly multiplied the intrusions of knowledge-gathering practices into the lives of many. Individuals are encouraged to see themselves as fitting under the categories of the new knowledge systems, for example, the intricate categories dealing with kinds of mental illness or of sexual deviance. He also traces the rise of "disciplinary" techniques that are worked upon bodies for the sake of a more rational organization of their powers, in the military, in factories, and in schools.[19]

Foucault talks about regimes of "power/knowledge"; systems of discourse and relations of power work together to form normalizing conditions that construct both selves and objects:

These 'power/knowledge relations' are to be analyzed, therefore, not on the basis of a subject of knowledge who is or is not free in relation to the power system, but, on the contrary, the subject who knows, the objects to be known and the modalities of knowledge must be regarded as so many effects of these fundamental implications of power/knowledge and their historical transformations.[20]

---

[17] "In the California cult of the self, one is supposed to discover one's true self, to separate it from that which might obscure or alienate it, to decipher its truth thanks to psychological or psychoanalytic science, which is supposed to be able to tell you what your true self is. Therefore, not only do I not identify this ancient culture of the self with what you call the California cult of the self, I think they are diametrically opposed." Foucault, "On the Genealogy of Ethics," a series of interviews with Hubert Dreyfus and Paul Rabinow in Dreyfus and Rabinow, *Michel Foucault: Beyond Structuralism and Hermeneutics* (Chicago: University of Chicago Press, 1983), p. 245.

[18] Foucault traces the development of a science of sexuality, with its normalizing power over us, in *The History of Sexuality*, Vol. I: An Introduction (New York: Random House, 1980).

[19] While this theme occurs frequently in Foucault, his most important work on the topic of the development of the modern "disciplinary technology" is *Discipline and Punish: The Birth of the Prison*, A. Sheridan, trans. (New York: Random House, 1979). See also *The History of Sexuality*, Vol. I, pp. 135–59.

[20] Foucault, *Discipline and Punish*, pp. 27–8.

Systems of knowledge are not simply in the business of discovery. They generate a field of objects that makes the application of power more effective and more easily justified. There is for Foucault no concentration of power toward a single point from which the rest of the field is determined. The determinative power is instead dispersed among the very many sites where knowledge and power intersect, in those everyday actions where social workers, teachers, forensic psychiatrists, and judges bring their knowledge to bear upon individuals. But that dispersal is part of a "totalizing" process that brings ever more aspects of life into the modern economy of confession, control, and surveillance, with coercion becoming less a matter of the state's policing power and more a matter of an internalizing of vocabularies by individuals.

The character of our interpretation of Foucault will depend on how strong a reading we give to his claim that both the subject who knows and the objects known are the "effects" of regimes of power/knowledge. The stronger and more controversial reading will repeat the familiar pattern of a theological system of determination. A relationship of self and other will be thought of as produced out of one side of the opposition, so that the otherness of what is set over against a certain determining power becomes empty and insubstantial. The relationship between discourse and the objects it speaks about will be itself generated out of a deeper self-positing "subjectivity," here the regimes of power/knowledge. On this reading, how the world is and what selves are like will offer very little constraint on how our discourses are to articulate the world into proper classifications, or on how cultural processes of self-formation ought to go if they are to be justified. For that which the discourses are supposedly measuring themselves against, when they look to the world as such a measure, are objects that they themselves have articulated and continue to secure as objects, through the inertia of the culture's conversational habits. (God, we are assured by a similar structure, can be sure of knowing the things that he has created and that he continues to hold in existence by the conserving power of his will.)

One is not, on this stronger reading, looking for social practices that respect, and allow to prosper, selves of the sort that humans are. For the regimes of power/knowledge are constructing both selves and the needs they wish to satisfy. A social change does not occur because institutions have learned to adjust themselves to what humans really need and desire, but because we have learned to form ourselves in accord with a new discourse, a new set of categories that bring their own kind of coercion. Let me refer again to a religious analogy I appealed to earlier. God creates me out of nothing and his causality is at all times underwriting my own; and there is no site from which I could justly complain about his treatment of me, as to whether or not I am saved, and no site from which I might genuinely resist his will. For it is his activity that defines what justice is, and his activity that has determined in advance just what moves I shall undertake while I exist. In the stronger reading of Foucault it is discourse/power configurations that seem to create selves and objects out of nothing, that seem to raise up by their own powers everything that might be thought of as carving out a space that is independent of them. No room is left for an account of self-development that can provide a criterion for evaluating various kinds of intrusion into, and coercion of, individual lives. As everything is swept up into the all-encompassing power of self-relating discursive practices, there can be no more sense in questioning the rightness of those practices than in questioning the rightness of God's interventions in the world. The ways they form selves and objects must be arbitrary enactments concerning which reason can say nothing at all, since it comes to life only as an artifact of those enactments. And any resistance to those regimes can only be what they themselves have generated *as* resistance. One must settle for describing the various ways that power is applied.

There is, on the other hand, a weaker reading of Foucault, a reading that does not lead to the extremely thin world that always accompanies a theological account of subjectivity, even when that subjectivity has become a matter of impersonal discourses. This weaker reading will present a picture of the relation between discourse and the world that resembles, in several respects, the account attributed earlier to the parochial realist, where coming to know what the world is like is a matter of both discovery and invention, both of adjustment to its articulations and of "lighting it up" so as to make some classifications significant and other ones not. Let us, for a comparison, consider two topics that followers of Foucault often discuss: homosexuality and madness.

The strong reading gives us an austere world of events that puts very little constraint on what categories we may successfully apply to it. So we can say, on that reading, that homosexuality and madness come into being only when the classifications available in a discursive practice begin to make certain groupings of acts or of traits of character significant. (Some will therefore say that homosexuality has been around for only a century or two.) When one large discursive practice is replaced by another in history, the character of the world itself will play very little role in bringing about the transition. Rather, one way of projecting classifications on the world will be replaced by another, and new objects will thereby become available to be talked about. 'Truth,' 'rationality,' and 'reality' are themselves products of those changing discursive formations. Freedom comes from recognizing that none of the ways in which societies classify us have any deeper basis than that; none have a more natural basis in how the world arranges matters.

The proponent of the weaker reading of Foucault will present an account that is quite different. We should not underestimate, he will grant, the ways that our categories do much more than reflect articulations of the world. We raise some possible boundaries to metaphysical prominence, and some ways of grouping people to social and cultural importance. The ways that people learn to describe themselves will very much affect how they live and what attitudes they take toward themselves. And many of our groupings are artificial ones that could be very different from what they are. So it is certainly to some degree up to us, or rather up to our institutions and our habits of talking, what categories relevant to sexuality and mental illness become important to us. A society that takes homosexuality to be a defining factor of identity will be different from a society that does not, and homosexuals in the former kind of society will be trained to live rather different lives from those lived by homosexuals in the latter kind. And the way we divide up the world into the mentally ill and the mentally well, and the subcategories we establish under the larger category of mental illness, will be due in important respects to what sort of society we inhabit.

But the one who supports this weaker reading thinks that something further now has to be said. The global picture of a very thin world upon which discourses project their classifications is simply wrong. The world's own way of articulating itself plays a much greater role in setting the conditions for our correct employment of categories; we learn in many areas to adjust our way of seeing things to its own arrangements, and those adjustments are often responsible for historical changes in our discursive practices. If the strong reading were not only the correct reading of Foucault but also an accurate account of how matters really stand, then we could know in advance, without investigation, that the social constructivist must give us the correct analysis of our social categories, such as those concerning sexuality and mental illness. But we do not know that in advance. Foucault would claim, correctly, that our notion of objective reality as guiding our beliefs itself arises within our practices; we cannot separate out the world that is doing the guiding as a simply external standard, untouched by our practices. But it does not follow that such a notion is a projection in the interests of power. Our idea of world guidance is itself world guided, and our evolving conception of how matters really stand may show us that the nonsocial world gives a very considerable basis to our classifications regarding sexuality and mental illness.

We are in a very real sense freer when we recognize how many of the ways in which we are described do not have as deep a basis as the social order often takes them to have. But it will do us no good to adopt the sometimes pleasurable illusion that all such categories are shallow and artificial. A resistance to all categories put forward by systems of discourse will make us blind to the causal processes by which selves are formed and by which they come to lead satisfying or unsatisfying lives.

That blindness will make it difficult to determine what sort of institutions of self-formation are needed to make individuals have a real chance at making their own lives, and at making their choices from a range of desirable options.

Now what is the importance of that distinction between the strong and the weak readings of Foucault? Simply this. Consider the topics mentioned earlier in the chapter: those of the self, the world, and reason. It is important that in each of these three areas, the Enlightenment thinker finds a space where some independence is available over against a culture's regimes of power/knowledge, so that there can be a measure of how those regimes must develop if they are to be justified. If the Enlightenment project is to make any sense, then there must remain certain pressures on our belief formation that are not just a product of the intersection of discourse and power. There must be a pressure from the world, as we try to make our beliefs more accurate; pressure from the standards of rational argument, as we try to assent to beliefs for which we have good inferential support; and pressure from what human selves are like, as we experiment to produce forms of life that we shall find satisfying to live. The strong reading would erode any independent space over against the regimes of power/knowledge, and would let those three sorts of pressures collapse into ongoing systems of power. On the weaker reading, in contrast, Foucault can come off as a skeptical and highly insightful friend of the Enlightenment project, one who has seen, better than most others, the ways in which liberating and "enlightening" discourse can introduce insidious new kinds of coercion and control, and the ways in which the modern belief in the metaphysical depth of subjectivity can be dangerous.

It should be clear, from a consideration of my arguments in earlier chapters, that I do not have much confidence that the strong reading can give us a correct global account of the relations between discourse and reality, though it may very well give a correct account of the position that Foucault himself has put forward, at least intermittently. It is significant that the stronger reading seems even more powerful when used against discourses that attempt to liberate marginal groups than when used against more traditional forms of coercion. Let us see how it goes wrong in a practical case, one that seems suitable for an analysis in the style of Foucault. He wants to see where liberal discourse that intensifies our interest in sexuality and in therapeutic intervention makes possible new kinds of control over the lives of individuals. So the issues of sexual harassment, child sexual abuse, and spousal relations, as discourse about them has developed in America, can be used to show how a new network of power/knowledge brings about greater opportunities for surveillance, regulation, and management, and trains individuals to accept a vocabulary and the classifications it assigns them.

Certainly there is something to be said for Foucault's point of view here. There is a discourse about child abuse, for example, that encourages a very high level of intervention in family life and that supports therapies by which adults are taught to "remember" being abused as children. Yet it is hardly the case that the discursive practices having to do with child abuse, spouse abuse, and sexual harassment construct their own objects. At least very many of our beliefs in these areas are caused by the fact, sorrowfully, that the world is a certain way. We can still accept the modest conclusion that it is due to the implicit codes of the new discourse, and to the ways of seeing supported by those codes, that we now are able to talk in certain ways, and to see as objects of concern features of the world that were there but too often ignored. And there is certainly a strong element of construction in the ways our discourse gives a specific shape to child abuse or sexual harassment as objects to be talked about. But we shall not be able to support a stronger, theological conclusion, according to which the world is, on these issues, a reflection of discursive networks, rather than an independent shaper of their content.

On the issue of selfhood and autonomy, it is again true that Foucault will give us useful warnings about self-discovery and liberation. But however much we are shaped by our cultures into finding some kinds of lives more satisfying than others, and however much our position in history limits what we can take to be worthwhile ways to live, still what humans are like is enough to place sharp constraints on what kinds of social institutions and practices can be acceptable. It is very likely *part* of the explanation that when we learn to form ourselves as beings for whom freedom is an important goal, we are learning to fit ourselves into categories defined by cultural discourse. But there is *discovery* here as well, as we come to understand better both the worth of a self that can relate to itself as something to be worked upon and chosen, and the processes of self-formation that produce humans who can do that sort of thing very well. In recognizing that earlier treatment of slaves and of women was wrong, we did not just pass over into a new discourse that invented a new way to be; we discovered that very many human lives were not being given a fair measure of an autonomy that is quite real and that is worth securing for humans generally, given the sorts of beings they are. And that notion of autonomy will be at least part of an account that shows why some increases in surveillance and control that the new discourses make possible are justified, because of the benefits they provide for women, children, and others. We are, of course, formed by our biology and by our culture. But if we are lucky we are trained in habits of reflection and argument that are not tools in the service of present systems, but that allow a genuinely critical stance toward what is taken for granted by those systems. And so we can have a proper, even if limited, sense of ourselves as self-reflective and self-determining, both individually and communally. Laziness is often more of a barrier to rational self-criticism and autonomy than is some mysterious coercive power of discursive regimes.

Foucault suggests that when we see a set of practices that are instrumental in a new sort of self-formation, we should make ourselves aware that those practices are contingent, and that the self constituted by them is contingent as well. But then we need to ask whether his own work is part of a discourse that is encouraging a new kind of self-formation. He appears to find attractive a self that can disengage itself from the disciplinary regimes of his society, that can mark their contingency, that can find new ways of inventing itself. But that is itself a particular kind of self that will be favored by certain cultures rather than by others. The sophistication of the contemporary consumer of information is reflected in a certain distance from texts that are being interpreted, and in an awareness of the artificial and the rhetorical that are present in any appeal to the natural and the true. A self emerges that is ambiguous in its commitments and skeptical about global programs, mobile in its employment of vocabularies and weak in its commitments to any of them. The modes of information by which the world reaches us make it less likely that we can see the world as having depth or enduring value, or that we can think of our projects as extending far into the past and into the future, in a stable field of meaning that gives a proper scale to what we do, and allows us to appreciate the way meaning takes shape over time. So there is a valuing of an ego made for playful, fluid maneuvering through symbol systems. We have here the sort of self that Rorty has praised, ready to move quickly on to new vocabularies when older ones become tired, and ready to stitch together old texts in novel and interesting juxtapositions.

But is that a worthwhile sort of self to be? I am quite certain that Nietzsche, so often a hero in postmodern thought, would look with scorn upon the kind of selves just described, and on a society that tended to produce them. Now it is true that Foucault's recent work on self-making in the ancient world suggests that there may be a kind of working we can do on ourselves that produces selves that it is worth being because they are aesthetically well made, and in being so may be more than mobile sites for the play of codes. Perhaps in that turn to material from the ancient world, we can see at least a hint that he would not find the life of the postmodern self, as I have described it, an admirable form of life.[21]

---

[21] In talking about techniques of working upon the self that are less Christian and more like some of those in the ancient world, Foucault by no means advises a return to ancient practices themselves: He says, "you can't find the solution of a problem in the solution of another problem raised at another moment by other people." ("On the Genealogy of Ethics," p. 231.)

Perhaps that sort of self is too fluid and shallow to be the point of a self-making worth endorsing. But the matter is very much unclear, and Foucault's death has left it that way, so far as his own work is concerned.

Foucault was happy to be considered an antihumanist philosopher. He thought that man was "invented" during the last couple of centuries, since it was only then that the human sciences arose and constituted humanity as an object of scientific study. He saw in structuralism and its descendants the beginning of a move by which man, having been thus invented, would in some sense disappear through a discursive revolution that no longer gave humans and their mental lives a central role. Now in certain respects one wants to endorse an understanding that makes humans and their lives less important in the universe. We know the world through a human perspective, and much of it is a world that we have made over through our labor, but it is not a human world, and its dimensions have no intrinsic link to the time span of our species. Perhaps others in the distant future, on this planet or on other ones, will take up and improve upon the scientific and cultural achievements that we have worked so hard to produce, and we recognize our responsibility to keep the only planetary biosphere we know of flourishing, not just for ourselves but for its other inhabitants. Antihumanism can be a spur to realist conceptions in philosophy, rather than to those that over-emphasize the importance of our human faculties.

But Foucault's antihumanism accompanies a severe underestimation of the human goods brought about and maintained by the institutions we owe to the Enlightenment, and of the very real improvements that our habits of self-criticism have effected in the disciplinary practices that he studied. There is sometimes in him a childish irritation at *any* of the ways in which a culture shapes and disciplines its members, and the suggestion that all the pressures that make belief formation go in some directions rather than others are akin to totalitarian coercion. That analysis will apply even to the ways that scientists form beliefs on the basis of evidence. The notions of subjectivity and authorship as well will be seen as forces limiting the free circulation of signs in a text. Yet at the same time he grants that it is the operation of these disciplinary and coercive forces that is a condition for generating meaning and the objects of discourse. One sometimes senses in him the appeal of the anarchic to those whose more rigid upbringing may have given them the habits and discipline needed for success, and whose sympathies seem unaroused by those growing up in truly anarchic family and social situations. So he is not going to be of much assistance when we come to very detailed questions about the forms of life for which our various kinds of education and habit formation ought to train individuals. And his picture is so onesided that it will be unhelpful in analyzing the complex ways we both control and are controlled by cultural forms, so that our sense of ourselves as to a considerable degree self-determining is not a myth.

Yet when these points have been made, it remains true that Foucault is an important philosopher whose influence will justly be felt in future decades. He reminds us, as Nietzsche did, that what seems an abstract tolerance for any form of life in modern liberal democracies is actually a set of powerful pressures that shape us into being some sorts of selves rather than others. Regarding the project of coming to a satisfying manner of weighing against one another the various goods possible for human lives, it is still unclear just what relative weight we ought to give, in the long run, to self-knowledge, autonomy, and the rational ordering of individual lives and social relations. We do not yet know whether, from the perspective of the distant future, the lives produced by our present form of life will appear admirable and well lived, and whether the culture that produced them will be seen as constituting a period in which the species flourished.

Bibliography

Apel, Karl-Otto. *Towards a Transformation of Philosophy*. G. Adey and D. Frisby, trans. London: Routledge and Kegan Paul, 1980.

Aquinas, Thomas. *St. Thomas Aquinas: Philosophical Texts*. Thomas Gilby, trans. London: Oxford University Press, 1951.

Arendt, Hannah. *The Life of the Mind*. Part One: Thinking. Part Two: Willing. New York: Harcourt Brace Jovanovich, 1978.

Bach, Kent. "*De Re* Belief and Methodological Solipsism." In *Thought and Object*, Andrew Woodfield, ed., pp. 121–52.

Baker, G. P., and P. M. S. Hacker. *Scepticism, Rules, and Language*. Oxford: Blackwell, 1984.

Bernstein, Richard. *Beyond Objectivism and Relativism*. Philadelphia: University of Pennsylvania Press, 1983.

(ed.). *Habermas and Modernity*. Cambridge, Mass.: MIT Press, 1985.

Bilgrami, Akeel. *Belief and Meaning*. Oxford: Blackwell, 1992.

"Meaning, Holism, and Use." In *Truth and Interpretation*, Ernest LePore, ed., pp. 101–22.

Blackburn, Simon. "Errors and the Phenomenology of Value." In *Morality and Objectivity*, Ted Honderich, ed., pp. 1–22.

"Moral Realism." In *Morality and Moral Reasoning*, J. Casey, ed. London: Methuen, 1971.

"Reply: Rule-Following and Moral Realism." In *Wittgenstein: To Follow a Rule*, Holtzman and Leich, eds., pp. 163–87.

Spreading the Word. New York: Oxford University Press, 1984.

"Supervenience Revisited." In *Essays on Moral Realism*, Geoffrey Sayre-McCord, ed., pp. 59–75.

Blumenberg, Hans. *The Genesis of the Copernican World*. Robert Wallace, trans. Cambridge, Mass.: MIT Press, 1987.

The Legitimacy of the Modern Age. Robert Wallace, trans. Cambridge, Mass.: MIT Press, 1983.

Bouveresse, Jacques, and Herman Parret, eds. *Meaning and Understanding*. Berlin: DeGruyter, 1981.

Boyd, Richard. "How To Be a Moral Realist." In *Essays on Moral Realism*, Geoffrey Sayre-McCord, ed., pp. 181–228.

Burge, Tyler. "Cartesian Error and the Objectivity of Perception." In *Subject, Thought, and Context*, Pettit and McDowell, eds., pp. 117–36.

"Individualism and the Mental." In *Midwest Studies in Philosophy* IV (1979), Peter French et al., eds., pp. 73–121.

"Individualism and Psychology." *Philosophical Review* 95 (1986): 3–45.

"Other Bodies." In *Thought and Object*, Andrew Woodfield, ed., pp. 97–120.

"Two Thought Experiments Reviewed." *Notre Dame Journal of Formal Logic* 23 (1982): 284–93.

Caputo, John. "The Thought of Being and the Conversation of Mankind: The Case of Heidegger and Rorty." In *Hermeneutics and Praxis*, Robert Hollinger, ed., pp. 248–71.

Cassirer, Ernst. *The Individual and the Cosmos in Renaissance Philosophy*. M. Domandi, trans. Philadelphia: University of Pennsylvania Press, 1963.

Davidson, Donald. "A Coherence Theory of Truth and Knowledge." In *Truth and Interpretation*, Ernest LePore, ed., pp. 307–19.

"Empirical Content." In *Truth and Interpretation*, Ernest LePore, ed., pp. 320–32. *Essays on Actions and Events*. Oxford: Clarendon Press, 1980.

"Expressing Evaluations." Lindley Lecture. University of Kansas (pamphlet from University of Kansas Library, 1982).

"First Person Authority." *Dialectica* 38 (1984): 101–11.

Inquiries into Truth and Interpretation. Oxford: Clarendon Press, 1984.

"Knowing One's Own Mind." *Proceedings of the American Philosophical Society* 60 (1987): 441–58.

"The Myth of the Subjective." In *Relativism: Interpretation and Confrontation*, Michael Krausz, ed., pp. 159–73.

"A Nice Derangement of Epitaphs." In *Truth and Interpretation*, Ernest LePore, ed., pp. 433–46.

"Paradoxes of Irrationality." In *Philosophical Essays on Freud*, R. Wollheim and J. Hopkins, eds. Cambridge: Cambridge University Press, 1982, pp. 289–305.

"Rational Animals." In *Actions and Events*, Ernest LePore, ed., pp. 473–81.

Davidson, Donald, and Gilbert Harman, eds. *Semantics of Natural Language*. Dordrecht: D. Reidel, 1972.

Dennett, Daniel. "Beyond Belief." In *Thought and Object*, Andrew Woodfield, ed., pp. 1–96.

Brainstorms. Montgomery, Vt.: Bradford Books, 1978.

Elbow Room. Cambridge, Mass.: MIT Press, 1985.

Consciousness Explained. Boston: Little, Brown, 1991.

Derrida, Jacques. "Differance." In *Margins of Philosophy*, pp. 1–28.

"Limited, Inc." *Glyph* 2 (1977): 162–254.

Margins of Philosophy. Alan Bass, trans. Chicago: University of Chicago Press, 1982.

"The Pit and the Pyramid: Introduction to Hegel's Semiology." In *Margins of Philosophy*, pp. 69–108.

Positions. A. Bass, trans. Chicago: University of Chicago Press, 1981.

"Signature Event Context." In *Margins of Philosophy*, pp. 307–28.

Speech and Phenomena and Other Essays on Husserl's Theory of Signs. D. Allison, trans. Evanston, Ill.: Northwestern University Press, 1973.

Devitt, Michael. *Realism and Truth*. Oxford: Blackwell, 1981.

DeVries, Willem. *Hegel's Theory of Mental Activity*. Ithaca, N.Y.: Cornell, 1988.

Dove, Kenley. "Hegel and the Secularization Hypothesis." In *The Legacy of Hegel*. J. J. O'Malley et al., eds., pp. 144–55.

"Hegel's Phenomenological Method." *Review of Metaphysics* 23 (1970): 615–41.

Dreyfus, Hubert, and Paul Rabinow. *Michel Foucault: Beyond Structuralism and Hermeneutics*. Chicago: University of Chicago Press, 1983.

"What Is Maturity?: Habermas and Foucault on 'What Is Enlightenment?'," In *Foucault: A Critical Reader*, David Hoy, ed., pp. 109–22.

Dummett, Michael. "Comments on Davidson and Hacking." In *Truth and Interpretation*, Ernest LePore, ed., pp. 459–76.

Truth and Other Enigmas. London: Duckworth, 1978.

"What Is a Theory of Meaning?" In *Mind and Language*, Samuel Guttenplan, ed., pp. 97–138.

"What Is a Theory of Meaning? (II)." In *Truth and Meaning*, Gareth Evans and John McDowell, eds., pp. 67–137.

Dunn, John. *The Political Thought of John Locke.* Cambridge: Cambridge University Press, 1969.

Ellis, Brian. *Truth and Objectivity.* Oxford: Blackwell, 1990.

Evans, Gareth, and John McDowell, eds. *Truth and Meaning.* Oxford: Clarendon Press, 1976.

Fackenheim, Emil. *The Religious Dimension of Hegel's Thought.* Bloomington: Indiana University Press, 1967.

Farrell, Frank B. "Iterability and Meaning: The Searle–Derrida Debate." *Metaphilosophy* 19 (1988): 53–64.

"Metaphor and Davidsonian Theories of Meaning." *Canadian Journal of Philosophy* 17 (1987): 625–42.

Findlay, J. N. *Hegel: A Re-Examination.* New York: Oxford University Press, 1976.

Fodor, Jerry. *The Language of Thought.* New York: Crowell, 1975.

Psychosemantics. Cambridge, Mass.: MIT Press, 1987.

"Why Paramecia Don't Have Representations." In *Midwest Studies in Philosophy* X, French, Uehling, and Wettstein, eds. Minneapolis: University of Minnesota Press, 1986, pp. 3–23.

Foucault, Michel. *The Archaeology of Knowledge.* Alan Sheridan, trans. New York: Harper Colophon, 1972.

Discipline and Punish: The Birth of the Prison. Alan Sheridan, trans. New York: Random House, 1979.

The History of Sexuality. Vol. 1: An Introduction. R. Hurley, trans. New York: Random House, 1980.

Michel Foucault: Language, Counter-Memory, Practice. D. F. Bouchard ed. Ithaca, N.Y.: Cornell University Press, 1977.

"On the Genealogy of Ethics." In Herbert Dreyfus and Paul Rabinow, *Michel Foucault: Beyond Structuralism and Hermeneutics,* pp. 229–52.

The Order of Things: An Archaeology of the Human Sciences. New York: Random House, 1973.

Fraassen, Bas van. *The Scientific Image.* Oxford: Oxford University Press, 1980.

French, Peter, Theodore Uehling, and Howard Wettstein, eds. *Contemporary Perspectives in the Philosophy of Language.* Minneapolis: University of Minnesota Press, 1979.

Midwest Studies in Philosophy IV: Studies in Metaphysics. Morris: University of Minnesota Press, 1979.

Midwest Studies in Philosophy XII: Realism and Antirealism. Minneapolis: University of Minnesota Press, 1988.

Gadamer, Hans-Georg. *Hegel's Dialectic.* New Haven, Conn.: Yale University Press, 1976.

Truth and Method. Rev. ed. D. Marshall and J. Weihsheimer, eds. New York: Continuum Press, 1988.

Guttenplan, Samuel, ed. *Mind and Language.* Oxford: Clarendon Press, 1974.

Habermas, Juergen. *Knowledge and Human Interests.* Jeremy Shapiro, trans. Boston: Beacon Press, 1971.

The Philosophical Discourse of Modernity. F. Lawrence, trans. Cambridge, Mass.: MIT Press, 1987.

Hacking, Ian. "The Archaeology of Foucault." In *Foucault: A Critical Reader,* David Hoy, ed., pp. 27–40.

"Language, Truth, and Reason." In *Hermeneutics and Praxis,* Robert Hollinger, ed., pp. 48–66.

"The Parody of Conversation." In *Truth and Interpretation*, Ernest LePore, ed., pp. 447–58.

Why Does Language Matter to Philosophy? Cambridge, Mass.: Cambridge University Press, 1975.

Harman, Gilbert. *The Nature of Morality*. New York: Oxford University Press, 1975.

Hartmann, Klaus. "Hegel: A Non-Metaphysical View." In *Hegel: A Collection of Critical Essays*. Alasdair MacIntyre, ed., pp. 101–24.

Haugeland, John. *Artificial Intelligence: The Very Idea*. Cambridge, Mass.: MIT Press, 1989.

Mind Design. Cambridge, Mass.: MIT Press, 1981.

Hegel, G. W. F. *The Difference between Fichte's and Schelling's System of Philosophy*. H. Harris and W. Cerf, trans. Albany: SUNY Press, 1977.

Hegel's Logic. Part One of the Encyclopedia of the Philosophical Sciences. W. Wallace, trans. Oxford: Clarendon Press, 1975.

Hegel's Philosophy of Mind. W. Wallace and A. V. Miller, trans. Oxford: Clarendon Press, 1971.

Hegel's Philosophy of Nature. A. V. Miller, trans. Oxford: Clarendon Press, 1971.

Hegel's Philosophy of Right. T. Knox, trans. Oxford: Clarendon Press, 1952.

Hegel's Science of Logic. A. V. Miller, trans. London: Allen and Unwin, 1969.

The Phenomenology of Mind. J. B. Baillie, trans. New York: Harper, 1967.

Heidegger, Martin. *The End of Philosophy*. New York: Harper & Row, 1973.

The Question Concerning Technology and Other Essays. New York: Harper & Row, 1977.

Henrich, Dieter. "Fichte's Original Insight." David Lachterman, trans. In *Contemporary German Philosophy* I. University Park: Pennsylvania State University Press, 1982, pp. 15–53.

Hollinger, Robert, ed. *Hermeneutics and Praxis*. Notre Dame, Ind.: University of Notre Dame Press, 1985.

Hollis, M., and S. Lukes, eds. *Rationality and Relativism*. Oxford: Blackwell, 1982.

Holtzman, Stephen, and Christopher Leich, eds. *Wittgenstein: To Follow A Rule*. London: Routledge and Kegan Paul, 1981.

Honderich, Ted, ed. *Morality and Objectivity*. London, Routledge and Kegan Paul, 1985.

Hoy, David C., ed. *Foucault: A Critical Reader*. Oxford: Blackwell, 1986.

Hurley, Susan. *Natural Reasons: Personality and Polity*. Oxford: Oxford University Press, 1989.

Husserl, Edmund. *The Crisis of the European Sciences and Transcendental Phenomenology*. D. Carr, trans. Evanston, Ill. Northwestern University Press, 1970.

Hyman, Arthur, and James J. Walsh, eds. *Philosophy in the Middle Ages*. Indianapolis: Hackett, 1973.

Inwood, Michael. *Hegel*. London: Routledge and Kegan Paul, 1983.

(ed.). *Hegel*. Oxford: Oxford University Press, 1985.

Kierkegaard, Soren. *Either/Or*. W. Lowrie, trans. Garden City, N.Y.: Doubleday, 1959.

Klein, Peter. "Radical Interpretation and Global Skepticism." In *Truth and Interpretation*, Ernest LePore, ed., pp. 369–86.

Kojève, A. *Introduction to the Reading of Hegel*. J. Nichols, trans. New York: Basic Books, 1960.

Krausz, Michael, ed. *Relativism: Interpretation and Confrontation*. Notre Dame: University of Notre Dame Press, 1988.

Kripke, Saul. "Naming and Necessity." In *Semantics of Natural Language*, Davidson and Harman, eds., pp. 253–55.

Wittgenstein on Rules and Private Language. Cambridge, Mass.: Harvard University Press, 1982.

Lear, Jonathan. *Aristotle: The Desire to Understand.* Cambridge: Cambridge University Press, 1988.

"Ethics, Mathematics, and Relativism." In *Essays on Moral Realism*, Geoffrey Sayre-McCord, ed., pp. 76–94.

"Leaving the World Alone." *Journal of Philosophy* 79 (1982): 382–403.

"Transcendental Anthropology." In *Subject, Thought, and Context*, Pettit and McDowell, eds., pp. 267–98.

Leff, Gordon. *Gregory of Rimini.* Manchester: Manchester University Press, 1961.

LePore, Ernest, and Brian McLaughlin, eds. *Actions and Events.* Oxford: Blackwell, 1985.

(ed.). *Truth and Interpretation.* Oxford: Blackwell, 1986.

LePore, Ernest, and Barry Loewer. "A Putnam's Progress." In *Midwest Studies in Philosophy* XII (1988), Peter French et al., eds., pp. 459–73.

Loar, Brian. *Mind and Meaning.* Cambridge: Cambridge University Press, 1981.

MacIntyre, Alasdair. *After Virtue.* Notre Dame, Ind.: University of Notre Dame Press, 1981.

Hegel: A Collection of Critical Essays. Notre Dame, Ind.: University of Notre Dame Press, 1972.

Marcus, Ruth B. "Moral Dilemmas and Consistency." *Journal of Philosophy* 77 (1980): 121–36.

Marx, Werner. *Hegel's Phenomenology of Spirit.* P. Heath, trans. New York: Harper & Row, 1975.

Heidegger and the Tradition. T. Kisiel and M. Greene, trans. Evanston, Ill.: Northwestern University Press, 1971.

McDowell, John. "Functionalism and Anomalous Monism." In *Actions and Events*, Ernest LePore and Brian McLaughlin, eds., pp. 387–98.

"Non-Cognitivism and Rule-Following." In *Wittgenstein: To Follow a Rule* Stephen Holtzman and Christopher Leich, eds., pp. 141–62.

"Singular Thought and the Extent of Inner Space." In *Subject, Thought, and Context*, Philip Pettit and John McDowell, eds., pp. 137–68.

"Values and Secondary Qualities." In *Essays on Moral Realism*, Geoffrey Sayre-McCord, ed., pp. 166–80.

McGinn, Colin. *Mental Content.* Oxford: Blackwell, 1989.

The Problem of Consciousness. Oxford: Blackwell, 1991.

"Radical Interpretation and Epistemology." In *Truth and Interpretation*, Ernest LePore, ed., pp. 356–68.

"The Structure of Content." In *Thought and Object*, Andrew Woodfield, ed., pp. 207–58.

Wittgenstein on Meaning. Oxford: Blackwell, 1984.

Millikan, Ruth. *Language, Thought, and Other Biological Categories.* Cambridge, Mass.: MIT Press, 1984.

Nagel, Thomas. *The View from Nowhere.* New York: Oxford University Press, 1986.

Nietzsche, Friedrich. *The Genealogy of Morals.* F. Golffing, trans. Garden City, N.Y.: Anchor Books, 1956.

Neuhouser, Frederick. *Fichte's Theory of Subjectivity.* Cambridge: Cambridge University Press, 1990.

Nozick, Robert. *Philosophical Explanations.* Cambridge, Mass.: Harvard University Press, 1981.

Papineau, David. *Reality and Representation.* Oxford: Blackwell, 1987.

Peacocke, Christopher. "Reply: Rule-Following: The Nature of Wittgenstein's

Arguments." In *Wittgenstein: To Follow a Rule*, Stephen Holtzman and Christopher Leich, eds., pp. 73–94.

Sense and Content. Oxford: Oxford University Press, 1983.

Pears, David. *The False Prison* (II). Oxford, Clarendon Press, 1988.

Pettit, Philip, and John McDowell, eds. *Subject, Thought, and Context*. Oxford: Clarendon Press, 1986.

Pippin, Robert. *Hegel's Idealism*. Cambridge: Cambridge University Press, 1989.

Platts, Mark. *Ways of Meaning*. London: Routledge and Kegan Paul, 1979.

Putnam, Hilary. *The Many Faces of Realism*. LaSalle, Ill.: Open Court, 1987.

Meaning and the Moral Sciences. London: Routledge and Kegan Paul, 1978.

Mind, Language, and Reality. Philosophical Papers, Vol. 2. Cambridge: Cambridge University Press, 1975.

Realism and Reason. Philosophical Papers, Vol. 3. Cambridge: Cambridge University Press, 1983.

Reason, Truth, and History. Cambridge: Cambridge University Press, 1981.

Quine, Willard Van Orman. *Ontological Relativity and Other Essays*. New York: Columbia University Press, 1969.

Word and Object. Cambridge, Mass.: MIT Press, 1960.

Railton, Peter. "Moral Realism." *Philosophical Review* 95 (1986): 163–207.

Ramberg, Bjorn. *Donald Davidson's Philosophy of Language*. Oxford: Blackwell, 1989.

Romanos, George. *Quine and Analytic Philosophy*. Cambridge, Mass.: MIT Press, 1983.

Rorty, Richard. *Consequences of Pragmatism*. Minneapolis: University of Minnesota Press, 1982.

Contingency, Irony, and Solidarity. Cambridge: Cambridge University Press, 1989.

"Foucault and Epistemology." In *Foucault: A Critical Reader*, David Hoy, ed., pp. 41–50.

"Habermas and Lyotard on Postmodernity." In *Habermas and Modernity*, Richard Bernstein, ed., pp. 161–76.

Philosophy and the Mirror of Nature. Princeton, N.J.: Princeton University Press, 1979.

"Postmodernist Bourgeois Liberalism." In *Hermeneutics and Praxis*, Robert Hollinger, ed., pp. 214–21.

"Pragmatism, Davidson, and Truth." In *Truth and Interpretation*, Ernest LePore, ed., pp. 333–55.

"The World Well Lost." *Journal of Philosophy* 69 (1972): 649–65.

Sayre-McCord, Geoffrey, ed. *Essays on Moral Realism*. Ithaca, N.Y.: Cornell University Press, 1988.

Searle, John. "Minds, Brains, and Programs." In *Mind Design*, John Haugeland, ed., pp. 282–306.

Steinkraus, Warren. *New Studies in Hegel's Philosophy*. New York: Holt, Reinhart, and Winston, 1971.

Stich, Stephen. *The Fragmentation of Reason*. Cambridge, Mass.: MIT Press, 1990.

Stroud, Barry. *The Significance of Philosophical Skepticism*. Oxford: Clarendon Press, 1984.

Taylor, Charles. *Hegel*. Cambridge: Cambridge University Press, 1975.

Tugendhat, Ernst. *Self-consciousness and Self-determination*. P. Stern, trans. Cambridge, Mass.: MIT Press, 1986.

Unger, Peter. *Identity, Consciousness, and Value*. New York: Oxford University Press, 1990.

Wiggins, David. "On Singling Out an Object Determinately." In *Subject, Thought, and Context*, Philip Pettit and John McDowell, eds., pp. 169–80.

Sameness and Substance. Oxford: Blackwell, 1979.
"Truth, Invention, and the Meaning of Life." In *Essays on Moral Realism*, Geoffrey Sayre-McCord, ed., pp. 127–65.
Williams, Bernard. *Descartes: The Project of Pure Enquiry*. Atlantic Highlands, N.J.: Humanities Press, 1978.
Ethics and the Limits of Philosophy. Cambridge, Mass.: Harvard University Press, 1985.
Moral Luck. Cambridge: Cambridge University Press, 1981.
Winfield, Richard D. "Conceiving Something without Any Conceptual Scheme." *The Owl of Minerva* 18 (1986): 13–28.
Wittgenstein, Ludwig. *On Certainty*. D. Paul and G. E. M. Anscombe, trans. Oxford: Blackwell, 1969.
Philosophical Investigations. G. E. M. Anscombe, trans. Oxford: Blackwell, 1953.
Woodfield, Andrew, ed. *Thought and Object*. Oxford: Clarendon Press, 1982.
Wright, Crispin. "Realism, Antirealism, Irrealism, Quasi-Realism." In *Midwest Studies in Philosophy* XII (1988), Peter French et al., eds., pp. 25–50.
Realism, Meaning and Truth. Oxford: Blackwell, 1987.
"Rule-Following, Objectivity, and the Theory of Meaning." In *Wittgenstein: To Follow a Rule*. Stephen Holtzman and Christopher Leich, eds., pp. 99–117.
Wittgenstein on the Foundations of Mathematics. London: Duckworth, 1980.

Index